HOLMAN
Old Testament Commentary

Exodus, Leviticus, Numbers

GENERAL EDITOR

Max Anders

AUTHOR

Glen S. Martin

HOLMAN
REFERENCE

NASHVILLE, TENNESSEE

Holman Old Testament Commentary
© 2002 B&H Publishing Group
Nashville, Tennessee
All rights reserved

ISBN: 978-0-8054-9462-4

Bible versions used in this book:

Dewey Decimal Classification: 222.1
Subject Heading: BIBLE. O.T. Exodus
BIBLE. O.T. Leviticus
BIBLE. O.T. Numbers

Martin, Glen
Exodus, Leviticus, Numbers/Glen Martin
            p.   cm. — (Holman Old Testament commentary)
      Includes bibliographical references. (p.).
      ISBN 0–8054–9462–6
      1. Bible. O.T. Exodus, Leviticus, Numbers—Commentaries.   I. Title.   II. Series.
      —dc21

Printed in China

9 10 11 12 13 14   19 18 17 16 15

To the Lord Jesus Christ—you have given me the privilege of being called your servant, and you continue to love me as your child. Thank you for the breath of life, the ability to love and understand your Word, and the passion to see others get on fire for you. I love you, Lord!

Contents

Contents

Editorial Preface

Today's church hungers for Bible teaching, and Bible teachers hunger for resources to guide them in teaching God's Word. The Holman Old Testament Commentary provides the church with the food to feed the spiritually hungry in an easily digestible format. The result: new spiritual vitality that the church can readily use.

Bible teaching should result in new interest in the Scriptures, expanded Bible knowledge, discovery of specific scriptural principles, relevant applications, and exciting living. The unique format of the Holman Old Testament Commentary includes sections to achieve these results for every Old Testament book.

Opening quotations stimulate thinking and lead to an introductory illustration and discussion that draw individuals and study groups into the Word of God. "In a Nutshell" summarizes the content and teaching of the chapter. Verse-by-verse commentary answers the church's questions rather than raising issues scholars usually admit they cannot adequately solve. Bible principles and specific contemporary applications encourage students to move from Bible to contemporary times. A specific modern illustration then ties application vividly to present life. A brief prayer aids the student to commit his or her daily life to the principles and applications found in the Bible chapter being studied. For those still hungry for more, "Deeper Discoveries" take the student into a more personal, deeper study of the words, phrases, and themes of God's Word. Finally, a teaching outline provides transitional statements and conclusions along with an outline to assist the teacher in group Bible studies.

It is the editors' prayer that this new resource for local church Bible teaching will enrich the ministry of group, as well as individual, Bible study, and that it will lead God's people truly to be people of the Book, living out what God calls us to be.

Acknowledgments

I have never written a book of this magnitude, so I owe thanks to many people who have influenced its development. A little of their impact and wisdom is within every page. The writing has been an exciting, transformative experience that would never have been completed without their help and support.

I owe an unbelievable debt of gratitude to Dr. Sam Petitfils because of his theological insights and love for the holy Scriptures. He has probably forgotten more details of biblical history and application than I have yet learned. He has been the encouragement, support, and fuel for this commentary.

To my wife, Nancy, I want to extend my deepest appreciation for her radiant, enduring love and unwavering personal support. She has always been at my side, and I truly love serving with her. And I want to say to my children—Kerry, Scott, and David—that I am proud of how God has molded them into godly adults and how they have supported my ministry.

I am grateful to Max Anders and Steve Bond, who expressed confidence in my abilities by asking me to be a part of this commentary series. Thanks to them for challenging me to a higher level of research and writing. Their excellence is an outstanding model to follow.

To David, Gregg, Chris, Ken, Ron, Bill, Gary, Rich and Dennis—a big thank you for being men of influence in my life. Their love for Christ, desire to impact the world for their Lord, and passionate belief in the church has been the wind in my sails. Like Barnabas, they have been encouragers and faithful friends to me.

Glen Martin

2002

Holman Old Testament Commentary Contributors

Vol. 1, Genesis
ISBN 978–0-8054-9461-7
Kenneth O. Gangel
and Stephen Bramer

Vol. 2, Exodus, Leviticus, Numbers
ISBN 978–0-8054-9462-4
Glen Martin

Vol. 3, Deuteronomy
ISBN 978–0-8054-9463-1
Doug McIntosh

Vol. 4, Joshua
ISBN 978–0-8054-9464-8
Kenneth O. Gangel

Vol. 5, Judges, Ruth
ISBN 978–0-8054-9465-5
W. Gary Phillips

Vol. 6, 1 & 2 Samuel
ISBN 978–0-8054-9466-2
Stephen Andrews

Vol. 7, 1 & 2 Kings
ISBN 978–0-8054-9467-9
Gary Inrig

Vol. 8, 1 & 2 Chronicles
ISBN 978–0-8054-9468-6
Winfried Corduan

Vol. 9, Ezra, Nehemiah, Esther
ISBN 978–0-8054-9469-3
Knute Larson and Kathy Dahlen

Vol. 10, Job
ISBN 978–0-8054-9470-9
Steven J. Lawson

Vol. 11, Psalms 1-72
ISBN 978–0-8054-9471-6
Steven J. Lawson

Vol. 12, Psalms 73-150
ISBN 978–0-8054-9481-5
Steven J. Lawson

Vol. 13, Proverbs
ISBN 978–0-8054-9472-3
Max Anders

Vol. 14, Ecclesiastes, Song of Songs
ISBN 978–0-8054-9482-2
David George Moore and Daniel L. Akin

Vol. 15, Isaiah
ISBN 978–0-8054-9473-0
Trent C. Butler

Vol. 16, Jeremiah, Lamentations
ISBN 978–0-8054-9474-7
Fred M. Wood and Ross McLaren

Vol. 17, Ezekiel
ISBN 978–0-8054-9475-4
Mark F. Rooker

Vol. 18, Daniel
ISBN 978–0-8054-9476-1
Kenneth O. Gangel

Vol. 19, Hosea, Joel, Amos, Obadiah, Jonah, Micah
ISBN 978–0-8054-9477-8
Trent C. Butler

Vol. 20, Nahum, Habakkuk, Zephaniah, Haggai, Zechariah, Malachi
ISBN 978–0-8054-9478-5
Stephen R. Miller

Holman New Testament Commentary Contributors

Vol. 1, Matthew
ISBN 978–0-8054-0201-8
Stuart K. Weber

Vol. 2, Mark
ISBN 978–0-8054-0202-5
Rodney L. Cooper

Vol. 3, Luke
ISBN 978–0-8054-0203-2
Trent C. Butler

Vol. 4, John
ISBN 978–0-8054-0204-9
Kenneth O. Gangel

Vol. 5, Acts
ISBN 978–0-8054-0205-6
Kenneth O. Gangel

Vol. 6, Romans
ISBN 978–0-8054-0206-3
Kenneth Boa and William Kruidenier

Vol. 7, 1 & 2 Corinthians
ISBN 978–0-8054-0207-0
Richard L. Pratt Jr.

**Vol. 8, Galatians, Ephesians,
Philippians, Colossians**
ISBN 978–0-8054-0208-7
Max Anders

**Vol. 9, 1 & 2 Thessalonians,
1 & 2 Timothy, Titus, Philemon**
ISBN 978–0-8054-0209-4
Knute Larson

Vol. 10, Hebrews, James
ISBN 978–0-8054-0211-7
Thomas D. Lea

Vol. 11, 1 & 2 Peter, 1, 2, 3 John, Jude
ISBN 978–0-8054-0210-0
David Walls and Max Anders

Vol. 12, Revelation
ISBN 978–0-8054-0212-4
Kendell H. Easley

Holman Old Testament Commentary

Twenty volumes designed for Bible study and teaching to enrich the local church and God's people.

Series Editor	Max Anders
Managing Editor	Steve Bond
Project Editor	Dean Richardson
Product Development Manager	Ricky D. King
Marketing Manager	Stephanie Huffman
Executive Editor	David Shepherd
Page Composition	TF Designs, Mt. Juliet, TN

Introduction to

Exodus

The Book of Exodus serves as a prequel to the unfolding theme of salvation in the Bible. Readers of the Bible can well relate to this book's emphasis on bondage, deliverance, thanksgiving, and worship. The very term *Exodus,* probably originally supplied by the Greek translators of the Septuagint, means "a going out" or "departure." The book chronicles the departure of Israel from Egypt, the house of bondage, toward the promised land.

The events of Exodus point to a turning point in Israel's history and spiritual development. As his covenant people they had grown into a thriving nation in Egypt. Now the Lord called them away from Egypt and led them to a land he would give them. In the course of their journey from Egypt to the promised land, God prescribed for them the true form of worship, the only kind that would please him, and supplied even the minutest details about every particular and nuance related to the sacrificial system. Of course, that system pointed to a greater reality that would be revealed in its own time.

CHARACTERISTICS OF EXODUS

The book forms a running narrative and highlights key events and people that relate to Israel's salvation and redemption. The book can be divided into three major divisions: (1) *Israel in Egypt* (chs. 1–12). Although the time from Jacob's original descent into Egypt until the birth and calling of Moses was considerable, Moses passes this over with a brief remark about Israel's surging population (1:7). This opening section emphasizes the sufferings of Israel in Egypt, the birth and call of Moses the lawgiver, the initial conflict and meeting with Pharaoh, the subsequent miracles and Pharaoh's responses, and the first Passover. (2) *Fleeing Egypt toward Sinai* (chs. 13–18). This section features the miraculous deliverance through the Red Sea, a song of thanksgiving, some religious and ceremonial instructions, bitter water and manna, water from the rock, and Jethro's visit. (3) *Israel at Sinai* (chs. 19–40). The final section introduces the law of God (otherwise called the law of Moses) and related covenant terms, supplementary civil and ceremonial laws, the design and measurements of the tabernacle and attendant furniture, apostasy and covenant renewal, and the construction of the tabernacle.

In Exodus, God reveals himself as Yahweh, the personal God of presence, who dwells with his people. He revealed himself in a theophany to Moses in the burning bush and promised to be with Moses in the daunting task of leading Israel out of bondage. God manifests his presence throughout this book as a deliverer, guide, lawgiver, and supreme object of worship. But more important, God offers the nation and its citizens forgiveness of their sins through blood sacrifice, developed later in the Book of Leviticus.

He demonstrated his love and care for the covenant community by giving them guiding principles for daily life, worship, and ethics. He protected them from certain death in the Red Sea and nourished them with heavenly food. He gave every indication that he longed to draw near to these people and establish permanent closeness with them.

AUTHORSHIP

Although the Torah (or Pentateuch, the first five books of the Bible) is anonymous, the Bible indicates Moses was the primary author of these books. God commanded him to faithfully record certain facts and events (Exod. 17:14; Num. 33:2), laws (Exod. 24:4, 34:27–28) and even a song (Deut. 31:22). Other Old Testament writers and books identify Moses as the author (see Josh. 1:7; 8:31–35; 1 Kgs. 2:3; 2 Kgs. 14:6; 21:8; Ezra 6:18; Dan. 9:13; Mal. 4:4). The New Testament also attributes these books to Moses (Mark 12:26; Luke 2:22; 16:29; 24:27; John 5:46–47; 7:19; Acts 3:23; 13:39; Rom. 10:5).

Certainly the author must have been an eyewitness of the events and somewhat educated. The writer was keenly aware of the exact number of springs (twelve) and palm trees (seventy, see Exod. 15:27). The writer was knowledgeable of Egyptian names and landmarks as well as trees, such as the acacia, which grew in Egypt and the Sinai Peninsula, but not in Palestine. When we compare these facts with Moses' own qualifications, the case for Mosaic authorship becomes even stronger. He grew up in elite Egyptian schools where he would gain the necessary intellectual and literary skills to help him compose the Pentateuch with greater ease.

Virtually every ancient authority cites Moses as the author of the Pentateuch. Not until the rise of Julius Wellhausen and the historical/critical school of the nineteenth century was Mosaic authorship even questioned.

DATE OF WRITING

The date of the Book of Exodus falls naturally with discussions on the date of the exodus from Egypt. Traditional scholars have assigned that date at around 1445 B.C. for many reasons, and below we cite three of these:

1 Kings 6:1. "In the four hundred and eightieth year after the Israelites had come out of Egypt, in the fourth year of Solomon's reign over Israel, in the month of Ziv, the second month, he began to build the temple of the LORD." If the fourth year of Solomon's reign was about 966 B.C., then the traditional date certainly makes sense.

Judges 11:26. God raised up Jephthah as a judge to rescue the Israelites from the cruel oppression of the Ammonites. Jephthah recounted to the king of Ammon that Israel lived in the towns of Heshbon for three hundred years. Bible scholars date the reign of Jephthah around 1100 B.C. Subtracting from this date the time Jephthah said Israel lived in the land (three hundred years) gives us the time of Joshua's conquest, around 1400–1405 B.C. Allowing for forty years for Israel's wanderings in the wilderness, we arrive near the traditional dating of the exodus from Egypt. If we allow that Moses compiled the book some time during the stay at Sinai, the date of the book could be assigned a few months following the exodus (see Exod. 19:1–2).

Acts 13:19–20. Paul comments that God destroyed seven nations in the land of Canaan and gave it to the Israelites. The time of the exodus through David's capture of Jerusalem took place in about 450 years. So if we include in this time frame the exodus through David (1445 to 995 B.C.), we arrive at Paul's figure and require an early exodus date.

THEMES OF EXODUS

Bondage. Before readers learned about Israel's Savior, Moses introduced them to the cruel hardships the Israelites faced under Pharaoh's regime. Their awful plight paved the way for a special revelation of God in theophany (Exod. 3:2–22) and a promise of deliverance.

Deliverer. The Book of Exodus highlights two deliverers, the Lord himself and Moses his servant. God raised up Moses and guided him in his leadership duties. The helpless people were now forced by their sufferings to listen to Moses the man of God as he told of his encounter with the God of Abraham, Isaac, and Jacob. The unfolding relationship between Israel and God revealed a not-so-perfect trust on the part of Israel and God's gracious willingness to forgive Israel for her sins time and time again.

The law. Although the law was formally unveiled in chapters 19 and 20, really the entire book reveals the character of God in his words and commands. The law became much more than a codebook or a constitution for Israel; it pointed to a divine standard of perfection. This standard displayed something of the very nature of God, perfect, holy, and separate from sin. The revelation of the law at Sinai came with attending phenomena so striking to onlookers that they trembled and feared for their lives (20:18–19). Such a display of God's holiness and divine character could drive men and women to look inwardly at their own need and yearn for a solution.

Sacrifice. Moses did not disclose the entire sacrificial system in this book as he would in Leviticus, but he laid a foundation. The Lord gave elaborate instructions on how to prepare for and observe the Passover, where blood was both shed and applied to the doors of the Israelite houses. In the Passover the Israelites could see both the avenging angel and the Redeemer. The avenging angel served to exact due punishment on those who were not covered by the blood of the Passover and who thus stood distant from God. But the Redeemer was close by to protect, deliver, and thereafter guide those who trusted in his gracious provision for salvation. While the elaborate sacrificial system, so detailed in Leviticus, carried significant meaning, so did the apparatus and instruments of sacrifice—the tabernacle itself.

The tabernacle. Readers of Exodus are struck by the attention that God gives to the smallest details of this edifice, from precise measurements to the coloring of the curtains. But the meaning is not spelled out in this book, at least not in any detail. Later God, through the writer of Hebrews, would tie all the loose ends together and untie the knots of rabbinic tradition. But even in this first instant the reader learns something of the way to God's presence. Only sanctified priests, duly adorned and anointed, could venture into the holy place. God commanded them to build special articles of furniture that would facilitate sacrifices, prayers, and lighting in the tabernacle. While only the priests could be anointed and set apart for this service, the entire community partook through these agencies of the presence of God.

Presence. God revealed himself to the Hebrews in several ways. Early on he disclosed his divine name, Yahweh, "I AM WHO I AM" (3:14). With this theophany came a promise of a great deliverance based on his covenant with these people's forefathers—Abraham, Isaac, and Jacob (3:7–8). Following the miraculous rescue from Egypt's clutches, the Lord further manifested himself in the cloud and pillar of fire during Israel's initial wanderings. He showed himself in the law given at Sinai (20:1–18) and its elaboration in succeeding chapters. God was present with his people through divinely chosen spokesmen and leaders who communicated his will to the people. When the tabernacle was completed the Lord took up residence in the tabernacle (40:34–38).

So whether in theophany, deliverance, covenant law, or worship, Yahweh manifested his desire to dwell with his people. As time went on, he would let the people know of his desire to dwell with them more permanently.

Response. While the Lord took the first steps in reaching out to his people, he expected the people to respond in kind. He expected them to accept freely the provisions of the covenant and cheerfully comply with its demands. For their part, the people did respond at times, such as in their song to God following their deliverance through the Red Sea (15:1–18), and contributing their resources toward the work of the tabernacle (35:20–29). But more often they responded in unbelief. They failed to believe God would provide adequately for them (15:23–25; 16:1–3; 17:1–3), or care for them in the absence of their leader (32:1–8). From the beginning they were carried along by the faith of their fearless leader Moses, himself no stranger to self-doubt and, at times, despair (4:1,10–17; 6:12). But he rallied to full faith once the Lord assured him of his abiding presence (33:12–23).

Continuation. The great themes that emerged in Genesis continued in Exodus with even greater clarity. There is but one God who made the universe and is greater than all other so-called gods, and he will execute judgment on the gods of Egypt. He will fulfill the promises to the patriarchs by leading them toward the promised land and providing protection along the way, both from enemies, the elements, and starvation. He will provide not only for their physical needs but spiritual ones also. He gave them the tent of meeting and tabernacle, where he would meet with them and forgive their transgressions through blood atonement. He instructed them in his principles and thus revealed more of himself to them.

Anticipation. The types and figures of Exodus prefigure the great New Testament themes about which the Bible looks forward to with anticipation. The Lord who partially revealed himself in the burning bush would one day dwell with his people. The elaborate worship and sacrificial system pointed to a greater reality that would provide complete and final salvation. The priests, animal sacrifices, tabernacle, and accompanying rituals all looked forward to a better solution and must have raised questions even in ancient days.

All these elaborate and beautiful features point to Christ, who embodies all the hopes and expectations of God's people. He is at once our sacrifice, Passover, and even high priest (1 Cor. 5:7; Heb. 8:1–2). Finally, the promise of a permanent dwelling place toward which Israel journeyed pointed to a lasting place of complete and eternal rest.

Exodus 1–2

Preparing for the Journey

I. **INTRODUCTION**
Life in the Balance

II. **COMMENTARY**
A verse-by-verse explanation of these chapters.

III. **CONCLUSION**
Learning a Careful Balance

An overview of the principles and applications from these chapters.

IV. **LIFE APPLICATION**
An Indian's Insight

Melding these chapters to life.

V. **PRAYER**
Tying these chapters to life with God.

VI. **DEEPER DISCOVERIES**
Historical, geographical, and grammatical enrichment of the commentary.

VII. **TEACHING OUTLINE**
Suggested step-by-step group study of these chapters.

VIII. **ISSUES FOR DISCUSSION**
Zeroing these chapters in on daily life.

Quote

"*S*ome providences, like Hebrew letters,

must be read backwards."

John Flavel

Exodus 1–2

IN A NUTSHELL

*T*he careful balance between deliverance, direction, and dedication unfolds in the Book of Exodus as we learn how a people are prepared for the journey awaiting them and how a leader is prepared for the task of leading a ragtag group of people into a long-awaited land of milk and honey.

Preparing for the Journey

I. INTRODUCTION

Life in the Balance

*H*ave you ever wondered why British sailors are called "limeys"? Well, hundreds of years ago, modern medicine was still in its infancy. Sailors would drop like flies from scurvy on long sea voyages. But British sailors accidentally discovered a truth that was to impact the health and lives of thousands. They found that the dreaded scurvy could be stopped with the addition of limes to the sailors' diet. This fruit, unknown to them, contained vitamin C. Who would have thought that the difference between life and death could be a humble lime! So, because British sailors sucked on limes, they became known as "limeys."

Life is delicately balanced. It can be negatively affected, and even ended, by the smallest deficiency or addition. Add an extra carbon molecule to oxygen, and you get carbon dioxide, which can be fatal if too much is inhaled. This substance, much like vitamin C, is unseen, yet potent.

What is true in the physical realm has similar parallels in the spiritual realm. You are about to make a journey that will demonstrate the fine balance of deliverance, direction, and dedication. The Book of Exodus paints three pictures for the careful student. First is the picture of God's deliverance of the people of Israel from Egyptian bondage. The second picture will be a beautiful portrayal of God's faithful guidance of these same people through the wilderness to the promised land. The third painting will show us the glory of God as the Israelites trusted his leading and dedicated a dwelling place for his holy habitation.

II. COMMENTARY

Preparing for the Journey

MAIN IDEA: *God saw the oppression of his people and prepared a deliverer for them.*

A The Oppressed People (1:1–22)

SUPPORTING IDEA: *God's chosen people were persecuted in a foreign land.*

1:1. Moses aptly opens this book with a listing of the tribes of Israel. The tribes represent the sons of Jacob, over which Jacob uttered profoundly prophetic words (see Gen. 49). From these tribes would come prophets, priests, kings, and other notable characters who would help create Israel's unique history. Of course, Israel's greatest contribution would be the giving of the

Messiah (Rev. 12:5). Moses mentions Joseph last because of his unique place in Genesis and because he comprises the two other tribes not mentioned here—Ephraim and Manasseh.

1:2–14. God had blessed these tribes abundantly so that they were **fruitful** and had **multiplied**. Yet their growth in Egypt was viewed as a threat by the reigning Pharaoh. His fears were twofold. These growing tribes in Egypt might align themselves with Egypt's enemies or be strong enough to escape from the land. In either case, the results would be disastrous for Egypt. To protect the interests of Egypt, the Pharaoh began oppressing the Israelites. He appointed tough **slave masters over them** as they built **store cities** for him. Yet Pharaoh's tactics backfired: The more Israel was **oppressed**, the more they grew in number. This, in turn, resulted in still more severe countermeasures.

1:15–22. Students of history tell us that when a nation uses terror tactics on a segment of its society, it will not achieve the desired result. In fact, such actions lead to further frustration, causing the perpetrators to sink to even lower depths of cruelty. Witness the twentieth century's fascist regimes that fell into such murderous evil as they attempted to destroy peoples with whom they felt they could not coexist. Pharaoh, realizing his previous attempts at controlling the exploding population growth of the Israelites had failed, now approached the **Hebrew midwives** with a scheme so unscrupulous it can only be called devilish. He commanded the midwives to kill all Hebrew male babies, while sparing the females.

The midwives, however, feared God and would not submit to Pharaoh's bloodthirsty scheme. Instead, they spared the male infants and told Pharaoh that the Hebrew women did not wait for their assistance but delivered the babies on their own. Such daring actions by the Hebrew midwives did not escape the eye of God, who rewarded their faithfulness by providing them with **families of their own**. Pharaoh then acted out of pure desperation. He sent his own soldiers on search-and-destroy missions. Whenever they located a Hebrew male baby, they were ordered to throw him **into the Nile**. Would Pharaoh have his way? Did Pol Pot, Stalin, or Hitler?

B Adoption and Life in Midian (2:1–25)

SUPPORTING IDEA: *God carefully prepared his servant.*

2:1–10. Moses, the writer of Exodus and God's chief instrument in bringing the people of Israel out of bondage in Egypt, now mentions something of his origins. Descended from Levi, the third child of Jacob and Leah (Gen. 29:34), Moses was the second son of Amram and Jochebed, who previously gave birth to Aaron and daughter Miriam (Num. 26:59). The baby Moses must have beamed with vigor and strength, standing out among other Hebrew babies (Heb. 11:23), and would have been a prime target for Pharaoh's brand of extermination.

Yet Moses' mother, well aware of the ongoing surveillance commanded by Pharaoh (Exod. 1:22), **hid him** for approximately **three months**, and then, possibly out of desperation (but also faith, Heb. 11:23), placed him in a **papyrus basket . . . among the reeds along the bank of the Nile**, so he wouldn't float away down the Nile. Jochebed also posted his sister Miriam to keep watch over him.

When **Pharaoh's daughter went down to the Nile to bathe . . . she saw the basket . . . and sent her slave girl to get it.** Soon the princess concluded the baby was one of the endangered Hebrew babies, and, at the prompting of the enterprising and skillful Miriam, sent for a Hebrew nurse to care for the child. Miriam, of course, didn't get just any nurse, but Moses' own **mother.** Pharaoh's daughter arranged to have the "nurse" feed and care for the child, after which she took him for her own, naming the adopted son **Moses,** which means roughly "to draw out."

2:11–14. Moses developed a close relationship and identification with his own people, even though he was raised and educated as an Egyptian. Year after year Moses witnessed untold instances of his adopted nation cruelly oppressing his people. These experiences had a cumulative effect on Moses' psyche. Soon his allegiance to his God-given heritage would find dramatic and life-altering expression. One day, after Moses had grown up, he **went out to where his own people were**, and watched them laboring. But this day was no ordinary day. Events unfolded quickly.

Moses **saw an Egyptian beating a Hebrew.** This angered Moses and prompted him to take justice into his own hands and kill the Egyptian. Although he thought his actions went undetected, he soon discovered his deed was known by at least one man. When he tried to break up a fight between two Hebrews, one of the men protested his intervention by pointing to Moses' own guilt in killing the Egyptian the previous day.

2:15–25. When Pharaoh learned of this deed, **he tried to kill Moses,** who escaped by fleeing to the desert of **Midian.** Moses, in whose life we see the close care and guidance of God, found his first refuge **by a well.** Here he met the daughters of a certain Midian **priest** named **Reuel** (see Jethro at 18:1), who came **to water their father's flock. Some shepherds,** who must have recognized only the nomadic adage "rule of the strong," tried to scatter the flock away from the well, but Moses came to the aid of these women. These grateful daughters reported Moses' good deeds to their father, who in turn invited Moses to stay with them. The stay lasted quite some time, and Moses married one of Reuel's daughters named **Zipporah.** They soon gave birth to a son whom Moses named **Gershom,** a name that summarized the history, call, and destiny of Moses himself. *Gershom* means "banishment," signifying "one who was driven out or thrust forth" (Durham, 23).

Moses seemed quite fortunate in his present circumstances, far removed from the Egyptian threat now endured by his people. But he was a stranger in a foreign land, estranged from the people of his birth. Certainly these feelings began to awaken a sense of calling and divine purpose in the inner recesses of his soul. At the same time, the Hebrews cries for deliverance from their slavery went up to God, who loved these people and who had made an irrevocable **covenant** with their forefathers, Abraham, Isaac, and Jacob. God heard their cries and would soon act on their behalf.

But how would all this come about, and who would God use to achieve this purpose, and what if that person was reluctant to obey?

MAIN IDEA REVIEW: *God saw the oppression of his people and prepared a deliverer for them.*

III. CONCLUSION

Learning a Careful Balance

Just as British sailors discovered the importance of vitamin C in their diet and were pronounced "limeys," the people of Israel had to learn the balance of patience and trust. The people needed to be prepared for the major undertaking ahead of them, and a leader needed a similar preparation in order to accomplish this daunting mission. The nation of Israel had grown and prospered in fulfillment of the promise that God had previously made to Jacob back in Genesis 46:3–4a: "I am God, the God of your father. Do not be afraid to go down to Egypt, for I will make you into a great nation there. I will go down to Egypt with you, and I will surely bring you back again." Just the fact that this nation had grown despite the persecution they had faced is a testimony of God's guidance and sovereignty. Learning the careful balance of deliverance, direction, and dedication had now begun.

PRINCIPLES

- God has always been working throughout history.
- God demands faithfulness of those who want his blessing.
- Suffering is a necessary part of God's plan.

APPLICATIONS

- Since no one who is against God will prosper, analyze your life for ways to be more obedient to him.
- Since faithfulness will be rewarded, don't fret over the things God asks you to give up.
- Remember what God has done in the past and trust his character for wisdom and strength for the future.

IV. LIFE APPLICATION

An Indian's Insight

Have you lived life long enough to feel a little like the story of a cowboy on the western frontier who came across an Indian lying flat with his ear to the ground? The Indian looked up at the cowboy sitting on his horse and said, "Wagon; four horses; two passengers; woman wearing calico gown; heavy man driving; thirty minutes away." The cowboy's jaw dropped as he said, "That is so amazing! You can tell all of that just by putting your ear to the ground?" "No," the Indian replied, "they ran over me half an hour ago!"

There are times in life when we all feel like that Indian. Maybe people have deliberately run over you—a friend, your spouse, a coworker, an employee—just knocked you down and left you deeply wounded. Or maybe circumstances have flattened you. Your health has broken. Your house has burned. That financial risk you took just didn't work out. And just when you needed encouragement the most, people seemed to be oblivious to your hurt, or they misinterpreted your actions and asked, "Why are you so down in the dumps?" Everyone needs encouragement and comfort at times. Know this, whatever place of bondage you are in right now, God knows. And whatever place of suffering you feel trapped within, God cares. And when you labor to remain faithful to God's leading and remain patient through the adversity, God will do something about it. That is the great news of the balance in Exodus—a balance of deliverance, direction, and dedication.

V. PRAYER

Heavenly Father, in the midst of my suffering and pain, remind me of your faithfulness to all generations. Remind me that before deliverance there must be a time of preparation. Thank you in advance for the way you are preparing me, and I commit to remain faithful to you as I continue my personal journey. Amen.

VI. DEEPER DISCOVERIES

A. The Civil Disobedience of the Hebrew Midwives

When Pharaoh told the midwives to destroy the Hebrew males as they were born, the midwives "feared God" and refused to comply. Here is an early example of civil disobedience in the Bible. Francis Schaeffer said in his *Christian Manifesto* that if Christians can never practice civil disobedience, then the state has become the object of worship. The Bible clearly teaches that at times believers must disobey civil laws in order to obey God's higher laws. The apostles were commanded not to speak about their faith in the early church, but they disobeyed (Acts 4:18–20; 5:40–42). They paid a penalty for their actions.

So when should a child of God disobey the state? Certainly he or she should pray and search the Scriptures about such matters. Certainly he or she should not obey the state if it means disobeying God in any matter. Many faithful Christians suffered in Germany during World War II because they refused to join forces with Adolf Hitler's regime. Today Christians are known to take a number of approaches when defending the life of the unborn. While we may never compromise the right-to-life stand, clearly taught in the Bible, we need to seek God's will when determining just how to participate in this great cause.

B. Midian

Midian, the land of Reuel, was a region in the Arabian desert bordered by Edom on the northwest. It measured approximately 175 miles from north to south. During Moses' day, Midian controlled the area near Horeb and the Sinai Peninsula. Later events in their history include the episode with Gideon (Judg. 6–8) and isolated references during the time of David (1 Kgs. 11:17–18). They joined with the Moabites in hiring Balaam to curse Israel, which was unsuccessful. Later they led the Israelites to commit immorality and idolatry (Num. 25:1–9).

VII. TEACHING OUTLINE

A. INTRODUCTION

1. Lead Story: Life in the Balance
2. Context: God sent Jacob and his sons to Egypt during a time of famine. While in Egypt, this family multiplied and became a nation within a nation. The Egyptians made slaves of them, fearing they might form alliances with Egypt's enemies. The more the Hebrews were oppressed, the more they multiplied.
3. Transition: Chapters 1–2 recount the stern measures the Egyptians took with the Hebrews and how Egyptian policy affected one family. In these difficult circumstances, the God of Abraham, Isaac, and Jacob worked through this one family in a way that would eventually result in the liberation of the Hebrews from their oppressors.

B. COMMENTARY

1. The Oppressed People (1:1–22)
2. Adoption and Life in Midian (2:1–25)

C. CONCLUSION: AN INDIAN'S INSIGHT

VIII. ISSUES FOR DISCUSSION

1. The story of Exodus cannot be read in isolation. Take a moment to read Genesis 45:8–11 and Genesis 46:1–4. How is the exodus from Egypt related to the plight of Joseph and his leadership in Egypt?
2. We are told that the midwives "feared God." How does the fear of God relate to doing what is right, doing what is wrong, and following through on your responsibility?
3. Were there risks involved in the disobedience of the midwives? Are there any risks involved in faithfulness to God's will? Why?

Exodus 3–4

The Call of God

"*If* a man is called to preach the Gospel, God will crush him till the light of the eye, the power of the life, the ambition of the heart, is all riveted on Himself. That is not done easily. It is not a question of saintliness, it has to do with the Call of God."

Oswald Chambers

Exodus 3–4

IN A NUTSHELL

While Moses is taking care of his father-in-law's sheep, God appears to him in a bush that burns but isn't consumed. God calls Moses to go back to Egypt and lead God's people out of slavery. He gives Moses all the evidence he needs that God will enable him to carry out this assignment. After arguing with God, Moses leaves for Egypt.

The Call of God

I. INTRODUCTION

My Call

*B*efore going into the ministry, I taught junior high school science for ten years. I thoroughly enjoyed those years, but I still remember vividly a restlessness developing in my heart over the final two years. I began offering Bible studies for the students who were interested during the lunch hours. God confirmed in my spirit that there would soon be a transition in my life. Then came what I would consider to be my "burning bush" encounter.

Driving home, I had to pass the Forest Home Mortuary and Cemetery every day just off the Interstate 10 freeway in southern California. This day, however, was going to be a little different. I found myself taking the off ramp toward the cemetery, just wanting a little solitude before I went home. At the end of the main drive, I came directly in front of a massive mosaic of the Lord's Supper. I climbed out of my car, walked to one of the wire chairs in front of the biblical portrait, and began to pray. It was at this moment God said to me about as clearly as anyone will ever hear the voice of God speaking in the depths of their soul, "It's time! I want you to leave teaching and preach my word." With tears on my face, I received the call of God into the ministry, a call that I have at times doubted and struggled with, but nonetheless a call to serve him.

My call follows a long list of servants before me. Throughout history, God has had a way of getting people's attention and compelling them into the ministry. Several centuries ago Moses received his call. He recognized his own personal inadequacies, but God confirmed to Moses his leading and a personal guarantee of protection and support. And Moses accepted his call to serve.

II. COMMENTARY

The Call of God

> **MAIN IDEA:** *God called, molded, and equipped his servant Moses.*

A Yahweh in a Burning Bush (3:1–6)

> **SUPPORTING IDEA:** *God appeared to Moses in an unpredictable, but unmistakable way.*

3:1. As the story of Moses unfolds, we learn once again how sudden and unpredictable our lives can be in the service of God. But behind the scenes of our lives is an invisible hand weaving a fabric with careful design. Perhaps the memories of his former life in Egypt and the knowledge of the still-oppressed people there slipped in and out of Moses' consciousness.

For unknown reasons, Moses drove his father-in-law's flock clear to the **far side of the desert**, all the way to **Horeb, the mountain of God**. Horeb was located in the peninsula of Sinai, where God later gave the law to Israel (18:5). *Horeb* and *Sinai* refer to the same mountain (cp. 33:6 with 19:11), but could also designate a series of mountains in the same vicinity.

3:2–6. Here the **angel of the Lord** appeared to Moses **in flames of fire from within a bush**. We could say that God appeared to Moses as the angel of the Lord (KD, 437; see "Deeper Discoveries"). With this appearance and continuing with the narrative that follows, the writer introduces to us something of the meaning behind the name *Yahweh* or *Jehovah* (see "Deeper Discoveries"), the covenant God who cares for his people. This God, who remembers his covenant (6:5), will direct, deliver, and bless his people through his *presence*, or "active reality" (Moyter, 260). God did not create and situate a people merely to live for themselves on earth. He created a people to love and worship him.

God, for his part, would protect these people with a jealous love that would lead them to the promised land. The history of man now becomes the history of redemption, with this covenant God revealing himself as Yahweh, the ever-existing God who reveals himself in mercy and judgment. He stands ready to deliver, or redeem, his people from bondage. Although this bondage begins with political bondage in Egypt, God's redemptive work goes far beyond that. With the revelation of God as Yahweh comes the unfolding teaching of the relation he sustains with a *particular* people. Subsequent writers of both the Old and New Testaments will develop this theme of God's gracious choice of a nation and a people who are the apple of his eye.

Furthermore, this God speaks to his people in manifold ways (Heb. 1:1) as we now see him speak from within a flaming bush that is not consumed. This peculiar sight caught the attention of Moses, who drew near to find out why the bush did not burn up. There he encountered an audible voice calling out to him, **Moses! Moses!** God forbade Moses from approaching him and commanded him to remove his sandals. Moses was on **holy ground**. God identified himself as the God of the patriarchs Abraham, Isaac, and Jacob—names that Moses knew something about. The announcement must have soothed Moses' initial fears somewhat, but perhaps only for a moment. Soon Moses **hid his face**, afraid to gaze directly into the appearance of God in the bush.

B God Promises His Presence to Moses (3:7–12)

SUPPORTING IDEA: *God cared for his people and provided for their deliverance.*

3:7–9. God had seen the miseries of his people in the land of Egypt and now came down to deliver them from their captors and bring them to an expansive land currently occupied by other nations. The expression **a land flowing with milk and honey** described the fertile and beautiful land of Canaan.

3:10–12. But Moses knew he must first appear before the Egyptian Pharaoh to make his case, something Moses recoiled from. While Moses was in Egypt, he once tried to deliver someone from a cruel oppressor by his own human force. But years in the desert taught him humility and a healthy distrust of his own power (KD, 440). God promised Moses that he would not have to go it alone, but he would accompany Moses all the way to Pharaoh's courts and beyond. God further encouraged Moses with a promise: The people of Israel will yet come all the way back to this very mountain to worship God.

C Yahweh Overcomes His Servant's Objections (3:13–22)

SUPPORTING IDEA: *Man's weakness is God's opportunity.*

3:13–18. Moses began a series of protests against this God-sized assignment. What if the people of Israel asked the name of God who had sent Moses? God told Moses to let them know the self-existing Yahweh, the God of their forefathers, had sent him to them. God promised to go with Moses and to be an abiding and unfailing presence with him and the people of Israel. The name of Yahweh, the face of Yahweh, the angel of Yahweh, and later the pillar and the cloud—all these expressed the permanence of God's presence among his people in contrast to the fleeting and temporary appearances that characterized his relations with the earlier patriarchs (Vos, 106). With Moses, God's presence would be more constant, an indication of what was to come in the future.

God commanded Moses to assemble the elders of Israel and announce to them that the same God who appeared to their fathers in the land of Canaan had appeared to him, promising to deliver them from their taskmasters in Egypt. Moreover, God promised to bring them to "a good and spacious land, a land flowing with milk and honey" (v. 8), now inhabited by other nations. These elders were to follow Moses' leadership as he went before Pharaoh.

There Moses would reveal first to Pharaoh that the LORD, **the God of the Hebrews**, had met with his people. He would then seek permission to make a three-day journey into the wilderness to offer sacrifices to God.

3:19–22. God warned Moses that he would meet resistance from Pharaoh. But God promised that he would support Moses by striking **the Egyptians with all the wonders** that he would **perform among them**. Supported by God's **mighty hand**, Israel would be allowed to leave Egypt and would **not go empty-handed**.

D God's Sufficiency for His Servant (4:1–17)

SUPPORTING IDEA: *God will provide supernaturally what man lacks naturally.*

4:1–5. The protest of Moses seems legitimate at face value. Moses believed. He experienced God in the burning bush. But what about his brothers in Egypt? Would his words, his description of what he had witnessed, be sufficient to bring them on board? God knew these people better than Moses. He was prepared to do what was necessary to convince them that Moses was his spokesman.

As a shepherd, one of Moses' key tools was a staff. God commanded him to **throw it on the ground**, where it turned into a **snake**. The snake represents diabolical evil embodied in the one great adversary, the devil. He was present in the garden of Eden and would join forces with Pharaoh and his armies in pursuit of the fleeing Hebrews. Moses didn't have the means to defeat or even compete against such an adversary, as God demonstrated to him. God told him to reach down and grab the snake by the tail. Moses did, and the snake promptly turned back into his staff. God told Moses that this sign would convince the Hebrews that **the God of Abraham, the God of Isaac and the God of Jacob** had appeared to Moses.

4:6–7. Similarly, God told Moses to reach his hand into his cloak. When he pulled it out, his hand was covered with leprosy. But at the command of God, Moses put it back into his cloak, and when he took it out again, **it was restored** and looked like the rest of Moses' body. Through these signs God told Moses he would enable him to fulfill his calling by supplying him with everything he needed.

4:8–17. Knowing the power of unbelief, God gave Moses one more authenticating sign to depend on if the first two signs failed to persuade the Egyptians. Moses was to take some water from the Nile River and pour it on the ground where it would turn into blood.

Even with all of this support, Moses persisted with still more objections. He cited his lifelong inability to speak well as a reason not to obey his commission from God. Even his personal encounter with God had not changed that. But God reminded Moses that he had created his mouth and his senses.

He promised that he would give him the words needed and enable him to speak them effectively.

Yet as God removed Moses' objections and excuses one by one, Moses showed his real motive: He just did not want to take on this mission. God became angry with Moses. God told him that his brother Aaron would be his spokesman. God would show both Moses and Aaron what to say and do. The mission would not fail because of reluctant servants. God would make them willing in the day of his power.

🄴 Moses' Farewell to Family (4:18–31)

SUPPORTING IDEA: *Sometimes God's service uproots us from familiar surroundings.*

4:18–23. Moses returned to his father-in-law Reuel and bade him farewell, not telling the true reason for leaving for a time. Reuel gave his blessing to Moses and allowed him to leave.

God further encouraged Moses by letting him know that the men who once sought him were now dead. At this Moses departed the land of Midian and, along with his wife and sons, began the long journey back to Egypt. God again assured Moses of his ultimate success, even though at first God would harden the heart of Pharaoh so as not to let the people of Israel go. To this Moses would reply, **This is what the LORD says: Israel is my firstborn son.** Egypt would learn that God distinguished between Egypt and Israel. Egypt had to obey God's command to let his nation go and sacrifice. Egypt's stubbornness would come only at great cost to them: God would take their firstborn children in death.

4:24–31. Verse 24 contains a puzzling and difficult account of the Lord actually seeking to kill Moses. No doubt Moses refused to circumcise his son. When Zipporah finally circumcised the child, the Lord let him go. This appears to be the best explanation of why God sought to kill Moses. Some interpreters object to the severity of the threatened penalty, but Israel was not to take lightly the covenant sign that God established between himself and Abraham. Indeed, God had before pronounced death on any who would violate this sacred rite, labeling them covenant breakers (Gen. 17:14).

God had spoken to Aaron as well, telling him to go to the desert and meet his younger brother. Moses related all that God said to him and what they were to do. Upon their return to Egypt, Moses and Aaron summoned the elders of Israel and told them everything God had said to Moses. They performed signs in the presence of the elders, who then believed their words. They also learned that the God of whom they spoke was no impersonal God, but one who cared for them in their misery. He was the covenant-making God of their fathers, their deliverer, and the object of their worship.

> **MAIN IDEA REVIEW:** *God called, molded, and equipped his servant Moses.*

III. CONCLUSION

"I Was Thrown into the Stream"

George W. Truett became pastor of the First Baptist Church of Dallas, Texas, at the age of thirty. He was converted at the age of nineteen, and it was obvious to people who observed Truett's life that God had a special work for him. He was preparing to teach school and thinking about going to law school. One Saturday night Truett's church held a business meeting. When Truett arrived, he realized the primary matter of business was for the church to vote to ordain him to the ministry. Truett, twenty-three at the time, rose to protest, but the church would not hear him. Looking back on this event, Truett said, "There I was, against a whole church, against a church profoundly moved. There was not a dry eye in the house . . . one of the supremely solemn hours in a church's life. I was thrown into the stream, and just had to swim."

George Truett was not the first to resist the call. Moses tried, but with a fresh revelation from God and a new set of values guiding his life, he could not. You might remember that forty years earlier this was Moses' dream, but God needed to place him in a school of learning where new values would change his heart and prepare him for the awesome task ahead. We pastors relate to Moses more than we want to admit. The call to service is a wonderful call but a momentous responsibility. If I had known everything I do now about the ministry, I may not have been so open to the Lord's leading to ministry. My own experience has caused me to lighten up a little on Moses. Forty years in the wilderness made him much more aware of the work ahead as a messenger and leader of God's people.

PRINCIPLES

- God speaks to us in a variety of ways if we are tuned in.
- God breaks up the hardened soil and hearts before us when we commit to his service.
- God will never ask you to do something without his presence to guide and protect you.
- God prepares and provides resources for the tasks to which he calls us.

APPLICATIONS

- Be sure to follow through on the things you think God wants you to do.
- When in doubt, never forget that God alone is faithful!
- Be sensitive to the pain in the people around you.

IV. LIFE APPLICATION

Get Busy

A bumper sticker read, "Jesus is coming . . . look busy!" Cute sticker—lousy theology! God knows what is going on in your life. He knows all the opportunities you have neglected, all the acts of servanthood you have performed, and all his attempts to get your attention that you have rejected. The Bible tells us that Jesus Christ is coming again and we are to accept his call to be busy, not to go through life trying to fool everyone around us. You cannot fool God by faking your involvement. He has a job for you to do in your family, in your community, and in your church. Are you listening for his call?

V. PRAYER

Lord, I confess I sometimes get so busy, I don't slow down enough to hear you speaking to me. I wonder what you have asked me to do even this week that I have failed to do because of conflicting priorities. Forgive me, Lord. I am going to sit here for a few minutes and just listen to you. Is there anything you want me to do today? Amen.

VI. DEEPER DISCOVERIES

A. Jehovah/Yahweh

Although the name *Jehovah* or *Yahweh* was not unknown in earlier years (Gen. 15:2), Moses and writers after him used it with more frequency. "Yahweh" is a term derived from the Hebrew verb "to be." The name denotes the self-existent, covenant God who lives and acts independent of outside influences. With this name God reveals himself as the faithful God of all grace (Berkhof, 49) who pledges himself to his people. This faithful God of the covenant does not change his being or purposes as it relates to his people whom he has redeemed. Other names of God include Lord of Hosts (probably referring to the hosts or armies of angelic beings), Elohim (God), El Elyon (God most high), Adonai (Lord or master), and El Shaddai (God all-sufficient), among others.

God reveals himself to us in his character, words, and even his names. Today people place little significance in a name. But in the ancient Middle East a "name often commemorated some great historical or religious event or denoted the parent's hope for or assessment of a child's character" (Reymond, 153). Hence God reveals something of his nature and relations toward his people through his names.

B. The Angel of the Lord (3:2)

The special designation "angel of the LORD" does not refer to ordinary angels. In Genesis 18 and again in Judges 6, the term becomes interchangeable with God himself. Moses saw a bush on fire but was not consumed (Exod. 3:2), heard the voice of God (3:4), and yet saw no "angel" as they are often pictured in art. He later led the Israelites (14:19), appeared to the prophet Balaam (Num. 22:22) and Joshua as the "commander of the army of the Lord" (Josh. 5:14–15), and manifested himself with special instructions to Samson's parents (Judg. 13). Most of the references above have led scholars to conclude this angel of the Lord to be none other than the second person of the Trinity, later to be incarnated as the Lord Jesus Christ.

C. Elders (3:16)

One of the more conspicuous offices of biblical leadership is that of "elder." Nowhere does the Bible formally introduce the concept of eldership, as it does priest or king. It simply appears early on. The elders of Israel assisted the other installed leaders of Israel in leading the nation (Exod. 4:29; Deut. 5:23; Josh. 7:6; Ezek. 8:1), a practice that continued through the New Testament era, as seen in Luke 22:66, where Jesus appeared before them along with the chief priests. The New Testament included elders from its inception (Acts 14:23; 1 Pet. 5:1–2), and Paul included the office in newly formed churches (Titus 1:5–9). Never do we see them function officially as individuals, but as a team. Originally the term referred to older men, who naturally stood as the wise representatives of the people.

The Bible teaches that God leads and directs his people through a specified order and by godly representatives. Today churches should be careful who they select as their leaders and always keep foremost in their minds the necessity of preparing and grooming godly leaders.

D. The Hardening of Pharaoh's Heart (4:21)

When addressing this difficult matter of God hardening Pharaoh's heart, we must remember that when Pharaoh first encountered God he already had a sinner's heart. The text clearly states that at times Pharaoh hardened his own heart. Still, other texts are quite clear that God fully intended to harden the despot's heart for the purpose of displaying signs and wonders and freeing his people from Pharaoh's tyranny. Furthermore, a problem still exists even for those who believe that Pharaoh first hardened his heart and only afterwards did God harden his heart: Why did God still harden his heart when he might normally allow for a time of repentance?

In Romans 9 Paul appeals to God's sovereign right to harden Pharaoh's heart much as a potter shapes a piece of clay after his own purposes (Rom. 9:17–21). The Book of Exodus elsewhere declares God's purpose in installing Pharaoh as leader in the first place: to show God's power and proclaim his name throughout the world (Exod. 9:16; Rom. 9:17, see Reymond, 359–60). Is God unrighteous? God forbid. Students of Scripture know that God is both sovereign and merciful. He is patient, kind, forbearing, and slow to anger (Nah. 1:3). While the Bible does contain some concepts hard to understand, we will travel safer ground by accepting Scripture at face value and relegating the more difficult passages to the realm of mystery. God is God.

VII. TEACHING OUTLINE

A. INTRODUCTION

1. Lead Story: My Call

2. Context: Moses was a man of two cultures. He was born a Hebrew but educated as an Egyptian. His identification with the Hebrews became clear when he killed an Egyptian for beating a Hebrew slave. When Moses realized his deed was known, he fled to the land of Midian. There he married and worked for his father-in-law Reuel over a period of forty years. In this setting, God appeared to him and called him to a task for which he had been prepared since his birth.

3. Transition: These chapters begin with Moses in the wilderness tending sheep and ends with Moses and Aaron in Egypt before the elders of Israelite explaining the mission God had for them.

B. COMMENTARY

1. Yahweh in a Burning Bush (3:1–6)

2. God Promises His Presence to Moses (3:7–12)

3. Yahweh Overcomes His Servant's Objections (3:13–22)

4. God's Sufficiency for His Servant (4:1–17)

5. Moses' Farewell to Family (4:18–31)

C. CONCLUSION: GET BUSY

VIII. ISSUES FOR DISCUSSION

1. What does it take for God to get your attention? Can you think of some "burning bush" experiences in your life that God has used to move you out of your comfort zone?
2. God's will for every believer is involvement. What is your involvement right now in the church? Is there something God has wanted you to do and you have not listened to his call?
3. Read Exodus 3:1–6 again. Describe the kind of relationship God desired Moses to have with him. What kind of relationship does God want with you?

Exodus 5–7

God's Deliverance from Tough Times

"*W*hoever is spared personal pain must feel himself called to help in diminishing the pain of others. We must all carry our share of the misery which lies upon the world."

Albert Schweitzer

Exodus 5–7

 IN A NUTSHELL

*M*oses stands before Pharaoh and demands the freedom of the people of Israel only to find Pharaoh is both stubborn and defiant. When Pharaoh does not comply, Moses feels like a failure and begins to question God. Through a series of promises God makes it abundantly clear he can be trusted and will follow through on his promise.

God's Deliverance from Tough Times

I. INTRODUCTION

Getting the Message

A shipping company had advertised a job opening for a ship's radio operator, and the outer office was crowded with applicants for the position. They were waiting to be called in turn and were talking to one another loudly enough to be heard over the sound of the loudspeaker. Another applicant entered the crowded waiting room, filled out his application, and sat quietly for a few moments. Suddenly, he rose and walked into the office marked PRIVATE. A few minutes later, he came out of the room with a huge smile on his face. He had been hired; the job was his. Someone in the waiting room began to protest. "Hey, we've been waiting a lot longer than you. Why did you go in there before us?"

The new radio operator replied, "Any one of you could have landed this job, but none of you were listening to the Morse Code signals coming over the loudspeaker. The message was, 'We desire to fill this position with someone who is constantly alert. If you are getting this message, come into the private office immediately.'"

Pharaoh could have been in that same waiting room, and he wouldn't have gotten the message either. He was a poor listener. In fact, we are going to see the great lengths God went to in order to get him to listen in a few chapters when we examine the plagues. But for now, there was no code for Pharaoh to decipher, simply, "God says to let my people go!" But when you fail to listen to God or his word, you are inviting trouble. Pharaoh didn't learn that right away because he decided to put up a fight. The only problem was that Pharaoh's poor listening didn't lose him a job; it lost additional security for the Hebrew people, who would now be forced to do additional work.

II. COMMENTARY

God's Deliverance from Tough Times

MAIN IDEA: *Moses is tested before Pharaoh.*

A Israel's Hardships (5:1–23)

SUPPORTING IDEA: *The Egyptian tormentors turn up the heat.*

5:1. God gave Pharaoh every opportunity to obey him by letting the Hebrews venture out into the wilderness in order to sacrifice to God. Judgment did not come first but rather an appeal through God's spokesmen Moses and Aaron. They made their appearance before Pharaoh and asked him to grant them a suitable leave so they could go into the desert to make a sacrifice to God. We do not know for certain how Moses and Aaron were granted such access into Pharaoh's own courts. Perhaps Pharaoh learned of the popular sentiment, by now widespread among the guest nation, that the God of Abraham, Isaac, and Jacob had once again visited his people with strict commands to worship him in a prescribed manner. The request to relocate the people for sacrifice should not have seemed an unusual request to Pharaoh. The particular rites that the Hebrew nation would follow could very well stir up religious animosity among their Egyptian hosts.

5:2–5. Pharaoh did not respond with objections of pure logistics, at least not at first. Instead he revealed his own heart by asking, **Who is the LORD, that I should obey him and let Israel go?** Questions of identity and authority form the essence of belief, certainly in the spiritual realm. Who is God, and what does he require of me? Pharaoh could not grant the request because he did not know the God of whom Moses and Aaron spoke. Consequently, he would not allow them to relocate to the desert however short that time might be. Moses and Aaron replied that God specifically met with them and commanded them to journey away from the environs of Egypt in order to make a sacrifice to him. Israel could not disobey this command lest they lose the favor of God and he would strike them with plagues or an invading army from the outside.

But Pharaoh did not give in to this appeal. He commanded them to return to their work of making brick. Perhaps Pharaoh's advisers whispered to him that a revolt was imminent, and he should put it down by discouraging its leaders Moses and Aaron. To Pharaoh the large number of Hebrews meant either economic disaster or opportunity. They would produce much for their host nation but could also cost it much by stopping their labors.

5:6–9. Pharaoh no doubt attributed the recent awakening for liberty among the Hebrews as simply having too much time to think. He therefore commanded his servants to enact stricter measures in the way the Hebrews labored. From now on they were not only to produce the prescribed quota but also to do so by gathering the straw themselves. Brick-making involved digging clay from the ground, tempering it, mixing it with straw, and then forming the brick tablets. The straw was used probably not so much as a binding agent as it was to prolong the life of the brick (Hannah, 116). But because Pharaoh forced the Hebrews to locate the straw themselves, their work would now double (Rawlinson, 124). Whether or not Pharaoh believed that the Hebrews were lazy, he certainly wanted his slave drivers to believe that.

5:10–18. These slave drivers faithfully reported Pharaoh's command to the Israelites, causing them to scatter frantically all over Egypt to locate straw. About the only place to locate it was on the ground in the cornfields, but then they had to grind it up into small particles to mix it in properly with the bricks. Part of Pharaoh's strategy might have been to divide and conquer the Israelites by imposing individual penalties on those slaves who did not produce. This might have the effect of fracturing the unity of the nation and turn them against one another. But Pharaoh's new restriction resulted in inevitable failure, and the Hebrews could no longer produce bricks at the same pace as before. Consequently, the appointed Hebrew foremen were beaten and interrogated.

The **Israelite foremen went and appealed to Pharaoh** that his demands were not only unreasonable but also impossible. Unless he lifted the requirement that they find their own straw, they would not be able to produce, and the fault would reside with them. Pharaoh replied that the laborers had grown **lazy** and needed to return immediately to their work.

5:19–23. The foremen, troubled by Pharaoh's insensitivity and apprehensive about their own near-term prospects, vented their frustrations and fears on Moses and Aaron, who had been waiting for their report. The foremen now blamed the two brothers for raising their hopes only to see them dashed on the ground by Pharaoh's contempt of their request. Surely Pharaoh and his leaders would now suspect them of initiating a revolt, and just as surely Pharaoh would put it down with brute force, if necessary.

Moses did not respond directly to the foremen. He found himself once again going before the Lord with nothing but questions. His only constituency—the people of his birth and the very people the Lord sent him to deliver—now railed bitterly against him. But now God would take Moses to the school of prayer and teach him that short-term failure would never be final when God is involved. God had previously stated that success would not come easy (3:19), but through hardship God would be with his servant (3:12).

Moses used an argument that there was a link between his recent troubles and God's sending him before Pharaoh. He also bemoaned God's delay in delivering his people from Egypt's clutches as if it were somehow contrary to God promise. But God would soon demonstrate to his servant that true strength would be perfected in weakness, and the wisdom of all who would follow God is their total trust in him.

B The Lord Encourages His Servant (6:1–30)

SUPPORTING IDEA: *The Lord reminds his servant of his unchanging purpose for Israel.*

6:1–8. God reassured Moses by reaffirming his promise that he would bring his people out of captivity and into the land of Canaan. Many hardships awaited Moses on this long journey to Canaan, and he needed to learn the strong consoling name of Yahweh was all he needed. Moses would need to lift up the hearts of thousands of travelers in the coming decades, and he would have to learn where to find encouragement in times of distress. He would also learn more and more about the God he now served. Part of this knowledge comes through knowing the names of God, which signified more than mere attributes but revealed something of the character of God.

But now the time of deliverance drew near. **Now you will see**, the Lord said to Moses, what he would do to Pharaoh. He would not only yield to the Lord's command and let the people go but would drive them out himself. God further encouraged his prophet by pointing out his original covenant with Abraham, Isaac, and Jacob. He did not reveal himself as fully to them as he would to Moses.

Although God did reveal his covenant name to Abraham (Gen. 15:7), he was primarily known to them as a God of power and might. With Moses he would more fully disclose his name and character, as the self-existing faithful God who would bring rest to the tired people of his covenant. The patriarchs Abraham, Isaac, and Jacob wandered through the land of Canaan as aliens, but Moses would lead the people to the brink of the land of permanent dwelling. The self-existing God of the covenant cared for his afflicted people and **heard the groaning of the Israelites**.

God offered them an **outstretched arm**, as if to reach out to pull them up from a slippery slope or a perilous pit. The wonders with which God would bring out the Israelites from Egypt were not mere signs to amaze but mighty acts of **judgment**, designed to punish the cruel nation of oppressors. When God performed all these mighty acts, the Israelites would then know that he was truly the Lord their God, the one who delivered them.

Of course, the greatest promise of all was the permanent dwelling of God with his people, his presence in their midst. The writers of Scripture all weave this thread through the unfolding theme of salvation. God longed to dwell with his people in perfect and permanent peace. They are, after all, the people of his possession. He would take them as his own people. In the centuries following, the budding nation would test this relationship to the limit by repeated acts of unfaithfulness in turning to other gods and idol worship. But God would never turn his back completely on them because of his faithfulness to his promise. In an interesting play on words, the Israelites would be the possession of God, and God, in turn, would grant the land of Canaan as their possession. Their hold on this land would always be linked to their relationship with God (see Lev. 26:3–45; Deut. 28:1–68).

6:9–12. The Israelites, who expected a mighty and speedy deliverance, were in no mood to listen to Moses now. They felt Moses had deceived them once; why should they listen to him now? God once again told Moses to return to Pharaoh and tell him to let the Israelites leave the country. But Moses complained to God that he lacked the oratorical skills to persuade the people. Moses must have attributed his recent disappointing dialogue with the people to his lack of speaking ability.

6:13–27. The narrative now includes an important genealogical account of Moses' origin, since he occupies such a prominent role in Israel's history. The nation was based on tribal affiliation, and Joshua would later assign their portions in Canaan according to tribe. Moses mentioned **Reuben** and **Simeon** because they were the firstborn of Jacob (Gen. 29:32–33), but quickly he came to **Levi**, the head of the tribe to which Moses belonged. The sons of Levi—Gershon, Kohath, and Merari—began the lineage of Levi and would represent the Levitical division of duties in the tabernacle and later the temple (Num. 4:1–33). Levi lived for 137 years.

Moses' immediate family is mentioned in Exod. 6:20–25, with Amram (not the Amram of verse 18, which would have made him a contemporary of Joseph) as the father of Aaron and Moses. Amram married his own aunt Jochebed, a practice up to this point allowed but later forbidden in Leviticus 18:12. The writer mentions more of the pedigree of Aaron than Moses, probably because Moses married a non-Israelite and Aaron's immediate sons would form the priesthood of Israel.

In verse 26 of this passage the narrative resumes by reviewing the commission of Moses and Aaron. The later Jews would place great value on genealogical roots, particularly of their leaders. The leaders of our present account could trace their ancestry to the origins of the nation.

6:28–30. The two great qualifications of a called prophet were to know the Lord God and faithfully to announce his words to the people. God called Moses and separated him for this very task. God disclosed himself to Moses in fuller measure than the patriarchs before him. To such a man he would entrust his message of deliverance and command him to **tell Pharaoh king of Egypt everything I tell you.** Although he felt ill prepared for this task and still complained of less than desirable speaking skills, Moses now embarked on the mission he was created for.

◖C◗ First Signs (7:1–25)

> **SUPPORTING IDEA:** *God begins to display his power before his servants and Pharaoh.*

7:1. Moses probably felt intimidated by the thought of venturing into Pharaoh's court with such a message. But God reminded him that he not only would successfully confront Pharaoh; in light of subsequent signs and wonders, he would appear as a god to Pharaoh. Aaron himself would appear as the interpreter of Moses' words to Pharaoh.

7:2–7. Moses was to report to Pharaoh what God commanded him. The probable order of dialogue was Moses spoke to Aaron and then Aaron to Pharaoh. We should not suppose, however, that Moses never spoke directly to Pharaoh at all. God had told him he could do so, but eventually he accommodated Moses' wavering faith in his ability to convince Pharaoh through his own tongue.

But God knew in advance that Pharaoh would not let the Israelites go. God would harden the king's heart, causing Pharaoh to defy God's words. Although the words of God about hardening Pharaoh trouble many today, the hearts of the leaders never slip out of God's sphere of control (see "Deeper Discoveries"). As God would later move Cyrus to proclaim emancipation to the captives of Persia, so he originally put it in the heart of Nebuchadnezzar to conquer Judah as an instrument of discipline. The result of these mighty judgments would be that Egypt would know that **I am the LORD**. Moses and Aaron now approached the sovereign throne of Pharaoh with the words of their God.

7:8–13. God quickly established the credentials of his spokesmen by performing a miracle with Aaron's staff. Aaron responded to Pharaoh's inevitable request for a sign by casting down his staff before Pharaoh. The staff became a snake. Pharaoh may have been prepared for the kind of sign Moses performed, as word may have got to him about previous signs (see 4:17,30) performed by Aaron and Moses. The "magicians" of Pharaoh's court duplicated this sign by casting down their own staffs that turned into snakes. Some have speculated that the Egyptian soothsayers were actually ancient tricksters or snake charmers who had the ability to charm snakes into a state of rigor mortis, only to bring them back to normal through similar means. Others believe evil spirits assisted the magicians. In the end, Aaron's snake swallowed the other snakes. But Pharaoh's heart grew harder even while beholding this sign.

7:14–21. When Pharaoh refused to let the Israelites go, God told Moses and Aaron to meet Pharaoh when he went to the water the next morning (possibly to offer a sacrifice to the Nile). There they were to repeat the word of the Lord to let them go into the desert to make sacrifice to him and also to announce another sign—the waters of the Nile turning to blood. The Egyptians relied on the resources of the Nile for virtually everything from fishing to irrigation (Isa. 19:5–10). But **the fish in the Nile** would die and along with it the fortunes of Egypt, at least for a time.

The Lord commanded Moses to tell Aaron to stretch his staff in the direction of the waters of Egypt. Moses and Aaron obeyed the word of the Lord, and Aaron stretched his staff over the waters of Egypt. These included both natural and man-made canals along the river, ponds, marshes, and pools, and even the water collected in buckets and jars. The effect of this judgment was an awful stench that filled the air and widespread scarcity of suitable drinking water.

7:22–25. Instead of joining in the search for water, the magicians, bent on duplicating this latest sign, **did the same things by their secret arts**. They probably found water by digging, as we see in verse 24. Pharaoh, quite content with what the magicians could do, turned toward his stately palace, undisturbed by the disaster before him. Pharaoh literally did not take this to heart and further hardened his heart. He would not lift the injunction against Israel and let them go to the desert to offer sacrifice to the Lord. He left his suffering people to dig around the Nile, where apparently the judgment of the blood did not affect the subterranean waters residing below the surface. This first plague lasted seven days.

MAIN IDEA REVIEW: *Moses is tested before Pharaoh.*

III. CONCLUSION

Questioning the Call

Moses did everything he was supposed to do. He was assertive before Pharaoh. "Let my people go!" sounded so straightforward. Then why didn't Pharaoh respond to God's word? This proud Egyptian leader insinuated that the Hebrews were trying to get out of work. So he gave them even more work. A delegation was formed to persuade Pharaoh of his injustice, but this didn't work. So all the pain caused the Hebrew representatives to turn on Moses and Aaron. Moses turned to God again. After all, it had been God who sent Moses on this mission. You might think that God would solve all the problems in advance. But he didn't. Moses asked, "Why?" and began to question his call.

PRINCIPLES

- Just because you have a message doesn't mean people will listen.
- Satan wants every spiritual leader to become discouraged.
- People rebel when in pain.
- Any disobedience in God's eyes is serious.

- God disciplines those he loves.
- God will address every idol in our lives because he is a jealous God.
- God's judgment will fall. Be patient.
- God's mercy gives us ample time to obey before he enters the scene and corrects the problem.

APPLICATIONS

- Remain faithful to your responsibility; God is not finished.
- Some people have hardened hearts, and we must trust in the Lord to break through those barriers.
- Never fear honesty with the Lord. He already knows your heart.
- Doubts are a normal part of accepting an assignment of faith, but you must work through them.
- When you are praying for God's leading in your life, pray for every other person and situation that may add to his leading even though you may not be aware of it yet.
- Quit whining and trust God.
- Be very careful whom you follow. Test the fruit of one's leadership.

IV. LIFE APPLICATION

The Devil's Yard Sale

The devil once had a yard sale. He put out all of his tools with a price sticker on each one. There were a lot of them, including hatred, envy, jealousy, doubt, lying, pride, and lust. Apart from the rest of the tools was an old, harmless-looking tool with a high price.

One of the devil's customers asked about this high-priced tool. The devil said, "Why, that's discouragement."

The customer asked, "Why do you have such a high price on it?"

The devil responded, "That's one of my most useful tools. When other tools won't work, I can pry open and get into a person's heart with discouragement. Once I get inside, I can do whatever I want. It's easy to get into a person's heart with this tool because few people know it belongs to me."

It's said that the devil's price on discouragement is so high that he's never been able to sell it. As a result, he continues to use it.

And he often uses it with his oldest tool: "Did God really say that?" "Are you sure he's called to do that?" "Wow, you sure have made a mess of things, haven't you?" These are very painful times and must be addressed by simply being honest with God. Ask the Lord why he is allowing these periods of stress and pain. Ask him for wisdom to walk through them graciously and humbly. But never allow any root of anger and bitterness to grow in your heart, because God is not finished with you yet.

V. PRAYER

Thank you, Father, for the reminder of this time in Moses' life. I think I get it Lord, at least for today. Help me trust you in the good and the bad . . . you're not done! And help me to listen. Amen.

VI. DEEPER DISCOVERIES

Bricks and Brick-making

The bricks in Bible times resembled bricks in our own time. The bricks that the Hebrews made were rectangular and were used for housing, architecture, and constructing various structures. They could be dried by either burning them in a kiln or drying them in the hot sun. Brickmakers could use straw as a hardening agent for the bricks. Some of the knowledge we now have of Egyptian language and culture we learned from inscriptions on bricks.

VII. TEACHING OUTLINE

A. INTRODUCTION

1. Lead Story: Getting the Message
2. Context: After Moses convinced the Israelite elders that God had called him to return to Egypt and lead them out of bondage, he went next to Pharaoh.
3. Transition: It's clear from the start that Pharaoh will not be easily persuaded by Moses. Pharaoh digs in his heels and makes the Israelites work harder with fewer resources. The Israelites begin to doubt Moses, and Moses questions both himself and God. God reassures Moses and begins to take a series of actions against Pharaoh.

B. COMMENTARY

1. Israel's Hardships (5:1–23)
2. The Lord Encourages His Servant (6:1–30)
3. First Signs (7:1–25)

C. CONCLUSION: THE DEVIL'S YARD SALE

VIII. ISSUES FOR DISCUSSION

1. You have no doubt heard, "When the going gets tough, the tough get going." Can you think of some setbacks in your life that have been difficult to overcome? Why do you think God allowed them?
2. Chapter 5 is a picture of a classic power struggle. What do you think is the root problem of this conflict? Who should take responsibility for reconciliation here? When you are in conflict, what are some things you can do while anticipating resolution?
3. When was the last time you responded in a way similar to that of the Israelites in this chapter? Was yours a correct response? How did you discover this answer?
4. How does a heart get hardened? Do you suppose God can still soften a "hardened heart"? How?
5. Describe the last time God gave you an assignment that appeared to be impossible but you accomplished it anyway. Describe the growth that takes place in a believer's life in such situations.

Exodus 8–11

Getting Pharaoh's Attention

I. **INTRODUCTION**
An Attitude Indicator

II. **COMMENTARY**
A verse-by-verse explanation of these chapters.

III. **CONCLUSION**
Pharaoh's "Nose-Down" Attitude

An overview of the principles and applications from these chapters.

IV. **LIFE APPLICATION**
Fixing the Problem

Melding these chapters to life.

V. **PRAYER**
Tying these chapters to life with God.

VI. **DEEPER DISCOVERIES**
Historical, geographical, and grammatical enrichment of the commentary.

VII. **TEACHING OUTLINE**
Suggested step-by-step group study of these chapters.

VIII. **ISSUES FOR DISCUSSION**
Zeroing these chapters in on daily life.

"*H*ow many a hardened rebel on shipboard, when the timbers are strained and creaking, when the mast is broken, and the ship is drifting before the gale, when the hungry waves are opening their mouths to swallow the ship up alive and quick as those that go into the pit— how many a hardened sailor has then bowed his knee, with tears in his eyes, and cried, 'I have sinned!' But of what avail and of what value was his confession? The repentance that was born in the storm died in the calm; that repentance of his that was begotten amidst the thunder and the lightning, ceased so soon as all was hushed in quiet, and the man who was a pious mariner when on board ship, became the most wicked and abominable of sailors when he placed his foot on *terra firma*."

Charles Haddon Spurgeon

Exodus 8–11

I N   A   N U T S H E L L

*E*xodus 8–11 represents the portion of the book where God addresses the idolatry in Egypt through a series of plagues on the land. God could have easily delivered the Hebrews without this demonstration of control, but his intent was educational. Now the whole world will see and know that he is God despite the hardness of Pharaoh's heart and defiance.

Getting Pharaoh's Attention

I. INTRODUCTION

An Attitude Indicator

An "attitude indicator" is an important piece of equipment on a plane. It shows the position of the plane in relationship to the horizon. As the plane climbs, there is a "nose-high attitude," meaning that the nose of the plane is above the horizon. A "nose-down attitude" for too long means it is going to crash. Monitoring a plane's attitude is important, and sometimes it's necessary to change the attitude in order to change the performance.

We reach the point of the story in Exodus where Pharaoh is about to crash. His "nose-down" attitude has made his heart impenetrable, but God continues his assault upon the Egyptian powers and idolatry for instruction purposes as various plagues are unleashed.

II. COMMENTARY

Getting Pharaoh's Attention

> **MAIN IDEA:** *If necessary, the Lord can carry out his plan by judgment.*

A The Plague of Frogs (8:1–15)

> **SUPPORTING IDEA:** *The Lord sends frogs to invade the land.*

8:1–15. Following an interval of unknown duration, the Lord once again commanded Moses to approach Pharaoh with the request to let God's people go so they might worship him. If Pharaoh again refused to grant the request, God would send innumerable frogs into the land to infest the Nile, Pharaoh's own palace, the houses of his officials, and the dwellings of all the people of the kingdom. The frogs would find their way into every place imaginable, including ovens and bedrooms and bread-making troughs. What would make this plague particularly annoying to the Egyptians was their trait of extreme cleanliness that characterized the entire country.

Although the narrative does not record the actual appeal to Pharaoh this time, God probably waited until Pharaoh once again refused to obey the request of Moses and Aaron before he commanded Moses and Aaron to begin initiating this judgment. Aaron again stretched his hand in the direction of the waters of Egypt, after which **the frogs came up and covered the land**. The magicians duplicated Aaron's act with apparent success, although the frogs they "called up" may have come from Aaron's original act. In any case, the magicians were by now outclassed and Egypt had a real problem.

Pharaoh then summoned Moses and Aaron before him and pleaded with them to call off the frogs. He gave his word that he would let the Israelites go offer sacrifices to God. Moses allowed Pharaoh to set the date. It is unclear from the text whether this date was when Moses called off the frogs or the date when Pharaoh would allow the Israelites to go into the desert.

John Calvin believed it unthinkable that Pharaoh would request Moses to call off the frogs the next day in view of the devastation they were causing in the land. More likely, he requested immediate relief from the judgment of the frogs while setting the next day as the time he would let the people of Israel go to sacrifice to God (Calvin, 163). Perhaps the text would allow for this explanation, and indeed Moses seemed to pray about the frogs immediately after his audience with Pharaoh (v. 12). Pharaoh could have set the time for the frogs to leave the next day for reasons unknown to us. Moses allowed Pharaoh to set the timing so he would know there was **no one like the LORD our God** and that stopping the plague was no accident or coincidence.

With the prayer of Moses, God called off the plague of the frogs, which soon died and **were piled into heaps**. But the land was now filled with the foul stench of the dead frogs. Once again, Pharaoh witnessed a mighty judgment of God, and once again, **hardened his heart** and did not let the Israelites leave.

B The Plague of Gnats (8:16–19)

SUPPORTING IDEA: *The Lord sends swarms of gnats.*

8:16–19. The Lord, seeing Pharaoh's continued refusal to let the Israelites go, unleashed the next plague unannounced. He directed Aaron to strike the dust with his staff. This would result in countless gnats, or mosquitoes, covering the land. The wording does not require the dust actually turned into gnats, only that the gnats were so plentiful that they covered all the land. The magicians again attempted to repeat this act but could not. They quickly acknowledged the work of God in this phenomenon, with the hint that Pharaoh might listen this time. The gnats were everywhere—on land, beast, and man. **But Pharaoh's heart was hard** and not in any mood to relinquish his hold on his income-producing slaves.

C The Plague of Flies (8:20–32)

SUPPORTING IDEA: *The Lord sends dense swarms of flies.*

8:20–32. The Lord next told Moses to meet Pharaoh as he went to the water (see commentary on 7:14) and announce to him the next plague: swarms of flies invading the land. The heaps of dead frogs had probably already attracted many flies to the region, but now dense swarms of these pests blanketed the entire land of Egypt except Goshen, where the Israelites lived. True to his word, the very next day God sent swarms of flies that covered the land, not sparing anyone or any place, including Pharaoh and his officials. Pharaoh hastily summoned Moses and Aaron into his presence and told them he would let the people go and sacrifice to God **here in the land**. Again Pharaoh did not fully loosen his hold on the Israelites but sought a clever compromise. Moses pointed out the political consequences of such a move. The Egyptians would not tolerate a rival practicing a different religion in the land and might even stone the Hebrew worshipers. Moses insisted that Pharaoh let the Israelites go into the desert for a three-day journey just as God had originally commanded them.

In verse 28 Pharaoh said he would let the Hebrews go if they didn't **go very far**. Moses did not seem to object to this latest caveat of Pharaoh and promised that the next day the flies would disappear from the land. However, he warned Pharaoh not to deal deceitfully with them. When Moses prayed to the Lord, the flies left almost as miraculously as they came, leaving no trace of their presence. But Pharaoh went back on his promise once again and would not let the people go.

D The Plague on Livestock (9:1–7)

SUPPORTING IDEA: *The Lord destroys the livestock of Egypt.*

9:1–7. While previous plagues harassed the Egyptians by disturbing their relative comfort, the Lord now directed his judgment toward the Egyptians themselves, beginning with their property.

As the Lord commanded, Moses and Aaron announced the next plague to Pharaoh. Following another appeal to release the Hebrew people to worship God away from the land of Egypt, the Lord now threatened Pharaoh with **a terrible plague on your livestock in the field** should he refuse to let the people go. The plague would result in the death of the Egyptian livestock, including horses, donkeys, camels, sheep, cattle, and goats. The economic consequences would be catastrophic on Egypt, since the livestock constituted a great deal of the production of the land, including food and dairy products. The result would certainly put political pressure on Pharaoh to do something quickly to remedy the crisis.

But the Lord would spare the livestock of the Hebrews, showing a marked difference between them and the Egyptians. The Lord did grant Pharaoh and the people a day to consider the pending judgment and to remove their livestock from the fields.

The following day the Lord struck the Egyptian livestock with an awful plague that resulted in their immediate death in the open fields. The livestock of the Hebrews, however, was left untouched. Pharaoh's apparent curiosity moved him to inquire of the Hebrew cattle, whether they had escaped this awful fate. Upon learning the Hebrew cattle was spared, Pharaoh further hardened his heart and refused to let the Israelites go.

E The Plague of Boils (9:8–12)

SUPPORTING IDEA: *The Lord sends festering boils on the Egyptians.*

9:8–12. The sixth plague came unannounced, but when it came it hit close to home, inflicting the Egyptians themselves. The Lord directed Moses and Aaron to **take handfuls of soot from a furnace** and have Moses release it to the open air in the presence of Pharaoh. As the God of the Hebrews was Lord over the water, air, earth, and life itself, so he was Lord over all elements, including fire. Following Moses' act God would strike the Egyptians and the remaining animals with severe boils. We cannot identify the specific kind of skin disease with any precision, only that it was severe. The magicians probably attempted to duplicate the sign but were themselves inflicted with painful boils. The Lord had still more signs and judgments to display, so he hardened Pharaoh's heart again. Pharaoh did not let the Israelites go and would not listen to Moses and Pharaoh, just as God predicted.

F The Plague of Hail (9:13–35)

SUPPORTING IDEA: *The Lord rains down hail upon Egypt.*

9:13–26. With the next plague, the worst hailstorm ever to fall on Egypt, came an announcement and fuller disclosure to Pharaoh of God's purpose and motive in unleashing such calamitous judgments upon the Egyptians. In fact, Pharaoh would now receive the final wave of God's fierce judgments with increasing intensity.

Moses rose up early and confronted Pharaoh with news of the impending judgment. As God predicted and later reaffirmed, he was now judging not only the Egyptians and their heartless stance toward his people, but their gods, who were no gods (1 Cor. 8:4–6). The Lord would convince the Egyptians, if only for a short time, that **there is no one like me in all the earth.** What they never considered was that God extended considerable mercy and patience toward them, because he could have wiped them off the face of the earth at any time. But the hidden purposes of God would now become manifest: God raised up Pharaoh for this very hour and purpose of displaying God's power and name in all the earth.

God warned Pharaoh to take heed to his words and bring his remaining livestock in from the open field where they would be vulnerable to injury from the falling hail. And, for the first time, human life was threatened. Some of those within earshot of Moses' words took the counsel and brought both man and beast inside for protection. But others did not listen to God and left their people and livestock in the open fields.

The Lord next directed Moses to stretch out his hand toward the sky, after which hail, accompanied with thunder and lightning, would fall on man and beast. Moses obeyed the word of the Lord, and the hail fell with such force that it crushed everything in its way, including the trees. The Egyptians faced death if things proceeded on the present course, but the hail did not fall in the land of Goshen where the Hebrews lived.

9:27–35. Pharaoh, now seized with panic, summoned Moses and Aaron and acknowledged his fault in treating the Hebrews with such severity. He requested Moses to pray to the Lord to remove this awful plague and he would let them go. Moses replied that upon his departure the plague would stop, but the servant of God knew the words of Pharaoh were tainted with deceit. The flax, used in making linen garments, and barley, a food source for horses, were destroyed in the plague. But the hail did spare **the wheat and spelt** (an after crop of the wheat, used in bread-making), so necessary for the sustenance of the Egyptians.

Once out of the city, Moses **spread out his hands toward the Lord**, and the hail stopped raining down on the land. But the respite brought no lasting change in Pharaoh's heart. Both he and his officials hardened their hearts and refused to let the Israelites go.

Ⓖ The Plague of Locusts (10:1–20)

SUPPORTING IDEA: *The Lord sends a plague of locusts.*

10:1–20. Pharaoh's persistent stubbornness and hardened stance played into the hands of God, who would display his great wonders before Pharaoh and the Israelites. The next plague, swarms of locusts (called "my great army" in Joel 2:25), would further endanger the nation's well-being, leading even Pharaoh to call it a "deadly plague" (v. 17).

The chapter opens with God telling Moses to go again into Pharaoh's presence and announce the next plague. The recent plagues were severe but had no effect on Pharaoh or his immediate officials. God would now display his power and might by striking the Egyptians with an awful judgment of locusts.

Moses and his brother approached the royal throne and asked Pharaoh how long he would refuse to humble himself before God. God was casting unmistakable judgment upon the so-called gods of Egypt, the gods that sought to seduce God's own people into false worship. It was time to let God's people go into the desert to worship, and Pharaoh should immediately allow this on pain of a deadly plague. The locusts would not spare anything in their path. They would eat crops, vegetables, trees, shrubs, and the eroding estates of the Egyptian people. Should Pharaoh refuse once again, God would unleash on them this latest plague, the eighth in number, the very next day.

While some suppose that loss of property and goods is the particular lament of the Western world, it is actually universal and timeless in scope and duration. The officials now begged Pharaoh to let the Israelites leave the "ruined" land of Egypt. Having lost the political support of his closest officials, Pharaoh admitted Moses and Aaron once again into his presence and granted another qualified release. Specifically, he asked, **Just who will be going?** Moses replied that all the Israelites plus their flocks and herds would need to depart to celebrate a festival to the Lord. In verse 10 Pharaoh answered sarcastically and dismissed Moses' request to let the women and children go. The original Hebrew of verse 11 implies Pharaoh had an official or bodyguard drive them out of his presence. Pharaoh's waffling now turned into rage as he drove off the two servants of God and with them the hopes for his nation's well-being.

The Lord told Moses to stretch out his hand over Egypt so that locusts would **swarm over the land and devour everything growing in the fields, everything left by the hail**. The Lord brought an east wind, a usual carrier of locusts that rely on such winds if they are to travel very far. With the wind came swarms of devouring locusts that settled in all regions of the country in vast numbers. The locusts (Heb. *'arbeh*) were two inches or more in length and had four wings. Although they had six legs, they walked on four, using the back legs for springing. God would later declare them clean food for consumption (Lev. 11:21–22), and they were eaten by John the Baptist (Matt. 3:4).

The locusts came in such numbers that they darkened the sky, consuming everything in sight. Pharaoh called for Moses and Aaron and pleaded with them to call off the voracious creatures before they destroyed the nation. He further responded with the most contrite words up to this point, confessing his sin and appealing to them to ask God to remove the locusts. Moses departed from Pharaoh and prayed to the Lord to remove the locusts. God graciously responded by whipping up a westerly wind, driving the locusts into the Red Sea. But again the Lord hardened Pharaoh's heart, and **he would not let the Israelites go**.

⊞ The Plague of Darkness (10:21–29)

SUPPORTING IDEA: *The Lord darkens all of Egypt.*

10:21–29. The ninth plague came with provocation but without warning, much like the third and sixth plagues. Darkness could come upon the land of Egypt at times when extreme wind kicked up the sand. But the next plague came with a divine signature and could not be mistaken for a natural phenomenon.

The Lord told Moses to stretch out his hand toward the sky **so that darkness will spread over Egypt**. The darkness would be so thick it could **be felt** (literally, "grasp"). Although some interpreters attribute this phenomenon to the effects of the sand upon the face, the acute nature of the blackened sky would better account for the expression. They would not be able to see one another and would fear even rising from their places lest they quickly fall. But the Israelites had light in Goshen and were relatively immune from the plague's effects.

Pharaoh responded to this plague by allowing Moses to depart with the women and children, but he would not allow him to take the flocks with him. Although Pharaoh may have stipulated this last condition out of greed or spite, more likely he would hold the flocks for security against the Israelites leaving for good. They could not long exist without the food provided by these animals. But Moses responded by restating the original terms of departure, which included taking with them all the animals. Moses did not know at the time how many animals they would need for sacrifice or precisely what kinds of animals would be required. With that Pharaoh flew into an irrational rage and expelled Moses from his sight, threatening him with death should he once again appear before him.

Ⅱ The Plague on the Egyptian Firstborn (11:1–10)

SUPPORTING IDEA: *The Lord kills the firstborn of all of Egypt.*

11:1–10. The first three verses are parenthetical and relate something that God previously told Moses. **One more plague** would afflict Pharaoh and the entire nation. This would be the means of Pharaoh not only allowing the Hebrews to venture away from the land but of Pharaoh actually driving them away. The plagues had increased in intensity, and soon God would lead the people out in a way that glorified his majesty, power, and holiness. The Lord told Moses he would grant them favor in the eyes of the Egyptians, and they were to ask the Egyptians for articles of silver and gold (probably "articles" to wear; see 3:22). Certainly the Israelites were entitled to these in view of their years of hardship and enslavement. God would cause the Egyptians to be willing to hand over these items to the Israelites, especially if it meant they would flee the land. Moses himself was afforded a lofty status among the Egyptians, not because of anything he had done, but because his God granted him special favor and chose to work mighty signs through him.

In the last interview between Pharaoh and Moses, he told Pharaoh the Lord's judgment would fall on the Egyptians in such a way that they would beg Moses and his people to leave the land. At midnight God would go throughout Egypt and strike all the firstborn, from the child of Pharaoh to the firstborn of slaves, not sparing any of them. He would also kill the firstborn of cattle. The firstborn represented the entire people (Gen. 49:3, see KD, 500) and often the best hopes and prospects of parents. Death remains the greatest fear of man. Man should fear and regard God, but instead will squeeze every drop out of his or her worldly existence, not caring for the will of God. But when faced with the ultimate fate, men even of careless disposition will sober up long enough to listen to a few wise words. The resultant cry from the Egyptians would be greater than ever before.

But among the Israelites, God's chosen people, not one child or animal would die. The expression, **not a dog will bark at any man or animal**, portrays the relative calm that would exist in Goshen in contrast to the upheaval throughout the rest of Egypt. The contrast would be striking, depicting the distinction between God's people and the Egyptians. The deadly stroke would prompt the officials of Pharaoh's court to do obeisance to Moses and beg him to leave the land. Following this announcement, Moses left Pharaoh's presence **hot with anger**. Pharaoh had already threatened Moses with death (10:28), and now the tyrant turned a blind eye to repeated warnings from God. Moses turned away in utter indignation. God would now fulfill his grand purpose of displaying his power through the land in order to bring the captive Israelites out of the land of bondage.

MAIN IDEA REVIEW: *If necessary, the Lord can carry out his plan by judgment.*

III. CONCLUSION

Pharaoh's "Nose-Down" Attitude

By now, everyone recognizes Pharaoh's "nose-down" attitude. Moses certainly knew as God again reminded Moses of the instructional value these miraculous signs would have for future generations. Pharaoh's officials also knew as they began to question Pharaoh's stubbornness and inability to get their nation out of this mess. After one more interrogation, down came the locusts on a land that was already desolate because of the earlier hailstorm. And just when you thought it might be over, Pharaoh's "attitude indicator" took another downward turn. Thus, the ninth plague—darkness—arrived, demonstrating God's supreme power over the Egyptian sun god. This was a darkness like nothing they had ever seen, a darkness they could feel. Amazingly, God's protection was maintained over the Hebrew people as their dwelling places remained full of light. This put Pharaoh into a "nose-down" attitude, and he threatened Moses' life.

PRINCIPLES

- God deals differently with his people than he does with idolaters.
- God gets to the root of the problem rather than dealing with the fruit of the problem.
- God uses the prayers of his faithful servants.
- God's power is so precise that one area can be destroyed while another area just a few blocks away can be spared.
- God in his sovereignty uses people, places, and events to reveal his glory, grace, and mercy.

APPLICATIONS

- Identify the areas of idolatry you struggle with and confess them to God.
- Trust God's power to deliver you from idolatry.
- Be specific with your prayers. Ask God to intervene in specific and tangible ways to the crises you face so when the answer arrives, there is no doubt that God intervened.
- Take actions which express your change of attitude.
- Trust God when the darkness of trials enters your life as a believer.

IV. LIFE APPLICATION

Fixing the Problem

Dealing with idolatry, as with any sin, is a lot like dealing with an electrical problem. We know there is a problem, but we can't figure out where it's located. We start the search, but the answer evades us. So we intensify the search and admit we need help, only to discover that most of the problems can be fixed with little effort. And once the problem is addressed, the electricity begins to flow.

As a believer, you know when there is a problem as well; the Holy Spirit will point it out to you. As you search your heart, the problem may be a little evasive because we live in a state of denial. If you intensify the search and say, "Search me O God . . . and see if there be any wicked way in me," God will break through the pride and help you understand how little effort it takes to confess the sin and move on. And suddenly the Spirit of God begins to lead and encourage in ways you may have not seen for a while. There is a return of the "joy of your salvation" (Ps. 51:12) and the energy begins to flow more freely. Let God go to war on those areas of idolatry in your life. As you have already seen, he's good at this!

V. PRAYER

Lord, search me and see if there is any wicked way in me. I want to serve you and enjoy our relationship more, and I realize that any idolatry will hinder my intimacy with you. I therefore give you permission and even invite you to go to battle on my behalf in the areas of idolatry that I struggle with. Amen.

VI. DEEPER DISCOVERIES

A. The Death of the Firstborn

Chapter 11 announces the deadly judgment of the firstborn in Egypt, an act that has troubled some Christians. We should keep in mind several significant truths about this event.

First of all, the Egyptians worshiped false gods, and they were leading the people of Israel astray by corrupting their relationship with God. What will it profit if someone gains the whole world and worships every god and then loses his or her own soul?

Second, God in his wisdom planned this event, knowing it would lead others to the true God, or at least give him a serious hearing.

Third, the Bible teaches that God alone controls the destinies of humans, and "no one has power over the day of his death" (Eccl. 8:8) and cannot even "discover anything about his future" (Eccl. 7:14). The future belongs to God, and he knows what's best for us.

Finally, we should remember that one day God will punish those who refuse his gracious offer of salvation through Jesus Christ with everlasting fire away from his presence (Matt. 25:46; Rom. 2:8–9). Unfortunately, most people have not fully realized just how holy God is and how much he hates sin. Many will learn too late. We should learn from this and other examples of God's judgment of sin and seek to live a life worthy of his name.

VII. TEACHING OUTLINE

A. INTRODUCTION
1. Lead Story: An Attitude Indicator

2. Context: From chapters 7–11 we see nine plagues visited on Egypt, climaxed by the tenth, the death of the firstborn.
3. Transition: Pharaoh's response to God's word is a mirror into which we can look and test our own hearts. How is my attitude similar to Pharaoh's? How is it different?

B. COMMENTARY

1. The Plague of Frogs (8:1–15)
2. The Plague of Gnats (8:16–19)
3. The Plague of Flies (8:20–32)
4. The Plague on Livestock (9:1–7)
5. The Plague of Boils (9:8–12)
6. The Plague of Hail (9:13–35)
7. The Plague of Locusts (10:1–20)
8. The Plague of Darkness (10:21–29)
9. The Plague on the Egyptian Firstborn (11:1–10)

C. CONCLUSION: FIXING THE PROBLEM

VIII. ISSUES FOR DISCUSSION

1. Do you think God was a little harsh with the leadership of Egypt? Why does God work this way occasionally while other times he appears gentle and mild?
2. Look at Exodus 8:19 again. Imagine the magicians saying this to you. If you were sensitive to God's leading, what would those words imply? Why is this important?
3. This Pharaoh was certainly a stubborn man. What is it within mankind that causes this root of stubbornness? Where and how has this trait appeared in your life?
4. Idolatry is just as alive today as it was in the days of Moses. How have you seen God break down some of the idols of your culture to reveal his power? Why do you think he does this?

Exodus 12–13

The Passover

I. **INTRODUCTION**
A Significant Sacrifice

II. **COMMENTARY**
A verse-by-verse explanation of these chapters.

III. **CONCLUSION**
From Passover to Exodus

An overview of the principles and applications from these chapters.

IV. **LIFE APPLICATION**
A Saving Sacrifice

Melding these chapters to life.

V. **PRAYER**
Tying these chapters to life with God.

VI. **DEEPER DISCOVERIES**
Historical, geographical, and grammatical enrichment of the commentary.

VII. **TEACHING OUTLINE**
Suggested step-by-step group study of these chapters.

VIII. **ISSUES FOR DISCUSSION**
Zeroing these chapters in on daily life.

"*A* true love to God must begin with a delight in his holiness, and not with a delight in any other attribute; for no other attribute is truly lovely without this."

Jonathan Edwards

Exodus 12–13

 I N   A   N U T S H E L L

*C*hapters 12–13 represent a significant change in the Book of Exodus. Moses has ushered into Pharaoh's presence nine plagues, and Pharaoh continues to break his promise of freedom. One more plague is promised—the death of the firstborn among the Egyptians. But through God's providence and love, the Passover is initiated. This would become a picture of the salvation God would offer to all mankind.

The Passover

I. INTRODUCTION

A Significant Sacrifice

*L*iving in California, especially near the beach, has its perks. I take long walks with my wife Nancy along the Strand, the walkway along the beach, just about every month of the year. But a disadvantage of living in California in 2001 is these rolling blackouts. We have a power crisis and need to be prepared for the electricity to go out without warning. Well over a decade ago, there was another power crisis at a nuclear power plant in Chernobyl in Russia. This power plant experienced a meltdown and created an enormous tragedy, probably beyond the bounds of what was reported on television here in the United States. To make the best of a catastrophic situation, the Russian authorities decided their best plan of attack for resolving this mess was to dump hundreds of tons of sand and concrete into the live reactor in order to seal it up and prevent its radioactive discharges.

One helicopter pilot was decorated for his heroism in making dozens of passes over the hot reactor to dump the huge cargos of sand and concrete. Each pass he made over the reactor increased his health risk, but the job had to be done or the reactor would keep bubbling out its deadly fallout for decades to come. This pilot exposed himself to the deadly radiation in order to save the lives of millions of people and many more who had not yet been born.

This one man's sacrifice saved many lives. But there was another sacrifice two thousand years ago that offered salvation for all humanity. When we say that Jesus Christ became sin for us (2 Cor. 5:21), we mean that he knowingly exposed himself to a world brutalized by sin. In the end, he was also brutalized by sin, even though he himself had lived a sinless life. In order to seal off and neutralize the power of sin, Jesus gave his life that we might find peace and life with God.

The significance of Christ's sacrifice is rooted in the story of the exodus. Paul wrote in 1 Corinthians 5:6: "Your boasting is not good. Don't you know that a little yeast works through the whole batch of dough?" The picture here shows the result of sin and how it can permeate everyone and everything related to it. Then in 1 Corinthians 5:7–8, we read, "Get rid of the old yeast that you may be a new batch without yeast—as you really are. For Christ, our Passover lamb, has been sacrificed. Therefore let us keep the Festival, not with the old yeast, the yeast of malice and wickedness, but with bread without yeast, the bread of sincerity and truth." Paul indicates that what the

Passover lamb meant to the Israelites in their bondage, the Lord Jesus should mean to us. But what did the Passover lamb mean? Let's find out!

II. COMMENTARY

The Passover

> **MAIN IDEA:** *The Lord provides deliverance for the Israelites and points to a future deliverer.*

A The Passover (12:1–50)

> **SUPPORTING IDEA:** *The inaugural Passover and redemption are established.*

12:1–20. With the Passover feast comes a reminder of the spiritual foundations of the nation of Israel and the importance of remembering the God who brought their nation into existence and redeemed them with a mighty hand. The festival contained rich symbolism depicting the grace of God in salvation and deliverance from bondage. The people of Israel would at times mechanically observe this and similar rituals while forgetting the meaning behind them. The means of protection from the wrath of God didn't come by outwardly performing certain religious functions, but by God providing the only means of salvation that would satisfy his holy demands.

The Passover would begin on the tenth day of the first month (called Abib before the Babylonian captivity, thereafter Nisan) with each head of household taking a lamb for his family. Smaller families would unite with another family to consume one lamb (later custom would limit the number of people consuming one lamb at ten; KD, 11). Since they would slaughter the lamb as a sacrifice, the lamb had to have certain characteristics. The Lord told them to choose **year-old males without defect . . . from the sheep or goats**. The male lamb would replace the firstborn males of Israel. They were to care for this lamb until the fourteenth day of the month, then publicly kill him at sunset.

The various tribes were not assembled for the purpose of slaughtering the lamb; they did it as individual families in their separate households. But they were to kill the lamb at the same time. They would apply some of the blood of the slain animal to the **sides and tops of the doorframes of the houses where they eat the lambs**. The blood would be a sign that God would not send the destroying angel against them, but would "pass over" them (v. 13). They would then eat the entire lamb that was **roasted over the fire** that night accompanied with **bitter herbs** and unleavened **bread**. The herbs did not represent a seasoning of sorts but depicted their bitter existence in Egypt.

If they could not eat the entire lamb, they were to burn the remaining portion. Furthermore, they were to consume it with their cloaks **tucked** into their **belts**, in order to be ready for a speedy departure, with their sandals on (not normally worn in houses), and with staffs in hand. The Passover belonged to the Lord, and his deliverance of the Israelites from Egyptian captivity could occur at any time.

There was a spiritual and religious dimension to the Passover and subsequent death of the Egyptian firstborns: God would thereby **bring judgment on all the gods of Egypt**. If the Hebrews sought refuge in God, he would spare them from the pending judgment. The destroying angel would take the firstborn of the Egyptians but would pass over the Hebrew households when he saw the blood on the top and side doorposts.

The Passover feast would become a lasting ordinance in Israel. It foreshadowed the future sacrifices and offerings for atonement, and the meal represented the fellowship they would enjoy with God. The Feast of Unleavened Bread would last seven days, following the Passover feast, during which they would **eat bread made without yeast**. Yeast spreads rapidly and thoroughly in bread, and the Bible elsewhere indicates it can symbolize the corrupting influences of evil (1 Cor. 5:6–8), although we should not strictly identify leaven as a type of evil. God would punish violators of this ordinance by cutting them off from Israel, a euphemism for the death penalty (see Lev. 20:2–3). On the seventh day they would hold another assembly during which they were not to work at all but to observe the feast.

12:21–30. Moses summoned all the elders of Israel and told them to prepare the Passover lamb. He instructed them to slaughter the lamb and then take hyssop and dip it in the blood before applying it to the door frames of their homes. Hyssop was a plant that often grew on walls that was thought to contain cleansing qualities. It was later used in the cleansing ritual with lepers (Lev. 14:4–7) and the water of cleansing (Num. 19:1–22). They were then told to observe the Passover after they arrived in the promised land as a perpetual reminder of the Lord's wonderful deliverance from Egyptian bondage.

The Israelites obeyed the words of Moses and **bowed down and worshiped**. Then at the stroke of midnight the Lord struck down all the firstborn in Egypt, **from the firstborn of Pharaoh, who sat on the throne, to the firstborn of the prisoner**. Panic and loud wailing spread throughout land; death was everywhere.

12:31–42. Pharaoh quickly sent for Moses and told him to take the Israelites and leave the land immediately with everything they had. He also asked Moses to bless him. The Egyptian people, also afraid for their own lives, sent Moses away. As the Israelites left, they took the dough, not yet leavened, and then asked the Egyptians to give them silver, gold, and clothing—something the Egyptians eagerly did. The Israelites **journeyed from Rameses to Succoth**, with what had to amount to an enormous multitude (six hundred thousand men besides women and children (over two million in all?). Others soon followed them, possibly some native Egyptians, to join, not oppose, them. The stay in Egypt had lasted 430 years.

12:43–50. The regulations mentioned in these verses supplement previous instructions concerning the Passover. Strict foreigners were not to partake of it, unless they were circumcised slaves purchased by the Hebrews (see "Deeper Discoveries"). Mere workers who were hired for their services were not to consume it. Foreigners who sought to align themselves with the nation and its God would have to be circumcised first; then they could join them in eating the feast. The Passover was a community festival, to be celebrated by all the people, each in their own households. They were not to break any of the bones of the sacrificial animals, a feature that carried prophetic significance (John 19:33–36).

B Dedication of the Firstborn (13:1–22)

SUPPORTING IDEA: *God commands the firstborn to be set apart for him.*

13:1–16. When God delivered the firstborn of the Israelites from the fate of the Egyptian firstborn, he set them apart for special consecration (Num. 3:13; 8:17). They were seen as the strength of the family and were thus given to God as the first fruits of God's blessing to each family. The same was true for all of the firstborn animals. God repeated the instructions for observing the Feast of Unleavened Bread and commanded them to observe the ordinance after they arrived in the land he promised them.

Part of the observance included instructing their children that it was God who brought them out of Egypt. He was the one who brought them out to take them as his own possession. In addition, they were to remember that the vital union between them and God included a strict observance of his holy law. Later he would command priests and kings to rule faithfully and instruct the people in the law. The law was the very expression of the will of God, a reflection of his nature. Jesus would later in the Sermon on the Mount give an exposition of the true meaning of the law in heart, life, and practice. Although the civic and ceremonial law was to be fulfilled in Christ, the law itself as an expression of God's will and nature will outlast the earth itself (Matt. 5:18).

Once in the land, the people were to give to God the firstborn by redeeming them with a set amount (fixed in Num. 3:47 at five shekels). Later, in place of the firstborn, God would set aside the entire tribe of Levi for his special service. The primary thought behind the consecration of the firstborn was a reminder of God's miraculous deliverance of the Hebrew people from Egypt.

13:17–22. God did not take the Israelites on the more direct route, one that would take them through the environs of the Philistines in and around Gaza. Any further crisis might scare them into turning back to Egypt. The Philistines were militarily superior to the Israelites in equipment, training, and psychological readiness. So the Israelites would venture out toward the desert of the Red Sea away from neighboring threats. They also remembered Joseph's last request and brought his bones with them in order to bury them in the land of Canaan.

The Israelites first journeyed to Etham, where they traveled for three days (Num. 33:8). God himself would directly lead them and did so by the appearance of **a pillar of cloud to guide them on their way and by night in a pillar of fire to give them light.** The pillar remained in front of them at all times. The pillar was an obvious sign of God's presence among them, a supernatural phenomenon of divine origin. They were led all the way to the promised land by means of this pillar. They were never to forget that if they were to survive as a nation, they would have to submit to God's leading in their lives after they settled in the land.

> **MAIN IDEA REVIEW:** *The Lord provides deliverance for the Israelites and points to a future deliverer.*

III. CONCLUSION

From Passover to Exodus

With no Passover, there would never have been an exodus from Egypt. This is why this chapter is so pivotal in our understanding of the entire Book of Exodus. After the ninth plague and all the broken promises of Pharaoh, God said, "One more; the death of the firstborn of Egypt." But God was also going to offer a provision for the people of Israel to escape his wrath. When the Passover lamb was killed, the blood was caught. Using the hyssop, the blood was put on the lintel—the crosspiece of the door—and on the two side posts. This is what God commanded so that when the destroyer came to take the firstborn as promised in the tenth plague, God himself would cover those houses with the blood on the doors so no harm would come to anyone inside. This truth became so important to the people because of its importance to God. Thus every generation was to learn and identify with God's deliverance.

When the people of Israel sat with their families and asked about the Passover feast and wondered about the importance of the Feast of Unleavened Bread and wondered about the sacrifice of the first clean animal to the Lord, each family had memories that they would pass on to the next generation. The story would be told of the first Passover and God's deliverance. Children would then have memories to build their faith upon. God wanted the Hebrew people and all who would read the Scriptures throughout history to remember that mankind has always lived under a penalty of death through their rebellion and only God can provide the deliverance we desire for our souls. And because of God's faithfulness to us, we are to be dedicated to him and pass this on to others who are trapped in personal bondage.

PRINCIPLES

- The true Passover Lamb is Jesus Christ.
- God is faithful even through our pain.
- God wants our memories to increase as we experience his leading.
- Mankind is trapped in a personal bondage to sin, and only God can provide deliverance.
- Mankind is helpless without God's intercession.
- God's leadership is obvious to those who are looking for it.

APPLICATIONS

- Learn the difference between the Israelites and the Egyptians in order to understand the difference between the saved and the unsaved.
- Think about what you deserve if God granted justice, not mercy.
- Thank God for the provision that he made for the Hebrews to avoid the death angel. Thank him for his provision for you through Jesus Christ's sacrificial death.
- What will you do in response to God's grace in your life?
- Live what you profess.

IV. LIFE APPLICATION

A Saving Sacrifice

To illustrate the principle of substitution, George Sweeting, chancellor of Moody Bible Institute, told of a series of tornados that caused extensive damage in eastern Ohio and western Pennsylvania. Nearly one hundred lives were lost. Before the storm, a man named David Kostka was umpiring a Little League baseball game in Wheatland, Pennsylvania. When he saw the black funnel heading toward the field, he rushed into the stands and grabbed his niece. He pushed her into a nearby ditch and covered her with his body. Then the tornado struck. When the youngster looked up, her uncle was gone. He had given his life in the deadly storm to save her.

Many lambs gave their lives in ancient Egypt so the death angel would pass over the homes of the Hebrews. Years later the Lamb of God gave his life to cover the sins of all those who by faith would receive his gift of salvation.

Jesus' sacrifice can be studied and contemplated, but until a person applies the blood of Christ by faith to his or her own heart, there is no hope of eternity in his presence in heaven. The writer of Hebrews declared, "By faith he kept the Passover and the sprinkling of blood, so that the destroyer of the firstborn would not touch the firstborn of Israel" (Heb. 11:28). What did Moses have faith in? The answer is God's word, his revelation to Moses. God said it; he believed it. Without faith, it is impossible to please God. You cannot ignore the truth from God's promises and have this kind of peace, security, and hope.

V. PRAYER

Lord Jesus, I believe you are the true Passover Lamb who died on the cross for my sin, was buried, and rose again on a day we celebrate as Easter. I need forgiveness for my sin, and I am asking you to cleanse me and come into my life as my Savior. Thank you that by faith I know the wrath of God will pass over me and allow me entrance into your kingdom. But until I stand before you, mold me into a person who points others to the Passover Lamb of God. Amen.

VI. DEEPER DISCOVERIES

A. Circumcision

Circumcision (literally, "cutting around") was instituted in Genesis 17:10–14. This ritual was to be performed on all males on the eighth day after they were born (Lev. 12:3; Phil. 3:5). It became a rite particularly observed on the Sabbath (John 7:23). Later Jews would require it for salvation (Acts 15:1), something the apostle Paul vigorously opposed (Rom. 2:25–28; Gal. 6:13). God instituted this rite to be the special sign of his chosen people, a permanent symbol of their separation to him. At times the practice was ignored or neglected, such as during the wilderness journeys of the Israelites, later resumed by Joshua before they entered the promised land (Josh. 5:2–8).

Circumcision carried some symbolic meaning, such as purity (Isa. 52:1) and clean hearts (Lev. 26:41). Many physicians today tell of the medical and health advantages of this procedure, without necessarily viewing it in any religious sense. Of course, the Christian need not be circumcised for any spiritual reasons, as the ceremonial law no longer is binding (Col. 2:11–12).

VII. TEACHING OUTLINE

A. INTRODUCTION

1. Lead Story: A Significant Sacrifice

2. Context: The memories we have shape who we become and how we live in the present and the future. Our knowledge of God is built on what he has done in history. As God prepared to perform two mighty miracles—Passover and crossing the Red Sea—he wanted his people to remember what he had done. So he instituted a way by which they would remember what he had done for them and to anticipate what he would yet do for them through his Son.

3. Transition: God has given Pharaoh numerous opportunities to obey him and to avoid judgment. Pharaoh's heart has only become harder. God is now ready to act on behalf of his people.

B. COMMENTARY

1. The Passover (12:1–50)

2. Dedication of the Firstborn (13:1–22)

C. CONCLUSION: A SAVING SACRIFICE

VIII. ISSUES FOR DISCUSSION

1. One of the most useful tools in studying the Scripture is answering the questions who, what, where, when, why, and how? Using these questions, what truths become more obvious in the study of the Passover?

2. Do you think there was any other way God could have used to accomplish the exodus of the people of Israel? Why such drastic measures?

3. This firstborn consecration is a big deal in God's eyes. Review Exodus 4:22–23, 12:12–13; 13:2,12,15. Why is God so concerned about this?

4. The Ten Commandments will arrive in the future for Moses and his people. Can you explain why the events and teaching of this chapter will be so important when these commandments are given?

5. What activities take place in your church to show the importance of consecration? Have you been involved in them?

Exodus 14–15

"Lord, We Need a Miracle"

I. INTRODUCTION
Habits Are Hard to Uproot

II. COMMENTARY
A verse-by-verse explanation of these chapters.

III. CONCLUSION
God at Work

An overview of the principles and applications from these chapters.

IV. LIFE APPLICATION
Burdens and Blessings

Melding these chapters to life.

V. PRAYER
Tying these chapters to life with God.

VI. DEEPER DISCOVERIES
Historical, geographical, and grammatical enrichment of the commentary.

VII. TEACHING OUTLINE
Suggested step-by-step group study of these chapters.

VIII. ISSUES FOR DISCUSSION
Zeroing these chapters in on daily life.

Quote

"*T*here was never miracle wrought by God to convert an atheist, because the light of nature might have led him to confess a God: but miracles have been wrought to convert idolaters and the superstitious, because no light of nature extendeth to declare the will and true worship of God."

S i r   F r a n c i s   B a c o n

Exodus 14–15

I N   A   N U T S H E L L

*F*reedom at last. The people of Israel are now only a few months into their journey and reach a dead end. Worse yet, Pharaoh has again changed his mind and is coming after them. These chapters show us the power of God as the Red Sea is parted and the people again rejoice over God's victory over the enemy. But bitter waters are ahead.

"Lord, We Need a Miracle"

I. INTRODUCTION

Habits Are Hard to Uproot

A grandfather and his grandson were on a walk. As they walked along the trail, the grandfather pointed to a small plant and told the young boy to uproot the small plant. The boy did so easily. They came to a slightly larger plant, and the grandfather told the boy to do the same to the larger plant. After some effort and a little more time, the boy was able to complete the task. The grandfather then pointed to a large plant and told his grandson to uproot this one. The boy's eyes widened as he examined the task before him but, in obedience to his grandfather, went to work. He struggled for some time but was unable to get the plant to budge. The grandfather stepped to the boy's side and helped him pull. Both of them were finally able to ease the plant from the ground. Along with the plant came a system of roots almost as long as the plant itself.

As the grandfather and the grandson continued their walk, the grandfather told the boy that the largest plant was the most difficult to pull out because of its roots; they had grown too long. He explained to the boy that our habits are much the same. If we catch them early, we can pull them ourselves. If we wait too long, we are powerless against their roots unless someone else comes into our lives and helps us to pry them loose.

The people of Israel had been in captivity for hundreds of years. Their habits of dependency and lack of faith had deep roots. Ten plagues may have broken up a little of the soil in these habits, but ahead of the Israelites were some major acts of prying and pulling to bring them to the point of being ready for the promised land God had told them about. Here comes the first huge plant—the Red Sea.

II. COMMENTARY

"Lord, We Need a Miracle"

MAIN IDEA: *The Israelites experience deliverance through the Red Sea and celebrate.*

A Escape from Pharaoh's Army (14:1–31)

SUPPORTING IDEA: *God provides a miraculous rescue through the Red Sea.*

14:1–4. The Lord next directed the Israelites **to turn back and encamp near Pi Hahiroth, between Migdol and the sea**. At this location they were to camp by the sea near Baal Zephon. Although the location of these cities cannot be determined with any precision, these cities were grouped together near the outskirts of Egypt near the Red Sea. Migdol may have been a military post on the way out of Egypt. The name of the last of these mentioned, Baal Zephon, suggests that the Canaanite god Baal was worshiped there. The sudden move east may have prompted Pharaoh to suppose the Israelites lost their way and had become vulnerable. But God would once again harden the heart of this tyrant and lead him to chase the Israelites down. But God would once again get the glory.

14:5–14. Perhaps Pharaoh now caught on to the true intentions of the Israelites and soon prepared his chariots to track them down. The Hyksos (possibly Canaanites or other foreigners who temporarily conquered the land of Egypt) brought horses to Egypt, and soon after the Egyptians used these vehicles in their military campaigns. Pharaoh took six hundred of the very best chariots and other chariots and pursued the Israelites and **overtook them as they camped by the sea**. Pharaoh approached to find a vast multitude paralyzed with fear and virtually defenseless. They cried out first to the Lord, then bitterly complained to Moses about the plight: **Was it because there were no graves in Egypt that you brought us to the desert to die?** For a moment it seemed better to the Hebrews to have endured slavery in Egypt than to be in such a predicament.

But Moses stood resolute in his confidence in the Lord and lifted the hearts of the people by reminding them once again of God's pending deliverance. Moses believed the word of the Lord, not just this once, but as a way of life (Heb. 11:24–29). Apparently the Lord revealed to Moses the nature of the deliverance would be quite miraculous—completely independent of human means. With this deliverance Moses could say to the Israelites, **the Egyptians you see today you will never see again**.

14:15–25. But God told Moses it wasn't time to cry to him but to arise with the Israelites and move toward the sea. There he was to raise his staff and stretch out his hand over the sea that God would then divide, allowing the multitudes to cross unharmed. Their Egyptian pursuers would follow close on their heels, but God would get the glory. The Egyptian army was vast and powerful and seemed to have the upper hand. But now events would take place that would be spoken of for centuries to come.

Then the angel of God (see "Deeper Discoveries," ch. 4), who had been traveling in front of Israel's army, **withdrew and went behind them**. Perhaps this is where we get the popular "avenging angel" slogan. The angel of God and the pillar of cloud, the token of God's nearness to them, surrounded the Israelites. What more did they need? These protective agents of God stood between the Israelites and their pursuers. The cloud seemed to have a two-fold effect, bringing light to the Israelites, who were about to flee full-force into the divided Red Sea, and darkness to the now halted Egyptian horsemen. Moses stretched out his hand over the sea, and all that night **the LORD drove the sea back with a strong east wind** and turned it into dry land. Between the divided walls, the Israelites fled, taking the entire night to cross over. The Egyptians pursued them, and all **Pharaoh's horses and chariots and horsemen followed them** into the sea.

Perhaps more than ever we see the hardness of Pharaoh's heart and that of his soldiers. They had already witnessed great signs and wonders, and were even now withheld from further pursuit by the cloud. But the moment a window of opportunity opened up, they charged forward after the Israelites. But sometime between 3:00 a.m. and 6:00 a.m. the Lord threw the entire army into confusion. This probably amounted to losing control of the horses and losing their own mental or emotional bearings. The wheels then fell off their chariots. Finally it dawned on them that the Lord was fighting for Israel and they would continue their mad rush to catch the fleeing nation in vain. But alas, it was too late!

14:26–31. Then the LORD told Moses to stretch his hand over the sea so **the waters may flow back over the Egyptians**. The waters that were previously divided and a means of deliverance for the Israelites now came together and became a means of destruction for the Egyptian army. The entire army perished, leaving no survivors, no one to tell the miraculous events of the day, and what the Hebrew God did. The Israelites continued to flee, protected by the walls of water on both sides. From afar they viewed the mass of dead Egyptians on the shore.

The effect of all this on the Israelites brings us back to God's original purpose: God displayed his power in the world, and many people took notice and feared. The Israelites not only began to fear God with a deep trust, but they also acknowledged God's hand on his servant Moses, now fully credentialed as God's spokesman.

B The Song of Moses (15:1–27)

SUPPORTING IDEA: *Moses composes a hymn of thanksgiving.*

The "songs" of the Old Testament were Hebrew poetical compositions, usually brief, that could be set to music (v. 21). The song may either acknowledge God or, in some instances, some great exploit of man (1 Sam. 18:6–7). Some songs were carefully composed, while others, such as the present song and the Song of Deborah (Judg. 5), seem to be more of a spontaneous outburst. Later King David would organize the temple worship and make singing a prominent feature (1 Chr. 15:16–23).

Moses began his song by acknowledging the exalted Lord who turned back the advancing army by drowning them in the sea.

15:1–8. Moses acknowledged God as his **strength** and **song**, the true source of his joy. The Old Testament concept of **salvation** (v. 2) may encompass both physical and spiritual deliverance. Moses probably referred to Abraham when he called God his **father's God**.

The song continues (v. 3) with a declaration of God's role as a protector for the people of God. Wherever God's people go, their enemies are not far behind. Although at times they may resort to arms, their true defender is God himself, as the account of the exodus makes evident. This is why the Egyptian army was cast into the Red Sea. The **right hand** of God signifies his strength (Ps. 20:6), and even in the majority of people it is the arm of action, particularly in combat. The fuel for wielding his power was God's **burning anger** against Egypt's cruelty and mistreatment of his people.

15:9–12. At first the Egyptians boasted as they captured the outpaced Israelites. God's motive in delivering them was to exalt his name, but the Egyptians sought only to **divide the spoils.** Indeed the sight of the defenseless Israelites must have spurred the violent aggressors on even more. But at the command of God the waters enclosed and swallowed the riders alive. Moses saw the attributes of God in his acts. He asked, **Who among the gods is like you, O Lord? Who is like you—majestic in holiness, awesome in glory, working wonders?** Moses was so enraptured with beautiful notions of God's greatness that the "grandeur of the subject transcends the power of words" (Calvin, 259).

15:13–18. The revelation of God's love for his people unfolds gradually in biblical revelation. By the time we reach the New Testament and see the fuller unveiling of God's intentions for his people, we marvel at his love (1 John 3:1). Still, God chose his people from the beginning in love and never failed to love them as his own. Moses called that love **unfailing**, a truth made more evident by the deliverance through the Red Sea. God's people often find themselves in such straits that they despair of ever finding this love, wondering where God's kindnesses went. But God's miraculous rescue of the Israelites proves once more that his love never left them for a moment.

Moreover, this love for his people will cause the surrounding nations to realize that God makes a distinction between those who know him and those who don't. By the time the Israelites arrived at the borders of Canaan and entered under Joshua's command, the nations melted in fear. The goal of their journeys would be **the mountain** of God's inheritance, the glorious land of Canaan. The rest afforded the Israelites under Joshua would not be final, however (Heb. 4:8–9). They awaited a better time in the future, something that even the most enlightened of them knew only in part (1 Pet. 1:10–12). Then the Lord would reign **for ever and ever.**

15:19–21. The name Miriam has been alternately defined by scholars as meaning "bitter," "obstinate," and even "corpulent" (Gehman, 623). Yet her brief song in these verses reflects her devotion to God and her thankfulness for his marvelous deliverance. She would later join Aaron in complaining to Moses about his marriage to a Cushite woman, an act that would leave her a temporary leper. Apparently she played the tambourine (timbrel), a percussion instrument often used by women while celebrating (Judg. 11:34; 1 Sam. 18:6–7).

15:22–27. Following the utter defeat of the Egyptians in the Red Sea, Moses led the Israelites into the Desert of Shur (literally, "wall"; perhaps stemming from the defensive walls in the city), a region in the northwestern Sinai Peninsula. There they looked for water without success. Finally they came to Marah ("bitter") where they found water, but it was unsuitable for drinking. The people grumbled to Moses about this, prompting him to cry out to God. The Lord showed his servant a piece of wood. Moses, probably at the direction of God (although it's not recorded), cast the wood into the bitter waters, making them **sweet**.

At this site the Lord promised the Israelites that if they walked in his counsels and obeyed his word he would not bring on them **the diseases** (probably some or all of the plagues) that he **brought on the Egyptians**. They would have to depend on him to give them their health and strength in the days and years ahead. The chapter closes with their arrival at Elim ("large trees"), where they found twelve springs and seventy palm trees to sustain and comfort them.

> **MAIN IDEA REVIEW:** *The Israelites experience deliverance through the Red Sea and celebrate.*

III. CONCLUSION

God at Work

The Israelites had hit a dead end. Mountains on both sides, the Red Sea in front of them, and Pharaoh's army behind them. The people grumbled. God told them to get going. His power was revealed through Moses, his servant, in parting the waters and destroying their enemy. The Hebrew people needed to uproot a bad habit of grumbling and distrust, and God provided some training for this on that day. He had guided and protected them through the pillar of cloud and fire. He had revealed his faithfulness over and over, and now it was time to pull a larger plant.

Do not read this chapter with the impression that the people of Israel just sat on the seashore, Moses lifted his rod, the waters parted just like the scene with Charlton Heston, and the people walked gingerly across on dry land. This was a major step of faith for these people, according to Hebrews 11:29:

"By faith the people passed through the Red Sea as on dry land; but when the Egyptians tried to do so, they were drowned."

When the Israelites finally finished the crossing, God sped up their learning curve. On one side of the sea, the people were filled with fear and complaints. On the other side of the sea, there was worship. In the midst of this worship experience primarily by Moses and secondarily by Miriam, we hear one of the key verses for the Book of Exodus: "In your unfailing love you will lead the people you have redeemed. In your strength you will guide them to your holy dwelling" (Exod. 15:13).

First, God leads his people by his mercy. Second, God continually reveals his omnipotence throughout the journey. Third, God's map may not be the shortest route so that lessons may be learned along the way. Each of these truths reveals God's unending mercy and compassion for his people. And God simply wants us to take him at his word.

After the brief celebration, God brought them to the bitter waters of Marah where the people went from singing and rejoicing to difficulty and complaining. They had experienced two water problems that week—too much water at the Red Sea and too little water at Marah. The Hebrew people still had a lot to learn.

PRINCIPLES

- God doesn't always lead us through the shortest path to get to the destination he desires for us.
- Following God is a walk of faith.
- God often wants us to wait on him.

APPLICATIONS

- Make an inventory of the major obstacles in your life. Bring those obstacles into God's presence one by one. How does each obstacle look in the presence of God, the mighty deliverer who saved his people from the death angel and opened the Red Sea for them?
- Ask God to show you how he will work with each of these obstacles.
- Ask God what he wants you to do next.
- Praise God for what he has done and will yet do in your life.

IV. LIFE APPLICATION

Burdens and Blessings

Your greatest burden can become a wonderful blessing when viewed correctly. One pastor of a small church in the Midwest learned this truth while visiting a widow in his church. As he talked with her, he noticed two large jars of beads on a shelf. He asked why one jar was nearly full of beads while the other jar had only a few.

"Through my life I have experienced many burdens that God has changed into a blessing for me," she told him. "The jar with a few beads represents my burdens, and the nearly full jar stands for the burdens God has turned into a blessing in my life. As he does so, I move a bead from one jar to the other. It doesn't help to complain when I hurt, but it does help to look for God's hand in turning things around."

During the course of life, you may hit a dead end much as the people of Israel did early in their journey. You can complain and doubt God's leadership, or you can trust for the bead to be transferred from one jar to another in the future.

V. PRAYER

Gracious Father, from your perspective I must seem to be one of those chronic complainers. I hit those dead ends of life with little or no expectation of you parting the seas before me. I forget your power. I forget your majesty. And I forget how easy it is for you to turn a burden into a blessing. I guess it is time to find a couple of jars and some beads, Lord, so I can keep track and thank you more often. Thanks for the reminder. Amen!

VI. DEEPER DISCOVERIES

A. Destroying the Egyptian Army

Critics have pointed out two problems with the account of the deliverance of the people of Israel through the Red Sea and the destruction of the Egyptian army. First, how could this have happened? Second, how could a loving God destroy an entire army? The two objections are actually related. If people believe that supernatural events cannot take place, no explanation will ever satisfy them. Some interpreters have tried to explain the Israelites' ability to cross on low tides. How would they then explain Pharaoh's army drowning in such tides? As far back as Calvin's day, critics were seeking natural explanations for this miracle (see Calvin, 252–53).

If we grant that God created the heavens and earth—a far greater task than parting the Red Sea—then we should have no trouble believing this miracle of the parted Red Sea. Likewise, people's presuppositions also govern their belief whether or not a loving God could destroy an entire army. The Egyptian nation had not only enslaved the Hebrews, imposing cruel bondage on them, but they began to seduce them with false gods. If true religion were to disappear from the face of the earth, no one would be saved. Those who presuppose a holy God with an absolute righteous nature do not nitpick his actions, knowing that whatever he does is for the spiritual welfare of the people. God will one day judge the world in righteousness (Rom. 3:6; 2 Tim. 4:1), and he will do so by perfect and holy standards.

VII. TEACHING OUTLINE

A. INTRODUCTION

1. Lead Story: Habits Are Hard to Uproot

2. Context: The tenth plague had done its work. Not only did Pharaoh agree to let Israel go; he wanted them out of Egypt. And yet his memory was short. No sooner had they begun their exodus than Pharaoh decided to pursue them. You would think he would have learned.

3. Transition: God is among the Israelites as the Egyptian army pursues them. Victory is followed by a song of praise.

B. COMMENTARY

1. Escape from Pharoah's Army (14:1–31)

2. The Song of Moses (15:1–27)

C. CONCLUSION: BURDENS AND BLESSINGS

VIII. ISSUES FOR DISCUSSION

1. Do you believe the Hebrew people are ready for the struggles of the promised land? If not, what are some ways God will prepare them, and what did they need to learn?

2. How did God lead the people? How does God lead people today?

3. Moses is facing his first huge test of his leadership. What does he need to learn from this event? What do you think the people learned?

4. Describe how the people of Israel may have described God on the Egyptian side of the Red Sea and then after their deliverance. Does this process happen in your life?

5. What is your first response to a great success in life? When was the last time you included worship in the celebration?

Exodus 16–18

The Global Whining of Israel

I. **INTRODUCTION**
Time to Take Off the Training Wheels

II. **COMMENTARY**
A verse-by-verse explanation of these chapters.

III. **CONCLUSION**
Growing Faith

An overview of the principles and applications from these chapters.

IV. **LIFE APPLICATION**
Living by Faith

Melding these chapters to life.

V. **PRAYER**
Tying these chapters to life with God.

VI. **DEEPER DISCOVERIES**
Historical, geographical, and grammatical enrichment of the commentary.

VII. **TEACHING OUTLINE**
Suggested step-by-step group study of these chapters.

VIII. **ISSUES FOR DISCUSSION**
Zeroing these chapters in on daily life.

"*T*rusting in Him who can go with me and remain with you, and be everywhere for good, let us confidently hope that all will be well."

Abraham Lincoln

Exodus 16–18

 I N A N U T S H E L L

*L*eading the people of Israel was no easy matter. They had water problems, bread problems, and meat problems, all of which are seen in these chapters. Yet Moses remains faithful as the leader. More importantly, Moses becomes an intercessor for the people who must defeat the Amalekites. But Moses has more to learn when his father-in-law pays him a little visit and prescribes a needed change in leadership styles for Moses.

The Global Whining of Israel

I. INTRODUCTION

Time to Take Off the Training Wheels

All three of my kids loved riding bikes when they were growing up. We began their training the same way most parents did, with training wheels. The age may not have been the same for all three children, but the day arrived when they watched me use some tools to remove the safety they had grown accustomed to, and I began the journey of running beside them as they put into practice the skills and muscles they had developed. That doesn't mean the kids like this stretching experience at first, but it was all a part of their maturity. So as their father I looked past their fears and told them to trust me.

We approach Exodus 16–18 with an understanding that God is about to remove Israel's training wheels. They have been marching in the desert for about six weeks, and we get the sense that they were not quite ready for the steps of faith necessary to trust the Lord totally for both deliverance and sustenance. And yet God was willing to run beside them for further training and help them discover the faith needed to "ride with God."

II. COMMENTARY

The Global Whining of Israel

MAIN IDEA: *Divine and human encouragement are available.*

A The Provision of Manna and Quail (16:1–36)

SUPPORTING IDEA: *Man does not live by bread alone, but God provides even that.*

16:1–3. From Elim the people of Israel journeyed to the Desert of Sin, which lay somewhere in the southwest interior of the Sinai Peninsula. While journeying, **the whole community grumbled against Moses and Aaron** because of the lack of food. Instead of trusting in God, the Israelites resorted to wild exaggerations of their difficulties and overstatements of how well they fared in Egypt.

16:4–8. The Lord announced to Moses that he would miraculously provide for the Israelites by raining down "bread" from heaven and that they were to gather it according to a prescribed order. In order to properly observe the Sabbath, they would collect twice as much on the sixth day (see v. 23). God would also provide meat for them in the evening, a hint of the quails that he would bring to cover the camp (v. 13). Moses also reminded them that when they raised their voices it was not to Moses and Aaron, who were nothing, but to God.

16:9–16. Moses directed Aaron to gather the community to come before the Lord, who had heard their grumbling. While Aaron was addressing the community, the glory of the Lord appeared toward the desert in a cloud. The Lord, not speaking directly to the people but rather to Moses, said, **I have heard the grumbling of the Israelites.** The Lord's response to this grumbling would be to give them meat in the evening and "bread" in the morning. In demonstrating his power over the elements and ability to create out of nothing, he would again display himself as the Lord their God.

That very **evening quail came and covered the camp**, and in the morning **there was a layer of dew around the camp.** When the mist evaporated, what remained were **thin flakes like frost on the ground**, the identity of which appeared mysterious to the Israelites. They asked, **What is it?** The substance, called "manna" (Heb. *Man*), was white in color (v. 31) and could be cooked or prepared in different ways to relieve monotony. Attempts to identify it with various plants that grow in the region (such as the *Tamarix gallica manniferat*) do not satisfy the biblical description. It was the proverbial heavenly food! Moses directed the people to gather as much as they needed, or about an omer (3.5 quarts) per day for each member of the household.

16:17–20. The Israelites at first obeyed and gathered the prescribed amount of manna. Although it may have averaged out to an omer each, some gathered more, some less. Moses again reminded them that **no one is to keep any of it until morning**. God would provide as needed. This spoke to the spiritual principle of waiting on him and trusting him for daily provision—a trait they would certainly need in the coming years. But some people did not obey. Instead they hoarded the manna until morning, causing it to spoil with maggots.

16:21–31. To prepare for the Sabbath Day, on the sixth day the Israelites gathered twice as much as previous days, and what was saved until morning neither smelled nor became infested with maggots. On that seventh day, the Sabbath, the Lord did not rain down manna at all, although some people in disobedience went out looking for it. The Lord reminded Moses again how important the Sabbath was.

16:32–36. The Lord commanded Moses to **take an omer of manna and keep it for the generations to come.** So Aaron, in accordance with the word of the Lord, put the manna in front of the testimony (the two tablets of the law; see 31:18). Later Jews may have moved the manna in the ark of the covenant (Heb. 9:4). The manna would sustain them through their wandering years in the desert until they approached the promised land.

B Miraculous Water and a Battle (17:1–16)

SUPPORTING IDEA: *God provides in thirst and battle.*

17:1–7. God next led the vast multitude **from place to place** until they came to Rephidim (literally, "expanses," "stretches"), where the people found no water and **quarreled with Moses**. In response, God led Moses and some elders to a rock at Horeb, where Moses, at God's command, struck the rock from which water flowed freely. The water possibly flowed down a hill into the camp of the Israelites where they could collect it. Moses struck the rock with his staff, used previously at the Nile (7:20). Moses called the place Massah and Meribah, which mean "testing" and "quarreling," respectively.

17:8–16. Without warning, **the Amalekites came and attacked the Israelites at Rephidim**. The Amalekites were descended from Esau (Gen. 36:12), and they lived for the most part in Kadesh Barnea. Here is our first real look at Joshua the warrior. Apparently he was a soldier of superior skill and stood out among the others. He no doubt possessed additional leadership skills that would enable him to lead an otherwise untrained army into battle. Moses did not hesitate to order Joshua to engage the enemy. The same staff that Moses raised toward the Red Sea and used to strike the rock would next be raised in battle.

Although Joshua must have fought courageously and competently, the battle belonged to the Lord, who demonstrated his power through the symbolic gesture of Moses his servant. When Moses raised his hands, **the Israelites were winning**, but whenever he lowered his hands, **the Amalekites were winning**. Naturally he grew tired, so some aides placed a stone for him to sit down, while Aaron and Hur each held up a hand of Moses. Hur (possibly from Hb. *huru,* "child") was probably a special attendant of Aaron. Moses later appointed Hur to assist Aaron in leading the congregation during Moses' absence (Exod. 24:14). The Jewish historian Josephus claimed Hur was the husband of Miriam, Moses' sister, something the Old Testament is silent about. Moses, with this assistance, continued to hold his hands up until sunset, allowing Joshua to overcome the Amalekites.

The battle against Amalek carried not only temporary significance but symbolic significance as well. God directed Moses to write down this account of the defeat of Amalek on a scroll. Furthermore, he was to make sure Joshua knew the full significance of this event. In times to come the Israelites would have to remember that God himself allowed them to prevail, and God would continue to help them against future enemies. Joshua would face discouraging times in the days to come and would have to resort to the oral and written memory of God's former deliverances in times of battle. Moses' words to him took effect, and one day Joshua would command his fellow Israelites not to let the word of God depart from their mouths (Josh. 1:8).

After this event Moses built an altar and called it **The LORD is my Banner**. Moses was quick to ascribe victory to the Lord. Because they attacked Israel with such unprovoked aggression, God pronounced a curse of sorts against Amalek, declaring he would be at war with Israel from generation to generation (forever).

The defeat of the Amalekites displayed the power of God and his willingness to come to the assistance of his people in times of crisis. But God usually uses human instruments in achieving such victories, and he did so here. He chose to use wise and skilled leaders and warriors, such as Moses and Joshua, who never forgot who was fighting for them. Later the apostle Paul would elaborate on this principle of God working through man: "Continue to work out your salvation with fear and trembling, for it is God who works in you to will and to act according to his good purpose" (Phil. 2:12–13).

Many people attempt to serve God in their own strength and in doing so strip God of the glory. Others, in what amount to a cop-out, do very little to serve him and instead invoke such tired slogans as, "If anything needs to be done, God will do it himself." God's defeat of Amalek teaches us that God will indeed fight for us, but we must stand ready to be his instruments in the battle in whatever way he chooses to use us.

◖C◗ Jethro's Visit and Wise Counsel to Moses (18:1–27)

SUPPORTING IDEA: *Jethro supports Moses through fellowship and wise advice.*

18:1–12. Jethro (called "Reuel" in Exod. 2:18), Moses' father-in-law, had **heard of everything God had done for Moses and for his people Israel, and how the LORD had brought Israel out of Egypt.** Previously Moses had sent his wife, Zipporah, and two sons, Gershom and Eliezer, to Jethro for safe-keeping while he attended his time-consuming duties for the Lord on Israel's behalf. The names of Moses' sons carried significance. *Gershom,* the elder son, meant "sojourner-stranger," and *Eliezer,* the younger son, meant "God is a helper." God helped Moses during his sojourn in Egypt and beyond, saving him from certain death by the vengeful hands of Pharaoh. Jethro, probably after gaining information from messengers, came to meet Moses at Horeb, where possibly Moses had previously told Jethro to meet him. Moses went out and bowed down in respectful greeting and then went into his tent. There Moses related to Jethro how God delivered them from the land of Egypt with a mighty arm, and how God had sustained them thus far in their journeys.

Jethro delighted in the news Moses told him and seemed to own the God of Israel for himself when he uttered, **Praise be to the LORD, who rescued you from the hand of the Egyptians and of Pharaoh.** Jethro, who probably had believed in a plurality of gods, now ascribed to God alone the supremacy over the other so-called gods. Jethro then offered to God sacrifices and shared a communion meal of sorts with Moses, Aaron, and the elders of Israel.

18:13–27. Moses served not only as the direct spokesman for God but also as the chief arbiter for the people. They would bring their daily disputes to him, and he would patiently listen to them, then decide the matter. The cycle lasted all day, no doubt day after day, prompting Jethro to ask Moses why he allowed this to take place. Moses replied that the people sought God's will from his mouth. Moses did indeed speak to God face-to-face (Num. 12:6–8), so how else could the people learn the will of God in any matter? Moses was no doubt well versed in the word of God, which up to this point was restricted to oral tradition (preserving God's word by each generation passing it down orally to the next generation). But, as mentioned above, he stood in close relation to God. Still, God would now teach a vital principle that leadership, if it is to be truly effective, should be shared.

Jethro told Moses that his procedure, or lack of one, in hearing the people was **not good**. Moses would soon wear himself out with the countless demands upon his time. Jethro advised him to think differently about things. Moses, Jethro told him, could actually expand his leadership base by delegating much of the decision-making to **capable men from all the people**. In doing so, Moses would not negate his own authority but enhance it. He would still be the primary teacher of the people and routinely teach them the word of God with its many laws and regulations.

Jethro specifically counseled him to organize the leaders into leaders **over thousands, hundreds, fifties and tens**. The chosen leaders were to be men of unblemished character who feared God and regarded him as sole Lord of Israel. They must be men who could be relied on and who would not give in to the dishonest solicitations of people bent on getting their own way. In short, Moses must select men of sterling character who would honor God and represent the people's true interests. Moses, Jethro advised, would still handle the more difficult decisions, but he would delegate more routine matters to the leaders he chose. Moses listened and heeded the advice of his father-in-law, and he chose wise, capable leaders from the people.

The wise counsel of Jethro gave impetus to Israel's budding governing structure that culminated in a triumvirate, of sorts, consisting of priesthood, monarchy, and prophets. Alongside these would be elders, whose official function remains largely undefined until the New Testament. Such structure gave way to even more elaborate organization under King David, who expanded the priestly service and functions of the Levites. But the true genius of Israel's government was its theocratic foundation that acknowledged God as the legitimate ruler. But structure alone would never ensure God's blessing upon Israel. They would have to protect these structures against foreign and sinful intrusions, something they continually failed to do.

Then Moses sent his father-in-law on his way, and Jethro returned to his own country.

MAIN IDEA REVIEW: *Divine and human encouragement are available.*

III. CONCLUSION

Growing Faith

Faith is a spiritual muscle that needs training. God wanted the people to recognize their need to trust him. That's why he gave the strict rule of collecting only about six pints of manna daily. When they disobeyed, they experienced the consequences: spoiled food. They had to learn the lessons of beginning to ride without their training wheels.

God took the people of Israel the long way through the wilderness for two reasons. One, because the warfare going on in the land of the Philistines that God knew the people of Israel were ill-equipped to handle; and two, because according to Deuteronomy 6, God wanted to learn what was in the heart of his chosen people, whether they were willing to be submissive and follow his leading. But didn't the all-knowing God already know what was in their hearts? Yes, but they didn't. They were ignorant of their real condition, and some extra journey trials would bring some clarity to them. They soon discovered deep within their hearts was a critical spirit, and they spent a great deal of time eating their words or wishing they could have them back. It was not enough that God had delivered these people from slavery. It was not enough that God had established a loving relationship with them. They wanted all their struggles resolved *now*.

PRINCIPLES

- God asks us to live each day to the fullest, trusting him for our tomorrows.
- Grumbling and complaining get you nowhere when you have not prayed and sought God's wisdom for the trials you are facing.
- Little steps of faith precede larger steps of faith.
- There is security in obedience.
- Unrealistic expectations almost always lead to grumbling and complaining when things do not go our way.

APPLICATIONS

- Wake up each morning with gratefulness, saying, "Good morning, Lord."
- Take an inventory of your blessings, and thank God for each one.
- Let this week be a time of "fasting" from complaints as they come into your mind.

IV. LIFE APPLICATION

Living by Faith

Living a life of obedience is a long ride. It means riding when we understand the safety of training wheels or are comfortable in what we see as true. It also means living by faith. Sadly, many people learning to walk this path of faith never learn the posture of training wheels. Moses never had to say to the Hebrew people, "Don't gather the manna for two days." They would have already learned this lesson the hard way and would have found it easier to obey. In your life, do you obey because of a walk of faith or because of the sad lesson you learn from the bumps and bruises that accompany moments of disobedience? The lesson may be learned, but it is the walk of faith that appeals to the heart of God.

V. PRAYER

Heavenly Father, provider of all that is good in my life, give me this day my daily bread. I confess those words are a little tough to say and mean because I am so used to praying "give me this week my weekly check," or "give me during these twilight years my earthly retirement portfolio." But the people of Israel had to learn, and so do I. So Lord, off with the training wheels; here goes nothing. Amen.

VI. DEEPER DISCOVERIES

A. The Glory of the Lord (16:7)

The term *glory* sometimes denotes beauty and dignity, especially when applied to humans. But the glory of the Lord refers to his power and majesty (1 Chr. 29:11). Sometimes this glory resembled physical form, as in Moses' later experience (Exod. 33:18–23). God would at times descend or appear in glory, such as at the temple dedication (1 Kgs. 8:10–11) and to the prophet Ezekiel (Ezek. 1). While God would not share his glory with man, he would allow man to reflect that glory in some sense (Ps. 84:11). A major consequence of man observing and recognizing this glory would be a holy life and outlook (Lev. 11:44–45). Once Israel took their eyes off God and looked on things that could not satisfy, God withdrew his glory from their midst (Ezek. 10:1–19). Of course, God carries his glory wherever he goes, and in that sense his glory is his presence. Man, through sin, has separated himself from God's presence and thus fallen short of the *glory* of God (Rom. 3:23).

VII. TEACHING OUTLINE

A. INTRODUCTION

1. Lead Story: Time to Take Off the Training Wheels
2. Context: It doesn't take long to travel from Egypt to the promised land. God could have taken Israel to the promised land in days rather than forty years. But these people weren't ready to take possession of the land. They had been slaves. They needed a period of education and testing before they were ready to possess Canaan. Growing in

faith means to grow in capacity to cope with and overcome obstacles through God's wisdom and power.

3. Transition: The obstacles faced in this passage are lack of water and enemies. A third obstacle must have been the large number of disputes that would inevitably arise within a community this size.

B. COMMENTARY

1. The Provision of Manna and Quail (16:1–36)

2. Miraculous Water and a Battle (17:1–16)

3. Jethro's Visit and Wise Counsel to Moses (18:1–27)

C. CONCLUSION: LIVING BY FAITH

VIII. ISSUES FOR DISCUSSION

1. How good is your memory while in a place of pain? Do you remember the hand of God on your life? Why or why not?

2. Do you really think the people of Israel thought they had packed enough for their extended journey? What resources were they lacking that only God could provide for them? Physically? Emotionally? Intellectually? Spiritually?

3. When you consider the miraculous intervention God provided for the people of Israel to escape bondage in Egypt, why do you think they complained so much?

4. Describe the faith that would be needed to have total dependency upon God's provisions? Do you have this depth of faith? What could God do in your life to help you develop these spiritual muscles?

5. What are the deeper issues in this chapter besides a group of thirsty, unsatisfied people?

6. How do you deal with stress? What can be lifted out of this text to help you deal with stress in a better way?

7. There are many lessons to learn about the leadership process in the defeat of the Amalekites. List three principles that will help you as a leader at church, at work, and in your home.

8. How is Moses' leadership style changing? Why will this be important in the future?

Exodus 19–20

God's Top Ten List

I. INTRODUCTION
Tell Them God Came

II. COMMENTARY
A verse-by-verse explanation of these chapters.

III. CONCLUSION
Check the Instructions

An overview of the principles and applications from these chapters.

IV. LIFE APPLICATION
Ten Commandments or Ten Suggestions?

Melding these chapters to life.

V. PRAYER
Tying these chapters to life with God.

VI. DEEPER DISCOVERIES
Historical, geographical, and grammatical enrichment of the commentary.

VII. TEACHING OUTLINE
Suggested step-by-step group study of these chapters.

VIII. ISSUES FOR DISCUSSION
Zeroing these chapters in on daily life.

Quote

"Doctrine is the framework of life—the skeleton of truth, to be clothed and rounded out by the living grace of a holy life."

A d o n i r a m   J .   G o r d o n

Exodus 19–20

IN A NUTSHELL

You have probably seen the movie. Charlton Heston climbs up Mount Sinai to receive the Ten Commandments from God. Only three months have passed since the opening of the gates of Egypt and the arrival at the holy mountain. Moses has had some face-to-face discussions with God and now in the midst of a cosmic light and sound display etches his "Top Ten List" on stone tablets for his people.

God's Top Ten List

I. INTRODUCTION

Tell Them God Came

A pastor in a southern state described how a special surge from the Spirit swept through his church one Sunday morning. To his knowledge nothing unusual had happened that week to hint of the event. In fact, the previous week's service, although uplifting, showed no sign that its successor would be unforgettable. At the outset that service was moving according to routine. The hymn they had sung to open the Sunday school, "Blessed Redeemer," they had sung a hundred times. Hardly anyone needed a hymnal for it. The Sunday school superintendent wasn't an orator even on his better occasions, and that morning was not one of his better occasions. He mumbled through a few opening comments as he usually did. Then he prayed his regular prayer and dismissed the people to Sunday school—all in one breath. But nobody got up to go. Thinking that he had not communicated clearly, he started back at the prayer and did the last part over again. Only this time when he gave the final dismissal, he made a flourish with his hands. They certainly couldn't miss that. But still nobody moved.

A little confused, but at the edge of a deep perception, the superintendent walked back to his seat on the platform. No sooner had he sat down than a red-haired man whose heart had recently been shredded by a divorce stood and raised his hand. "I just wanted to thank God for how good he's been to me," he said, then sat down.

The pastor later said, "When that man testified, it was like opening a bottle of fragrance from heaven. The Spirit spread around like divine perfume. For two hours the people testified and prayed and sang and wept. Over one hundred people voluntarily visited the altar. It was a day that will live forever in my heart and in my memory."

But true to form, every silver lining also has a cloud. At the end of the service, the Sunday school secretary, who had missed most of the power because she was in the basement counting pennies, came running up the stairs frustrated. "Pastor, pastor, I don't know what to do about the attendance. Nobody went to class. I don't think anybody got counted. What are we going to do? What about the numbers on the board?"

"Forget the numbers," the pastor told her. "Today was more than numbers. Just cut a piece of cardboard and slip it in the slot of the board and write on it, 'God came.'"

The people of Israel are now three months into their journey, and they stop in the desert of Sinai. Moses is then summoned to the mountain and has good news for the people: "God came." What was his message? Let's find out.

II. COMMENTARY

God's Top Ten List

MAIN IDEA: *The divine law is revealed through Moses.*

A Preparation for the Law (19:1–25)

SUPPORTING IDEA: *God prepares Moses for the law by instruction and phenomenon.*

19:1–15. In the third month after their miraculous deliverance from Egypt, the Israelites arrived at Sinai, setting camp in front of the mountain. Sinai, also called Horeb, was located among the mountains in the Sinai Peninsula, some eleven days away from Kadesh Barnea by the road to Mount Seir (Deut. 1:2). Although scholars admit they cannot locate the actual mountain with certainty, the traditional site is Jebel Musa, which rises to a height of seventy-five hundred feet.

Soon after the arrival, Moses went up to God, and **the LORD called to him from the mountain** with the words he was to share with the Israelites. They witnessed firsthand the mighty hand of God that brought them to God on eagle's wings, soaring high above any real threat. God told Moses he should remind the nation if they kept his covenant (see "Deeper Discoveries") and obeyed him fully, God would elevate them above the existing nations of the world and earmark them for special blessing. They would exist as God's unique possession and enjoy his presence. Although God claims the entire earth as his possession, Israel would stand out as a unique people, the people of God.

Moses returned to the camp and summoned the elders and related to them all the words God had shared with him. The people, in turn, promised to obey the words of God. The nation's relationship with God would be built on faith from the very outset, if they were to prosper. God would not bless them simply because they observed some rituals in honor of the Lord. The sacrifices God prescribed were to be made in faith.

God told Moses to set the people apart and prepare them to meet God. He would do this by commanding them to wash their clothes (and, no doubt, bodies, the probable meaning of "consecrate," Gen. 35:2, KD, 101) and abstain from sexual intercourse. On the third day God would descend from the mountain and meet with them. But they were not to go near the actual mountain on threat of death. The precise penalty would come by either stoning or being shot by arrows. This injunction included all animals. The only time God permitted them to climb the mountain was when they heard a long blast from a ram's horn.

Moses obeyed the Lord's words and separated the people just as God prescribed. He told them to prepare themselves **for the third day**. He probably at this time gave instructions to build a fence of some kind around the front of the mountain to prevent anyone from wandering near it (see vv. 12,23).

19:16–25. On the morning of the third day, there was thunder and lightning with a thick cloud over the mountain and a very loud trumpet blast. The people awoke to thunder (literally, "voices") and related phenomena and the loud trumpet blast which the Lord had previously spoke to Moses about. All this was to announce the Lord's appearance. God could have produced the trumpet sound through either natural or supernatural means. Some have speculated it came through angels.

The Lord descended the smoke-filled mountain in fire, demonstrating his majesty and holiness. The people trembled in response as Moses led them to the foot of the mountain. By now the mountain trembled violently, with the trumpet sound growing louder and louder. Although God chose these people to be his special people, sin still created a barrier between people and Creator, and they could only approach him through carefully prescribed means.

Moses next spoke to God, probably asking for his commands. But now God drew back to the top of Sinai, and he summoned Moses to meet him at the summit. There he warned Moses to command the people not to break through the barrier to look upon the Lord. To do so could bring death. The priests may have supposed themselves exempt from consecrating themselves like the others because of their special status. So God gave them a special warning in verse 22 to consecrate themselves properly lest God break out against them. God next commanded his servant to get his brother Aaron and bring him up with him. But he was not allowed to bring any of the priests or people with him. Moses faithfully shared these words with the people.

B The Law of Moses (20:1–26)

SUPPORTING IDEA: *The Lord gives Israel the Ten Commandments.*

20:1–17. The words God spoke next have come to be known as the Ten Commandments. The commandments became the official code of the covenant but were much more than that. They clearly echoed the will of God for man. Although Jesus Christ would later give the law a searching exposition in his Sermon on the Mount, describing the obligation to keep it in the heart as well as externally, these words would become the primary moral code of Israel. Moses repeated these commandments in Deuteronomy 5:6–21.

God began by identifying himself as the Lord their God, who brought them **out of Egypt, out of the land of slavery**. In so identifying himself, God established his rights as the sovereign Lord over Israel. The first command was that the Israelites **have no other gods before me**. The command itself is quite general and would outlaw not only any species of polytheism but also idolatry of any sort and all erroneous depictions of God.

The second command comes close on the heels of the first in both sequence and thought. Here God defines what is proper worship. Since God is spirit (John 4:24), God forbids any attempt to capture an image of God, whether by comparing him to another man-made image or any natural phenomenon. Perhaps this command especially prohibits constructing images for the purpose of worshiping them.

God appended a threat to this command, describing himself as a **jealous God** who would inflict such fury on violators of this command that their third and fourth generation descendants would suffer some consequences if they broke it. By contrast, he would bless and smile upon the succeeding generations of those who loved and obeyed him.

The third command instructed the Israelites not to **misuse the name of the LORD your God**. We should apply this command as broadly as possible. These words forbid any frivolous use of God's name, whether in swearing over trivial matters or in emotional outburst. God's people should use his name only in reverent contexts and never in questionable worship.

The fourth command sets apart the seventh day as a **Sabbath** (Heb. "to cease," "rest"). Although formally instituted here, the Sabbath originated with the giving of the manna (Exod. 16:23). Man should work six days and rest on the seventh. God himself symbolically "rested" on the seventh day of creation, thus sanctifying the day. The command applied to "both man and beast without exception" (KD, 119). God knew the effects of constant physical toil not only on the body but on man's spirit as well. The later Hebrew writers would repeatedly decry Sabbath-breaking (Neh. 13:15–18; Jer. 17:19–23). Modern authors continue to debate the relevance of the Sabbath for today and whether the Lord changed its observance to the Lord's Day, Sunday. The writer of Hebrews links the Sabbath to the final rest that all of God's people will one day enjoy (Heb. 4:3–11).

None of the formal institutions escape the rule and involvement of God, including that of family. The fifth command enforces the parent-child relationship as one of obedience of the latter to the former. Father and mother represent God to a child. And as children should **honor** God in all they do, so should they honor their parents as well. The promise attached to this command applies to individuals as well as the nation. Children who obey their parents could expect, under normal circumstances, to live long lives. But a nation of compliant children could expect to rear generations of God fearers who would reap the general promises of national longevity (Lev. 26:1–13; Deut. 28:1–14).

The next five commands involve man's treatment and relation to his neighbor. The command against **murder** goes back to the image of God within man (Gen. 9:6). To destroy man is to destroy the pinnacle of God's creation. We shouldn't wonder why God insists so often that we love our neighbor (Lev. 19:18; Luke 10:27). The opposite of love is hate, which may lead to murder (1 John 3:15).

A man or woman displays hatred toward his or her neighbor and the institution of marriage itself when he or she indulges in **adultery**. God made this violation a capital crime in ancient Israel, punishable by death (Lev. 20:10). But going beyond the mere physical act of adultery, the marriage union must cherish the strictest code of inner trust and sacred faithfulness, beginning with the couple's relationship with God. Flowing from a right relationship with God must come a "one-flesh" union characterized by the utmost faithfulness, admitting no rivals.

The command not to **steal** included more than outright removal of another's property but also injury to another's possessions and fraudulent practices of any kind. Paul would later speak out against theft of any kind, directing his readers instead to give of their possessions to those who were in need (Eph. 4:28). This command teaches the divine sanction of individual property rights.

The remaining commands caution against giving **false testimony against your neighbor** and coveting of any kind. The first would apply to any kind of such testimony, formal or not. Jesus would later cite Satan himself as the originator and "father of lies" (John 8:44), an outright "liar." Hence the God of all truth desires "truth in the inner parts" (Ps. 51:6). Today society blurs the lines between truth and lies, allocating both to the realm of personal choices.

The final command warns us not to **covet** anything God prohibits us. For example, God prohibits us to take something that does not belong to us. But God also might prohibit us from enjoying something, whether a possession or a lifestyle, that he readily grants another. The last command anticipates the unlawful lusts so clearly explained in the New Testament, especially in the Sermon on the Mount. The thought precedes the act, as in the case of lustful Achan, who "saw," "coveted," then finally "took" (Josh. 7:21). Solomon, no stranger to self-indulgence, instructs us to "guard your heart, for it is the wellspring of life" (Prov. 4:23).

20:18–21. The people trembled in fear when they saw the thunder and related phenomena on the mountain. They kept their distance and instead relied on Moses to communicate God's words to them. But Moses reassured them that God did not seek their undoing but was testing them to see what was in their hearts and to keep them from sinning.

20:22–26. This monumental chapter closes with a reminder not to worship other gods, including man-made gods of silver and gold. Furthermore, God directed them to make their altar out of the earth he created or stones not shaped by human hands. Upon the approved altar God would accept their burnt and fellowship offerings (see Lev. 1–6).

MAIN IDEA REVIEW: *The divine law is revealed through Moses.*

III. CONCLUSION

Check the Instructions

When I get something new, I look at it, determine how to use it and how it runs, and then try it out. Only if I find I am not getting it to work will I look at the instructions. When microwave ovens first came out, in my impatience to cook something quickly, I threw an item into the unit, turned the handle to three minutes, and watched through the little window. The only problem was that sparks were flying everywhere! A small fire started. Why? Because I had left the aluminum foil on the item. I had not read the instructions that warned me not to do this if I wanted to avoid problems. So I turned to the instruction book and learned how to operate the microwave correctly before using it again.

The same thing is true with our lives. God never designed his Top Ten List to be a rigid system of rules so your life would be miserable. His list displayed his character: He knew that we would live life to the fullest and have the most joy if we lived in a way that showed his character in all we did and thought. God knows how people think, how they respond in different situations, and what they need to have the healthiest relationships with him and with one another. Therefore, he gave warnings, similar to those in the microwave book. These are healthy rules. When people follow his ways, their lives reflect the fact that they are living their lives well, are following the "Manufacturer's Instructions."

What an unbelievable display of God's love and power. These Ten Commandments were given to mankind for several reasons. No one would ever be able to keep all the commandments until the Lord Jesus arrived on earth, but God still gave them to show mankind just how far we fall short of God's standards for our lives. Paul wrote in Romans 3:19–20:

> Now we know that whatever the law says, it says to those who are under the law, so that every mouth may be silenced and the whole world held accountable to God. Therefore no one will be declared righteous in his sight by observing the law; rather, through the law we become conscious of sin.

No one could ever stand before someone and proclaim his or her own personal righteousness. God would simply need to point to the law. Through their conviction of sin, however, people begin to recognize their desperate need of salvation. Where our culture has drifted from God's Top Ten List, sin abounds all the more. But don't be surprised. Romans 5:20 states, "The law was added so that the trespass might increase. But where sin increased, grace increased all the more."

PRINCIPLES

- God's standards are much higher than the average person understands.
- The Ten Commandments demonstrate human weaknesses and our inability to follow God completely.
- Break one of the commandments, and you have broken the entire law.
- The Ten Commandments are primarily relational: The first four deal with our relationship with God, and the last six address our earthly relationships with people.
- Our God is a jealous God who wants our undivided loyalty and allegiance.

APPLICATIONS

- Do not trust willpower to make yourself acceptable to God.
- Ponder what God has done to provide your salvation and take joy in his love for you.
- Belive that the Ten Commandments were given for your welfare.
- Christ fulfilled the righteous demands of the law on the cross. Never let a day pass without thanking your Lord for his love and sacrifice for you.

IV. LIFE APPLICATION

Ten Commandments or Ten Suggestions?

The Ten Commandments were never intended to be suggestions or opinions. They came directly from God and were meant to be followed. Living in a new millennium certainly has its advantages. Easier travel, great medical provisions, and information at your fingertips are all examples of the benefits of the twenty-first century. But these advantages do not translate into spiritual well-being. Some 65 to 95 percent of the people responding to a national survey state they pick and choose which of the Ten Commandments to obey. According to Roger Rosenblatt:

> Only 15% thought the majority of Americans curse and use profanity; only 22% thought that the majority attended a house of worship regularly and refrained from envying the things someone else had. Only 49% of those responding thought Americans in general worshipped the true God (*Family Circle,* 21 December 1993, p. 30).

The real problem is our hesitation to commit to obedience and personal holiness. Like any sporting event, success and victory will be found in the life of the person who finishes the game, who fights to the finish, who has the endurance and passion to win. You cannot sidestep God's Top Ten List, thinking there is an easier way to live. The people of Israel had to learn this truth, and so do we.

V. PRAYER

Lord, I often look at your Word through the eyes of a person in line at the smorgasbord, not wanting to fill up in the beginning because I may miss the good stuff at the end of the line. But the Ten Commandments are the good stuff. These guidelines for genuine living have been given to me to provide a reflection of where my heart may be at any given moment and remind me of how thankful I should be for you, Lord Jesus, in fulfilling the law and providing salvation for me. You are so right, Lord: I may not have seen the clouds and lightning, but I have seen your heart. Help me to take these things seriously, because you do. Amen.

VI. DEEPER DISCOVERIES

A. Covenant

In ordinary terms a covenant (literally, "bond") is an agreement between two or more persons. The Bible speaks of such agreements (Gen. 21:27,32; 1 Sam. 18:3). At times God condescended to be a party to a covenant with man. The Old Testament concept of "covenant" begins with a one-sided declaration of God, such as "I will establish my covenant with you" (Gen. 6:18). There God makes his intentions known to man. God promises to be faithful to his covenant. Although God alone decides the nature of his covenant with man, he accomplishes it with man.

God's covenant with man is therefore a promise based on grace upon certain conditions being fulfilled by man. God actually enacts several covenants with man in the Old Testament. Some say these are different covenants, while others insist they are different features of the same covenant. Although the pact God makes with man cannot be abrogated by anyone, man himself may disqualify himself from enjoying the blessings of the covenant through his disobedience.

Of course, behind all of this is God's gracious election of a people for himself—people who will follow him because God will work in their lives to make it so. When the nation rebels against God through disobedience, God will receive them back only through repentance (2 Chr. 15:12; Neh. 9:38). The fullest development of this covenant looks forward to a time when God and man will live in harmony and perfect fellowship (Isa. 42:6; Jer. 31:31–32; Heb. 8:8–9). When the Bible was translated into Latin, the word *testament* for the most part replaced the word *covenant*.

B. Israel and the Nations of the World

One promise God made to Israel granted them a unique status among the nations of the world. In Exodus 19:5–6 God promised them "privileged nation" rights as long as they kept his commands and trusted him. But God never promised them "worldruler" status, nor did he command them to colonize the world. Of course, in the future those in a trusting relationship will partake of the kingdom of God—the one kingdom that will dominate and even crush the other kingdoms of the world (Dan. 2:44). Until then, Israel was to obey their God and not fraternize with the nations and idols of the surrounding world.

Upon fulfillment of this condition, God would do the following for Israel: He would grant them safe and prosperous living conditions in the land (Lev. 26:5–6), domination of their enemies (Lev. 26:7–8; Deut. 28:7), an exalted position among the nations (Deut. 28:1), both militarily (Deut. 28:7) and economically (Deut. 28:12). But never did God promise the Israelites immediate world-ruler rights even if they were obedient. The kingdom of God in its fullest realization (sometimes called the "eschatological kingdom") would be a stone cut without human hands, and God would bring it about in his own time.

VII. TEACHING OUTLINE

A. INTRODUCTION

1. Lead Story: Tell Them God Came
2. Context: To be God's people, Israel had to know God. Sinai was the place where God revealed his nature to Israel in the form of "Ten Words" or "Ten Laws." These people who grew up in a polytheistic culture are beginning to experience the holiness of God and his call for them to be holy.

3. Transition: In these chapters we experience the fear of the Lord and come to know that "the fear of the LORD is the beginning of knowledge" (Prov. 1:7).

B. COMMENTARY

1. Preparation for the Law (19:1–25)
2. The Law of Moses (20:1–26)

C. CONCLUSION: TEN COMMANDMENTS OR TEN SUGGESTIONS?

VIII. ISSUES FOR DISCUSSION

1. Chapter 19 is a significant chapter for leaders. Read verses 4–6 again and identify what God expects from his leaders.
2. What is involved in becoming a "holy nation"? Why all the special effects in the middle of this chapter?
3. Would you like to meet God face-to-face? Why or why not? What does it mean to walk on holy ground?
4. Are the Ten Commandments just as relevant today as they were in the days of the Book of Exodus? Why or why not?
5. Which one of the Ten Commandments do you struggle most with? Why? What steps can you take this week to improve in this area?
6. Reword each of these commandments to read as a freedom you can enjoy this week.

Exodus 21–24

Civil and Religious Law

I. **INTRODUCTION**
Laws of the Land

II. **COMMENTARY**
A verse-by-verse explanation of these chapters.

III. **CONCLUSION**
Times Haven't Changed

An overview of the principles and applications from these chapters.

IV. **LIFE APPLICATION**
The Power of Encouragement

Melding these chapters to life.

V. **PRAYER**
Tying these chapters to life with God.

VI. **DEEPER DISCOVERIES**
Historical, geographical, and grammatical enrichment of the commentary.

VII. **TEACHING OUTLINE**
Suggested step-by-step group study of these chapters.

VIII. **ISSUES FOR DISCUSSION**
Zeroing these chapters in on daily life.

"The first law that ever God gave to man was a law of obedience. . . . From obedience and submission spring all other virtues, as all sin does from self-opinion and self-will."

Michel Eyquem de Montaigne

Exodus 21–24

IN A NUTSHELL

After receiving the Ten Commandments, God continues the education process for Moses and his followers by addressing specific illustrations and applications of his law. In these chapters God provides guidelines on personal responsibility toward servants and property and responsibility toward social issues and matters of justice. Then God reminds the people once more of a promise he had made to the Hebrews.

Civil and Religious Law

I. INTRODUCTION

Laws of the Land

*I*n the city of Philadelphia, a group of fifty-five men met in mid May of 1787 to discuss the creation of a new system of government. Each of these men were representatives of the colonies that had won a war to establish their independence from Great Britain. The Articles of Confederation had previously been drawn up as a temporary guide for governing the colonies, but these articles had failed to meet the needs of the colonies. The colonies, therefore, determined to create a permanent document by which they could be governed.

The representatives met behind closed doors for four months. They met in a final session on September 17, 1787, and signed the document they had created. The document was submitted to the various colonies and was approved. The document they approved was the Constitution of the United States of America. It is a rather brief document that contains the general principles upon which our government is based. It is the foundational document that provides the guiding principles for all of our national life.

The Constitution is the guiding document of our legal system. It is the basis of thousands and thousands of laws that apply its principles in specific situations. The specific situations are then governed by what is called case law, and these laws declare that if you do this particular deed, then you could receive this particular punishment. In other words, case law provides the practical application of the broad principles asserted in constitutional law.

The Bible contains Ten Commandments. We have already determined that these are the foundational principles God gave to his people. In a sense, they are similar to our Constitution. They serve the same purpose regarding our relationship with God as the Constitution does with regard to our nation's government. The Old Testament, however, also contains case law or legislation that applies those principles to specific situations. The moral law was outlined in Exodus 20, the civil law in chapters 21–23, and the religious law at the end of chapter 23 and on into chapter 24.

II. COMMENTARY

Civil and Religious Law

> **MAIN IDEA:** *God requires his children to live righteously in the new community.*

A Jewish Servitude (21:1–11)

> **SUPPORTING IDEA:** *God protects the rights of both masters.*

21:1. The vast multitude now began to settle into community life, and with it they experienced many new challenges. We must remember that the Hebrew law governed the religious, civil, and moral life of the community. All three were rolled into one, although all three were separately and clearly addressed. God expected the life of the community would reflect his own righteousness and care for individuals, particularly those who could not easily fend for themselves. So God now specifically addresses the relationships between master and servant and neighbors (used in the broad sense of "fellowman").

21:2–6. We must remember that the Jewish nation was really born into slavery. God did not immediately forbid some forms of servitude (see "Deeper Discoveries") but instead carefully regulated it to prohibit the inhumane treatment of individuals. The first regulation governed the duration of the master-servant relationship. God limited it to **six years**. In the seventh year (i.e., the seventh year of his servitude, not the sabbatical seventh year), the servant could go free without any remaining obligations to his master. If he contracted the servant relationship when he was single, then the master would release him single. But if he was married at the time he made the contract, then his wife would accompany him upon his release. However, if the master gave him a wife after he became a servant, then the wife and any children born to the couple would remain with the master, and the man would go free.

Sometimes the servant could probably fare no better on his own, and he wanted to remain a servant all his days. Or he might want to remain with his family who were not eligible to be released for the reasons stipulated in verse 4. In that case the master could not simply "make it happen" but must get official sanction before the judges. Then he must participate in a "servant forever" ceremony that consisted of piercing the servant's ear with an awl to the door or doorpost as a symbolic gesture of permanency. Thereafter the relationship between servant and master would last for life.

21:7–11. God regulated the female servants somewhat differently. If a father sold his daughter as a servant to a master, then the seven-year release did not apply to her. Often this kind of transaction included the master actually marrying the female servant, or taking her as a concubine, in addition, perhaps, to his existing wife or new wife (see v. 10). If things did not work out and the master no longer desired her, then he must **let her be redeemed** by selling his rights over to another Hebrew, give her to his own son, or turn her over to her father without demanding any refund money. In no case could the master deprive her of her physical needs. If somehow the master failed to keep any of the above stipulations, then the female slave could go free without further restrictions of any kind.

B Personal Injuries (21:12–36)

SUPPORTING IDEA: *God regulates human behavior by punishing criminal acts and protecting the rights of the innocent.*

21:12–17. Community order was further maintained by punitive regulations, the first of which dealt with murder. Outright murder was never to be pardoned for any reason. It would be punishable by death, even if the perpetrator went into the sanctuary area and pleaded for his life. But accidents did not amount to murder. If a man accidentally caused the death of another, then he would flee to a place specifically designated for this purpose (later called "cities of refuge"; see Josh. 20:1–9). Also included in capital crimes were patricide, matricide, kidnapping, and cursing or swearing at one's parents. To a contemporary mind, this might seem harsh, but we must keep in mind that Jewish law combined civil and religious elements, something not in vogue in most nations today.

21:18–36. The law further governed personal altercations that resulted in injury of some sort or death. In a fight, if one person struck another with a stone or his fist and this resulted in injury but not death, the perpetrator had to compensate the man for time lost (at work). If a man beat his male or female slave and this resulted in death, then he must be punished (how we're not told). In such a case, it might have to be determined whether the actual death was intended or not. The regulation did not apply, however, if the slave recovered in a few days.

Perhaps two men were fighting and accidentally struck a pregnant woman (perhaps the wife of one of the combatants) so that she gave premature birth. If neither she nor the baby received a permanent injury, then the court and the woman's husband would litigate the settlement. In everything, the law dictated fairness: **eye for eye, tooth for tooth, hand for hand, foot for foot**. If a master should strike a servant and this resulted in the permanent loss of sight in one eye or the loss of a tooth, the slave could go free.

If a bull gored a person to death, that bull would be stoned to death. But the owner would not be held responsible unless he had allowed a bull that was aggressive and known to gore to wander freely. In the later case both the bull and owner would be put to death. If the bull killed a slave, the owner of the bull would make compensation to the owner of the slave consisting of thirty shekels of silver. A man would also have to pay an animal's owner if he dug a pit and the animal fell into it and died.

Finally, two bulls with separate owners that had a fight in which one was killed resulted in the owners selling the live bull, splitting the proceeds, then also sharing the dead bull. The latter regulation would be voided, however, if the owner of a particularly aggressive bull killed another bull, in which case that owner must make up the difference to the other.

C Property Rights and Social Relations (22:1–31)

SUPPORTING IDEA: *Following God's will includes adhering to community and moral codes of responsibility.*

22:1–6. The laws respecting compensation for lost or stolen property do not contradict New Testament principles of forgiveness. Furthermore, these codes serve three purposes: (1) maintaining justice in the land, (2) granting justice and compensation to victims, and (3) teaching thieves that crime not only doesn't pay; it forces you to suffer loss.

In the case of stolen and resold animals, the law required the thief to pay back five times the worth of the ox and four times the worth of a sheep. Such protection of victims extended to extenuating circumstances where the victims were forced to kill the thief at night. If, however, the homeowner killed the thief by day, he would be held liable. The reason, although not specifically mentioned, was probably that day thieves could be easier apprehended than night thieves, and the homeowners may not have been able to determine whether the thieves who came by night had hostile intentions. In any case, the thief was to make double restitution, even if that meant being sold into slavery for a season.

If a man grazed his livestock and allowed them to wander off and feed in another's field, the owner of the animal would make restitution from his own crops or vineyard. Since there did not appear to be any willful violation, simple restitution was all that was required. Similarly, if a man failed to trim back flammable bush that bordered another's field, or a similar instance of carelessness, he must make simple restitution.

22:7–15. Some cases were more complex than others. For example, if one man held another's valuables for safekeeping and the items were stolen, of course the thief would be held liable and must make reparations according to the law (see above). But if the thief was not apprehended, the case reverted to judges, who determined whether the "safe keeper" had a part in the crime. Cases where two people claimed ownership of disputed property also went to the judges for official judgment. If they determined one of them was the true owner, the other must pay back twofold, as if he had stolen the property. This law would discourage widespread slander.

If one neighbor handed over an animal to another for safekeeping and the animal died in his care, the latter must take an oath **before the LORD** (the judges, who ruled for God), in which case the owner must rest content with his neighbor's oath. But if it was stolen, then the guilty neighbor must make restitution. But if the animal was mauled to death by another animal, then the safekeeping neighbor would not be held responsible. This provision did not, however, extend to *borrowed* animals that died or were killed in another's care outside the presence of the owner (who would have cared for the animal had he been present). If the neighbor "rented" an animal from his neighbor, the sum of the lease would satisfy the demand.

22:16–17. If a man seduced a girl not betrothed to another, he would have to pay a dowry, even if the father refused to give her to him in matrimony. (For instances where a man seduces a girl betrothed, see Deut. 22:23–24.)

22:18–31. Any person who practiced sorcery would pay with his life. We must remember that Israel's civil and religious life, unlike the majority of Gentile nations, were vitally linked. God prescribed penalties that, if followed, insured the people against seeking power or knowledge of the future from evil spirits. The idolatrous and demonic practices that came with such assaults often involved sexual deviation and other dark behavior of the grossest sort. Accordingly, God outlawed bestiality (v. 19), idolatrous sacrifices (v. 20), and blasphemy of God or a ruler (v. 28).

When a nation declined spiritually, the devaluation of life soon followed. Hence, God protected aliens, or visitors, from mistreatment. He also protected the nation's widows and orphans—those who could not easily fend for themselves—from the oppression of those who were stronger. The penalty for such offenses was stiff (v. 24). In the case of the needy borrowing money from wealthy individuals, the latter were to treat the former with dignity and not charge them interest (see "Deeper Discoveries"). If they secured the borrower's cloak as a pledge, they were to return it to him by nightfall. People of the Middle East often slept using their outer garment or cloak as a blanket. Again, the needy often used a weapon not often utilized by their rich counterparts—prayer to God. Since God is a **compassionate** God, he would work on their behalf.

Sometimes people might be tempted to sin in ways not easily detected by others. For example, it would be difficult to ascertain whether a man properly tithed from large quantities of grain or vats. But God would see and bless or curse the land according to how people obeyed him in such matters. Of course, the greatest tithe would be the giving up of the firstborn sons, by redeeming them with payment (see 13:15), and cattle and sheep in sacrifice (see Lev. 22:27–28) following the natural weaning time with their mothers. When God chose Israel, he did so with the purpose of making them a holy people. This even pertained to their diet, a theme developed more thoroughly in the next book of the Pentateuch, Leviticus. For now, they were not to eat an animal that had been torn by wild beasts.

D Justice, Faithfulness in Spiritual Observances, and God's Protection (23:1–33)

> **SUPPORTING IDEA:** *God's protection of Israel would depend on their faithful observance of laws of justice and maintaining prescribed ceremonial rituals.*

23:1–5. Moses now elaborates on the ninth commandment and forbids slander. Slander would include spreading false reports or serving as an "expert" witness, being hired by a malicious person for the purpose of false testimony. Even if a multitude tried to incite someone to spread such reports or bear false witness, he or she should resist. The multitude is not always on the side of the truth, and God certainly protects the rights of the minority in the Bible and especially in the Pentateuch. Since God is compassionate and demonstrates his mercy to the people, the people should exercise the same kind of compassion toward others. If one man saw even his enemy's donkey or ox wandering off or fallen under its load, he was to assist him in any way possible. Here we see incipient New Testament themes already in play (Matt. 5:43–48).

23:6–9. God would jealously watch over the land in matters of justice, especially where the wealthy could abuse the poor and defenseless. Judges were to settle lawsuits fairly, giving no preference to the rich over the poor. They were not to be a party to false charges or rule of the mob, particularly where human life was at stake, such as in a capital trial. Often some judges were tempted to give or receive bribes in such cases, but God was watching over the land and the actions of its rulers and would not overlook such violations. Finally, God commanded the host nation, Israel, to remember its lowly status in Egypt, to respect the rights of aliens or foreigners in the land.

23:10–11. God provided Israel with a "land flowing with milk and honey" but forbade misuse of the land. One such example of misuse was overworking the land. The animals, workers, as well as the land itself needed rest. God also intended the seventh year land rest to be a time of increased spiritual reflection (Deut. 31:10–13) and an opportunity for the poor to glean from the idle fields.

23:12–13. The normal Sabbath observance would follow six days of work. This would provide rest and refreshment for workers and animals alike. God required scrupulous observance of all he enacted in the way of rule or ceremony. God set forth the conditions of his blessing and presence in the land. He was their God and they his people. Therefore they were not to pray to or even acknowledge the names of other gods.

23:14. Three times per year the Israelites were to set apart a prescribed period of time to participate in a thankful remembrance of God's gracious presence among them. Such festivals encouraged national unity under their one and only God, enhanced group and individual spiritual devotion, and paved the way for God to bless them as a people.

23:15–17. The three festivals included the **Feast of Unleavened Bread**, the **Feast of Harvest**, and the **Feast of Ingathering** held at the end of the harvest year. The first feast began with the Passover and continued for seven days (see Lev. 23:4–8). The second, "Pentecost," or first fruits, lasted but a single day and began fifty days after the Feast of Passover. It celebrated the wheat harvest (Lev. 23:10–14). The last feast mentioned, Ingathering, celebrated the general harvest and was also called the Feast of Tabernacles (Lev. 23:33–36).

23:18–19. The **fat** of the festival probably refers to the "best" of the lamb, or the part normally eaten (distinct from the fat of other sacrifices; see Exod. 34:25) at the Passover. It was not to be left until the morning but was to be consumed that night. They were to drain the blood as prescribed and not allow the bread to become leavened. The final rule mentioned in verse 19 forbids cooking **a young goat in its mother's milk**. Some people supposed the kids were most palatable when boiled in their mother's milk. Was this restriction a humane or ceremonial consideration? Probably the former.

23:20–26. Human nature tends to mess up a good thing. The task of conquering the nations presently occupying the land of Canaan would prove far less demanding than obeying God in all he commanded. Yet this was the key to the success and longevity of the Israelites in the land. God obligated himself to protect the people by sending his angel, a probable reference to the angel of the Lord, who would go before them. He would make God's will known to them, and they would have to obey everything he said. He would reward such obedience by routing their enemies and bringing them safely into the land of Canaan. But if they learned the practices of the people of the land and worshiped their gods, they would soon forfeit this protection and succumb to all forms of disease and other curses.

They were to leave no trace of the native religion, even to the point of smashing **their sacred stones to pieces**. Pluralism and toleration weren't virtues in ancient Israel.

23:27–33. By way of encouragement, God spelled out what he would do to their enemies in the land. He would instill fear in them and chase them out as a hornet. He would do this gradually, however, because of the difficulty of dealing with the rising population of wild predators. But drive them out he would, until the people found full and complete rest in the land. But they must obey him. Israel's specific border would extend from the Red Sea (on the southeast) to the **Sea of the Philistines** (the Mediterranean Sea on the west), all the way to the Euphrates River to the north (see 1 Kgs. 4:21). The only threat to these borders would come from within: Israel's own reluctance to honor their God by ridding the land of idol worship.

Ⅰ Sealing the Covenant (24:1–18)

SUPPORTING IDEA: *The covenant between God and man is based on trust and spiritual fellowship.*

24:1–2. God selected key leaders to approach him on the mountain for the purpose of formally ratifying the covenant. Moses, Aaron, Nadab, Abihu, and seventy elders of Israel were to climb the mountain, but only Moses could draw near to the Lord.

24:3–6. The people not only heard the words of the covenant but also voiced a willingness to heed the words it contained. Once the covenant was affirmed, Moses wrote down the words the Lord had told him. The very next morning Moses arose and built an **altar at the foot of the mountain, and set up twelve stone pillars** (boundary marks of sorts) that represented the twelve tribes of Israel. Then Moses had young men collect and offer burnt offerings and fellowship offerings to the Lord. The young men were allowed to perform Levitical functions because this event preceded the formal institution of the priesthood. Young men were probably selected because of their strength. Moses then took the blood and sprinkled it on the altar and put some blood into bowls (basins). In this sense Moses was the mediator of the covenant.

24:7–8. The people again affirmed their commitment to keep the words of the covenant. Moses then set the people apart for God by sprinkling the blood on them. Without this they could not be clean in God's sight (Heb. 9:22). This covenant had all the earmarks of grace written on it, although some have mistakenly called it "graceless." Moses solemnized the covenant by identifying the blood as **the blood of the covenant** the Lord made with them.

24:9–12. Moses, Aaron, Nadab, Abihu, and the seventy elders of Israel climbed the mountain and saw the God of Israel (see "Deeper Discoveries"). While we don't know precisely what they saw, they did see feet of sorts, under which was **a pavement made of sapphire, clear as the sky itself.** They saw God and lived because God sanctified them for this occasion. The Jews supposed no one could see the Lord without dying, and they even discouraged pronouncing his name. The Lord commanded Moses to climb higher and remain for the formal giving of the law contained on tablets.

24:13–18. Moses along with Joshua, his aide and eventual successor, climbed the mountain again to meet with God. Aaron and his assistant Hur would oversee the congregation in their absence. Upon their arrival the cloud covered the mountain for six days. We don't know if Joshua followed Moses all the way. We learn in 32:17 that he was actually with Moses on the mountain, but he probably did not go into the vicinity of God's presence (see 24:2). To the inhabitants at the camp below, the sight resembled a wildfire. Moses entered the cloud and remained there for forty days and forty nights.

> **MAIN IDEA REVIEW:** *God requires his children to live righteously in the new community.*

III. CONCLUSION

Times Haven't Changed

A recent study reported in the Northern Arizona University School of Hotels and Restaurant Management newsletter, *Hospitality Trends,* relates some disturbing facts about ethics in America today. The article cites a recent study of five thousand Americans from a wide spectrum of backgrounds and demographics. The findings were startling:

- 93 percent said their judgment about right and wrong was based solely on personal belief. They feel no impact from law, threat of police action, religion, or family values.
- 74 percent said they would steal from those who would not miss it.
- Almost 50 percent of college students cheat.
- Upwards of 24 percent of all résumés contain false information.
- The study found an increased willingness to lie on financial aid forms.
- 64 percent would lie when it suits them if it caused no "real" damage.

Despite what Bob Dylan may have written years ago, the times haven't changed all that much. We continue to be a depraved, sinful people in need of God's moral law and God's civil law if we hope to live according to his will for our lives.

PRINCIPLES

- God has a purpose and a plan for every person.
- The Bible is a universal book that applies to all walks of life and every segment of culture.
- God's desire for his people is to reach out and care for the needs of the less fortunate.

APPLICATIONS

- As you have read this portion of God's law, has God brought to mind any sins you need to confess to him?
- Are there people to whom you need to make restitution?
- Take some time to reflect on how God values you as an individual and your community, desiring his best for you.

IV. LIFE APPLICATION

The Power of Encouragement

Psychologists conducted an experiment to determine the capacity of people to endure pain. They measured how long a person could stand barefooted in a bucket of cold water. They discovered one factor that could allow some to stay in the water twice as long as others: encouragement. If someone was offering encouragement and support, the sufferer could endure the pain twice as long as one who did not receive such encouragement.

Isn't that what God is reminding us of in these chapters? Become a person of influence by being both obedient and caring. Never lose sight of the people around you and how your choices will impact their lives. Respond to the needs of those less fortunate who are in desperate need of the touch of God's hand in their lives.

V. PRAYER

Lord, you care about the universe, and you care about the individual. I must do the same. Help me to be sensitive to your leading in the lives of others. Where I have hurt others, remind me to make restitution. Where there is a need, encourage me to respond. Use me as one of your angels of mercy in the lives of others. Amen.

VI. DEEPER DISCOVERIES

A. Hebrew Servitude

Slavery was a common practice in the Near Eastern world. Slaves could be obtained during war (Num. 31:9), through purchase (Gen. 37:28), by birth from existing slaves (Gen. 17:12), as a payment of debt (Exod. 22:3), or because of poverty (Lev. 25:39). Of course, the price would vary according to circumstances. But Hebrew slavery, if we can call it that (some prefer "servitude"), was quite different. A slave could go free after six years of service, and he was not to be harshly treated by the owner. Non-Israelite slaves could be whipped but not disfigured in any way (Exod. 21:20–27). Women who were acquired as slave wives were given special rights (Deut. 21:10–14). Most of the glimpses we have of Hebrew slavery practices compare favorably with pagan practices. Among most nations of the ancient world, slaves were treated with brutality and considered subhuman. It goes without saying that ancient and modern slave markets did not follow any humanitarian laws. The motive was profit. Paul's letter to Philemon in the New Testament gives us a look into the heart of God, who considers all men and women equal in his sight and demands respect for all. Christianity, rightly and compassionately applied, has led to many successful abolition movements throughout history.

B. The Nature of God

God is spirit (John 4:24), indeed "a most pure spirit, invisible, without body, parts, or passions" (Westminster Confession). So what did Moses and his companions see when they met God on the mountain? Let Keil explain: "At the same time we must regard it as a vision of God in some form of manifestation which rendered the divine nature discernible to the human eye. Nothing is said as to the form in which God manifested Himself" (159). The form is probably not mentioned so the people would not attempt to make likenesses of the Lord.

C. Borrowing

During the times of the early Hebrew nation, loans were not made to obtain capital or to engage in business ventures but for the necessities of life. The Israelites were commanded to exercise compassion toward their needy brothers (Deut. 15:7–11). Those who made loans to fellow Hebrews could not charge them interest (Exod. 22:25), but they could charge interest to foreigners (Deut. 23:20). Lenders could request pledges from borrowers, but they could not enter the house to obtain them. If the pledge for the loan was a garment, the lenders must return it to them by sunset (Exod. 22:26–27). A lender could not take as a pledge anything needed to produce food (Deut. 24:6) or a widow's garment (Deut. 25:17). At the end of every seven years, all debts were to be forgiven (Deut. 15:1–11).

VII. TEACHING OUTLINE

A. INTRODUCTION

1. Lead Story: Laws of the Land
2. Context: God is just, and he calls his people to be just. The last six of the Ten Commandments contain broad principles of justice. These

chapters spell out in greater detail how the Ten Commandments are to be applied in specific situations.

3. Transition: Human beings have a tendency to wander from God. Times of worship and celebration are instituted as reminders of God, what he has done on our behalf, and what he expects us to do from day to day.

B. COMMENTARY

1. Jewish Servitude (21:1–11)
2. Personal Injuries (21:12–36)
3. Property Rights and Social Relations (22:1–31)
4. Justice, Faithfulness in Spiritual Observances, and God's Protection (23:1–33)
5. Sealing the Covenant (24:1–18)

C. CONCLUSION: THE POWER OF ENCOURAGEMENT

VIII. ISSUES FOR DISCUSSION

1. If the Hebrews had had enough insight to compare the previous laws regarding serving the Egyptians and the laws regarding serving one another, what insights would they have seen?
2. Can you detect a hierarchy of values in these chapters? How do these chapters further develop the Ten Commandments?
3. Look at the inventory of property owned by the people of Israel in Exodus 22. Attempt to describe the kind of lifestyle these people enjoyed. Compare their lifestyle with yours.
4. Three festivals are outlined in chapter 23. What do these festivals tell us about celebrations we should be enjoying in the Christian faith?

Exodus 25–28

Blueprints for God's House

I. INTRODUCTION
The Heart of God

II. COMMENTARY
A verse-by-verse explanation of these chapters.

III. CONCLUSION
Building the Tabernacle

An overview of the principles and applications from these chapters.

IV. LIFE APPLICATION
A Multiple Perspective

Melding these chapters to life.

V. PRAYER
Tying these chapters to life with God.

VI. DEEPER DISCOVERIES
Historical, geographical, and grammatical enrichment of the commentary.

VII. TEACHING OUTLINE
Suggested step-by-step group study of these chapters.

VIII. ISSUES FOR DISCUSSION
Zeroing these chapters in on daily life.

"*The* Lord showed me, so that I did see clearly, that he did not dwell in these temples which men had commanded and set up, but in people's hearts. . . . His people were his temple, and he dwelt in them."

George Fox

Exodus 25–28

IN A NUTSHELL

We now approach a series of chapters devoted to the blueprints and layout of the temporary worship center known as the tabernacle. When the directions are given, God begins with the most holy place and the ark of the covenant and proceeds to the outer courts. Without the shedding of blood, there would be no remission of sin (Heb. 9:22). So this literal building with numerous pieces of symbolism becomes a picture of a future deliverance and deliverer.

Blueprints for God's House

I. INTRODUCTION

The Heart of God

*I*n his book *Faith, Hope, and Hilarity,* Dick Van Dyke told about a Sunday school teacher who asked her students to talk about how they felt about their church. The students responded in the usual ways: some said something silly to get the rest of the class to laugh, while others tried to be more serious. One of the girls was new to the class, and she felt uncomfortable about entering into class discussions, so she never raised her hand or volunteered an answer. That Sunday, however, she did have an answer for her Sunday school teacher, and it was unforgettable. She said that going to church was "like walking into the heart of God."

You are about to walk into the heart of God by walking into a study of the tabernacle. In chapters 25–31, we are going to examine a blueprint for the tabernacle just as God gave it to Moses on Mount Sinai. We then will watch the actual building of this masterpiece in chapters 35–40. You will learn more about the parenthetical chapters 32–34 a little later. This tabernacle was an actual building for not only the meeting of God with his people but also where the priest would offer sacrifices for the sins of the people to bring about a complete fellowship with God.

In the first fifteen chapters of Exodus, we enjoyed God's leading of Moses and the people of Israel out from captivity in Egypt. The next nine chapters reveal God's sovereignty in his leading of this motley band of wanderers through the wilderness and right up to the borders of the land they had only dreamed about. Now we are going to learn about the tabernacle where God was to make his holy habitation and speak to man. A study of the tabernacle is vital for the maturity of the Bible student because fifty chapters in Scripture are devoted to a discussion of the tabernacle.

II. COMMENTARY

Blueprints for God's House

MAIN IDEA: *God gave detailed instructions for the proper place and practice of worship.*

A The Initial Offerings and Furniture for the Tabernacle (25:1–40)

SUPPORTING IDEA: *The heart of worship begins with a willing giver, sacrificial gifts, and a prescribed order of service leading to God's glory.*

25:1–2. Worship always comes first. God did not wait until Israel was settled in the land to instruct them in proper worship. He saw it as a special priority and planned for it from the outset. This taught the Israelites always to place God first in their lives and that no inconvenience should ever bar them from honoring God. The purpose for them "plundering" the Egyptians of their goods was not for personal or national enrichment but to provide for the worship of the living God. Accordingly, God instructed Moses to tell the people to bring a freewill offering. In Scripture, God requires gifts from willing worshipers. This seems almost like a contradiction but yet quite true (see 2 Cor. 8–9).

25:3–7. From their precious metals they were to offer gold, silver, and bronze. The craftsmen would use these to overlay boards, make dishes, and other like items for the tabernacle. Next they were to offer up cloths of blue, purple, and scarlet (probably wool dyed by some of the natural resources from Egypt, such as indigo from Egypt and, for the purple, shellfish). Other items included goat hair, ram skins, and the hides of sea cows, all of which would be made into cloths and various coverings. They needed to provide wood for the tabernacle furniture, olive oil for the lamp, and spices (such as myrrh, cinnamon, and cassia; see 30:23–25) for the scented oil and incense. The precious stones would be set in the ephod and breastplate.

25:8–9. From these materials they would make a sanctuary for God's dwelling, one in which—if they made everything according to the pattern God showed them—God would be pleased to dwell. God allowed for no deviation from the precise pattern he showed them.

25:10–16. Perhaps the most important feature of the tabernacle furniture was the ark of the covenant (see "Deeper Discoveries"). They were to construct it from acacia wood, taken from the shittah tree, quite plentiful in the Sinai desert area. The wood is quite hard and close grained (Gehman, 874). The ark would be two and one-half cubits long (a cubit measured approximately eighteen inches) by one and one-half cubits wide. It would measure one and one-half cubits high. The ark itself would be overlaid with gold (inside and out) with gold trim. The ark would be carried by poles, which were to be constructed of wood overlaid with gold and inserted into rings also made from pure gold.

25:17–22. Next they were to make **an atonement cover of pure gold,** with two cherubim (see "Deeper Discoveries") places on each end. This was the mercy seat (from the Hebrew root *kaphar,* meaning "to cover") which was a lid, of sorts, on the ark. The cherubim were to have their wings facing upward, their faces facing each other but looking downward. Inside the ark would go the testimony (no doubt the Ten Commandments). It was here that God said **I will meet with you and give you all my commands for the Israelites.**

25:23–30. The table for the bread of the presence, often called "showbread," would also be constructed from acacia wood overlaid with gold. Its length would be two cubits long by one cubit wide and one and one-half cubits high. It would be bordered by a gold molding or trim, and it would contain a ring on all corners for the poles, also made of acacia wood overlaid with gold, by which it was carried. The utensils to be used included plates, dishes, pitchers, and bowls, all made of unmixed gold. Upon this table went the bread of the presence (see "Deeper Discoveries"). The table was never to lack this bread.

25:31–40. The candelabrum, or "lampstand," would assist the priests as they performed their various duties. It was an elaborate structure full of detail and beauty. The workers were to fashion this by hand, as they did the cherubim (v. 18). They would then make the base and shaft from gold, six branches extending from its side, three on each side, and three ornamental cups shaped like almond flowers on each branch. In all, the lampstand contained **seven lamps.** The entire candelabrum would weigh exactly one talent of gold (a specified weight, approximately seventy-five pounds, used in determining the worth of precious metals). As in the case of the entire tabernacle, they were to make everything **according to the pattern** revealed to Moses by the Lord.

Ⓑ The Tabernacle Proper (26:1–37)

SUPPORTING IDEA: *God reveals the unique design of the tabernacle.*

26:1–6. God next showed Moses the elaborate structure that would house his holy presence during the journeys ahead. The tabernacle would prepare the way for a more permanent structure years ahead. The **ten curtains,** which would be fastened together to form one large curtain, were to be made from twisted linen and blue, purple, and scarlet yarn. The twisted linen was formed by twisting together several fine strands, as was done in Egypt.

An artist would then weave into the fabric figures of cherubim. Each curtain would be twenty-eight cubits long by four cubits wide, with five curtains joined to one another. The curtains would be held together by fifty "loops" made of blue material, each held together by gold clasps.

26:7–14. God instructed Moses to make the external hangings, or curtains, of goat hair. These curtains would serve as coverings over the outside of the structure to protect it from the elements. He was to make eleven of these curtains, each measuring thirty cubits long by four cubits wide. They would be joined as two separate units (probably to transport it easier), with one containing five curtains, the other six. The sixth curtain would be folded over double and hang at the front of the tent. These too would be held together by fifty loops and clasps. The additional length overhanging the linen covering would hang down on the back portion of the tabernacle. Moses was to make a final covering to protect the roof of the tabernacle. While nothing is mentioned of the size of the covering, it was long enough to hang over the structure. The covering was to be constructed from ram and cow hides.

26:15–25. Next God described the boards that would serve as the actual structure of the tabernacle. These boards, or **frames**, would measure ten cubits long by one and one-half cubits wide, with each board containing two projecting rods parallel to each other. The skilled craftsmen would make twenty boards on the south side, and twenty on the north. The boards would contain two silver sockets, or **bases**, each of which received one of the projecting rods. The back (west) of the tabernacle would contain only eight boards (six plus one double strength board at each end held together by a single ring) with sixteen sockets (each board containing two).

26:26–29. The crossbars provided stability to the structure, keeping the boards in place especially when it was moved. They were to make five bars for each side, including the back. The bars would pass through rings that kept them in place. The center bar would extend the entire length of a side, with two boards above and below it, extending half of the length of a side. We may deduce the latter measurement by noting the middle bar alone was to cover the entire length of one side. The frames and crossbars were to be overlaid with gold.

26:30. God reminded Moses that he was not to change this original plan. God intended the measurements as well as the individual furniture parts to be precisely made and set in order **according to the plan** revealed on the mountain. God himself was the lifeline for the Israelites, and God instituted proper worship as the foremost and enduring priority of the nation. Israel would forfeit certain blessing if she departed from God's specific instructions for worship.

26:31–37. God next described how Moses should make the veil that would overlay the holy of holies. This curtain would be made of blue, purple, and scarlet yarn and twisted linen (see above), with figures of cherubim woven into the fabric. This curtain would hang on four hooks and clasps that were attached to four pillars, or posts. The posts were to be overlaid with gold and to stand on silver bases. The curtain would **separate the Holy Place from the Most Holy Place**. Inside the curtain (i.e., in the holy of holies) would go the ark of the testimony, now covered by the mercy seat (atonement cover). Outside the curtain the table (of showbread, or bread of the presence) would be placed against the north wall. The lampstand would be placed near the table in the south side. A final hanging would cover the front of the structure, and it was to be hung over five posts made of acacia wood overlaid with gold standing on five bronze bases.

The Altar, Courtyard, and Sacred Oil (27:1–21)

SUPPORTING IDEA: *God gives detailed instructions for completing the tabernacle and preparing for worship.*

27:1. The next article of furniture that God instructed Moses to make was the altar of burnt offering. It would also be made of the native acacia wood and would measure three cubits high by five cubits wide and extend five cubits in length. This altar would stand in the outer court directly in front of the door of the tabernacle.

27:2–8. The square altar would be hollow and would contain four projections called **horns** that may have resembled oxen horns. The horns would not be affixed to the altar as removable parts, but they were to be built into the actual structure. The craftsmen would overlay the altar with bronze (hence, the altar was sometimes called the bronze altar). The altar was furnished with rings into which went poles made of acacia wood, so that the altar could be transported. To facilitate use, the craftsmen also would make several utensils, including pots and shovels used to remove ashes, sprinkling bowls, forks, and firepans. The altar, as everything else Moses was to construct, was to be made according to the pattern revealed to Moses on the mountain.

27:9–11. God then commanded Moses to have the skilled men construct a courtyard that would form a perimeter around the tabernacle. The courtyard would be constructed as a rectangle, with its longer sides measuring one hundred cubits, and the shorter sides fifty cubits. The material of the courtyard would include **curtains of finely twisted linen**, held by twenty posts on each side standing on bronze bases. The posts also contained silver hooks and bands on the posts to hold it together.

27:12–15. Both the west and east ends of the tabernacle would measure fifty cubits long and also contain posts (ten in number) with bases (also ten) and curtains. The front would be divided into two separate sidepieces, each measuring fifteen cubits in length and hung over three posts and bases.

27:16–19. The entrance curtain would measure twenty cubits long, would stand on four posts with four bases, and would be made of blue, purple, and scarlet-colored yarn. An artist (or **embroiderer**) would be used to fashion this design. The posts that supported the courtyard would have rods, or **bands** (to connect the structure), made of silver. The posts would also contain silver hooks and would stand on bronze bases. The tools used in putting up and taking down the tabernacle and any other articles were to be made of bronze.

The courtyard illustrated the effect that sin had in restricting man's access to God. The very first article in the courtyard was the altar of sacrifice, beyond which no ordinary Israelite could go. Members of the nation could approach God only through divinely appointed mediators, who performed worship rituals prescribed by God himself. The system of sacrifice and ritual should have awakened in the nation a yearning for a more permanent solution to the problem of sin.

27:20–21. God now began to prepare the Israelites for the actual functioning of the tabernacle. He instructed Moses to command the Israelites to bring him **clear oil of pressed olives** for the light in the tabernacle. The oil was not to be extracted from the olives by man-made olive presses but "beaten" (i.e., crushed and put into a basket where the oil would then seep out).

Aaron and his sons would prepare the lamps in the tabernacle but outside the holy of holies. The lamps would provide light all night long. The "lit" tabernacle was a **lasting ordinance among the Israelites** for future generations.

Ⓓ Priestly Attire (28:1–43)

> **SUPPORTING IDEA:** *The priests were to be adorned with sacred and beautiful attire.*

28:1–5. These verses introduce the special attire to be worn by those who served as priests—Aaron and his direct descendants. God instructed Moses to gather Aaron and his four sons—**Nadab, Abihu, Eleazar,** and **Ithamar**—and to begin the process of preparing them for priestly service. The skilled men who would make so much of what would comprise the tabernacle itself would next make special clothes to be worn by the priests. These craftsmen were chosen by God for this task and endowed with special skills that enabled them to make these articles precisely as God directed.

The priestly garments would include a breastplate, an ephod, a robe, a tunic, a turban, and a sash. God further instructed these items to be made of gold, blue, purple, and scarlet yarn, and with the fine linen mentioned in the previous chapter.

28:6–8. The **ephod** was a sleeveless vest worn close to the body that probably extended to just below the hips. The materials that comprised the ephods were expensive (see above) but reflected the dignity of the office. The ephod included two shoulder pieces fastened by clasps. The ephod would include a girdle, or **waistband**, also made with gold, blue, purple, and scarlet yarn and with finely twisted linen.

28:9–14. Moses was to take two onyx stones and engrave on them the tribal names of the people of Israel (by the order of their birth). They would next mount the stones on the shoulder pieces of the ephod. In this sense, Aaron would **bear the names on his shoulders** as a testimony before the Lord that Aaron represented the tribes before God. The skilled craftsmen would next make golden filigrees (ornamental pieces) that could be buttons or sockets, of sorts, fastened to the ephod, upon which were placed two cords (chains) of twisted gold wire.

28:15–21. The Hebrew word for breastplate means "ornament," and this distinctive item probably stood out from the rest of the priest's attire. A skilled craftsman would construct this item made of the same material as the ephod. He was to make it square and folded over double, possibly to form a bag of sorts to hold the urim and thummim (others suppose it was doubled to create greater strength). Upon the breastplate would go four settings of expensive stones. The first row included ruby, topaz, and beryl. The second had turquoise, sapphire, and emerald. The third row contained jacinth, agate, and amethyst. The final row would have chrysolite, onyx, and jasper. The stones numbered twelve in all, with each bearing the name of a tribe of Israel.

28:22–28. The breastplate would also contain chains made from pure gold fastened to the breastplate by rings. A blue ribbon was to pass through both lower rings to connect it to the waistband in order to fasten it securely to the ephod.

28:29–30. God makes an important distinction in this verse between Aaron's heart and breastplate. Aaron is not simply to wear the names on his breastplate, but he is to bear them on his heart. He and his sons were priests, representing man before God (Heb. 5:1). The urim and thummim (literally, "lights" and "perfections") went on the breastplate (see "Deeper Discoveries").

28:31–35. The outer robe would be made of blue cloth with a collared opening for the head. The edge (or hem) of the garment would contain pomegranates made of blue, purple, and scarlet yarn with finely twisted linen. Between these pomegranates would go golden bells that enabled the people to hear the priest when he ministered (thus assuring them of the priest's intercession on their behalf).

28:36–43. The turban of the priest would contain a gold plate, fastened by a blue cord, with the words HOLY TO THE LORD inscribed on it. Without this plate and these words, Aaron's intercession for them would be incomplete and ineffectual. The skilled craftsmen would next weave **the tunic of fine linen** (a long coat) with a belt (sash) worn around the waist. The final items were undergarments worn directly on the body from the waist to the thigh. The priests would wear these at all times while performing priestly service.

MAIN IDEA REVIEW: *God gave detailed instructions for the proper place and practice of worship.*

III. CONCLUSION

Building the Tabernacle

The tabernacle was a literal building with significant symbolism. Included in God's instruction were six literal pieces of furniture divided into two rooms—one called the most holy place and the other, the holy place. The purpose of this temporary structure was not merely a meeting place for the people. The people would gather on the outside of the tabernacle while the priests went inside to offer sacrifices for the sins of the people and thus temporarily restore fellowship with God.

Three pieces of furniture inside the tabernacle are described in this chapter. The ark of the testimony was a chestlike structure with a mercy seat on top surrounded by two cherubim. The ark was recognized as the presence of God and thus was housed in the holy of holies where access was permitted only once a year on the Day of Atonement. The three items inside the ark were the two stone tablets of the law, Aaron's rod that budded, and the golden pot of manna. Together these items formed the testimony (Exod. 25:21), hence the ark is called the ark of the testimony. The table of showbread would hold twelve loaves of unleavened bread, one for each of the twelve tribes of Israel. The lampstand was permanently lit and ultimately points to Jesus Christ as "the light of the world" (John 8:12).

PRINCIPLES

- Our God is a God of details.
- God gives us physical pictures designed to foreshadow spiritual truths.
- God gives us testimonies of his faithfulness, guidance, and deliverance, such as the ark of the covenant.

APPLICATIONS

- How do individuals and congregations need to prepare for worship?
- What do you bring and offer to God as your act of worship?
- How has Jesus' death, resurrection, and ascension changed our worship of God from what we read in Exodus?

IV. LIFE APPLICATION

A Multiple Perspective

On my tenth anniversary at Community Baptist Church in Manhattan Beach, California, my family was given a trip to my homeland, England. We began the process of researching where we wanted to visit, all the sites we could not miss, and how we were going to get to each place. In England, the "tube" is the best way to get around; it is their subway. What I found difficult was aligning the maps of the tube, maps of the throughways, and maps of the city streets. All three maps needed to be used when trying to get to Westminster Abby or Leeds Castle. England does not provide a three-dimensional map, so maps needed to be examined one layer at a time to get the benefit of the transportation system.

This is how you might be feeling about the tabernacle right now. As we study the tabernacle, we read of a literal building as well as a portrayal of spiritual dimensions of the Christian life. We will need to examine multiple levels to get us to the destination of understanding. The Bible says, "The Word became flesh and made his dwelling among us . . . full of grace and truth" (John 1:14). Suddenly the picture of God's sacrifice for us on the cross becomes more clear. God is near to us as demonstrated in the ark of the covenant. God will sustain us and supply our every need as seen in the showbread. And Christ is our light so we can walk with God as portrayed in the lampstand. Notice how dimensions were not given for all three pieces of furniture. Why? No one can measure the glory, majesty, and deity of our Savior. He truly is King of kings and Lord of lords.

V. PRAYER

Father, this is a great time to be reminded of how the entire Bible is linked together and how I must never forget the importance of passages like Exodus 25–28 where I see a picture, if only one layer, of my Lord. Thanks for being a God of the details. I can't wait to see what else I will learn from this design of yours. Amen.

VI. DEEPER DISCOVERIES

A. The Ark of the Covenant

The ark of the testimony (or covenant), as the chief object of the tabernacle, has always aroused curiosity and speculation. Even Hollywood has produced full-length feature films that highlight one aspect or another of the ark. The

Levitical family of the Kohathites had the responsibility to care for the ark. It traveled with Israel in her journeys toward the land of Canaan (Num. 10:33) and went in ahead of them once they reached the Jordan River (Josh. 4:9–11). In the days of Samuel, it was removed to Shiloh (1 Sam. 3:3; cp. 1:24) and was later stolen by the Philistines, only to be returned to Beth Shemesh (1 Sam. 6:10–15). David brought it to Jerusalem where he placed it in a temporary tent (1 Chr. 16:1–6). Finally, Solomon placed it in the permanent holy of holies in the new temple (1 Kgs. 8:1–9). Later writers seldom refer to it at all, and the ark disappeared following Nebuchadnezzar's invasion of Judah. Although many have circulated stories, mostly apocryphal, of reported sightings, Nebuchadnezzar probably valued its gold more than its religious significance and had it melted down.

B. Cherubim

The angelic beings that faced each other on the ark of the testimony were called cherubim, and they are mentioned as far back as the garden of Eden as guardians of paradise (Gen. 3:24). They represent the holiness of God. Solomon had two large cherubim constructed to adorn the temple (1 Kgs. 6:29). Ezekiel labeled the creatures he saw by the river Kebar *cherubims,* beings that figure prominently in the Book of Ezekiel. The Bible never identifies these beings in specific terms, but they are associated with carrying out his will and residing near his presence.

C. The Bread of the Presence

This bread, sometimes called "showbread" (derived originally from Luther's translation into German), consisted of twelve loaves of bread placed on the table for use by the priests. The priests were to maintain this table at all times and to replace the bread each Sabbath. The priests could eat the loaves in a sacred place (Lev. 24:5–9). Jesus discussed the symbolism of bread and life in his discourse in John 6. From this we gather the ancient bread of the presence expressed a special communion with God without which man could not live.

D. The Urim and Thummim

Scholars differ over the true meaning and significance of these two items. We do know they were a certain means, undoubtedly supernatural, by which God imparted guidance to Israel through the high priest. We don't know the precise method by which this was done. The urim and thummim were apparently material objects of some sort, separate from the breastplate, and added after the other stones were placed in it. They could have been images or emblems of some kind or perhaps stones (Hos. 3:4) through which the high priest could receive or impart a divine message. They were probably lost during Nebuchadnezzar's invasion.

VII. TEACHING OUTLINE

A. INTRODUCTION

1. Lead Story: The Heart of God

2. Context: Israel was God's people even when they were slaves in Egypt. He redeemed them or bought them from slavery and was bringing them to a good land. He was their God, and they were to be his people. Communion with God was vital to their being his people. He showed them the acceptable way of worship and communion. At the heart of what he showed them was the tabernacle.

3. Transition: Chapters 25–28 show in minute details the instructions God gave to Israel about their worship of him. Although the tabernacle and the temple are no longer a part of our worship, these chapters contain principles that God's people need to know in order to love him and magnify his holy name.

B. COMMENTARY

1. The Initial Offerings and Furniture for the Tabernacle (25:1–40)

2. The Tabernacle Proper (26:1–37)

3. The Altar, Courtyard, and Sacred Oil (27:1–21)

4. Priestly Attire (28:1–43)

C. CONCLUSION: A MULTIPLE PERSPECTIVE

VIII. ISSUES FOR DISCUSSION

1. What motivated these people to be so generous with their freewill offerings? What motivates you?

2. Why do you think God placed a table in the tabernacle?

3. Why was this tabernacle going to become so important to the people of Israel?

4. Comparing chapters 26 and 27, what differences can you detect between God's throne room and the altar of burnt offering?

5. What was the significance of the special clothes worn by the priests? Why would God go to such great lengths to give the details for their creation?

Exodus 29–31

Set Apart for Service

I. **INTRODUCTION**
Going Beyond Ourselves

II. **COMMENTARY**
A verse-by-verse explanation of these chapters.

III. **CONCLUSION**
All We Can Do Right Now

An overview of the principles and applications from these chapters.

IV. **LIFE APPLICATION**
Let's Huddle Up

Melding these chapters to life.

V. **PRAYER**
Tying these chapters to life with God.

VI. **DEEPER DISCOVERIES**
Historical, geographical, and grammatical enrichment of the commentary.

VII. **TEACHING OUTLINE**
Suggested step-by-step group study of these chapters.

VIII. **ISSUES FOR DISCUSSION**
Zeroing these chapters in on daily life.

"*W*hat we have done for ourselves alone dies with us. What we have done for others and the world remains and is immortal."

Albert Pine

Exodus 29–31

IN A NUTSHELL

*T*hese three chapters provide snapshots into the priesthood of the Old Testament. The priests' outfit, their anointing, and their offerings were of highest importance for the future of the Israelites and the freedom of salvation we would enjoy through Christ thousands of years later. We also meet the architect of the tabernacle and again see the call of service upon God's chosen.

Set Apart for Service

I. INTRODUCTION

Going Beyond Ourselves

*C*oach Bill McCartney, founder of Promise Keepers and former football coach, tells about the time in 1991, while coaching football at the University of Colorado, that he challenged his entire team to play beyond their normal abilities. He had heard that we spend 86 percent of our time thinking about ourselves and 14 percent of our time thinking of others. The coach was convinced that if his team could stop thinking about themselves and begin to think of others, there was a whole new source of energy that would be available to them. He challenged each of the team members to call someone he admired and loved and tell that person that he was dedicating the game to that person. The team member was to encourage this person to watch carefully every play he made, because it was all dedicated to this special person. McCartney planned to distribute sixty footballs, one for each player to send to the person he had chosen, with the final score written on the football.

The team that Colorado was playing was their archrival, the Nebraska Corn Huskers, on their home turf in Lincoln, Nebraska. Colorado had not won a game there in twenty-three years. But Coach McCartney had just challenged his players to play beyond themselves, to play for love. The Colorado Buffaloes won that football game. The score that was written on sixty footballs was 27–12 (adapted from *What Makes a Man?*, 12–13).

Love is a powerful motivator. Love empowers a mother to run into the flow of merging traffic to save her child. Love compels a husband to dedicate his life to his dying wife. Love provides added energy at work when you do for a living what you love to do. But have you ever thought about the fact that love motivates service and obedience? God has called a select group of men as priests who will play a vital role in the life of the people of Israel. These needed to be men not only called but so in love with their God that their motivation was always to please him through service and obedience.

II. COMMENTARY

Set Apart for Service

MAIN IDEA: *The Lord consecrates the priests, who will offer prayerful incense on a special altar.*

🅰 The Consecration of the Priests (29:1–46)

SUPPORTING IDEA: *The Lord sets apart the priesthood.*

29:1–4. God told Moses how to prepare Aaron and his sons for the priesthood. Moses was to take a young bull and two unblemished rams (male sheep) along with unleavened wheat flour from which he would make bread, cakes, and wafers. The food items would be put into a basket to be presented with the offering animals. Aaron and his sons would also appear at the entrance of the tabernacle and would be bathed with water.

29:5–9. Next Moses was to adorn Aaron and his sons with the special garments (see the previous chapter). The priesthood would belong to Aaron and his descendants forever or as long as the ceremonial law was in effect.

29:10–14. God next directed that the bull be brought to the entrance of the tabernacle, where Aaron and his sons would slaughter it and apply the blood to the horns of the altar of sacrifice. The remaining blood would be poured out at the base of the altar. The inward parts of the bull would also be burned on the altar, but the hide and any other part normally cut off from a sacrifice (the "offal") would be burned outside the camp. The sin offering was necessary for purging the priest from his own sin. His office conferred on him no special grace that earned merit from God. On the contrary, the fact that the priests also needed blood cleansing demonstrated their need before God.

29:15–21. Moses directed that Aaron and his sons should **lay their hands** on one of the rams and slaughter it. They then would apply the blood to the sides of the altar of sacrifice. Aaron would then cut the ram into pieces and wash its inward parts and place it on the altar. There it would be consumed by fire, as explained in Leviticus 1. They would then kill the other ram and take its blood and apply it to the right ears, right thumbs, and right big toes of Aaron and his sons. The right arm stood for a man's strength. Aaron and his sons were to serve with vigor but not in their own strength. Their efforts would amount to nothing but ceremonialism apart from the grace of God. Finally he (perhaps Moses was now officiating) would sprinkle blood and anointing oil on the newly invested priests.

29:22–28. From the latter ram he would take the waste parts of the dead animal and with the bread and cakes in the basket, have Aaron and his sons wave them before the Lord. Thereafter he would take them from their hands and offer them on the altar. The breast of the ram they would also wave before the Lord after which the priests (and those priests who would follow Aaron and his sons) could consume it.

29:29–30. The priestly garments, which were specially set apart for priestly use, were to be worn by Aaron's descendants from then on. Officiating priests would have to wear them always.

29:31–34. Aaron and his sons could consume the prescribed meat from the ordination ram, but this could be done only at the entrance of the tabernacle. No other Israelite, including officiating Levites, could eat them. They were the food of the priests alone who were duly set apart for this service. If any meat or bread remained over until morning, it was to be burned up.

29:35–41. The time of ordination of the priests would take seven complete days. Each day of the week of ordination they would sacrifice a sin offering to sanctify the altar itself. Also, each day the priests would offer two one-year-old lambs, one in the morning and one at night along with a meal and drink offering.

29:42–46. The glory of God would attend these carefully followed regulations. He would attend the sacrificial and worship functions of the congregation, and forgive their sins. God would take them as his own people and **be their God.**

B An Altar and Provision for Incense (30:1–38)

SUPPORTING IDEA: *An altar of incense and other items are set apart for special use; they carry special significance.*

30:1–6. The Lord further commanded that incense would burn before him continually (v. 8). To this end he commands Moses to build an altar made of the usual acacia wood. The altar would measure one foot long, one foot wide, and two cubits high. They must build horns into the structure (without adding the horns as removable objects). The entire top side and sides, including the horns, were to be overlaid with gold, and they must also make a border of gold (**gold molding**) on the top to prevent anything from falling off. The altar would be transported by means of poles, made of acacia wood and overlaid with gold, inserted through gold rings. The ark was to be placed in front of the curtain **before the ark of the Testimony.**

30:7–10. As to the order of burning incense, Aaron would begin the procedure by burning incense every morning when he trimmed and cleaned the candlestick. Upon lighting the candlestick, or lamp, he must also burn incense. In other words, God commanded that the priests burn incense continually before him. But not just any incense could be burned on this altar. In fact, this altar was not to be used as an altar for any other reason than specifically prescribed here. The altar itself would be set apart each year for this use by Aaron (and thereafter his descendants, the duly appointed priests), who would make atonement for it. According to Leviticus 16:18–19, this would take place on the Day of Atonement.

30:11–16. One obvious feature of the general service of the tabernacle would be the cost involved. So God gave Moses specific instructions on how to raise the funds. During a general census Moses was to exact a half shekel from each Israelite. Failure either to enact or comply with this feature would result in a general plague. Some interpreters have supposed that the sin of David in numbering the people stemmed from his failure to raise this money at that time (2 Sam. 24:15), but this is only speculation.

30:17–21. The proper washing of the priests would be facilitated by a laver, or **basin**, made from bronze and placed between the tabernacle and the altar of sacrifice. The priests were to supply an ample amount of water so the officiating priests could wash themselves before entering the sacred tent. This procedure would continue beyond Aaron and his immediate sons, and be **a lasting ordinance**.

30:22–29. It is interesting to note how God varied his instructions to Moses from general to specific. The directions he gave Moses here are quite specific, even including the type and quantity of spices. Moses was to gather five hundred shekels of myrrh and cassia and half that much of cinnamon and fragrant cane. He would add to that a hin of oil. He (or one skilled in this procedure) would then blend them into sacred oil used in anointing the priests. He then would anoint the other articles used in the sacred service.

30:30–33. Moses would take the oil and anoint Aaron and his sons, then say to the people: **This is to be my sacred anointing oil for the generations to come**. God would add to this a command not to use it for any other purpose than that described here. Those who violated this command would be put to death.

30:34–38. The holy incense, to be burned continually before the Lord, would come from **fragrant spices**. The spices included gum resin, onycha, galbanum, and frankincense, **all in equal amounts**. The priests were to add salt to the blend, then grind it to powder. Finally, they were to place it in front of the curtain which stood before the ark of the covenant. The smell must have been tantalizing, and no doubt it was a temptation for one to duplicate it. But God commanded them not to do so on threat of death.

Ⓒ A Special Calling and Sabbath Reminder (31:1–18)

SUPPORTING IDEA: *God provides gifted people to accomplish his work and reminds us in the Sabbath that work is not our life.*

31:1–11. Although God committed to Moses the precise instructions and designs of the furniture and materials to be used in the tabernacle, he did not want Moses to build these items himself. For that he raised up gifted workers and endowed them with the skills to carry out the construction of these elaborate materials.

The first man he called was **Bezalel, son of Uri**, from the tribe of Judah. While Bezalel probably already had superior artistic abilities, God filled him with skill, wisdom, and special knowledge in craftsmanship and artistry. God's people have always had the tendency to single out and exalt certain gifts, usually visible ones, at the expense of others. But such a mentality goes against God's design for his work (1 Cor. 12:23–25). In addition, we learn that artistic talent should not be used for purely selfish reasons, but for God's glory, since he is a God of beauty and splendor.

God also called, set apart, and endowed with skill a man named **Oholiab**, from the tribe of Dan, as Bezalel's primary assistant. To these two workers God added other **craftsmen** for the purpose of making the materials of the tabernacle.

The primary articles that the craftsmen would make included the actual tent of meeting, the ark of testimony with the mercy seat covering, the table of the bread of the presence, altar of incense, the lampstand, along with the various curtains and related furnishings. They also were charged with making the priestly clothing and the perfume for the sacred ordination of the priests.

31:12–13. God charged Moses with strict enforcement of the Sabbath (see "Deeper Discoveries") because it was a special sign between him and the Israelites. The other **sign** was the covenant of circumcision. The Sabbath would be unique to Israel, a nation that God set apart from the nations to be **holy**.

31:14–18. The specific conditions of the Sabbath would now follow, along with the penalties for violations. Those who broke the Sabbath by either not observing it or failing to comply with its restrictions would **be put to death**. God instituted the Sabbath as a day of rest for man and beast. Violators of this ordinance severed their ties with God and the terms of the covenant. Hence they would be put to death since the covenant relationship constituted a theocracy (God ruling the religious and civil institutions of the nation), and violators would prove their disloyalty to this rule.

The Sabbath day of rest points out another obligation—God's requirement that man work for six days each week.

When the Lord **finished speaking to Moses** on the holy mount, he gave him the two tablets (promised in 24:12) upon which were inscribed the commands of God. God also described the means he would use in inscribing these commands: **the finger of God**. God supernaturally etched these commands upon the tablets as a reminder of their divine origin and Israel's obligation to observe them.

MAIN IDEA REVIEW: *The Lord consecrates the priests, who will offer prayerful incense on a special altar.*

III. CONCLUSION

All We Can Do Right Now

In his book *The Fall of Fortress,* Elmer Bendiner describes one bombing run over the city of Kassel:

> Our B-17 (the *Tondelayo*) was barraged by flak from Nazi antiair-craft guns. That was not unusual, but on this particular occasion our gas tanks were hit. Later, as I reflected on the miracle of a twenty-mil-limeter shell piercing the fuel tank without touching off an explosion, our pilot, Bohn Fawkes, told me it was not quite that simple. On the morning following the raid, Bohn had gone down to ask our crew chief for that shell as a souvenir of unbelievable luck. The crew chief told Bohn that not just one shell but eleven had been found in the gas tanks—eleven unexploded shells where only one was sufficient to blast us out of the sky. It was as if the sea had been parted for us.
>
> Even after thirty-five years, so awesome an event leaves me shaken, especially after I heard the rest of the story from Bohn. He was told that the shells had been sent to the armorers to be defused. The armorers told him that Intelligence had picked them up. They could not say why at the time, but Bohn eventually sought out the answer. Apparently when the armorers opened each of those shells, they found no explosive charge. They were as clean as a whistle and just as harmless. Empty? Not all of them. One contained a carefully rolled piece of paper. On it was a scrawl in Czech. The Intelligence people scoured our base for a man who could read Czech. Eventually, they found one to decipher the note. It set us marveling. Translated, the note read: "This is all we can do for you now."

What an incredible story of sacrifice and service! "That's all we can do; we wish we could do more." These are the people God will bless, people who will do whatever they can with whatever they have to serve him and others.

God continues to search for Spirit-filled workmen. And God will not only enlist these people into service and fill them with his Spirit; he will also pro-vide specifics in their acts of service. And they will be motivated by God's love. The funds were raised for this project through willing hearts. The taber-nacle was built by willing hearts. The priests served with willing hearts.

PRINCIPLES

- Blood is a symbol of cleansing that comes from God.
- God desires our sacrifice of continual praise.
- God gifts some people as the architects of ministry while others are the servants in ministry.

APPLICATIONS

- For what kind of service has God set you apart?
- What is God asking you to do in helping others in your church discover God's call?
- How can you encourage your ministers in their service to God?
- Evaluate your practice of taking time off from the routines of your life to focus on God and his will for you. What changes do you sense God is asking you to make about rest times?

IV. LIFE APPLICATION

Let's Huddle Up

Let's imagine that your favorite football team is in a huddle; they're behind by one point with ten seconds to go, and the ball is on the five-yard line. They're just about ready to score. The fans in the stadium are on their feet. They know the next play is crucial, but the team just stays in the huddle and talks. Eventually, the referee blows a whistle, throws his yellow flag, and steps off a five-yard penalty for delay of game. But the team seems oblivious to what's going on. They remain in their huddle, just holding hands and talking. And finally they burst out of the huddle cheering, run to the sidelines and out of the stadium, and get in their cars and go home.

Every fan would be frustrated and angry about that kind of action because a huddle is not an end in itself. The purpose of the huddle is to plan the strategy for the next play and to give encouragement to those who are participating. And it would never happen that a team would just huddle and then hurry home. Or would it?

Sometimes this is an accurate portrayal of the church. There's a spiritual conflict going on in the world, and we gather for church. Granted, worship is a time for inspiration and strategy for everyday life. But the problem is that we tend to see this gathering as an end in itself. We measure the church's effectiveness by the number of people in the holy huddle and by the inspiration of the hour, and then we disperse and disappear until next week. Worship is a time for us to be inspired and to receive instructions on how to make an impact for Jesus Christ in the world. We are to serve the Lord as priests.

Did you know that you are part of a royal priesthood? As a believer, you have been anointed to serve the king and offer sacrifices of praise and service every day. And know this: God is watching, and God will judge your availability and service in the future. Believers will not face any judgment for their sin, but they will face the judgment for their servanthood. One day I will be standing before Almighty God giving an account of my service for God's church. Take this time you have been given on earth seriously. After all, you are the salt of the earth and the light of the world. Get those priestly outfits and go to work.

V. PRAYER

Lord, what a great picture of your model for every servant of God. I want to be consecrated wholly to you. I want to serve you with a willing and tender heart. I want to remember your sacrifice every day, knowing that your shed blood has cleansed me from all my sin. Make this day a time where I look back on and see the sacrifices I have offered to you at work, at school, or wherever you direct me. And when I am tired, remind me to take that day off to reenergize for the next round of sacrifices. Amen.

VI. DEEPER DISCOVERIES

A. Hebrew Money

Although barter was the ancient way of exchange, some form of money or coinage surfaced around the eighth century B.C. in Asia Minor. Later these coins were stamped with the values on them. The earliest Hebrew references to money emphasized weight, as opposed to standard-sized coins as we understand them today (Gen. 23:16; 43:21). In fact, the early shekel meant a certain weight in silver, not a value. Subsequent weights were variously named and valued. They were talent, mina, shekel, gerah, and beka (half shekel).

The Jews became acquainted with coins during the reign of the Persians. In the Lord's time Greek and Roman coinage circulated along with Jewish money.

B. The Sabbaths of Israel

The Hebrew term for "sabbath" is *shabbath* ("cease" or "rest"). We first see the Sabbath principle in Genesis 2:2 while man was still in a state of innocence. It is mentioned in connection with the gift of manna to the people of Israel in the wilderness (Exod. 16:23). Then it is mentioned when the law was given from Sinai where God commanded the people to "remember the

Sabbath day by keeping it holy" (20:8). In the Mosaic Law strict regulations were laid down regarding observance of the Sabbath (Exod. 35:2–3; Lev. 23:3; 26:34). Throughout Jewish history frequent references are made to the sacredness of the Sabbath (Isa. 56:2–7; 58:13; Jer. 17:20–22; Neh. 13:15–22). The Old Testament also mentions Sabbaths of different sorts, including Sabbath years every seventh year, and the Jubilee Sabbath (see Exod. 23:10–11; Lev. 25). By the days of the Maccabees and later in the time of our Lord, the Sabbath generally became legalistic and empty. Jesus restated the Sabbath's purpose on several occasions (Matt. 12:9–13; Mark 2:23–27; Luke 13:10–17). The apostle Paul also instructed his Colossian readers not to let others judge their liberty in Christ by appealing to a legalistic interpretation of the Sabbath (Col. 2:16–17). The Sabbath concept provides man with many benefits, including physical rest, spiritual refreshment, and reflection.

Is the Sabbath for today? Has the Old Testament day changed to the Lord's Day? More specifically, is the Lord's Day the Christian Sabbath? The only New Testament reference to the Lord's Day is Revelation 1:10, a probable reference to the first day of the week, Sunday. On this day the Lord rose from the dead, and Sunday became the traditional day of worship for Christians (Acts 20:7; 1 Cor. 16:1–2). Opponents of a New Testament Sabbath cite the lack of any formal change from Sabbath to the Lord's Day in any of the New Testament writings and also Paul's brief discussion alluded to above (Col. 2:16–17).

But proponents of the perpetuity of the Sabbath remind us the Lord established this principle as a creation ordinance occurring before the fall (Gen. 2:2–3) and that because the Ten Commandments included the Sabbath it must be part of God's moral law that endures (Matt. 5:17–18).

VII. TEACHING OUTLINE

A. INTRODUCTION

1. Lead Story: Going Beyond Ourselves

2. Context: There's a saying that "everyone's responsibility is no one's responsibility." Knowing that's how we are, God gave special assignments among his covenant people for serving as mediators between God and his people.

3. Transition: God commanded Moses to set apart priests who would represent God to the people and the people to God. Special ceremonies for the priests not only purified them for service but also impressed on all observers the holiness of God. Sabbath was a time of rest—a time to come to God in a focused way.

B. COMMENTARY

1. The Consecration of the Priests (29:1–46)
2. An Altar and Provision for Incense (30:1–38)
3. A Special Calling and Sabbath Reminder (31:1–18)

C. CONCLUSION: LET'S HUDDLE UP

VIII. ISSUES FOR DISCUSSION

1. What experiences have you enjoyed in your life where you knew they included sacrifice and service? What made them so enjoyable?
2. Can you think of reasons why blood played such a big role in the consecration process?
3. Why do you think the consecration of the priests was more important in Old Testament times than the consecration of pastors in the twenty-first century?
4. Why did God include instructions on the Sabbath in a section devoted to service and commitment? How does this principle relate to your life?

Exodus 32–34

Aaron's Sin

I. INTRODUCTION
Is God Listening?

II. COMMENTARY
A verse-by-verse explanation of these chapters.

III. CONCLUSION
Radar for the Birds

An overview of the principles and applications from these chapters.

IV. LIFE APPLICATION
Faith of a Child

Melding these chapters to life.

V. PRAYER
Tying these chapters to life with God.

VI. DEEPER DISCOVERIES
Historical, geographical, and grammatical enrichment of the commentary.

VII. TEACHING OUTLINE
Suggested step-by-step group study of these chapters.

VIII. ISSUES FOR DISCUSSION
Zeroing these chapters in on daily life.

Q u o t e

"*It* is as supreme folly to talk of a little sin as it would be to talk of a small Decalogue that forbids it, or a diminutive God that hates it, or a shallow hell that will punish it."

C h a r l e s   S e y m o u r   R o b i n s o n

Exodus 32–34

IN A NUTSHELL

Chapters 32–34 are an interlude between the blueprints of the tabernacle and the actual building process. Aaron, Moses' brother, falls into idolatry and orders the making of a golden calf, representative of an old pagan god from Egypt. This is a flagrant violation of God's commandments. When Moses becomes aware of this, he throws the tablets containing the Ten Commandments to the ground and burns the false god. Now Moses becomes more than the voice of God to the people; he becomes the voice to God on behalf of his followers.

Aaron's Sin

I. INTRODUCTION

Is God Listening?

*H*ave you ever wondered if God listens to your prayers? Have you sometimes felt like it's a waste of time, that the heavens are closed to your petitions? Consider this: When Franklin Roosevelt was President of the United States, he often endured long receiving lines at the White House. He complained that no one really paid any attention to what was said. One day, during a reception, he decided to try an experiment. To each person who came down the line and shook his hand, he murmured, "I murdered my grandmother this morning." The guests responded with phrases like, "Marvelous!" "Keep up the good work." "We are proud of you." "God bless you, sir." It was not until the end of the line, while greeting the ambassador from Bolivia, that his words were actually heard. Bewildered, the ambassador leaned over and whispered, "I'm sure she had it coming."

I wonder how many times I have looked toward the heavens and wondered, "Lord, do you care? Are you too busy for me right now? Why do I sense that I am getting a busy signal right now?" Despite how you feel or what you might think, please be assured that God is listening. This is a truth that Moses knew and deeply counted on. Remember, chapters 25–31 allowed us to view the blueprint of the tabernacle when God presented the plans to Moses. Later in chapters 35–40, we enjoyed a study of the building process itself. But now we look at a parenthetical series of chapters (32–34), where some of the saddest moments in Israel's history are revealed. In this tragic situation, Moses became more than a leader; he became an intercessor for his people, knowing God would listen.

II. COMMENTARY

Aaron's Sin

MAIN IDEA: *The Lord shows his erring people the way to his presence by once again giving them his law.*

A The Making of a God (32:1–35)

SUPPORTING IDEA: *The Israelites attempted to make a visible, material god that would lead them.*

32:1. Moses stayed on the mountain longer than expected. As a result, the Israelites grew impatient. They were far away from familiar environments and leaderless, although they did have Aaron, whom Moses had appointed to lead them in his absence. But Aaron had neither the moral fortitude nor the force of will to resist the popular uprising. The people probably sensed a void in Aaron, so they conspired to make themselves gods who would lead them.

32:2–6. Aaron seemed only too willing to oblige the corrupt desires of the people. He caught the drift of where they were headed in their request and suggested they make a god from existing materials—their gold earrings recently obtained from the Egyptians. Keil believed Aaron actually attempted to arrest the uprising by appealing to the vanity of the women (Keil, 221). But if this were the case, it backfired. The people wanted a visible manifestation of a god, just like the other nations around them. Aaron probably made the idol from wood, then covered it with gold. The people, in response, said, **These are your gods, O Israel, who brought you up out of Egypt.** We shouldn't infer from this expression that they attempted to make an Egyptian god of sorts. They attempted to materialize the Lord, whom they acknowledged brought them out of the land of Egypt.

Aaron then constructed an altar. The next day the people offered sacrifices and began to engage in **revelry**.

32:7–14. God reacted to the commotion by telling Moses to go down and see what the people were doing in his absence. They not only corrupted themselves; they did so with particular haste, proving the superficial nature of their faith. God labeled them **a stiff-necked people** and sought to destroy them and make a great nation from Moses' own stock. But such a judgment moved Moses to plead for his people. The incident revealed something of the faith of Moses, who used logic in his plea to God and sought to protect God's honor should word get out to the Egyptians that God destroyed the people he delivered from Egypt. Moses then appealed to God's previous promises and his covenant with the patriarchs who preceded him. He reminded God of his promise to make of these people a great and lasting nation that would inherit the land before them. Upon this the Lord relented (see "Deeper Discoveries") and withdrew his judgment.

32:15–18. Moses, armed only with the tablets God had given him on the mountain, went down toward the commotion. Joshua, whom Moses evidently left somewhere lower on the mountain, feared that war had broken out (either among the Israelites or by a surprise attack from an enemy). But Moses heard the voice of singing and celebration.

32:19–29. When Moses drew closer, he recoiled in disgust and anger, smashing the tablets on the ground. The Israelites despised the covenant with God and probably were worthy of God's original judgment of virtual extinction. Moses seized the calf and melted it in the fire, then scattered the ashes on the water. He then made the Israelites taste the bitterness of their sin by forcing them to drink the remaining dregs. The action was symbolic of the wages of sin (Rom. 6:23).

Moses then turned to his brother Aaron and asked, **What did these people do to you, that you led them into such sin?** Moses was right on target with this remark. Aaron demonstrated a reprehensible cowardice in his actions and manifested a flawed character. He was to blame, because he should have tried to stop the downward spiral of the Israelites.

Aaron replied characteristically and invented a wild story. He might have thought Moses would sooner believe a big lie rather than a small one. He admitted to taking from the Israelites their golden earrings and throwing them in the fire, out of which appeared a god on its own accord. This lie brought no response from Moses.

Moses immediately forced the Israelites to a decision (1 Kgs. 18:21), ordering any who stood with the true God to stand near him. The Levites complied at once and came near Moses. Moses then commanded each Levite to destroy **his brother and friend and neighbor.** The command seems harsh, and Moses may have left some details out. Some have suggested that the ringleaders were identified and set apart from the others. The Levites complied with Moses' order and killed about three thousand people.

32:30–35. Moses next scolded the Israelites for their apostasy and then sought audience with God in order to intercede for them. He pleaded to God on their behalf, even offering his own soul as a ransom for the lives. He asked God to blot his name out of the book God kept (see "Deeper Discoveries"). Moses was a true shepherd who would give his life for the sheep. But God replied by showing Moses the impossibility of this request. God taught Moses that every individual's fate rests with his or her own faith. This eventful chapter closes with God recommissioning Moses to go forth and lead the people to the land he promised them. God would not withdraw his angel from their presence. The plague mentioned in the last verse was fulfilled at some time in the future.

Ⓑ The Glory of the Lord (33:1–23)

SUPPORTING IDEA: *The presence of God is not to be taken for granted but humbly and eagerly sought.*

33:1–6. What follows here may be hard to understand, but it becomes quite plain when we see the whole picture. At first God seemed simply to renew his covenant with the Israelites and promised to take them successfully into the land. He would even send an angel to go before them to ensure their safe arrival. The covenant, the same one he made with **Abraham, Isaac and Jacob,** would be renewed with them and their descendants. But one key element would be missing: God's presence. The angel would indeed go before them, but God's own presence would not. What Israel lost in their sin was the *near presence of God.* The greatest priority for any child of God is to walk with God at all times so that he or she does not grieve the Holy Spirit (Eph. 4:30).

God's words shook the Israelites, and they began to mourn and strip themselves of their customary ornaments. Their sorrow was heightened when Moses told them precisely what God had said. If God went with them, he might destroy them on account of their presumptuous ways. God then enforced what they already had begun to do—take off their ornaments (probably permanently) as a sign of true repentance. They divested themselves of these things at **Mount Horeb**.

33:7–11. Before the actual construction of the tabernacle, Moses **used to take a tent and pitch it outside the camp some distance away.** The tent was used to seek God's presence. But when Moses himself went into the tent, the people watched carefully because they knew he enjoyed a unique relationship with God. In fact, God spoke to Moses face-to-face in the most intimate fashion. Subsequent men and women of God would not enjoy this kind of relationship with God. When Moses entered, the pillar of cloud stood at the entrance of the tent of meeting. During this time God spoke with Moses, and as the people beheld this, they worshiped God at a distance. When Moses departed from the camp, he left behind his faithful aide, Joshua, to stand guard over the tent.

33:12–17. Moses asked God to clarify his relationship with him and the people. Would he go up with them personally or not? Moses wanted to know more about God, and this tells us something about Moses' dynamic faith. Through all his adverse circumstances he grew in his faith and spiritual hunger. He wanted to know more of God's ways so the favor of God would rest not only upon him but on his people as well. God reassured Moses that his presence would go with them.

33:18–23. When Moses asked to see God's glory, God agreed but with certain restrictions. He would pass by Moses and proclaim his personal name Yahweh to him. But Moses would not see the essence of God's presence. To see God in the sense Moses wanted involved knowing something of his person and character. God was not a man that he should lie nor the son of man that he should change his mind (Num. 23:19). God is sovereign and answers to no one, offering mercy and compassion only to chosen vessels.

God chose to display his glory before Moses, who would stand upon a rock to behold the sight. As God passed by, he would put Moses in a cave or small enclosure in the rock and cover Moses. So Moses did not see God's face but his back. The expression was "anthropomorphic," which meant God used language that Moses could understand, although it did not convey with absolute precision every detail of Moses' encounter with God.

Ⓒ Covenant Renewal (34:1–35)

SUPPORTING IDEA: *The compassionate God renews his covenant with the erring nation.*

34:1–3. Soon after God assured Moses of his abiding presence, he renewed his covenant with the nation. The first matter at hand was to renew the terms of the covenant contained in God's law. He directed Moses to **chisel out two stone tablets like the first ones**, and then God would write on them the words contained in the first set.

34:4–9. Moses obeyed God's command to chisel out the new tablets and climb the mountain, where he would receive further directions from God. Once there, God again passed by Moses and proclaimed his name, **the LORD**. But in proclaiming his name, God also provided his servant with something of a description of his person. Moses had asked God to teach him more of his ways (33:12–13), and now God granted that request. The covenant God is a **compassionate and gracious God, slow to anger, abounding in love and faithfulness, maintaining love to thousands, and forgiving wickedness, rebellion and sin.**

No doubt Moses drew encouragement just speaking with God face-to-face. But how much more encouraged Moses was when he began to discover just what kind of God he served. He was not the impersonal deity of the surrounding nations but a personal God who held Israel as the object of his affection. But God did not betray his own nature in giving his love to the Israelites. He still was a just God who would punish them for their sins, as they discovered in the golden calf affair (see ch. 32). Armed with this new discovery of the knowledge of God, Moses **bowed to the ground at once and worshiped**. Moses wanted to go forth with the presence of the covenant God, who demonstrated his love by forgiving their sins and chose them as his inheritance. All Moses felt he needed was God's presence.

34:10–15. In order for God to work on Israel's behalf, she must scrupulously keep the terms of the covenant—observe the law of God. God would rout the enemies who occupied the land of Canaan—enemies whom Israel was not to make treaties with. Israel was to prove her faithfulness to Yahweh by obliterating any trace of foreign gods in her midst. The Lord, **whose name is Jealous**, demanded complete faithfulness of the Israelites.

34:16–28. God next renewed his summary commands for Israel but again reminded them of the danger of getting too close to the native inhabitants. They would bring them down as a nation if Israel failed to guard against foreign influences. Israel certainly was not to intermarry with these people, or she would soon make spiritual compromises with their gods. Israel was not to **make cast idols**.

God required Israel to prioritize the feasts, including the **Feast of Unleavened Bread**, to be observed in the month of **Abib**, the month they departed from Egypt, and the feasts of **Weeks** and **Ingathering**. Furthermore, the firstborn sons as well as the firstborn of livestock were to be redeemed. The Levites would serve in the firstborn's stead, but God required payment from the firstborn's parents (13:12–13). God reiterated his command that they set aside the seventh day as a day of rest, even during the plowing season. God reinforced other commands previously given, such as Israel's sacrifices and treatment of young goats (see 23:18–19).

God miraculously sustained Moses during his stay on the mountain, which amounted to **forty days and forty nights**.

34:29–35. Moses' direct encounter with Yahweh caused his face to become radiant, and the people withdrew from him in fear. But Moses calmed them and summoned them to appear before him. Apparently when he first spoke with them he did not wear a veil. Thereafter he did put on a veil when he spoke with them after being in God's presence. But when he entered God's presence, he did not have a veil. He probably drew great assurance from beholding God's glory without a veil, a precursor to the glorious privilege that new covenant believers would enjoy one day (2 Cor. 3:18).

MAIN IDEA REVIEW: *The Lord shows his erring people the way to his presence by once again giving them his law.*

III. CONCLUSION

Radar for the Birds

Not long ago great flocks of migratory birds overwhelmed airport radar systems at Des Moines, Iowa, Omaha, Nebraska, and Kansas City, Missouri. The computerized radar systems were "knocked out" for hours after they tried to process information on thousands of transient geese. FAA radar systems are supposed to filter out the radar echoes that come from birds by tracking their speed, but often controllers will turn off primary radar (the one that reads echoes from objects in the sky) and rely upon transponder signals from aircraft. But on that fateful day the birds appeared so suddenly that FAA controllers had no time to act. The birds appeared in such vast numbers that the radar filtering system (which screens out echoes from birds) quickly failed. The Des Moines radar system can process seven hundred bona fide aircraft returns and three hundred non-aircraft returns simultaneously. But that day the system was overwhelmed with over nine hundred bird echoes within minutes.

Life is like that sometimes. The background noise of contemporary life competes for our attention and overwhelms our ability to filter out the static.

We lose sight of what's really important in life. Our spiritual radar gets over-whelmed, and we lose God in all the static. That's when it's time to turn off the television, turn off the radio, put away the Christian music, fold up the paper, and close the magazines. It is time simply to "be still and know that I am God." Moses was in such a predicament in Exodus 33. When Moses requested to see God, God gave him just a glimpse of his "back." Hiding in a crevice, Moses' spiritual radar was tuned in, and all he could do was be still as God passed by.

PRINCIPLES

- God never ignores rebellion.
- When God calls a person to lead, intercession becomes a part of the call.
- Prayer is not to change God's mind but to allow us to see God's heart.

APPLICATIONS

- Pray for those for whom you are responsible.
- Thank those who pray for you.
- Read your Bible for an encounter with God each day.
- Remember God's past faithfulness, and trust him for the future.

IV. LIFE APPLICATION

Faith of a Child

A little boy in one of the schools in Edinburgh, who had attended a prayer meeting, had much better faith. He said to his teacher who had con-ducted the prayer meeting, "Teacher, I wish my sister could be made to read the Bible. She never reads it."

"Why should your sister read the Bible, Johnny?"

"Because if she should once read it, I am sure it would do her good, and she would be converted and be saved."

"Do you think so, Johnny?"

"Yes, I do, sir, and I wish the next time there's a prayer meeting you would ask the people to pray for my sister that she may begin to read the Bible."

"Well, it shall be done, John."

So the teacher mentioned that a little boy was very anxious that prayer should be offered that his sister might begin to read the Bible. John was observed to get up and go out. The teacher thought it very rude of the boy to disturb the people in a crowded room, and so the next day when the lad came, he said, "John, I thought it was very rude of you to get up in the prayer meeting and go out. You ought not to have done so."

"But sir," said the boy, "I did not mean to be rude. I thought I would just go home and see my sister reading her Bible for the first time."

Do you have this kind of faith? As God's people, we ought to believe and watch with expectation for answers to our prayer. Don't say, "Lord, turn my darkness into light," and then go out with your candle as though you expected to find it dark. After asking the Lord to appear for you, expect him to do so, for according to your faith he will answer. How badly do you want to see God work in the lives of the people you care about? How sincere are you in your prayers?

V. PRAYER

Lord, grant me the courage to be ready to lay my life on the line for my family, my friends, and the lost people I come in contact with each week. Help me develop muscles of faith to go before the people in my life and intercede for them—just like Moses did and just like my Lord does for me every day. Amen.

VI. DEEPER DISCOVERIES

A. Does God Repent?

In several places the Bible affirms the immutability of God—he does not change (Mal. 3:6; Heb. 13:8; Jas. 1:17). Part of God's perfection is that he does not change anything, including his mind. He cannot grow in knowledge, for example, because he is perfect in knowledge. Nor can he decay in any aspect of his person or character. Yet Scripture uses language at times that seems to indicate God can and does change his mind (Exod. 32:10–14; Jon. 3:10). But this is a misunderstanding of Scripture and the nature of God. Divine immutability (changeability) does not imply immobility (God has no movement, see Berkhof, 59). Man, on the other hand, does change, and God has relations with man. Often God stipulates terms to man which, depending on how man responds, cause God to administer justice or mercy. When David numbered the people, God sent an angel to destroy Jerusalem (1 Chr. 21:15). But God, upon viewing the grief of the people and David's own repentance, stopped the plague.

Sometimes the Bible uses "anthropomorphic language" (God speaking like a man or language that helps man to understand God) and will speak of God from man's vantage point. He appears to have changed his mind but, in fact, never altered his eternal mind or decree. These are mysteries, to be sure, and the Bible neither explains itself in every particular nor apologizes for its language. Yet every child of God can be confident that God will never change his mind about the eternal welfare of his children (Rom. 8:28–39).

B. The "Book of God"

The book spoken of here refers to the book of life (Dan. 12:1; Rev. 20:12). This phrase comes from the custom of writing the names of citizens of towns in a list in order to accord them full rights (Keil, 231). This book of life (Phil. 4:3) includes the names of the children of God from all ages. Missing from this book are names of people from every age and locale who do not have true fellowship with God. When we hear the phrase "blot out of the book of life," it simply means to cut off from fellowship with God or to deliver people over to eternal death. We grant that some of the language about books, and books of remembrance, may be figurative (Mal. 3:16; Rev. 20:12, see Berkhof, 734), and we equally should shun the clumsy attempts to label and classify all these books as some have attempted.

The kernel of this teaching is that God will recall all the actions, thoughts, attitudes, and responses of both his children and unbelievers. He will hold us all accountable (Rom. 2:16; 1 Cor. 4:5). No child of God need ever fear that God will ultimately forsake him. God's children are safely etched in that book of life from which, blessedly, there is no escape.

C. God's Jealousy

Most people today would not identify jealousy as an attribute of love, but that is what it is. True love, or God's love, places value on the object it loves. The Holy Spirit, for example, longs zealously to possess us (Jas. 4:5). When a party to a relationship becomes unfaithful in any regard, the other party can become jealous. Sometimes this jealously emits bad vibes and therefore is not from God. But true love promotes loyalty and purity, and the unfaithful party to a relationship can mar the union so badly that it causes the other party to become jealous.

God longs to possess fully his people and will fight for his own honor when a rival threatens that relationship. Jesus himself, the meekest of all men and lowly in heart (Matt. 11:29), did not hesitate to cast out the money-changers from his Father's house (John 2:12–17). Most manifestations of jealously we hear about do little to promote healthy relationships. But God exercises all his attributes in perfection and can never fall out of balance. We should rejoice when we see God exercising a holy jealousy over our lives because this means he really loves us. And he really does!

VII. TEACHING OUTLINE

A. INTRODUCTION

1. Lead Story: Is God Listening?

2. Context: God had delivered his people from slavery in Egypt. He was preparing them to give them the promised land. On the way from Egypt to Canaan, the people stopped at Mount Sinai. There God gave Moses the Ten Commandments, the basic principles by which Israel was to live. While Moses was on the mountain, the people became impatient and created a representation of God in the form of a golden calf.

3. Transition: Chapters 32–34 tell the consequences of Israel's making a golden calf. Moses intercedes with God on Israel's behalf, and the covenant is renewed.

B. COMMENTARY

1. The Making of a God (32:1–35)

2. The Glory of the Lord (33:1–23)

3. Covenant Renewal (34:1–35)

C. CONCLUSION: FAITH OF A CHILD

VIII. ISSUES FOR DISCUSSION

1. How long had Moses been away from his people? What happens when there is a void in leadership?

2. How can a student of these events describe Moses' leadership style in the face of dramatic sin? Did he go overboard? Why or why not?

3. How much does a leader have to care for the people he has been called to shepherd? Can you list some specific examples in your life that demonstrate your care for others?

4. What was the big deal about the stone tablets on which the Ten Commandments were written? Could the people of Israel have gotten by without a new set?

Exodus 35–40

Building the Tabernacle

I. INTRODUCTION
Mummy Fever

II. COMMENTARY
A verse-by-verse explanation of these chapters.

III. CONCLUSION
Planning Versus Follow-Through

An overview of the principles and applications from these chapters.

IV. LIFE APPLICATION
A New Football Position

Melding these chapters to life.

V. PRAYER
Tying these chapters to life with God.

VI. DEEPER DISCOVERIES
Historical, geographical, and grammatical enrichment of the commentary.

VII. TEACHING OUTLINE
Suggested step-by-step group study of these chapters.

VIII. ISSUES FOR DISCUSSION
Zeroing these chapters in on daily life.

"*I* never made a sacrifice. We ought not to talk of 'sacrifice' when we remember the great sacrifice which He made who left His Father's throne on high to give Himself for us."

David Livingstone

Exodus 35–40

 I N   A   N U T S H E L L

*I*n chapters 25–31, the blueprints were given for the tabernacle, and in chapters 35–40, the tabernacle is erected. Great detail is given for the fund-raising efforts and the contents of this building designed for God's holy habitation. The Book of Exodus then concludes with the glory of God filling the tabernacle.

Building the Tabernacle

I. INTRODUCTION

Mummy Fever

I took my family to the World's Fair in 1984. One of the most popular exhibits was the King Tut exhibit. Students of archeology remind us of the secret behind the historical discovery of this king's tomb. In 1922, archeologist Howard Carter and his patron George Edward Carnavon did not heed the curse of the pharaoh inscribed on the tomb entrance which said: "Any man who enters this tomb I will pounce upon like a cobra." The next year they didn't heed the words engraved on the burial chamber: "May he inside remain uninjured, the son of Ra." The discovery of King Tutankhamen's tomb in Egypt's Valley of the Kings was an immediate media sensation. The world contracted mummy fever.

Although a cobra did not pounce on the archeologists, the Egyptian government did. Officials accused the team of specialists of grave-robbing and defiling a sacred site and eventually demanded that all the findings be donated to the Cairo Museum for the entire world to enjoy. Two months after the burial chamber's seal was broken, a mosquito bit Carnavon while he was visiting the tomb, and he died of infections and complications.

Any undertaking needs to be driven by more than greed, ambition, or the desire for prestige and popularity. This is the lesson for all to learn when studying Israel's commitment to build the tabernacle.

II. COMMENTARY

Building the Tabernacle

> **MAIN IDEA:** *The tabernacle designed becomes the tabernacle built.*

Materials and Anointed Men (35:1–35)

> **SUPPORTING IDEA:** *The people provide precious materials and the Lord provides skilled craftsmen.*

35:1–3. Moses assembled the people and reminded them of their sacred obligation to set aside the seventh day for rest. Moses probably feared that the people of Israel, in their zeal to erect the tabernacle, might neglect the Sabbath day. But Moses reinforced the importance of keeping that day and appended a sobering threat of capital punishment for any who might violate its provisions.

Apparently someone or several people from the community had recently violated this command by kindling a fire on the Sabbath. Back then starting a fire involved rubbing two sticks together or using other friction-causing devices. In any case, it was work and a violation of the Sabbath regulations.

35:4–9. Moses next repeated God's command to take an offering from among the people to furnish the materials for the tabernacle (for more, see ch. 25:2–7).

35:10–19. For the specific materials for the tabernacle proper, see 26:1–6; for the tent items, 26:7–13; for the boards, 26:15–25; and for the ark, tables, and related furniture items, see 25:10–40.

35:20–29. The people withdrew from Moses and returned to their dwelling places to secure items for the offering. Apparently the people responded with an almost unanimous willingness. The offering itself would provide the materials needed for building the tabernacle, the priestly garments, and all related functions. They brought to Moses gold jewelry, brooches, rings, linen, spices for the oil, and related items covered in chapters 25–28. God also used the talents of the people, such as women who could spin goat hair into fine linen.

No doubt the general offering allowed for such a community participation that the people now possessed ownership in setting up the elaborate worship center. The sacrificial system and worship rituals would form the center of Jewish life and serve as the primary vehicle for God's blessing to rest upon the community. But if the people neglected this spiritual provision or observed its features in a mechanical or hypocritical manner, they would risk losing God's presence among them.

35:30–35. While God gave Moses the concept of the entire tabernacle system, he chose others to convert it to reality. To lead the effort, God chose Bezalel, son of Uri, and Oholiab, son of Ahisamach. Their task included teaching others how to build the various items needed for the tabernacle. But we see how God's grace presided over the entire enterprise by noticing how he filled these workers with the Spirit. The Spirit endowed these artists and workers with the necessary skills and talents to convert the divine plans into reality.

🅱 The Construction of the Tabernacle (36:1–38)

SUPPORTING IDEA: *The plans and purposes of God now come to fulfillment in a new tabernacle.*

36:1. Great plans amount to nothing if no one is willing to carry them out. But when God plans, he provides—as this chapter clearly teaches. The Lord raised up a master craftsman in Bezalel, and he would oversee the construction of the tabernacle. The details were so minute that this man must have possessed extraordinary keenness of intellect and the ability to convert elaborate plans into reality. To assist him God also endowed Oholiab and others with similar skills.

36:2–7. Moses summoned Bezalel and Oholiab and other skilled workers to build the tabernacle. To this end the Israelites willingly contributed offerings of materials that would go toward the building. In fact, they gave so freely that the spirit of generosity soon moved them to give more than was actually needed to complete the task. Moses then gave an order for them to hold back on their contributions because they now had enough for the task at hand.

36:8–18. The men first set out to make the beautiful and intricate curtains that would adorn the structure (see 26:1–11 for more details).

36:19–34. See 26:14–29 for explanation.

36:35–36. See 26:33–34.

36:37–38. See 26:36–37.

C The Furniture of the Tabernacle (37:1–29)

SUPPORTING IDEA: *The workers construct the altars, tables, and other sanctuary items according to divine plan.*

37:1–9. Bezalel next constructed the intricately designed ark of the covenant and mercy seat (for fuller explanation, see 25:10–20).

37:10–16. See 25:23–30 for explanation.

37:17–24. See comments on 25:31–39.

37:25–29. See comments on 30:1–5, 30:23–25, and 30:34–35.

D The Remaining Furniture of the Tabernacle (38:1–31)

SUPPORTING IDEA: *The skilled men complete the tabernacle proper by building the altar, basin, and courtyard.*

38:1–7. The workers next proceeded to build the altar of burnt sacrifice according to the instructions God gave Moses (for explanation, see 27:1–8).

38:8. These mirrors have not been previously mentioned. They were probably made from bronze plates, highly polished, and used by the women as mirrors in the same way as today. Both the British and Royal Ontario Museums host similar Egyptian articles, many of which contain handles and beautiful designs. That the women gave up these possessions showed their commitment to the entire tabernacle enterprise.

38:9–20. See comments on 27:9–19.

38:21–24. Moses recorded the precise amount (or weights) of the contributions from the Israelites. The precious metals obtained went to the ark of the testimony or the tabernacle that contained the tablets of the covenant. To aid him Moses had Levites under Ithamar do the actual recording. They observed Bezalel as he built the furniture, and Oholiab, as he worked with linen. The gold contributions amounted to 29 talents and 730 shekels.

38:25–28. Although the silver amounted to almost four times the weight of the gold, its worth was actually far less. The silver that went to the sanctuary was exacted from the people during a census (which amounted to 603,550 men).

38:29–31. The people willingly gave of their bronze (35:24), and from these offerings the workers made the entrance bases, bronze altars, courtyard bases, and tent pegs.

Ⓔ The Making of the Priestly Attire (39:1–43)

SUPPORTING IDEA: *The workers make the elaborately designed attire to be adorned by the officiating priests.*

39:1. From 35:22–25 we learn the colorful yarn (see "Deeper Discoveries") came from freewill offerings of the people. From these and others materials came the sacred garments for the priests.

39:2–7. See 28:5–14.

39:8–21. For a more detailed commentary, see 28:15–38.

39:22–31. For comment on 39:22–26, see 28:31–34; for 39:27–29, see 28:39–40; for 39:30–31, see 28:36–37.

39:32–43. All the completed materials were brought before Moses (probably not all at once), and he pronounced them complete and accurate. We are not told that he rejected any of the work as inferior or not up to divine standard, but if that had been the case, he would have had it redone. When Moses blessed the people, he conveyed not only his own approval but God's as well. We can estimate that they completed the tabernacle in about six months. They arrived at Sinai the third month after they left Egypt (19:1), Moses was in dialogue with God about three months, and they completed the project before the end of the year (40:17).

Ⓕ Erecting the Tabernacle and the Glory of God (40:1–38)

SUPPORTING IDEA: *God blessed the constructed tabernacle by filling it with his glory.*

40:1–8. Once Bezalel and Oholiab had completed their tasks, God commanded Moses to set up the tabernacle on the first day of the new year (Abib or Nisan). He was to place the ark of the testimony behind the curtain in the most holy place, then place the table of bread, lampstand, and altar of incense on the other side of that curtain opposite the ark of the testimony.

God next commanded Moses to place the altar of burnt offering in front of the tabernacle entrance, with the washbasin going between it and the tent.

He was to fill the basin with water. He then was to erect the tabernacle border, or courtyard, with its curtain at the entrance (see 27:16; 38:18).

40:9–16. God next gave Moses the directions for the setting apart of the tabernacle and related items and the priests. Because of the time it took to set up the sanctuary, Moses probably delayed the anointing ceremonies for a day or so. With Aaron, it appears the anointing procedure was different. The oil was first poured upon his head (Lev. 8:12) and then sprinkled (Lev. 8:30). With subsequent priests it was simply sprinkled.

40:17–33. The design of the tabernacle allowed for a quick setup and takedown, probably in less than a day. The bases probably rested on the bare desert sand (v. 18), weighing enough to support the entire structure. Moses put each piece in place, then overlaid it with the curtains. He then placed the tablets, or testimony, in the ark, attached the carrying poles, and set the mercy seat upon the ark itself. The ark was placed in the most holy place followed by the other items (see vv. 2–11). Moses lit the first incense (v. 27) and offered the first sacrifice (v. 29).

40:34–38. God now granted his own approval to all that had been done. He descended upon the tabernacle and filled it with his glory. We could say God took up residence there, although God is not spatially limited (1 Kgs. 8:27). It became the dwelling place of God's unique presence. From then on, when the people sought God, they would think of the sanctuary or Jerusalem (see Dan. 6:10). The way of immediate access to God was not yet available (Heb. 9:8), but he still was present with his people. They had to rely on the elaborate sacrificial system in order to meet with and please God.

With Adam's transgression came the fall of man, followed immediately by God's intervention on man's behalf. God always desired to share an intimate relationship with man, much closer than meeting with him through a detailed sacrificial and priestly system (see Isa. 66:1–2, cp. Acts 7:48–50). But the road to that place would be neither immediate nor trouble-free. The tabernacle served as a temporary "house of God," moving toward the ultimate goal of dwelling with man permanently (Rev. 21:3).

God would hereafter direct the Israelites in their journeys by means of the guiding cloud by day and fire by night.

MAIN IDEA REVIEW: *The tabernacle designed becomes the tabernacle built.*

III. CONCLUSION

Planning Versus Follow-Through

On January 7, 1913, William Burton was granted a patent for a cracking process that enabled him to obtain gasoline from crude oil. It was this patent that would change the way the world moves from one end of the globe to the other. Most people today don't even recognize the name of William Burton, let alone appreciate his contribution to the transportation industry. But people do complain about how his invention has adversely impacted our environment. No one ever thought greater wisdom was needed in handling this invention.

For the same reason, President Harry S. Truman should have heeded sounder advice when he announced on the same date in 1953 that the United States had developed a hydrogen bomb. Both inventions had tremendous potential. Both inventions offered the world hopeful technology. But both inventions make an important statement: Planning something and carrying out those plans are distinctly different. It is how we carry out the plans drawn that will demonstrate our faithfulness in following through on our commitments.

The plans drawn for processing gasoline and for developing a hydrogen bomb were flawed because no one had the whole picture as to their use, function, and maintenance. But the blueprint for the tabernacle and related items had already been given to the people of Israel, and it was perfect. Nothing was unforeseen by God or left out. After all, this was God's plans and God's building. Moses offered a challenge to the people, and they responded. Not just a few, but everyone got involved. This is God's design.

PRINCIPLES

- Leadership must always seek the face of God when launching into anything new.
- God wants people to be sold out to his will and his leading.
- When God challenges, responsive people give, serve, and obey.
- Consecration precedes blessing.

APPLICATIONS

- Give abundantly. Never hold back when the Spirit of God encourages you to build or grow.
- Get involved. Games are not won by cheerleaders.
- Participate in what God is doing in your church. Use your gifts.

IV. LIFE APPLICATION

A New Football Position

The little boy's first-grade teacher asked him, "What position does your older brother play on the football team?" The boy knew that his brother played football; he had been to many of his games. But flustered by the unexpected question, all he could say was, "I think he's a drawback."

Drawback . . . a term used for a retreat from battle, or the posture of a shy kid in a crowd. But this is also a term that could describe many Christians in the church today. God told the people of Israel, "You are my fullbacks, not drawbacks. I will do the blocking for you. Now pick up the ball and run with it! There's work to be done." The same is true for kingdom workers today. There are no benchwarmers in the Bible.

V. PRAYER

Heavenly Father, where I have been lazy, instill within me the desire to work harder. During those times where I was cheap with my possessions, remind me where it all came from. And as I read your Word, allow me to catch glimpses of your splendor as I serve you and until I get to see you face-to-face, like Moses. In Jesus' name. Amen!

VI. DEEPER DISCOVERIES

A. The Significance of the Tabernacle

The tabernacle carried more significance than simply a religious relic that the Israelites carted from place to place. The edifice, so intricately planned and designed by God himself, breathed rich meaning and symbolic truth that the New Testament writers would later develop. So we must understand the tabernacle in its original historical context but also in relation to the remaining biblical text (Poythress, 38). Below we mention several prominent meanings of the tabernacle of Moses.

A place of meeting. The idea of the tabernacle must not be conceived as though God needs a specific place of dwelling here on earth. Nor should we suppose the tabernacle limits God in any way. It was a means of allowing the people to meet with God in some way. Thus the tabernacle "embodies the eminently religious idea of the dwelling of God with His people" (Vos, *Biblical Theology,* 148; see Exod. 25:8; 29:44–45).

Was the tabernacle God's house or man's? Clearly it was God's house, but God received people as guests. Nor was the tabernacle constructed for God's sake, but *for* man, just as the priesthood was. Man needs God, yet sin banished him from unrestricted access to God. Yet God provided a solution through a salvation that not only forgave sinners but also maintained the integrity of God's righteous standards of holiness. So God and man could meet once again, under certain conditions.

Yet such a setup does not imply that God does not long for fellowship with man. "The dwelling with His people is to satisfy God's desire to have a mutual identification of lot between Himself and them" (Vos, 149). The term "tent of meeting" does not describe the people meeting together but meeting with God. When God's people gather today in churches across the globe, do they come together to network among themselves, to exchange pleasantries or gossip, or otherwise huddle in close-knit groups to meet some social need? The community of the redeemed should gather to encounter the living God, who has provided for their salvation. Clearly the "tent of meeting" was a place where God and man could come together.

The tabernacle proclaims not only the loving nature of God but his holiness as well. His dwelling inspired both fear and awe. Even people in God's favor had to worship at a distance, with only the ordained priests approaching, and then only under strict guidelines. But later Christ would bridge this distance. Still, the people of God should never view the presence of God as something to run from. The freewill offerings of the people were designed to express their desire to have God dwell among them. The New Testament links the dwelling of God with man by presenting the incarnate Christ as one who "made his dwelling among us" (John 1:14, literally, "tabernacled"). Thus access to God is through Christ (John 14:6), in whom dwells the Godhead. The designated name of our Lord, *Immanuel,* means "God with us" (Matt. 1:23). The ultimate realization of perfect fellowship between man and God culminates in Revelation 21:3, where a loud voice proclaims, "Now the dwelling of God is with men."

A place of worship. The articles of furniture contained in the tabernacle also exude specific worship themes later brought out by the New Testament writers.

(1) *The altar of incense.* This altar, located near the curtain, would emit a smoke and special fragrance that filled the tabernacle, ascending upward. The Bible links this beautiful scene with prayer ascending to heaven (Rev. 5:8; 8:3).

(2) *Table of bread of presence.* The priests of God relied on God for their daily provision—a reminder to us that God provides food to us daily, even as he provided the Israelites with food during their wilderness wanderings (thus a portion of manna was kept in the holy place; Exod. 16:32–35). But the bread from heaven came not only in physical form but spiritual form as well (John 6:32–35; Poythress, 20–21). We who name the name of Christ must seek spiritual sustenance from him alone to stay strong in the Lord.

(3) *Lampstand.* The illuminating lampstand provided the priests sufficient light so they could perform their duties within the tabernacle. Such light reminds us that if man would see, he must seek light from God, who gives light to men (John 1:9). Those who remain in unbelief cannot see the

light of the gospel (2 Cor. 4:4), but they remain in darkness. The light God gives his children shines in their hearts—something that Paul describes as the light of the knowledge of the glory of God in the face of Christ (2 Cor. 4:6).

B. Relationship of the Tabernacle and the Church

Can we find a relationship between the tabernacle and the church? In one sense, we can find anything we want, provided our imaginations are lively enough and duly stimulated. But it seems we can safely arrive at some close associations between the tabernacle of God and the church for which Christ died. The New Testament writers compared the church to the house of God (Eph. 2:21–22; 1 Tim. 3:15; 1 Pet. 2:5). Some today, with at least some justification, call their place of worship the house of God. Paul calls the Christian the temple of God (1 Cor. 6:19) and then draws some serious ethical conclusions (see also 2 Cor. 6:16).

Yet we should also note some differences. The people could not gather inside the tabernacle, and even the priests needed to observe the restrictions imposed by God. The New Testament household of God, where God also dwells (Eph. 2:21–22), need not observe such restrictions. God provides the church an advanced access to himself, which will one day result in face-to-face permanent fellowship (Rev. 21:3). In this sense the Old Testament tabernacle reflected the imperfect condition between God and man (Vos, 155), a condition that dramatically improves in the New Testament church.

Finally, God will one day remove all obstacles and mediums to his presence. John observes that the very "throne of God and of the Lamb will be in the city, and his servants will serve him" (Rev. 22:3). John saw no temple there, because "the Lord God Almighty and the Lamb are its temple" (Rev. 21:22).

VII. TEACHING OUTLINE

A. INTRODUCTION

1. Lead Story: Mummy Fever

2. Context: God heard Moses' intercession on Israel's behalf. He forgave Israel for their sin of idolatry. Israel responds to God's forgiveness by getting to work on the tabernacle, the place of God's abiding presence with his people.

3. Transition: Chapters 35–40 tell of the peoples' generosity in giving to the construction of the tabernacle. God used skilled artists and craftsmen to lead the people in building the tabernacle. When the tabernacle was completed, Moses consecrated it. A cloud settled on it, and

the glory of the Lord filled it so that Moses could not enter the tabernacle.

B. COMMENTARY

1. Materials and Anointed Men (35:1–35)
2. The Construction of the Tabernacle (36:1–38)
3. The Furniture of the Tabernacle (37:1–29)
4. The Remaining Furniture of the Tabernacle (38:1–31)
5. The Making of the Priestly Attire (39:1–43)
6. Erecting the Tabernacle and the Glory of God (40:1–38)

C. CONCLUSION: A NEW FOOTBALL POSITION

VIII. ISSUES FOR DISCUSSION

1. Why do you think God gave attention to Bezalel and Oholiab? What skills did they have that were so important to this campaign? How did they acquire these skills?
2. The Bible gives a lot of attention to details in the tabernacle. What does this say about God? How important do you believe these details became to Israel? Why?
3. What do some of the representative pieces of tabernacle furnishings say about God?
4. Where does God dwell today? Why do believers need these reminders? Is there any danger in attempting to localize God?
5. What was the most important element added to the tabernacle? Why was this so important to the people of Israel?

Introduction to

Leviticus

The title of this book also serves as it central theme: *that which pertains to the Levites* (Archer, 239). The name "Leviticus" comes from the Greek word *Levitikon*, meaning "or the Levites." The Hebrew title *Wayyiqra* means "and he called." The entire writing spells out the essence of Hebrew worship, both for the transitional time before the erection of the permanent temple in Solomon's time, but even following that time. All of it subthemes—priestly functions, sacrificial procedures, various cleansing rituals, and even brief biographical features (e.g., 10:1–7)—funnel into its chief theme: the holiness of the Lord.

The nation of Israel, comprised of twelve tribes, was separated by God from the other nations to be a people unto the Lord. Accordingly, their entire life was a regulated existence. No part was untouched by God's commands and influence. Although many Christians choose to stay away from this book because they do not see its immediate relevance, the book contains some of the richest symbolism in the Bible. Readers today will enrich their spiritual lives by probing deeply into the contents of Leviticus, an endeavor that will require more than a cursory effort. It is not the "one-minute" book.

CHARACTERISTICS OF LEVITICUS

Leviticus contains no formal introduction. It launches directly into successive themes, beginning with the authorized offerings of Israel. Connected with the offerings, the priestly regulations that stipulate the formula for acceptable intercession offer the reader another core theme of the book: the importance of holiness in all aspects of life.

Profoundly theological. Leviticus is "one of the most theologically oriented books in Scripture" (House, 126). From sacrifice to priestly service, Leviticus weaves a fine theological fabric with some of the richest doctrinal concepts in the entire Bible. Yet so many people get bogged down in the minutia of seemingly unrelated details, failing to grasp its wider significance. Leviticus needs to be examined in its broadest context, and readers need to discover how it relates to the rest of the Bible.

Leviticus addresses how to remedy sin, although it does not establish the fact of sin. It assumes that sin exists and has affected the nation's walk with God. The book also assumes a monotheistic deity who admits no rivals, whether in sacrifice, worship, or community regulations. "No other god exists to be offended" (House, 128). For Israel there is but one sanctuary, one altar (8:3; 17:8–9), and only one priesthood (1:5).

Assuming the reader is now acquainted with the periodic self-disclosures of God in Genesis and Exodus, he or she discovers in Leviticus that God inches ever closer to man in presence and self-revelation. As Israel draws close to God, she must take on family characteristics or become like God in some way. The Lord had previously given Israel her divine purpose: becoming a holy nation (Exod. 19:6), now she takes steps in that direction. At no time does the nation conduct its life as though God were distant, because he is close at hand. He involves himself in all aspects of the people's lives, revealing more and more of himself with each new revelation. The trappings of the sanctuary and the intricate functions of worship all point to the divine attribute of holiness.

The law of sacrifice, especially the Day of Atonement (Lev. 16), serves as the foundation for individual and community cleansing. Moses never revealed the significance of the sacrifices but did specify their character and quality. The annual Day of Atonement witnessed the high priest offering a sacrifice for atonement (16:6,10–11,16–17,20) for himself and the people (16:24). Thus the atonement does not merely "cover" the sins of the people but makes expiation. God pronounces real "forgiveness" (4:20,26,31,35; 6:7) for specific sins (Lindsey, 164), but the sacrifices remained limited in their ability to remove sin permanently. They could not, for example, remove sins done with a high hand such as murder or blasphemy (Num. 15:30–31). Yet Christ could remove such sins, as the apostle Paul would later declare (1 Tim. 1:12–17). Thus "the sacrifices of animals is inadequate to achieve final cleansing, and it cannot cleanse anything more than the copies of heavenly things" (Poythress, 46).

Orderly structure. The book unfolds as a logical and orderly unit, with clearly defined sections and natural transitions. Moses begins with the law of sacrifices (chs. 1–7) and related procedural matters. These chapters form the foundation for the sacrificial system in Israel, laws and regulations that would govern the nation's worship. Next Moses introduces the Aaronic priesthood (chs. 8–10), including ordination, initial offerings, and even an unfortunate incident that resulted in the deaths of Aaron's priestly sons, Nadab and Abihu. In keeping with its theme of holiness in individuals and the nation, the book then describes what constitutes uncleanness and how to remove it (chs. 11–16). The final lengthy section (chs. 17–27) discusses matters of community holiness, ranging from sexual behavior to the law of vows.

Revelational character. Evangelicals believe the entire Bible is an inerrant and infallible book, but some books of the Bible seem to be particularly dictated by God. Leviticus is one such book. Over and over we read, "The LORD spoke to Moses" (16:1), or, "The LORD said to Moses" (17:1). The Book of

Leviticus was written during the wandering years of Israel when Moses had plenty of time to hear from God and record what he heard. We later find a similar scenario with Paul in Roman imprisonment where he penned his prison epistles, and still later John on the Island of Patmos receiving apocalyptic visions that would later comprise the Book of Revelation. The contents of Leviticus demanded precision and clarity because it laid a foundation for worship in Israel. Without the Book of Leviticus the Book of Hebrews would make little sense. The writer of Hebrews looks back to the entire sacrificial system and transposes our thinking to see fulfillment in Christ. In a real sense, Leviticus demands Christ, in whom we discover the fullness of revelation (John 1:1–3,17).

Theocratic anticipation. Although scholars speak of the threefold character of the law with a bit of arbitrariness (Wenham, 32–33), Leviticus combines the law's moral, civil, and ceremonial aspects without clear distinction. Certainly this seems strange to Western minds which are accustomed to the separation of private and public living that pluralism demands. The Lord prescribes behavior for every sphere of life, from sexual conduct (ch. 18) to public worship (ch. 16). But such a union only brings home the truth that God's children will one day dwell under God's clear rule forever. Then, the Lord will perfectly write his law in our hearts and banish from his presence any who did not believe, including those who broke the moral, civil, and ceremonial laws (see Rev. 21:8, where the Lord banishes violators of religious, civil, and moral laws from his presence forever).

With the sacrifices we rejoice in temporary "covering" of sin, but we look to Christ for complete removal of sin (Heb. 10:10). In the elaborate community regulations we see laws that could possibly facilitate a people striving to keep God laws, but we look for a new heart upon which the Lord inscribes these laws (Heb. 10:16). The Old Testament worshipers looked to the priests for faithful mediation between all the people and a holy God, but they peered out into the hazy future longing for a better priesthood, one that would bridge the gap between God and man (Heb. 7:11–21). Truly the priestly ministry was glorious, but the ministry Jesus has received is as superior to theirs as the covenant of which he is mediator is superior to the old one, and it is founded on better promises (Heb. 8:6). So in Leviticus the Lord lays the groundwork for a theocratic kingdom, the perfection of which can only be realized in Christ.

Sacred numbers. Although the Bible clearly hints at some special significance to some of the numbers used in Leviticus (e.g., forty years of wandering, Num. 14:34), these sacred numbers figure prominently in Leviticus. The year of Jubilee, where land returns to the original tribal owners, occurs following "seven sevens" (forty-nine) of years. The Feast of Unleavened Bread follows the Passover for seven days. The weekly Sabbath falls on the seventh day, and the seventh month, Tishri, hosts three major observances: the Day of

Atonement, the Feast of Trumpets, and the Feast of Tabernacles, the last of which lasts for seven days. Seven is the number of perfection, God's own number, whereas six is the number of man (Rev. 13:18).

AUTHORSHIP

The internal evidence for Mosaic authorship of the Pentateuch is strong (see Introduction to Exodus). As to the Mosaic authorship of Leviticus, Ezra cites some of the worship procedures from the Book of Leviticus, calling it "the Book of Moses" (Ezra 6:18). God revealed the contents of the book to Moses himself (Lev. 7:37–38). Jesus, when citing the law for cleansing from leprosy (clearly given in Lev. 14), tells the cleansed leper, "But go, show yourself to the priest and offer the sacrifices that Moses commanded for your cleansing" (Mark 1:44).

DATE OF WRITING

Although Leviticus is part of the Pentateuch and, as such, is dated closely with its other books, we can perhaps suggest a more precise time line for the composition of this book based on some internal factors. The tabernacle was assembled and put up one year following the exodus from Egypt (Exod. 40:2,17). A month later the Israelites set out in the direction of the promised land (Num. 1:1; the first time of course, before the wandering years). The intervening month would allow Moses sufficient time to compose this book, a particularly urgent need assuming the Israelites would begin the prescribed rituals immediately as commanded by God. Although we don't know exactly when Moses composed this book, the above scenario seems as likely as any. See the introduction to Exodus for more on the dating of the Pentateuch.

THEME OF LEVITICUS

The holiness of Yahweh as Lord and Redeemer of Israel forms the central theme of the entire book. The Lord admonishes the entire nation to present themselves holy before the Lord in heart and community (Lev. 19:2; cp. 1 Pet. 1:15–16). He at times singles out particular groups for this admonition. In Leviticus 10:3 he reminds the grieving Aaron following the judgment of the Lord on his two sons that "among those who approach me I will show myself holy." Aaron and his sons represented the people to God, serving as priests. The office itself did not insulate its priests from contamination, and they must at all times guard against any defilement. The priests were to be holy.

Individuals must also present themselves to the Lord as holy by following the sacrificial, community, and individual commands given by the Lord. The nation as a whole was to cleave to the Lord's commands if it expected to prolong its days in the land (26:14–39).

Leviticus 1–7

God's Provision Through Sacrifices

I. **INTRODUCTION**
The Measure of Progress

II. **COMMENTARY**
A verse-by-verse explanation of these chapters.

III. **CONCLUSION**
A Little Boy's Sacrifice

An overview of the principles and applications from these chapters.

IV. **LIFE APPLICATION**
Caterpillar Confusion

Melding these chapters to life.

V. **PRAYER**
Tying these chapters to life with God.

VI. **DEEPER DISCOVERIES**
Historical, geographical, and grammatical enrichment of the commentary.

VII. **TEACHING OUTLINE**
Suggested step-by-step group study of these chapters.

VIII. **ISSUES FOR DISCUSSION**
Zeroing these chapters in on daily life.

"*E*very Christian truth, gracious and comfortable, has

a corresponding obligation, searching and sacrificial."

H a r r y   E m e r s o n   F o s d i c k

Leviticus 1–7

IN A NUTSHELL

*L*eviticus 1–7 gives us snapshots of the human condition. Through the study of five offerings demanded of the Hebrew people, we learn how these sacrifices deal with our relationship with God and our relationship with one another. Your understanding of the sacrifice of Jesus Christ on the cross will never be the same after you have studied how God's eternal plan started with these instructions thousands of years ago.

God's Provision
Through Sacrifices

I. INTRODUCTION

The Measure of Progress

How do you measure progress? Every generation has its own distinct way of measuring growth and progress. February 6 has been a date infamous for proving this truth in the area of technology and national security. On this day in 1959, the United States successfully test-fired the first Titan intercontinental ballistic missile from Cape Canaveral. This demonstration of progress seemed to show that the world's safety was now assured through this newfound technology. Twelve years later, on the same date, progress was again shown through two astronauts preparing to head back to earth from the moon after an incredible thirty-three hours on the distant moon. This event gave the United States some assurances that not only is the earth we live on safe and secure, but now the skies above us have the same hope. Progress had prevailed.

By 1985 national security took on a whole new meaning when Australian prime minister Robert Hawke began the process of allowing Americans to monitor MX missile tests from Australian military bases. Progress now allowed the land "down under" to become the first antinuclear nation. The span of time between all three events spanned a little over a quarter of a century, but each represented a step forward. But the problem mankind faces is that we can take steps backward instead of forward.

The study of Leviticus represents a return to truths often neglected and rarely studied. How many Christians have started reading their Bibles, enjoyed their travels through Genesis and Exodus, and come to Leviticus, only to become discouraged and confused. The regulations for the priests seem so detailed. All the talk about blood and sacrifices doesn't seem to relate to life as a modern believer.

Get ready for an exciting ride through a book that will change your perspectives and bring more personal progress than you expected. You are about to learn about the presence of God and his holiness. You will finally understand the role of the sacrifices. The term *covenant* will take on a new relevance in your life.

Our study begins with an analysis of the various offerings God set forth for the priests. The offerings that God spoke to Moses about were a means of worship as well as sacrifice for personal forgiveness and restoration with God.

Many of the offerings were associated with the burnt offering outlined in Exodus 27. The priests sacrificed various offerings to God in order to atone for their own sins as well as the sins of the people.

II. COMMENTARY

God's Provision Through Sacrifices

> **MAIN IDEA:** *God provided a way for the people to demonstrate total dependence on him and to offer up various sacrifices depicting a yielded life.*

A The Burnt Offering (1:1–2)

> **SUPPORTING IDEA:** *God showed Moses the prescribed manner to receive the freewill burnt offerings of the people.*

1:1–2. God spoke to Moses from the inner sanctuary (within the **Tent of Meeting**) and gave him general directions for the various offerings to be brought. Before this, God spoke from the mountain, but now he spoke from the mercy seat of the ark of the covenant.

The **when** in verse 2 is significant. Although the public offerings, such as in the Passover and Day of Atonement, involved set times and places, the individual offerings were voluntary. Sometimes the person wanted to express self-surrender to God and did so with a burnt offering. When God reminded the sinner of a particular shortcoming, he would then offer a sin or guilt offering.

B An Offering from the Herd (1:3–9)

> **SUPPORTING IDEA:** *Moses is instructed on the regulations governing a burnt offering from the herd.*

1:3–9. The burnt offering, or "whole offering," involved the entire offering being consumed on the altar. If the person brought an animal from the herd, the animal was to be a male without defect. He would bring the animal to the front of the tent of meeting. He then was to place his hand on the head of the animal and slaughter it **before the LORD**. The priests would then apply the blood to all inner sides of the altar. The entire offering was to be placed on the altar, then washed and burned. If the offering was performed according to regulation, God would accept it.

C An Offering from the Flock (1:10–13)

> **SUPPORTING IDEA:** *Offerings from the flock require the same procedure as those from the herd.*

1:10–13. Although Moses mentions that a person who offers an animal (whether sheep or goat) from the flock must do so on the north side of the altar, the same was probably true of an offering from the herd. Moses mentions it here with more precision. The procedure is the same as that for the herd offerings.

D An Offering of Birds (1:14–17)

> **SUPPORTING IDEA:** *God allowed the substitution of a bird for those who could not afford a larger animal.*

1:14–17. We learn from Leviticus 12:8 that God made a special provision for those who, because of insufficient means, were not able to offer a regular animal from either herd or flock. In such cases the individual could substitute either a dove or a pigeon.

The bird offering also differed from the animal offering in that the person was not required to lay his hand on the bird or kill it himself. The priest would perform that function. The priest would sever the head of the bird from the body and burn it on the altar. He would then **remove the crop with its contents** and dispense of it on the east side of the altar. The priest would have to divide the bird by the wings, making sure he didn't sever it completely. He then would burn the bird on the altar as a whole offering.

E Introduction to the Grain Offering (2:1–3)

> **SUPPORTING IDEA:** *Man acknowledges God's sovereignty over all things in the grain offering, by presenting to God a portion of his labors.*

2:1–3. The grain offering (called "meat offering" in some versions) consisted of an offering from the products of the earth needed to support life (flour and oil). It recognized God who gave the product (whether corn, grapes, or olives). The grain offering consisted of **fine flour and oil**, and it was mixed with incense as an offering **pleasing to the LORD**. And, unlike the burnt offering, the priests could eat the remaining portion of this offering. This expressed a communal element where priest and offerer enjoyed the blessings brought about by God's gracious provision.

F Preparing the Grain Offering (2:4–10)

> **SUPPORTING IDEA:** *God gives procedures for making the grain offering into a variety of forms.*

2:4–10. If the offerer brought the offering from the oven (probably a large pot in the room), he was to make it from fine flour without any trace of yeast. From the oven one might prepare either cakes or wafers. If from a pan, it also had to be made from flour and oil. The offerer then must present the offering to the priest, who would take it to the altar. The priest then took out a portion of the offering, **the memorial portion**, and offered it upon the altar so the fire could consume it. The remaining portion belonged to the priests.

Ⓖ Final Instructions for the Grain Offering (2:11–16)

SUPPORTING IDEA: *God gave specific instructions on what to add to the grain offering.*

2:11–16. God gave several instructions of significance concerning grain offerings. First, the people were to offer nothing leavened (except during firstfruits). Second, they were to salt each offering. Salt had the power to preserve food and signified a pure sacrifice (see "Deeper Discoveries"). Previously God instructed those who brought an offering not to bring any unblemished animals from the flock or herd.

God allowed an offering of firstfruits to serve as a grain offering. For example, the people could burn the ears of corn before they ripened, then rub them out in a sieve. Wheat could be gathered in small bundles, then roasted. These toasted grains could then be brought as an offering.

Man has always had the tendency either to idolize or to become preoccupied with the things of this earth. In the grain God reminded the Israelites of the source of all material provision. These regulations remind us to reflect upon the rich significance of the elements of the offering and to bring it with a willing heart.

Ⓗ Instructions for Offerings from the Herd (3:1–5)

SUPPORTING IDEA: *The fellowship offering from the herd explored and explained.*

3:1–5. Sometimes called the "peace offering" or "thank offering," the **fellowship offering** highlights the feast portion of the offering (see 7:11–21). The offerer did not approach God to appease him with this offering, nor was he seeking restoration. He was simply seeking God. This offering reminded the worshipers of the covenant between them and God. Three kinds of fellowship offerings are distinguished: the thank offering (thanking God for blessings, often unexpected), the vow offering (in payment of a vow), and the freewill offering (as an expression of love to God).

If someone offered an **animal from the herd**, he could present an unblemished male or female to the Lord. He would then kill the animal at the front of the tent of meeting. The priests would collect some of the blood and sprinkle it on all sides of the altar. Several parts of the sacrifice were to be burned on the altar. The first part was the fat from the inner parts of the animal, then both kidneys, followed by the "covering," or "net" of the liver (not the liver itself). The priests would then burn these waste items on top of the burnt offering.

Ⅰ Instructions for Offerings from the Flock (3:6–17)

SUPPORTING IDEA: *The fellowship offering from the flock explored and explained.*

3:6–11. Both the worshiper and the priest were to follow the same procedures as they did for the herd animals. The only exception would be burning the tail of the sheep.

3:12–17. The final instructions relate to the goat being offered as a fellowship offering. These procedures duplicate the previous instructions. The goats were tended with the sheep by a single shepherd, but in separate groups. Their hair could be woven into cloth (Exod. 35:26), and they could be consumed along with their milk (Prov. 27:27; Deut. 14:4). Sometimes people would wear the skin of goats as a thick covering (Heb. 11:37).

Ⅱ Introduction to the Sin Offerings (4:1–2)

SUPPORTING IDEA: *God restores fellowship through the sin offering.*

4:1–2. God commanded sin offerings to be offered by individuals (4:1–2,27–35), priests (4:3–12), the aggregate community (4:13–21), and the leaders (4:22–26). No one was excluded from the possibility of violating one or more of God's commands, and all who did needed restoration. When one person or one of these groups became aware of any infraction, atonement must be provided. The nature of the sin offering taught the Israelites that no one is immune from guilt and no one is outside of God's grace.

The Lord introduced this offering to Moses, and he, in turn, offered instructions for the entire community. The "unintentional" sins included those committed without the knowledge of the offender and any noncapital offenses. The capital crimes, or sins committed with a "high hand," brought the death penalty (Num. 15:30–31). The sins covered by the sin offering included those brought on by carelessness, error, oversight, and those stemming from human weakness (as opposed to outright defiance).

Ⅹ The Sin Offering for the Priest (4:3–12)

SUPPORTING IDEA: *The priests who intercede for others also need to be cleansed.*

4:3–4. The mischief caused by virtually all sacerdotal schemes (priestly rule) cannot be easily calculated. The people soon set apart the priests as some special class of "untouchables" (untouched by sin), and such is simply not the case. Such a belief not only sets the people up for disillusionment, but it also raises the priests above the people—a luxury God did not allow even for kings (Deut. 17:20).

When a priest sinned, he brought **guilt on the people**. If his sin was not dealt with, he could lead the people astray. The guilty priest was to bring an unblemished bull to the front of the tent of meeting and to slaughter it there.

4:5–12. The officiating priest then carried some of the blood from this bull into the tent of meeting and sprinkled it **seven times** in front of the inner sanctuary curtain. He applied some of the blood on the horns of the incense altar, then poured the remaining blood on the base of the altar of burnt sacrifice.

The priest next removed all the fat and kidneys from the bull's insides as in the fellowship offering and burned them up on the altar. Finally, the priest removed the bull's carcass and burned it up in a sanctified place outside the camp.

L The Sin Offering for the Community (4:13–21)

SUPPORTING IDEA: *The entire congregation needed atonement.*

4:13–21. When the entire congregation sinned, perhaps without knowing it, they were to make atonement for it as soon as it was known. The elders represented the congregation in this offering. God required them to lay their hands on the young bull's head and then kill it. The remaining instructions followed previous instructions (vv. 3–12).

M The Sin Offering for the Leaders (4:22–26)

SUPPORTING IDEA: *Leaders needed forgiveness for sin.*

4:22–26. Moses probably refers here to the tribal leaders of Israel (see "Deeper Discoveries"). For his sin offering, God commanded him to bring an unblemished male goat and then lay his hand on its head and slaughter it. The priest would then perform the same ritual as in previous sin offerings.

N The Sin Offering for the Common Person (4:27–35)

SUPPORTING IDEA: *Each individual needed atonement and restoration to fellowship with God.*

4:27–35. The sin offering for the common Israelite consisted of an unblemished female goat or a lamb (v. 32). The person was to lay his hand on the goat's head and slaughter it as in other sin offerings. The remaining ritual followed the instructions for the male goat (vv. 22–26).

O Examples of Sins that Require a Sin Offering (5:1–4)

SUPPORTING IDEA: *Moses now cites some instances of offenses requiring the sin offering.*

5:1–4. Examples of sins of this sort included failure to testify and provide evidence in some official venue of community justice, touching anything ceremonially unclean or any species of human uncleanness, or taking a thoughtless oath.

P The Regulation for Such Offenses (5:5–19)

SUPPORTING IDEA: *God gives both offenders and priests specific instructions on restoration through the sin offering.*

5:5–10. God required the offender to confess his wrongdoing before offering a sacrifice. Once confession had been made, the sinner was to bring either a female lamb or goat (or, if he could not afford either of these, two doves or two young pigeons) to the priest. The priest then made **atonement for him for his sin.** In the case of the doves or pigeons, the priest partially severed the neck from the head, then sprinkled some of the blood against the side of the altar. The remaining blood he poured out at the base of the altar. The second pigeon or dove was then offered as a burnt offering.

5:11–13. Offenders who were unable to afford the bird offerings were allowed to offer a grain offering instead. This offering was to be **a tenth of an ephah of fine flour** without oil or incense. The priest then took the offering and burned a handful on the altar of burnt sacrifice. The priest was allowed to consume the remaining offering (as in the case of the grain offering).

Q General Directions for the Guilt Offering (5:14–19)

SUPPORTING IDEA: *Atonement for sins plus an accompanying payment must be made.*

Some sins also involved expiation of sins against God, but included violations against other people. Although the forgiveness was complete and a product of God's grace, God did require restitution in the case of sins against others. At times such reparations were quite costly to the offender.

5:14–19. Those sins that required the guilt offering fell under a separate category. Moses mentioned some examples. He first cited offenses related to tithes, offerings, firstfruits, and related violations. The offender was to bring **a ram from the flock,** one that approximated the value of the offense, and then to add one fifth to that. The priest would then offer the ram as a **guilt offering.**

The next case involved a person who committed a sin of commission (although not aware of it at the time of the violation). The offender would bring to the priest an unblemished ram from the flock. The priest would then offer the ram as a guilt offering before the Lord.

R Sins Against Others (6:1–7)

SUPPORTING IDEA: *The offender must make a guilt offering and compensate the victim of fraudulent practices.*

6:1–7. The practice of distortion or cheating one's neighbor was also an example of unfaithfulness to the Lord. The offender must first of all restore what he took or cheated his neighbor out of, plus add one-fifth of the value to it. The day of restoration coincided with the day of the guilt offering for this sin. God directed the offender to bring his guilt offering to the priest, who would make atonement for him.

The offering consisted of an unblemished **ram from the flock**. The payment to the offended party did *not* expiate the sin. That was done through God's gracious pardon through the guilt offering. The reparation was a damage award of sorts. With sin came consequences and subsequent damages.

Ⓢ The Burnt Offering (6:8–13)

SUPPORTING IDEA: *The procedure for handling the burnt offering is detailed.*

6:8–13. God required that the priests leave the burnt offering and accompanying fire on the altar the entire night. The priest would adorn himself properly and dispose of the ashes of the burnt offering in a sanctified place outside the camp.

Ⓣ The Grain Offering (6:14–23)

SUPPORTING IDEA: *The priest must follow a procedure for his own grain offering.*

6:14–18. For the grain offering, the priests would **bring it before the LORD, in front of the altar**. By far the largest portion of the grain offering went to Aaron and his sons. God directed them to eat it in the **courtyard of the Tent of Meeting**. When a priest properly partook of this holy offering, he himself became holy (or set apart, consecrated).

6:19–23. The priest's own grain offering was brought on the day of his ordination. He offered half of it in the morning and the other half in the evening. Since it was the priest's own offering, the succeeding son would prepare it, and all of it would be consumed on the altar.

Ⓤ The Sin Offering (6:24–30)

SUPPORTING IDEA: *The priest must follow procedures for eating the sin offering.*

6:24–30. This brief section supplements the general directions for the sin offering given in chapter 4. The priest could partake of the normal sin offerings in a holy place (the courtyard). He could not, however, eat the sin offering of either the high priest or the congregation when the blood was taken into the sanctuary. Just as in the grain offering, the priest would become holy when he touched the sin offering. If some of the blood of the sin offering should spill on the priest's garments, he was to wash them in a holy place.

Ⅴ Regulations for the Guilt Offering (7:1–10)

SUPPORTING IDEA: *Moses gives further directions governing the guilt offering.*

7:1–6. The law prescribed that the slaughtering of the guilt offering follow the same procedure as that used for the burnt offering (see 1:5). The blood would be sprinkled against all sides of the altar. The fat was to be burned on the altar (as in the fellowship and sin offerings) (3:9–11; 4:8–10). Any member of the priest's family could eat the meat portion of this offering, but this could be done only in a ceremonially clean place.

7:7–10. In the burnt offering the skin of the animal would fall to the priest (as payment for his duties; K&D, 322). Although this was probably true of the guilt and sin offerings as well, the skin of the peace offerings went to the owner of the animal.

When the grain offering was cooked in either an oven or a pan, the offering (other than the small portion burned on the altar) went to the officiating priest. Those grain offerings that were either dry or mixed with oil went to the entire family of the priest.

Ⅵ Supplemental Regulations for the Fellowship Offerings (7:11–21)

SUPPORTING IDEA: *God gives special procedures for eating and accompaniments to the fellowship offerings.*

7:11–15. When a person offered a fellowship offering to the Lord **as an expression of thankfulness**, he was to bring unleavened cakes and wafers mixed or spread with oil and cakes of flour mixed with oil in addition to the offering itself. These special items served as a contribution to the Lord and would fall to the officiating priest.

7:16–18. If the fellowship offering stemmed from a freewill vow offering, the sacrifice itself would be eaten on the day of the offering, but remaining portions could be eaten on the next day. Anything remaining on the third day was to be burned up.

7:19–21. The Lord now forbade anyone from consuming the flesh of an offering that came in contact with anything unclean. A person who was unclean could not eat any portion of a fellowship offering to the Lord on penalty of death.

Eating Fat or Blood (7:22–27)

SUPPORTING IDEA: *The Lord forbade eating unclean portions of the offerings.*

7:22–27. The owner or priest could eat only the meat portions of the sacrifices. But the fat or blood of a sacrifice could not be consumed by anyone. The blood of any animal or bird could never be eaten. God viewed this as the soul of the offering, the very medium through which atonement would be made (17:11). Violators would suffer the highest penalty (see "Deeper Discoveries").

The Priests' Portion (7:28–38)

SUPPORTING IDEA: *God stipulates which portions of the offerings went to the priests.*

7:28–38. We should remember that the sacrifices essentially belonged to the Lord and not to the priests. The sacrifices were offered for atonement, as expressions of thanksgiving, or as acknowledgments of the peace that existed between God and his people. They were, therefore, offerings to the Lord. God did apportion some of these sacrifices to sustain the priests and their families.

The priests would burn the fat of the sacrifices on the altar, but they were allowed to consume the breast of the wave offering (see "Deeper Discoveries") and the right thigh (or leg) portions. This later portion was sometimes called the "heave" offerings, or that which was "lifted off."

MAIN IDEA REVIEW: *God provided a way for the people to demonstrate total dependence on him and to offer up various sacrifices depicting a yielded life.*

III. CONCLUSION

A Little Boy's Sacrifice

In his book *Written in Blood*, Robert Coleman tells the story of a little boy whose sister needed a blood transfusion. The doctor had explained that she had the same disease the boy had recovered from two years earlier. Her only chance for recovery was a transfusion from someone who had previously conquered the disease. Since the two children had the same rare blood type, the boy was the ideal donor. "Would you give your blood to Mary?" the doctor asked. Johnny hesitated. His lower lip started to tremble. Then he smiled and said, "Sure, for my sister."

Soon the two children were wheeled into the hospital room—Mary, pale and thin; Johnny, robust and healthy. Neither spoke, but when they met, Johnny grinned. As the nurse inserted the needle into his arm, Johnny's smile faded. He watched the blood flow through the tube. With the ordeal almost over his shaky voice broke the silence. "Doctor, when do I die?" Only then did the doctor realize why Johnny had hesitated, why his lip had trembled when he had agreed to donate his blood. He had thought that giving his blood to his sister meant giving up his life.

If anyone knows what this child was feeling, it's God. In the opening chapters of Leviticus, God sets the stage for what will be the ultimate sacrifice in history, the death of Christ on the cross. It will be a sacrifice of love (the burnt offering); joy (the meal offering); peace (the peace offering); forgiveness (the sin offering); and reconciliation (the trespass offering). God made his decision in eternity past to fulfill all of these sacrifices in one event!

PRINCIPLES

- Everyone has a knowledge of God and is aware of having fallen short of God's standards.
- God alone can provide the means of making sinful human beings right with him.
- All that brings joy and fulfillment into life comes from God.
- God knows everything that is going on in your life and will use these things to grow you and honor him.
- The peace of God transcends our circumstances.
- God offers a cure for our alienation from him as well as our alienation from one another.

APPLICATIONS

- Bring unconfessed sins of commission and omission before God and accept his forgiveness through the death of his Son, Jesus Christ.
- Take some time to reflect on the price that Jesus has paid for you to be forgiven and cleansed from sin.
- Reflect on where you would be without God's forgiveness.
- Thank God for his forgiveness and love offered at so great a price.
- In light of God's forgiveness, what will you do to those people who have wronged you?

IV. LIFE APPLICATION

Caterpillar Confusion

Peter Perry tells the following story of a vacation he took on Orcas Island.

"I sat one morning looking out the picture window in our little cabin by the sea. On the deck was a picnic table, and on top of the table was a caterpillar. I watched him in the morning light as he crawled across the top of the table and reached the edge. He poked his head over the edge into the vast openness below the table's edge. He wavered about in confusion for a while. He then turned around and crawled in the other direction. Soon he reached the opposite edge of the table. Again he poked the front half of his body over the edge. His fear quickly returned him to the safety of the table. But there was no place to go. I walked outside, picked up a twig, and tried to coax the reluctant caterpillar onto the twig. But the caterpillar was afraid to walk onto the twig. He could not understand that I would then deliver him from the prison of this tabletop.

"Like that caterpillar, we desperately seek a way out of our confusion and lostness, but we are not sure whom to trust. God offers us a way out, but he is just so different from us and his universe is beyond our comprehension. So he sent us Jesus."

Only a human being who has struggled as we have struggled and felt pain as we have felt it can lead us to freedom and peace. Only through Jesus Christ can we love and trust God and accept the lovingkindness God offers to all who are lost and alone.

V. PRAYER

My Father, these chapters are so detailed yet so personal. I long for your love, joy, peace, and forgiveness, and these qualities are found only in complete surrender to you. Thank you for the provision of my Savior Jesus. Amen.

VI. DEEPER DISCOVERIES

A. The Significance of the Burnt Offering

The common English rendering for the Hebrew term, *olah*—burnt offering—does not really do it justice. The original describes something ascending (Soltau, 128). The Hebrew terms occurs about 280 times in the Old Testament (Unger, 275). The central thought of the whole burnt offering, where the entire animal was consumed on the altar, is the complete self-surrender of the offerer to God. Everything placed on the altar was for God alone. This one offering "perpetually kept burning" (Vos, 171), even as the child of God needs to offer his or her life to God continually (Rom. 12:1–2).

We also see Christ in the burnt offering. In his death he offered himself completely to God on our behalf. In doing so, he displayed a holy obedience in death by dying on the cross for our sins. Such an offering was acceptable to God.

We also see complete destruction of the animal in the burnt offering. In fact, Deuteronomy 13:16 describes an entire city destroyed as a "burnt offering." Clearly Moses spoke of complete destruction there. How do we reconcile this with the previous thought of life and self-dedication? If in one sense the animal represents the worshiper, we would think the worshiper would be destroyed. But really the opposite occurs—he lives. How so? By substitution, of course. The "entire dedication is accomplished by an entire destruction of the substitute, superimposed on an entire preservation or even resurrection of the worshiper" (Poythress, 48). In other words, the substitute died in order that the worshipers might live. Hence God portrays another picture of the multifaceted nature of Christ's life, work, and death.

B. Covenant of Salt

Because salt was included in food as a necessary ingredient and was also included in the sacrifices, a connection was drawn between salt and covenant-making. In the ancient Eastern world when one ate with another, they "shared salt together." Such fellowship over a meal sealed a friendship. Covenants were sometimes accompanied by meals, with salt as a fixture on such occasions. A lasting covenant could be confirmed with the salt, an apt symbol of an enduring agreement. The offerings themselves were to be a lasting ordinance in the nation of Israel (Num. 18:19), and David's own kingdom was a lasting kingdom, as illustrated by the covenant of salt (2 Chr. 13:5).

The covenant of salt spoke of the lasting fellowship between the worshiper and God, the one offended, who is now appeased by the sacrifice offered in faith. Such a relationship yielded all the benefits of fellowship and invited the blessing and protection of God upon faithful worshipers.

C. The Deeper Significance of the Fellowship Offering

The fellowship offering allowed the worshiper to partake of the offering. Hence the one making and consuming the offering somehow shared with God. The offering itself could describe the communion and sharing between worshiper and God and the mutual enjoyment of such fellowship. In the broadest and greatest sense, the offerer would thank God for salvation, since we can imagine no true blessing or sharing apart from this truth. In fact, sometimes these offerings accompanied a prayer for salvation or temporary deliverance (Judg. 20:26; 1 Sam. 13:9). We are reminded of the alienation between man and God through man's sin and how Christ's death brought peace (Rom. 5:1). Even now both Jew and Gentile alike enjoy Christ's benefits because his death brought peace between these former enemies (Eph. 2:11–18).

The peace offering or thank offering emphasizes partaking, since that is what the offerer does—partakes of his own sacrifice. Likewise the child of God does not simply collect upon a heavenly insurance policy that keeps him or her out of harm's way. These worshipers should long for and enjoy that peace which surpasses all understanding (Phil. 4:7), something unknown to those who are alienated from God (Isa. 57:21).

D. The Meaning of the Guilt Offering

Guilt offerings remind us that sin never comes without cost. Since God made man in his image (Gen. 1:26; 9:6), sins against man grieve God's heart and demand restitution. Of course, man cannot remove the guilt of his sin by merely paying a price, something that smacks of the medieval scandal of indulgences. But God did in some circumstances require repayment for damages done to one's neighbor. Thus atonement came through the appropriate offering, but it was finalized by payment to a wronged party (House, 130–31).

The New Testament writers echo this truth by relating the sincerity of the sinner's contrition to his or her willingness to make things right with friend or neighbor. God did not accept offerings when the person making the offering harbored hate or resentment against his neighbor (Matt. 5:23–24). Paul reminded his Galatian readers to restore erring believers in the spirit of gentleness and meekness (Gal. 6:1). These and other passages remind us that our relationships with others are dear to God's heart. The guilt offering proclaimed both the need for atonement through blood sacrifice for forgiveness and due restitution toward our brethren in Christ as a demonstration of the sincerity of our repentance.

E. The Sin Offering Versus the Guilt Offering

The guilt offering seemed to be a specialized kind of sin offering (Unger, 276). The sin offering was presented when an individual or community committed some sin, even without knowing it. Sin offerings highlighted the necessity of punishment in the payment of sin (Poythress, 47). The punishment was borne by the substituted animal instead of the offerer. The guilt offering included this general meaning but also added the feature of restitution for damages done. The guilt offering thus removed guilt (1 Sam. 6:3) and sought to restore community harmony.

Through sin the offender really commits two offenses. First, he transgresses the law of God. For this God prescribed the sin offering. No act of subsequence obedience could remedy the consequences of the sin except blood atonement. Second, through sinning the offender withholds the positive obedience he would have rendered if he had not sinned, something that could only be atoned for in blood offering. But what of the value-added feature of the trespass offering? Vos suggests the addition of the value makes restitution for the obedience withheld (171).

The guilt offering "is the only class of sacrifice with which the sacrificial death of Christ is directly connected in the Old Testament" (Vos, 171). In Isaiah 53:10 the predicted offering of Christ is designated a "guilt offering." Hence the Lord not only atones for the sins of the people but gives to God the obedience withheld by the people through sin.

Beyond this, the offering of Christ assimilated the meaning of all the offerings into one act, including the guilt offering (Isa. 53:10). The church should abandon any notion of future payment beyond death as a means of appeasing God or winning his favor. Christ's guilt offering covered forever any offense we committed or may commit against God or others.

F. What Is Wrong with Eating Blood?

The Bible condemns the practice of eating blood (Hb. *dam*). In Genesis 9:4 blood is equal to life, and God forbids the practice of consuming blood, a prohibition to last forever (Lev. 3:17). The Israelites had to drain blood from their sacrifices before offering them. They could not consume meat unless the blood had been drained from it (1 Sam. 14:33). Why did God prohibit this practice?

First, the notion of eating blood is repulsive to most people. Nature itself teaches us to avoid this. Consuming blood certainly has no hygienic value and is actually unhealthy.

The second reason was to separate Israel from the pagan nations and their pagan practices. The custom of eating blood probably prevailed in heathen nations as some form of religious ritual (Clippinger, *ISBE*, I, 526). God expected Israel to separate herself from the customs of the nations surrounding Canaan and to establish biblical religion.

But the chief reason for prohibiting this practice came from the meaning of blood itself. It stood for life in all its forms, and blood was considered the soul of the animal (Kiel, 327). God had set apart the animal in sacrifice to atone for man's sin (Lev. 17:11). Along with this thought comes the value God places on life itself. The Lord first mentions capital punishment in relation to the taking of human life (Gen. 9:6). We conclude therefore that the "high value of life as a gift from God led to the prohibition against eating 'blood'" (Unger, 31).

VII. TEACHING OUTLINE

A. INTRODUCTION

1. Lead Story: The Measure of Progress
2. Context: The central theme of the Bible is redemption. God is holy. Human beings are sinful. Only God can bridge the chasm between holiness and sin. As Israel draws close to God, she must take on family characteristics of God. The Lord had previously given Israel her divine purpose: becoming a holy nation (Exod. 19:6); now she takes steps in that direction. The trappings of the sanctuary and the intricate functions of the worship point to the divine attribute of holiness.
3. Transition: Five kinds of sacrifice are described in chapters 1–7 and their forms and purposes are given.

B. COMMENTARY

1. The Burnt Offering (1:1–2)

C. CONCLUSION: CATERPILLAR CONFUSION

VIII. ISSUES FOR DISCUSSION

1. Given the Old Testament model for sacrifices, what might you offer as a twenty-first-century definition of *sacrifice?* What sacrificial offerings have you given to the Lord this week?

2. When an offering is taken in your church, what is your initial feeling? Why? How does God feel about your reaction?

3. The root word for *fellowship* is a word that can be translated "peace" or "completeness." How would this relate to the fellowship offering of chapter 3?

4. What is your definition of *sin?* What is the difference between an intentional sin and an unintentional sin?

5. The Old Testament priests were never allowed to own any land and had to maintain a complete dependence upon God's faithfulness and provision. What lessons can a Christian learn from God's model?

Leviticus 8–10

A Look at the Priesthood

"*T*here is one proposition in which the whole matter, as it is relevant to human duty, may be summed up; that all our works, alike inward and outward, great and small, ought to be done in obedience to God."

William Ewart Gladstone

Leviticus 8–10

IN A NUTSHELL

*T*his section of Scripture offers a detailed account of the consecration of the priesthood and the dress code and guidelines these priests were to follow. As Aaron begins his life as a priest, he offers several offerings, following the strict guidelines ordained by God. The glory of God appears as he asks for God's blessing on the people. The section concludes with the sin of Nadab and Abihu, Aaron's sons, who learned how important it was to follow their instructions as priests very carefully.

A Look at the Priesthood

I. INTRODUCTION

Take a Stand

*M*artin Luther was excommunicated from the Roman Catholic Church, the flagship of Christianity at that time, because of his stand against abuses on the part of clergy and laity.

There are those times when people feel so strongly about something or someone that they will do whatever they can to maintain their support. One of my favorite stories is the story of David's "Mighty Men" (see 2 Sam. 23:13–17). David finds himself on the run and hiding out in a cave and says in passing, "You know, I sure would like a drink of water from the well in Bethlehem." Bethlehem was a long way off, and the Philistines were encamped there. But David had surrounded himself with men who were always ready to take their stand. They traveled to Bethlehem, fought off the Philistines while one of them dunked his canteen in the well, then ran back many miles to David's cave. When they arrived, David was moved by their devotion, but he poured out the canteen of his prized water as an offering to the Lord.

All of us need such "mighty men" who will come alongside us. I have a group of men who meet in my office each Tuesday night to study the Word of God and pray for me. The tired mother needs this support. When mom is at the end of her rope, it is encouraging to have another woman come alongside and say, "Been there, done that." A Sunday school teacher, exhausted from spending several hours in a packed classroom of nine-year-olds, needs the reminder of how great his or her contribution is to the kingdom. We all need our advocates.

God knows we needed a sacrifice for personal cleansing, and this is why we were given Leviticus 1–7. He also knew we would need an advocate, a priest if you will, to offer the sacrifices for us. This priesthood would help us learn about our sinful condition, our guilt, and our hostility toward God. Chapters 8–10 provide in great detail the attire and the role of the Old Testament priests whom God ordained and the result of the failure of some to follow God's guidelines.

II. COMMENTARY

A Look at the Priesthood

MAIN IDEA: *Aaron and his sons are solemnly set apart for priestly duties.*

A The Consecration of the Priests and Tabernacle (8:1–36)

SUPPORTING IDEA: *Even the priests are not made holy until sanctified by the Lord.*

8:1–4. God had given Moses precise instructions on the proper way to set apart the priests for their holy duties (see Exod. 29:1–36; 40:12–16). Moses now brought the priests and accompanying anointing items to the sanctuary entrance.

8:5–9. Moses reported to the congregation what the Lord showed him about the consecration of Aaron and his sons into the functioning priesthood. He first bathed the priests in water, then adorned Aaron with the tunic, robe, and ephod. Upon the ephod he placed the breastplate with the mysterious urim and thummim through which they would inquire of the Lord. Finally, he placed the turban with gold plate and sacred diadem on Aaron's head.

8:10–13. Moses next anointed the sanctuary with the special oil. He also sprinkled oil on the altar seven times and poured oil on Aaron's head. He then adorned Aaron's sons as he did Aaron and probably then anointed them also. Although Moses does not mention the anointing of Aaron's son, we may safely conclude he did, since this was expressly commanded in Exodus 28:41.

8:14–29. Aaron and his sons laid their hands on the bull for the sin offering after which Moses slaughtered the bull. He then applied some of the blood to the horns of the altar and poured the remaining blood out in the basin. He burned the fat and waste portions of the bull on the altar and burned the remaining parts of the carcass outside the camp.

Moses presented the ram for the burnt offering to Aaron and his sons, who laid their hands on its head as in the case of the sin offering. Moses then killed the ram and sprinkled its blood **against the altar on all sides**. After washing the inner parts, he offered the animal on the altar of burnt offering.

Moses then slaughtered the other ram, but this time he applied some of the blood to the lobe of Aaron's right ear, his right thumb, and the big toe of his right foot. The priest was to listen continually to the Word of God and perform his functions according to the precise instructions contained in God's Word. Hence his ear and thumb were consecrated for divine use.

Moses took an unleavened cake and wafer from the breadbasket and placed them on **the fat portions and on the right thigh**. Aaron and his sons waved them before the Lord; then Moses burned them all on the altar.

8:30–36. Finally, Moses took the anointing oil and some of the blood and sprinkled it on the heads and clothes of Aaron and his sons. He again specified where the sacred place for eating was—at the entrance to the tent of meeting. They were to burn the uneaten portions (see 7:17). They were to remain at the entrance for the seven days of their ordination.

God demonstrated to us in the consecration of Aaron and his sons that all true and acceptable service stems from divine grace. God alone makes us presentable to him and renders our deeds acceptable in his sight.

B The Beginning of the Priestly Ministry (9:1–24)

SUPPORTING IDEA: *With God's blessing the priests begin their ministry.*

At the end of God's previous instructions that closed the Book of Exodus, God blessed the making of the holy articles by filling the worship sanctuary with his holy presence (Exod. 40:34–35). Chapter 9 also shows the blessing that attended faithful service (see 9:23–24).

9:1–14. On the day following the period of ordination for Aaron and his sons, the priests along with the elders of Israel appeared before Moses. He directed the priests to take a bull and ram for their sin and burnt offerings and to offer them before the Lord. Then the Lord directed the Israelites to **take a male goat for a sin offering** and a calf and a lamb that were one year old to present as a burnt offering. An ox and a ram for a fellowship offering, plus a grain offering would follow the priest's own offering. Aaron obeyed the Lord's instructions and offered the sin and burnt offerings for himself, according to previous instructions.

9:15–21. Aaron then offered the sin, burnt, and grain offerings for the congregation. He killed the ox and ram for the people's fellowship offering **as Moses commanded**. Just as the priests needed divine forgiveness and reconciliation to serve God, the people needed the same to stand in fellowship with God. Although the Israelites were centuries removed from the garden of Eden, God was now providing the means by which they might be brought back to God. God had banished the inhabitants of the world from the garden, then placed cherubim and a flaming sword to guard it (Gen. 3:24). But now God was pointing man a way back to him.

9:22–24. The priests obeyed the word of the Lord as found in the precise instructions given by God to Moses, so God blessed their obedience with the highest favor of all—his presence. Moses and his older brother went into the tabernacle, probably to pray for God's blessing to attend their sacrifices. **When they came out, they blessed the people.** The Lord then sent fire out from his presence and consumed the sacrifice. The people then **shouted for joy and fell facedown**. Hence the people reacted to the divine manifestation far differently than they had before at the mountain of God (Exod. 20:18–19). They now began to rejoice at God's presence and the privilege of having him as the Lord of their nation.

C Priestly Sin and God's Judgment (10:1–20)

SUPPORTING IDEA: *Exceptional privileges carry grave responsibilities.*

10:1–11. Aaron's sons **Nadab and Abihu . . . offered unauthorized fire before the LORD**. The Lord, in turn, sent out a fire of judgment that consumed both sons. We are not certain what this involved, but we know God was not pleased with their actions. Some interpreters have speculated that due to the injunction against drinking wine while performing sacred service (10:9), Nadab and Abihu may have performed their duties while drunk. But the evidence for this is lacking. The point made by the narrative is that they offered incense that was not sanctioned by the word of the Lord.

Moses asked Aaron's cousins to carry the bodies of the dead priests outside the camp. Moses restricted the two remaining sons of Aaron, Eleazar and Ithamar, from becoming disheveled from grief, or God would judge the entire community. The priests stood not only as intercessors but also as teachers of **all the decrees the LORD has given them through Moses**. Teachers cannot successfully teach what they do not model before the people.

10:12–20. Moses directed Aaron and his other sons to eat the remaining grain offering in a holy place. Their wider family could eat the breast and right thigh portions as previously directed.

When Moses learned that the goat of the sin offering had been completely burned up and not eaten in a holy place, he became angry with Eleazar and Ithamar. Scholars have offered various interpretations of this passage. The most likely view is that Aaron felt that if God so judged his sons for their disobedience, how could he, Aaron, be qualified to eat the sin offering in a holy place? He felt ashamed and unworthy to eat it. Some feel that Aaron did not eat the sacrifice because he was too overwhelmed with grief at the death of his sons to eat at all.

MAIN IDEA REVIEW: *Aaron and his sons are solemnly set apart for priestly duties.*

III. CONCLUSION

The Fable of the Birds

The fable of the birds is a story directed back to the very beginning of creation. God had divided the light from the darkness and the land from the sea and had now created the animals. All of these creatures were wandering around seeking to understand what it meant to be alive. All except the birds! They were not happy and spent all their time complaining because God had given them a heavy burden that he had given no other animal: those awkward appendages on their shoulders. God must be punishing them for something, they thought. Why did they have to carry these things around, making it so tough to walk and enjoy life? "Why?" they asked. "Why us?"

Finally, two or three of the more adventurous birds began to move their appendages. They soon began to flutter them, and it wasn't long before they discovered that the things they had regarded as a burden actually made it possible for them to fly. And none of the other animals could fly like they could. The "heavy burden" turned out to be a beautiful gift.

Too many believers act like those silly birds. We sit back complaining about our lot in life and the heavy burden of God's call on our lives and see God's hand as a massive appendage of expectations holding us down. And guess what? This will continue to be a heavy burden until you open your eyes and discover that God's word and regulations are designed to be the wind of the Spirit to launch you to a new level of maturity in your walk with God. Aaron and his family were the beginning of a heritage of servants and priests, a group to which you belong as a Christian. Work? Yes! Burden? Start flapping! God has great things in store for those who are obedient to his call.

PRINCIPLES

- Human evil must be dealt with at its core.
- As God's people serve him, he often asks us to wait on him and trust him for the outcome.
- The results of our service and activities done in our personal priesthood are always to manifest the glory of God before others.
- Those whom God calls into leadership are subject to higher standards.

APPLICATIONS

- Trust God as you face the struggles of life.
- Assimilate the truths of Scripture deep within your heart.

- Serve God and others, knowing he has saved you and consecrated you for a purpose.
- Rest in the truth that God is more concerned with making changes in your life than keeping you comfortable.

IV. LIFE APPLICATION

The Carpenter's Tools

Imagine the Master Carpenter's tools holding a conference: Brother Hammer presides, but several suggest he leave the meeting because he is too noisy. Brother Hammer replies, "If I have to leave this shop, Brother Screw must go also. You have to turn him around and around again and again to get him to accomplish anything." Brother Screw then speaks up: "If you wish, I'll leave. But Brother Plane must leave as well. All of his work is on the surface. His efforts have no depth." To this, Brother Plane responds, "Brother Rule will also have to withdraw, for he is usually measuring folks as if he were the only one who is right." Brother Rule then complains about Brother Sandpaper: "He ought to leave too, because he's so rough and always rubbing people the wrong way."

And so goes the discord. In the midst of all this discussion, in walks the Carpenter of Nazareth. Putting on his apron, he goes to the bench to make a pulpit from which to proclaim the gospel. He uses Hammer, Screw, Plane, Rule, Sandpaper, and all the other tools. After the day's work, when the pulpit is finished, Brother Saw arises and remarks, "Brethren, I observe that all of us are workers together for the Lord."

As Christians we have a long list of titles: Christian, child of God, children of the light, salt of the earth, light of the world, believers, friends, brothers and sisters, sheep, saints, soldiers, witnesses, fellow citizens, the elect of God, ambassadors, dearly beloved, servants, disciples, followers, overcomers, victors, and stewards. One title we often neglect is *priest*. The Bible says that all of us belong to a royal priesthood and have all the rights and privileges of this title. But each priest must do his part and serve the King.

V. PRAYER

Lord God, you have ordained in eternity past that I am to serve you in a way that brings you honor and edifies your church. I will be careful to follow through on what you have called me to do and not to make the mistakes I have read about in this section of Leviticus. It is a high calling and a great honor to serve you, Lord. Thanks for the opportunity. Amen.

VI. DEEPER DISCOVERIES

A. Ordination

When the Lord set apart Aaron and the priests for service in the tabernacle, he consecrated them for special service. This service, if performed correctly and with the right heart, would receive God's blessing and approval. Sometimes this procedure is called "ordination." To ordain is to install someone formally in a capacity of service. The passage before us presents a clear and formal recognition of certain priests as special servants who perform sacred duties.

Elsewhere the Bible teaches a similar divine-human recognition of a special appointment for divine ministry, including Mark 3:14; John 15:16; 20:21–23; Acts 6:1–6; 13:1–3; 1 Timothy 4:14; and 2 Timothy 1:6. All of these references point to some kind of special appointment to spiritual service in either a formal or informal manner. Throughout church history people with ministry gifts have been recognized and duly set apart for service.

Some people today insist on formal ordination by an ecclesiastical body before any public service, while others condemn formal ordination as a creation of man without scriptural warrant. Perhaps the church should adopt a middle ground. The priests were set apart for special duties in a sacred ceremony, but such formality did not carry over into every ministry even in the Bible. Yet the church should have a mechanism that screens potential candidates for ministry followed by a public presentation.

B. The Old Testament Idea of "Blessing"

When the priests began their public ministry, Aaron lifted up his hands and "blessed" them. Then he and Moses entered the tent of meeting and soon came out and blessed the people once again. The idea of blessing can mean to give or grant favor, worship, praise; to greet; or to congratulate. Humans can bless God in homage and adoration. In this sense the term means "praise." The idea is prominent in Psalms 103 and 104:1.

Usually to bless means to grant prosperity or a sense of well-being. Usually God grants the blessings to faithful servants who do his will. In the Old Testament the nature or content of blessing often included material prosperity. The dynamics of the conflict surrounding Jacob who stole Esau's blessing involved this idea. God's blessings can result in increased fertility (Gen. 1:28), food, water, and health (Exod. 23:25). God grants blessing to those who obey him and do his will (Deut. 7:12–14; Ps. 1:1–3).

When one "blesses" a person of higher rank, especially in greeting or formal address, he speaks out of respect and acknowledgement of dignity (Gen. 47:7; 1 Kgs. 8:66). People may bless themselves too. In such cases they acknowledge a general state of happiness or well-being (Ps. 49:18), whether rightly or wrongly. When used in the passive sense, blessing indicated that a person received favor from God. Such a person considers himself happy or fortunate.

C. Wine, Alcohol, and the People of God

The Jews discouraged excessive wine-drinking. This passage from Leviticus forbids priests to consume wine during the course of their normal duties. Kings and those who decreed judgment on behalf of God and the nation also could not drink wine, lest they compromise sound judgment (Prov. 31:4–5; Isa. 28:7–8). Hence the Bible warns against drunkenness and overindulgence. The Bible warns against the abuse of wine and other alcoholic drinks and provides telling examples of the sad consequences of ignoring this warning (Gen. 9:20–24; 19:33–38).

The apostle Paul's lengthy discussion in Romans 14 on Christian liberty provided some insight for arriving at a sane position. He cautioned against offending weaker believers. Perhaps one may arrive at a position of total abstinence another way. Paul also cautioned against allowing anything to control him (1 Cor. 6:12) or furnish an occasion of stumbling in his brother's path (Rom. 14:21). Of course, the child of God would not want to offend someone whom he or she might be witnessing to either (2 Cor. 6:3). If drinking wine somehow diminished the testimony of a Christian, he or she should be prepared to give it up altogether.

The law of love should override any selfish considerations or demands for liberty. The church should also teach weaker Christians not to judge stronger Christians (see Rom. 14:3). The solution suggested by Paul suggests posits a desire for peace as the prevailing consideration when discussing such questions (Rom. 14:19). Somehow the church should seek a happy medium in such cases, especially where the Bible is silent.

VII. TEACHING OUTLINE

A. INTRODUCTION

1. Lead Story: Take a Stand
2. Context: God desires that his people come to him in worship. Since they are sinful and God is holy, they can approach him only through propitiating sacrifices offered by priests of God's choosing and in the manner God prescribed.
3. Transition: Both the priests (ch. 8) and the tabernacle (ch. 9) are to be dedicated to God. God disciplined Aaron's two older sons, Nadab

and Abihu, for offering incense in a manner that was not in accord with God's directions (ch. 10).

B. COMMENTARY
1. The Consecration of the Priests and Tabernacle (8:1–36)
2. The Beginning of the Priestly Ministry (9:1–24)
3. Priestly Sin and God's Judgment (10:1–20)

C. CONCLUSION: THE CARPENTER'S TOOLS

VIII. ISSUES FOR DISCUSSION

1. The priests were not given any land, and they were dependent on God's faithfulness. What lessons can a Christian learn from God's model?
2. Consecration is obviously a big deal in God's eyes, since he placed so much emphasis on the ceremonies of the priesthood. What does this truth mean in your life? How does God's priority of consecration relate to your career, home, and family?
3. The people of Israel needed a priest to stand in the gap between them and God. Do you? Why or why not?
4. God never wastes an example. What is the significance of the fireworks display at the conclusion of chapter 9? And why did God include the death of Aaron's sons? (Their example is important enough to be mentioned seven other times.)
5. Read Leviticus 10:10–11. Relate this passage to modern life and the impact of Christianity in the twenty-first century.

Leviticus 11–15

Establishing Your Compass

Leviticus 11–15

Quote

"*If* you love me, you will obey what I command."

John 14:15

IN A NUTSHELL

In order to set Israel apart from other nations as well as to protect the people from diseases, God gives instructions in chapter 11 about which animals are acceptable to eat and which animals are not acceptable to eat, as well as dealing with dead carcasses. In chapters 12–15, God gives Israel instructions on hygiene and health.

Establishing Your Compass

I. INTRODUCTION

Point True North

"*C*lose your eyes and point to true north." This is how I began my message. I was preaching a series of messages on marriage and wanted to begin the series with a call to understand why we were going to use the Bible solely as our standard for learning about this important institution. "Everyone of you today, trust me and close your eyes. On the count of three, I want you to keep your eyes closed and point to true north. Ready? 1–2–3." Up went the hands. Some knew the direction of north; most did not. Some even pointed straight up. "Now, keep pointing and open your eyes."

As the laughter subsided, I told my audience that some of them were right and some were wrong, especially those who were pointing up. Then I took a compass from my pocket and explained how I can know for sure the accuracy of their choices as compared to true north: "I have a compass. This compass is a standard that reveals the accuracy of your decision."

As we begin this study of Leviticus 11–15, we have already laid a foundation of our personal need for sacrifices and the priesthood. We have a better understanding of how Jesus Christ fulfilled both these roles in going to the cross for our sins and serving as our advocate in heaven at the right hand of the Father. This section of Leviticus provides us with a look at a compass for measuring what is true north, what is beneficial for God's people and what will be harmful.

II. COMMENTARY

Establishing Your Compass

> **MAIN IDEA:** *The Lord set apart certain food items as clean and unclean and also gave other instructions on the theme of cleanliness.*

Clean and Unclean Animals (11:1–23)

> **SUPPORTING IDEA:** *God restricts the eating of flesh to certain animals.*

11:1–8. The first group God addressed were land-dwelling animals. The Israelites could eat **any animal that has a split hoof completely divided and that chews the cud.** The camel had a split hoof, but it was not completely divided, so it was considered unclean. The coney (similar but not identical to the rabbit) and the rabbit did not split the hoof and were rendered unclean. They did "chew the cud" in some sense by appearance and some of their chewing movements. The language Moses used here was phenomenal language, or "that which appears to the observer." Still, they were unclean. The pig was unclean because it did not chew the cud.

11:9–12. The Israelites could eat fish with fins and scales (the external covering of the fish). The Lord stated this allowance positively, prohibiting all other **swarming things or among all the other living creatures in the water.**

11:13–19. Most of the unclean birds were those that were predators by nature or "birds of prey" that sought to devour the flesh of another animal. He mentioned twenty such creatures but did not mention the remaining suitable birds for consumption. The latter included sparrows, quail, pigeons, and doves.

11:20–23. The restrictions prohibited eating any flying insects that also walked on all fours. The clean insects suitable for eating were restricted to the locust family. The locusts were eaten by many ancient societies, including the Greeks.

B Touching Dead Carcasses (11:24–47)

SUPPORTING IDEA: *Touching or eating a dead carcass was defiling.*

11:24–28. If a person touched the dead body of any of the unclean land animals, he or she would be unclean until evening. That person would also have to wash his or her clothes. Animals that walked on all fours, such as the common cat or dog, were also forbidden. Anyone who came into physical contact with their dead bodies was rendered unclean.

11:29–38. The Lord next declared as unclean certain **animals that move about on the ground,** such as the **weasel, the rat,** and **any kind of great lizard.** Such animals were detestable, and God declared unclean anything that came into contact with their dead bodies. He did, however, make an exception for a **spring . . . or a cistern** into which a carcass fell—probably because water was scarce.

11:39–40. Even those who came into contact with the dead body of a clean animal were declared unclean, and they had to go through the same ritual as for unclean animals.

11:41–47. The closing verses of chapter 11 form a summary and reminder not to violate any of the restrictions given by the Lord. He made these regulations sacred and put the Israelites under solemn obligation to obey them. They were to **consecrate** themselves, or set themselves apart, by following these precepts exactly.

The Purifying Process for Mothers (12:1–8)

SUPPORTING IDEA: *Moses details the steps toward purification following childbirth.*

12:1–4. When a woman gave birth to a male child, she would be **unclean for seven days** much as she would during her normal menstrual period. The male child was to be circumcised on the eighth day following birth (see Gen. 17:12). Following the child's circumcision, the woman would remain unclean for another thirty-three days. During this time she was to refrain from going to the sanctuary or from touching any of the vessels or items set apart by God.

12:5. If the woman gave birth to a daughter, she would be initially unclean for two weeks, followed by another sixty-six days before she could be purified. We don't know exactly why God doubled the period of uncleanness for women who gave birth to daughters. Perhaps it's because these daughters themselves would one day give birth and experience similar uncleanness, or they would later experience menstrual uncleanness. Others have suggested the reason may be related to the male child receiving the circumcision rite and thereby becoming cleansed in a way the female child could not.

12:6–8. The order of the offerings seems reversed here, with the sin offering following the burnt offering. But the chief idea in this sort of cleansing was not sin, but the self-dedication reflected in the burnt offering. The idea in the sin offering was the effects sin brought into the world as seen in a painful and somewhat loathsome delivery process. The priest offered a lamb for the burnt offering and a young pigeon for the sin offering, after which the mother would be **ceremonially clean from her flow of blood.** She could substitute a pigeon or a dove for the lamb if she, like Mary, could not afford the lamb (see Luke 2:24).

Skin Diseases (13:1–46)

SUPPORTING IDEA: *Moses tells how to identify and treat skin diseases.*

13:1–17. When a noticeable and abnormal blemish appeared on a person's skin, he or she **must be brought to Aaron** (or the officiating priest) for examination. If the priest determined that the infection was more than a surface blemish, he would pronounce the person ceremonially unclean. If upon inspection the priest could not determine whether the person actually had a skin disease that required cleansing, he would isolate him or her for seven days, then inspect once again. If the person still had the spot but it had not spread, he or she was isolated another seven days. If the sore began to disappear, the priest would pronounce the person clean. But if it spread or the priest determined the person had contracted a skin disease, he would be declared unclean.

The person did not have a true infectious skin disease if the skin turned white as opposed to **raw**. The person in this case probably contracted psoriasis, a condition where reddish patches with white scales broke out on the scalp, back, and elbows. Or the noticeable but harmless disease could have been vitiligo, caused by deficient skin pigmentation. But when ulceration occurred ("raw" flesh), the priest pronounced the person unclean.

13:18–28. The priest would also inspect those with a burn or perhaps a scar. The criterion for determining whether the person had contracted an infectious skin disease was very much the same as in the earlier case. If the sore spread, the priest would pronounce the person unclean.

13:29–39. If a disease broke out on the scalp or beard area, the priest would inspect for infection. What determined this was both the degree of skin penetration, the amount of hair loss, and a color change in the hair to yellow. The condition may have indicated a form of ringworm, but if it involved significant hair loss, it indicated an infectious disease. White spots on the skin did not constitute uncleanness.

13:40–44. The priest would not pronounce someone unclean on the basis of baldness. But a bald man with a **reddish-white sore** erupting on his head did have an infectious disease.

13:45–46. The priest would treat the individual who was pronounced unclean by having him wear torn clothes, refrain from normal grooming, cover his or her lower face, and **cry out, "Unclean! Unclean!"** The unclean person, so identified, would keep unsuspecting persons from coming near to prevent spread of the disease.

Ⓔ Mildew (13:47–59)

SUPPORTING IDEA: *Moses explains how to identify and treat mildew that has affected various articles or materials.*

13:47–59. If someone suspected that material items, such as cloth or leather garments, had developed mildew, the priest would look for a greenish or reddish tint. If after seven days of isolation the mildew had spread, the priest declared the item unclean. He then had the items destroyed by burning. If the mildew did not spread, the items were washed, then inspected again. If the mildew had spread, the items were to be burned.

⊞ Purification from Skin Diseases and Mildew (14:1–57)

SUPPORTING IDEA: *Restoration is provided through ritual cleansing.*

14:1–7. When the victim of the disease reported for examination and cleansing, he was **brought to the priest**. The priest then examined him outside the congregation in a separate place. The priest then examined the person for any remnants of a skin disease, probably in the same manner prescribed by God in making the original diagnosis. If upon examination the priest determined that no disease remained, he ordered that **two live clean birds and some cedar wood, scarlet yarn and hyssop be brought**.

The priest directed that one bird be killed over fresh water, probably in such a way that the bird's blood would pour into the fresh water already in a **clay pot**. Then the priest took the live bird accompanied with some cedar wood, scarlet yarn, and hyssop, and dipped them into the blood of the bird. He sprinkled the victim seven times with the blood and let the live bird go free. Once pronounced clean, the leper was free to go.

14:8–32. The victim then must shave, bathe, wash his clothes, and remain away from his tent for seven days. He repeated this procedure on the seventh day, then he was declared clean. The next day he **must bring two male lambs and one ewe lamb a year old** plus a grain offering with oil so the priest could make a guilt and wave offering. The priest applied some of the blood of the guilt offering on the right earlobe, thumb, and big toe of the victim. He sprinkled some of the oil **seven times before the LORD**, and then applied it to the victim in the same manner as the blood. The priest then applied the remaining oil to the head of the victim.

Next, the priest took the ewe lamb and offered it as a sin offering followed by the remaining lamb for a burnt and grain offering to complete the cleansing.

If the victim did not have the means to supply the needed animals for the prescribed cleansing, he could substitute a pair of doves or pigeons for the sin and burnt offerings, and he could supply only a tenth of an ephah for the grain offering. The priest would then repeat the same procedure as in the typical case above.

14:33–57. The Lord gave the following procedure for houses infected with mildew. When the owner first noticed the mildew, he was to notify the officiating priest, who would come and examine the house. If he noticed the signs of mildewing (a green or red appearance), the person was required to vacate the house for seven days. The priest then inspected it again, and if the mildew had spread, he had the infected materials and stones removed and the walls scraped down. The owner then replaced the stones and plastered the house. If after a further inspection the mildew still spread, the priest would then order the house destroyed and torn down. If, however, the priest discovered that the mildew had not spread, he declared the house clean and free of contamination. He then followed the same ritual for cleansing the house as he did for the infected victim.

The Lord displayed both his grace and sovereignty in dealing with skin diseases and mildew. The infected beings and items needed cleansing. Man alone could not effect the cleansing. Instead, God cleansed him through a properly administered procedure that utilized both sacrifice and oil. The sacrifice displayed the need for removal of the stain and consequences of the disease by the blood of another. The oil symbolized the work of the Spirit in consecrating individuals and their possessions for the Lord's use.

G General Bodily Discharges (15:1–15)

SUPPORTING IDEA: *Moses discusses ceremonial defilement and cleansing from bodily discharges.*

15:1–3. We cannot tell with certainty what sort of discharge Moses spoke of in these opening verses. It was not necessarily a seminal emission, since this is addressed specifically beginning in verse 16. Was it hemorrhoids or a venereal sort of discharge? Keil supposed some sort of mucus discharge caused the flow from perhaps an infected urethra. Whatever it was, the Lord prescribed a specific ritual of cleansing for such cases.

15:4–12. The man with a discharge would defile whatever he touched. Verses 4–12 mention touching a person, bed, chair, or spitting on someone as examples of such infection. Those he came in contact with would have to wash themselves and remain unclean until evening. Even the clay pots he touched would have to be broken, and wooden articles were to be washed with water.

15:13–15. When the man recovered from the discharge, he was to wait seven days and wash both himself and his clothes. **On the eighth day** he was to bring two doves or pigeons to the front of the tent of meeting and give them to the presiding priest. The priest would then prepare one for a burnt offering and one for a sin offering.

H Seminal Emissions (15:16–18)

SUPPORTING IDEA: *Moses discusses ceremonial defilement and cleansing from seminal emissions.*

15:16–18. A man with a seminal emission defiled any garment or skin he came in contact with. This required that he wash anything he touched and bathe himself. He should not conclude that sexual intercourse itself defiled man, an act sanctioned by God within marriage. Perhaps what defiled the man had something to do with the manner of emission. When this occurred, both the man and woman must bathe themselves and remain unclean until evening.

▌ Female Discharges (15:19–33)

SUPPORTING IDEA: *Moses discusses ceremonial defilement and cleansing from female discharges.*

15:19–24. The woman who experienced her regular menstrual period would remain unclean for seven days. Anyone who touched her during her menstrual period would be unclean until evening. As in the case of the male discharge, anything that she came in contact with, such as a bed or chair, would defile others who touched it.

15:25–31. The woman who had a discharge beyond her normal period would remain unclean as long as it continued. Whoever touched anything she slept on or sat on would be unclean until evening. He would have to bathe himself and wash his clothes. The woman was to wait seven days, then follow the steps for purification described in verses 13–15.

15:32–33. The biblical writers do not always explain themselves in detail when prescribing such rituals, but we must remember that the Lord gave Israel the ceremonial law to observe as a covenant sign between them. The Old Testament unveiled a series of glorious and symbolic representations that foretold of some kind of future meaning. The writers did not always know the import of the words in every detail, nor did even angels (1 Pet. 1:10–12). But God prepared something better for us who gaze back with wonder through the eyes of the cross. We should never cease thanking God for his marvelous provision on our behalf and for the rich meaning he supplied us in the New Testament Scriptures.

MAIN IDEA REVIEW: *The Lord set apart certain food items as clean and unclean and also gave other instructions on the theme of cleanliness.*

III. CONCLUSION

God Knows It All

The guillemot is a small sea bird that lives on the rocky cliffs of the northern coastal regions. These birds flock together by the thousands in comparatively small areas. Because of the crowded conditions, hundreds of females lay their pear-shaped eggs side by side on a narrow ledge, in a long row. Since the eggs all look alike, it is incredible that a mother bird can identify those that belong to her. Yet studies show that she knows her own eggs so well that when even one is moved, she finds it and returns it to its original location.

Is that not remarkable? But let me tell you what is even more remarkable: We are told in the Bible that God knows it all! Everything! He is so well acquainted with his flock that he knows the thoughts and the desires of our hearts and our motives. He knows and understands the pain we have in life. He knows when we have been moved to where we should be in life and is ready to pick us up and bring us back into the center of his will. Because he does know everything, doesn't it make sense to follow the compass for living that he gives to his people?

PRINCIPLES

- Leaders have a high calling to protect the people under their care.
- God has the power to heal or change even the most vile diseases or situations.
- God knows what is best for his people.

APPLICATIONS

- Seek to fulfill God's will for your life, knowing he has established guidelines for our lives.
- Be willing to listen carefully and respond in a godly way to the admonishment and encouragement of others.
- Be patient with the leaders of your church when they must make a decision or judgment.
- Seek personal purity in your life so you may remain all that God intended you to be.

IV. LIFE APPLICATION

Faking It

Roy Robertson is a name that few people recognize. But God had to get his attention and point him back to true north. He wrote the following account of a life-changing experience.

"My ship, the *West Virginia,* was docked at Pearl Harbor on the evening of December 6, 1941. A couple of the fellows and I left the ship that night and attended a Bible study. About fifteen sailors sat in a circle on the floor. The leader asked us to each recite our favorite Scripture verse. In turn each sailor shared a verse. I grew up in a Christian home, went to church three times a week, but I sat there terrified. I couldn't recall a single verse. Finally, I remembered one verse—John 3:16. I silently rehearsed it in my mind. The spotlight of attention grew closer as each sailor took his turn. It was up to the fellow next to me. He recited John 3:16. He took my verse! As he commented on it I sat there in stunned humiliation. In a few moments everyone would know that I could not recall from memory even a single verse. Later that night I went to bed thinking, 'Robertson, you're a fake.'

"At 7:55 the next morning I was awakened by the ship alarm ordering us to battle stations. Three hundred and sixty planes of the Japanese Imperial Fleet were attacking our ship and the other military installations. My crew and I raced to our machine gun emplacement, but all we had was practice ammunition. So, for the first fifteen minutes of the two-hour battle, we only fired blanks hoping to scare the Japanese airplanes. As I stood there firing fake ammunition I thought, 'Robertson, this has been how your whole life has been—firing blanks for Christ.' I made up my mind as Japanese bullets slammed into our ship, 'If I escape with my life, I will get more serious about following Jesus.'"

Do you recognize the name yet? Roy Robertson went on to help Dawson Trotman found the Navigators. He also was involved in the follow-up ministry for the 1990 Billy Graham Crusade in Hong Kong that saw more people hear the gospel at one time than any other meeting in history. But all of this happened after God reminded him what compass to follow.

The quickest way to determine if you are faking it is by personal obedience. Are you pretending? Do you read God's Word and then fail to apply the truths you receive? Are you faking it? Have you been told over and over through God's still voice to get back on track, and yet you live your life in denial and defy everything God is telling you to do? Then you too will only fire blanks when it comes to making a difference with your life. Make the decision: "If God said it, I believe it and will follow! No more pretending while the enemy has the upper hand."

V. PRAYER

My omniscient Father, how many times have I thought I knew everything I needed only to fall into the trap of pride? How many times do I need to be reminded that you are God and I am not? I am going to try to cut down on the number of reminders you will need to bring. Thanks for your patience in my life. Amen.

VI. DEEPER DISCOVERIES

A. How Did God Determine What Was Unclean?

God did not fully detail the reasons why certain foods were unclean to him, although he did give us some hints. Not all matters declared unclean by God were for sanitary reasons. Many of the stipulations he made regarding food or some of the skin diseases did indeed conform to common laws of health. But that did not constitute the essence of such laws. Some suppose the clean and unclean designations convey allegorical truth (e.g., "the clean animals represent the Jews, and the unclean the Gentiles"), but such speculation does not help. Other suggestions include the animals used by pagan nations in cultic worship, their repulsive looks or habits. The pig was indeed used in some pagan religious ceremonies, and God commanded that it not be used in sacrifice (Isa. 66:17). But the bull was also used in pagan ceremonies, yet God allowed its use in sacrifice. Some scholars attribute an animal's uncleanness to its habit of wandering in the desert waste places, long thought to be the habitation of unclean spirits.

The nations that bordered Israel did offer some of these animals in their rituals and ate them during their celebrations. Perhaps God sought to draw some strict ritual boundaries in order to discourage the Israelites from attending these gatherings. While we can't be certain of all the reasons why God designated some animals clean and some unclean, we do know the reasons came from a holy desire on God's part to keep his people clean and unspotted from the world.

B. Ceremonial Uncleanness and Childbirth

Why did God have the mother who had given birth wait for a time before entering the sanctuary? Another way of putting this is that she had to wait a certain amount of time before resuming her normal duties (House, 137). Both she and the baby needed time to rest and to recover physically from the birthing process. Perhaps the law was intended to separate childbirth from the sanctuary lest some link the process with fertility rites, as was common with some Canaanite groups.

These laws set Israel apart from the nations as a people intimately related to their God. If followed, these laws accorded Israel certain benefits, including hygienic, health, rest, etc. When Israel observed these laws, she protected herself from the intrusion of polytheistic teachings and practices that would have spelled her doom. Through the purifying process the "participant is made aware of his basic alienation from God, and he knows that he must prepare himself to take advantage of the opportunities to approach God. In so responding he demonstrates his obedience to God and discovers the meaning of the confession that Yahweh is the Holy One of Israel" (Hartley, "Clean and Unclean," *ISBE*, I, 721).

C. The Life of the Leper in Bible Times

Leprosy remains one of the most feared and dreaded diseases of our time. When we see pictures of people or communities infected with the disease, we naturally draw back in horror. Just think how the victim must feel. He senses not only the personal discomfort and loneliness that comes from the condition but the ostracism of those who look on in horror. From the Bible we can catch a glimpse of how the leper might have lived and how the community dealt with this disease.

The careful reader will note that Leviticus 13–14 did not prescribe a treatment but dealt with symptoms of the disease, procedures to take when determining whether the healing occurred, then prescribed the proper offerings associated with cleansing from the disease. For the most part, the lepers in Israel faced community ostracism, and the common people long associated leprosy with God's disfavor. Hebrews 13:13 alluded to bearing shame "outside the camp," which was a probable reference to the leper. We have evidence that Israel evolved from the practice of individual isolation prescribed by God (Lev. 13:45–46) to establishing parallel communities of sorts where lepers would dwell together but not within Israel's environs. In 2 Kings 7:3–10, four lepers seemed to dwell outside the gates of the city (see also Luke 17:12).

The new dispensation witnessed the kingdom of God come in power to demonstrate God's designs to defeat disease in general, including the repulsive leprosy (see Matt. 8:1–4; Mark 1:40–45; Luke 5:12–14; 17:11–17). Although it was not God's purpose to eliminate disease entirely at this time, he did demonstrate his power over disease. The consequences of Jesus' mission would indeed one day banish disease from the universe.

As with Israel, most nations relied on ostracism or quarantine to control the disease, a condition not as contagious as most feared. In medieval times, some constructed large "leprosariums" in order to care for and isolate those who were infected with leprosy. Not until modern times did the fear associated with the disease ease. Leprosy was always viewed as a dreaded fate that wrought fear in people. In medieval times, a priest would sometimes perform a burial reading over the leper before he was ostracized.

Today the church needs to reach out to those who have fallen victim to all kinds of diseases, including those, such as AIDS, that naturally ostracize the victims from the community. We also need to remind the sick and diseased that Jesus Christ came to relieve suffering of all kinds. Trust in him leads to peace, eternal life, and the promise of perpetual health in the kingdom of God.

VII. TEACHING OUTLINE

A. INTRODUCTION

1. Lead Story: Point True North

2. Context: God redeemed Israel from slavery in Egypt. As his people, Israel was to be holy because God is holy. They were to be different from other people.

3. Transition: Chapters 11–15 contain a series of "cleanness" prescriptions, standards for the separations of God's people from impurity.

B. COMMENTARY

1. Clean and Unclean Animals (11:1–23)
2. Touching Dead Carcasses (11:24–47)
3. The Purifying Process for Mothers (12:1–8)
4. Skin Diseases (13:1–46)
5. Mildew (13:47–59)
6. Purification from Skin Diseases and Mildew (14:1–57)
7. General Bodily Discharges (15:1–15)
8. Seminal Emissions (15:16–18)
9. Female Discharges (15:19–33)

C. CONCLUSION: FAKING IT

VIII. ISSUES FOR DISCUSSION

1. God has always promised to honor obedience. Some will read this section of Leviticus and wonder why God needed these guidelines. But God promised to honor those who follow through in obedience. Read Daniel 1 and discuss how these regulations were used by God to bring strength and victory.

2. Think about the people of Israel living temporarily in the wilderness. Why do you think the discussion on infectious diseases would have been important to them? What could have been the ramifications if God had never given them those regulations?

3. How do you think the priests felt when they were given their responsibilities in this section? What elements of leadership do you think they would have to practice in order to care for the people?

4. Knowing God can heal a disease and expecting him to heal the disease are two different things. Given the expectation for isolation of some who were very ill, do you think the people ever expected them to return to the camp? When they did return, what do you think may have been the initial reaction of the rest of the people?

5. What rules on personal hygiene can a student of the Bible learn from Leviticus 15? Are there any spiritual lessons you may have picked up as you studied this chapter?

Leviticus 16

Understanding the Atonement

"*I*n the cross, God descends to bear in his own heart the sins of the world. In Jesus, he atones at unimaginable cost to himself."

Woodrow A. Grier

Leviticus 16

 I N   A   N U T S H E L L

*A*lthough not mentioned as the Day of Atonement until Leviticus 23:27, Leviticus 16 provides insight into the substitutionary atonement God offers for the sins of his people and the subsequent removal of their guilt. The symbolism in this single chapter takes on even greater meaning when understood through the life and death of Jesus Christ as the ultimate sacrifice for the sins of all mankind.

Understanding the Atonement

I. INTRODUCTION

The Divine Scapegoat

*O*n January 28, 1968, the North Korean navy captured Commander Lloyd M. Bucher's ship, the *USS Pueblo,* an old coastal freighter used by the navy to gather intelligence. The North Koreans held Bucher and eighty-two officers and crew for eleven months. His captors tortured Bucher, and he finally signed a false confession to spying inside Korean waters. After they were released, a court of inquiry recommended that Bucher be court-martialed for surrendering the ship without firing a shot—the first such surrender in peacetime for the navy—and for failing to destroy all secret documents and equipment before capture. The navy vetoed the court-martial, saying Bucher had suffered enough. In 1973, seventy-eight of the *Pueblo* crew were decorated for heroism, but Bucher wasn't. His last years in the navy were spent in out-of-the-way jobs in quiet obscurity until his retirement in 1974.

Bucher believes that the navy made him a "scapegoat" to hide its own failure to answer Bucher's radio appeals for help when the North Korean gunboats attacked. He commented in an interview, "There was no way they were going to court-martial me. It would have brought out so many people who were implicated because of their involvement and responsibility."

The Christian concept of a "scapegoat" and atonement comes from the Jewish Day of Atonement, where the sacrifice prescribed for this holy day required two goats. One goat was killed in the usual manner. The second goat was not killed but was led away outside the camp of the Israelites. Sin was confessed over this goat, and he was set free in order to portray the removal of sin from God's presence. This concept is both precious and vital to our understanding of the Lord Jesus Christ's death as not only covering our sins, but also taking them away. Let's learn where the original instruction came from and God's guidelines for this symbolism.

II. COMMENTARY

Understanding the Atonement

> **MAIN IDEA:** *God provides a solution for the sin of Israel.*

A Preparation for the Day of Atonement (16:1–10)

> **SUPPORTING IDEA:** *God prepares the priests to offer the atoning sacrifice.*

16:1–2. The most holy place was God's sacred dwelling place. Neither Aaron nor his sons were to enter that place except once a year on the Day of Atonement. Verse 1 reminded Aaron of the sin of his two deceased sons when they did not perform their priestly functions according to the prescribed ritual given by God (see comments on ch. 10).

16:3–5. Items that were necessary to observe this day included a young bull for a sin offering, a ram for a burnt offering, special garments to wear for the ceremony, water to bathe with, and two goats—one for a sin offering and one that would serve as a "scapegoat."

16:6–10. Aaron was to offer the bull as a sin offering for himself. God was quick to remind Aaron and all who would follow in his steps that they themselves were sinners in need of forgiveness and grace. The two goats were placed at the door of the tent of meeting where Aaron would cast lots to determine which goat would serve what purpose. One lot fell to **the LORD**, and would be offered as the sin offering, and one fell to **the scapegoat** that would eventually flee to the desert.

B The Ceremony (16:11–28)

> **SUPPORTING IDEA:** *The Lord provided specific directions to Aaron how to perform this ceremony.*

16:11–14. The Lord directed Aaron to offer the bull **to make atonement for himself and his household**. Three times Aaron would enter the most holy place during this ceremony. The first time he would bring burning coals from the altar to the incense altar upon which he would burn incense. The incense would create a sort of smoke screen that would shield Aaron from God's glory and so prevent his death. Aaron then would sprinkle some of the blood of the sin offering on and in front of the atonement cover.

16:15–19. The Lord next directed Aaron to offer a sin offering for the congregation, which would form his third entrance into the holy of holies. Moses notes that the sanctuary itself, that had somehow been contaminated with Israel's sins, would be cleansed with the blood of the sin offering. The altar itself needed to be cleansed by atonement, and Aaron did so by applying some of the bull's and goat's blood on the horns of the altar. After this he would sprinkle blood on it **seven times to cleanse it and to consecrate it from the uncleanness of the Israelites**.

16:20–22. Following the consecration of the tent of meeting and altar, Aaron was to present the remaining goat, the live one, and lay both hands on its head. Then he would **confess over it all the wickedness and rebellion of the Israelites**. In this one act God would transfer the guilt of the nation to the goat, which would "escape" to the desert by the hands of an appointed man.

16:23–28. Aaron concluded the ceremony by taking off his linen garments, bathing, putting on his priestly garments, and then offering the two remaining rams for burnt offerings for himself and the congregation. The fat of the sin offering was to be consumed on the altar, and the man who escorted the live goat into the desert was to wash himself and his clothes before entering the congregation. The hides and inner contents of the sin offering animals were to be burned up outside the camp. The man appointed to this latter task was also to bathe and wash himself before coming back into the camp.

Formal Institution of the Day of Atonement (16:29–34)

SUPPORTING IDEA: *God set apart this day as a permanent statute in Israel.*

16:29–34. During this sacred ceremony, the Israelites were to deny themselves, or "afflict themselves," a general expression for humiliation that probably included fasting. Sometimes they would use sackcloth and ashes for this purpose (Ps. 35:13). During this time they were to observe a Sabbath and do no regular work.

MAIN IDEA REVIEW: *God provides a solution for the sin of Israel.*

III. CONCLUSION

So You've Sinned Again!

A farmer owned a very beautiful horse of which he was very proud. One day he rode him into town and tied the animal to the hitching post in front of the general store. Two thieves, passing through town, spied the handsome horse and decided to steal it. They also decided on a clever strategy to carry out their plan. One of them untied the horse and rode swiftly away. The other remained by the post. When the farmer emerged from the store and saw that his horse was gone, he was about to shout for help when the conspirator walked up to him. In a soft, low tone he said, "Sir, I am your horse. Years ago I sinned, and for my sins I was punished. In order to atone for my guilt, I was changed into a horse. Today my sentence is over, and I can be released if you will be so kind." The farmer was dumbfounded yet touched by the story. So he sent the man away wishing him luck in his new life.

Several weeks later the farmer went to a fair in a neighboring town. Great was his surprise to see his own horse for sale there. After gazing long at the animal to make sure that his own eyes did not deceive him, he walked over and whispered in the horse's ear, "So you've sinned again!"

People sin, and they need forgiveness and atonement for their sin. The Day of Atonement offered the people of Israel a once-a-year opportunity for forgiveness and freedom from the weight of their guilt. The priests were extremely busy. They never rested because there were always sacrifices to be offered. After all, people sin! But the perfect sacrifice of Jesus Christ, God's perfect Lamb of God, provides us with a once-for-all sacrifice with perpetual atonement for all who appropriate his finished work on the cross.

PRINCIPLES

- God has always provided for the forgiveness of sin and the removal of guilt.
- God is holy, and he requires repentance and confession of those who come into his presence.
- The forgiveness offered by God came at a high price.
- God's forgiveness brings his peace and rest.

APPLICATIONS

- Only through the substitutionary death of Christ will forgiveness and freedom from guilt become realities in your life.
- One of Satan's attacks in a person's life is in the area of doubting God's forgiveness. During these attacks, reflect on God's faithfulness through his atonement.
- When feelings of doubt and fear arise, turn your eyes to God.

IV. LIFE APPLICATION

The Lesson of the Toy Boat

A father and son had worked hard to build a toy sailboat. It was a labor of love—love for each other and for the thing they were creating. Finally, it was time for the toy boat's first sailing experience. Traveling to a nearby lake, the father tied a strong cord to the boat's stern to keep it from sailing too far. The boat performed beautifully until a motorboat crossing the lake cut the string, and the sailboat drifted out of sight. Attempts to find it were fruitless, and both father and son wept over their loss.

A few weeks later the boy passed his favorite toy store and was amazed to see his sailboat in the window. He ran inside to claim the boat, telling the owner about his experience on the lake. The store owner said he had found the boat while on a fishing trip. Then he said, "You may be its maker, but as its finder, I am the legal owner. You may have it back—for fifty dollars." Since the sailboat was so precious to him, the boy set about earning the money to buy it back. Months later he joyfully walked into the toy store and handed the owner fifty dollars. As he left the store, he held the boat up to the sunlight. "I made you, but I lost you," he said. "Now I've bought you back. That makes you twice mine, and twice mine is mine forever."

The atoning work of Jesus Christ on the cross makes you twice his if you have appropriated the finished work of Calvary to your life. You once were lost but now are found. You were once sailing on a lake of destruction away from your Creator, but now he has purchased you back. This is the picture of the Day of Atonement in the Old Testament and the death, burial, and resurrection of Jesus Christ in the New Testament.

V. PRAYER

Lord, acknowledge the gift you have provided for me, a gift of continual forgiveness and acceptance. I know that when I invited Jesus into my life, I was transferred from the kingdom of darkness to the kingdom of light. Help me to keep my sails in the wind of your Spirit's leading, steering toward your will for my life. Amen.

VI. DEEPER DISCOVERIES

A. Casting Lots and the Will of God

The term *lot* in the Bible comes from the Hebrew word *goral*, which comes from the Semitic root *grl*, meaning "stony" or "stony ground" (Aune, "Lots," *ISBE*). The Hebrew term *pur* was a direct transliteration of the Akkadian term for "lot." These stones originally were probably small stones or objects kept in a container and then shaken until one fell out. They were thought somehow to reveal the will of God.

In the Old Testament God prohibited some methods of divination (Deut. 18:10), but he never forbade casting lots. Proverbs 16:33 provided the biblical foundation for the function of the lot: "The lot is cast into the lap, but its every decision is from the LORD." Joshua casts lots to decide how to allocate the land of Canaan (Josh. 18:8–10). Sometimes lots were cast to narrow a choice until a final lot was cast (see Josh. 7:16–18, where lots were probably used, and 1 Sam. 10:20–21). The priests in Nehemiah's day cast lots to decide on when to bring contributions (Neh. 10:34), as did David when deciding the divisions of priests (1 Chr. 24:5).

The New Testament mentions this practice on several occasions. The soldiers cast lots to decide who would get Jesus' clothes (Matt. 27:35; Mark 15:24). The apostles chose Matthias over Barnabas by means of casting lots (Acts 1:26).

Did God honor and even encourage such a practice as a means of determining his will? It seems clearly he did, at times, do just that. We no longer have sufficient warrant to suppose God still makes his will known in this manner, particularly since we now possess all things for life and godliness (2 Pet. 1:3) and have the greater security of a completed canon of Scripture (2 Tim. 3:16–17). The child of God who lives under the new covenant must first consult the Word of God to learn the moral will of God (1 Thess. 4:3), then trust God for his clear leading in all situations.

The Christian should not resort to man-made devices or bewitching "Gideon's fleeces" in attempts to determine the divine will. Instead, he or she should follow the moral will of God contained in Scripture, pray without ceasing for God's blessing and guidance in decision-making, then make wise, Scripture-based decisions that honor God.

B. Fasting in Israel

Fasting refers to abstinence from food for a prescribed period of time or the period itself during which it takes place. Sometimes fasts were involuntary when no food could be found or conveniently provided (2 Cor. 6:5). But usually the Bible speaks of fasting from religious motives. The Bible contains many references to fasting, but it prescribes only one fast—on the Day of Atonement. On this day the Israelites were to "deny" themselves, generally thought to refer to fasting (Lev. 16:29). Although the Bible does not prescribe any other days of official fasting, it did control the self-imposed fasts of the nation and individuals (Zech. 8:18–19). One danger was the tendency to slip into hypocrisy, a temptation that both the Old and New Testaments warned against (Zech. 7:4–7; Matt. 6:16–18).

In general, people fasted to show humility or sorrow and to seek God's face (Isa. 58:3–4). David fasted when his child was deathly ill (2 Sam. 12:16–23). Sometimes people would observe fasts by wearing sackcloth and putting ashes on their heads. Fasts were sometimes proclaimed during times of national crisis (Jer. 36:9; Joel 1:14). Anna the prophetess served God with fasting (Luke 2:37) as did John the Baptist's disciples (Matt. 9:14–15).

VII. TEACHING OUTLINE

A. INTRODUCTION

1. Lead Story: The Divine Scapegoat
2. Context: The writer of Hebrews states a biblical principle that runs through both the Old Testament and the New Testament: "Without the shedding of blood there is no forgiveness" (Heb. 9:22).
3. Transition: The most important day in the Hebrew calendar was the Day of Atonement. The present chapter, which details the events of this day, forms a natural transition between the two major sections of Leviticus: access to God (chs. 1–16) and living for God (chs. 17–27).

B. COMMENTARY

1. Preparation for the Day of Atonement (16:1–10)
2. The Ceremony (16:11–28)
3. Formal Institution of the Day of Atonement (16:29–34)

C. CONCLUSION: THE LESSON OF THE TOY BOAT

VIII. ISSUES FOR DISCUSSION

1. As you watch the news and read the newspaper, describe the condition of our world. Why is this chapter so important and so relevant to this condition?
2. The Day of Atonement was a once-a-year ritual. How important was this day in the lives of the Israelites? How important is Christ's daily forgiveness and cleansing in your life?
3. List the difference between this verse and the principle of Leviticus 16.

Leviticus 17–20

Great Expectations

Leviticus 17–20

Quote

"*O*bedience must be the struggle and desire of our life. Obedience, not hard and forced, but ready, loving and spontaneous; the doing of duty, not merely that duty may be done, but that the soul in doing it may become capable of receiving and uttering God."

Phillip Brooks

IN A NUTSHELL

*E*very great truth in Scripture points either directly or indirectly to Christ, God's source of power and true living for his people. Upon recognizing God's provision in Christ, our attention must be directed at living a life that honors God and meets the expectations he has for his followers. Chapters 17–20 unwrap some of God's expectations on food, intimacy, authority, and various situations of life.

Great Expectations

I. INTRODUCTION

Who Are the Phonies?

I have never been one to purchase products or services being marketed on the television. I have always taught my children how things appear so much nicer when advertised aggressively by the right spokesperson. But on one occasion I was taken! Being your average male, I was "clicking" around the channels, watching my usual nine shows, when there it was—the most magnificent telescope I had ever set eyes on. Included in the package were the multi-balancing stand, an external focusing device, and special cleaning wipes for the lenses. Galileo would have been proud as I dialed the phone and ordered this thirty-dollar steal. Two weeks later I came home to discover a small box on the front steps of my home. No way—couldn't be! I had been taken. This telescope was not the real deal; it was a phony.

We now arrive at the second section of instructions in Leviticus, a section designed to reveal the phonies. God's instruction to his people is unfolding great truths that will take on greater significance and clarity when we study the New Testament. All the ceremonies and rituals were designed to prepare the world for the arrival of Jesus Christ, God's only Son. As we approach chapters 17–20, we begin to recognize what God's expectations will be for his people—expectations to reveal "who are the phonies."

II. COMMENTARY

Great Expectations

> **MAIN IDEA:** *Instructions are given on offering and eating sacrifices, maintaining sexual purity, relating to God and others, and forsaking all false gods.*

The Place of Sacrifice (17:1–9)

> **SUPPORTING IDEA:** *The Lord carefully prescribed the place where he would accept sacrifices.*

17:1–2. Most of this chapter relates to laymen who offered sacrifices. Because the entire sacrificial system was specifically laid out by God in rich detail, and because its numerous features carried such profound theological and typical significance, the people of Israel were to pay strict attention to the various procedures associated with their sacrifices.

17:3–9. Perhaps the entire scope of the present section dealt with animals that were designated to be slaughtered as sacrifices. Some scholars have concluded that these sacrifices referred not to regular sacrifices as explained in the first seven chapters of this book but to any killing of animals. If this were the case, then the Law of Moses did not allow the killing of any animal commonly used in sacrifice. The upshot of this law is that "no secular slaughter is permitted" (Wenham, 241). See below for restrictions on hunting game. If an Israelite desired to eat meat, he must first designate it as an offering to the Lord. The law would discourage open sacrifices, sacrificing to false gods, and channel all sacrifices through the priestly system as ordained by God. The penalty for breaking this law was death.

B Eating Blood (17:10–12)

SUPPORTING IDEA: *The Lord prohibited the Israelites from consuming blood.*

17:10–12. From antiquity the Lord commanded his people not to eat blood (Gen. 9:4). The practice of eating blood may have been a common practice among the heathen nations. The restriction made sense once the significance of blood was explained. The life of a creature is in the blood. Although the word for *life* is sometimes translated "soul" or "person," the term *life* is the most fitting term in this context. Since the shedding of blood destroys life, consuming blood, the life of the animal, devalues life. Another reason not to eat blood is that the Lord gave it to the Israelites to make atonement on the altar. Since the blood makes up the essence of physical life, the Lord requires it to make a ransom. The blood, so representative of life, must be given as an atonement for sin. A secondary reason for not consuming blood was hygienic.

C Hunting Game (17:13–16)

SUPPORTING IDEA: *The Lord prohibits all eating of blood, including that of game animals.*

17:13–16. The Lord gave an exception to the rule above about killing animals in the tabernacle area. He allowed the Israelites to hunt and consume wild game under certain conditions. First of all, the blood of all such animals must be poured out and covered with dirt. Secondly, if a person ate a clean animal that was already dead, it would be difficult to determine if the blood drained out completely. This meant the person risked becoming unclean. Accordingly, that person would have to wash his clothes and bathe himself with water.

D Foundations for Sexual Morality (18:1–5)

SUPPORTING IDEA: *Israel must reflect vital union with the Lord by adhering to his standards of sexual behavior.*

18:1–5. The Lord was more than a guardian angel or terrifying entity meant only to appease. He was their God who had already worked mightily on their behalf. He is quick to compare his desire for the well-being of their nation's life with that of other nations, such as Egypt, or the land of Canaan, where they were headed. Their longevity as a nation depended on their adherence to God's revealed will.

E Specific Unions Forbidden (18:6–18)

SUPPORTING IDEA: *Specific instances of sexual defilement are described.*

18:6. Verse 6 summarizes the entire passage by prohibiting sexual relations with any close relative other than one's spouse. Of course, marriage itself fell under specific restrictions that are, for the most part, assumed in this chapter. The reader may also assume other unlawful sexual acts not specifically mentioned in this passage, such as adultery (although v. 20 later alludes to this).

18:7–18. The Lord forbade the following unions, all of which included sexual and contractual marital unions. A man could not marry or have sexual relations with his mother (v. 7), stepmother (v. 8), aunt (vv. 12–13), aunt by marriage (v. 14), sister or half sister (v. 9), stepsister (v. 11), stepdaughter (v. 17), sister-in-law (v. 16), daughter-in-law (v. 15), granddaughter (v. 10), or stepgranddaughter (v. 17). Although the Lord also prohibited a man marrying both a woman and her sister (v. 18). Although the Lord did not mention marrying one's daughter, it is assumed throughout the narrative that this was prohibited. The Lord held marriage in such high esteem that he even called this union "one flesh" (Gen. 2:23–24). Because of this close union, the Lord considered any physical union with in-laws in the manner mentioned above incestuous.

A woman was forbidden to marry her brother-in-law even after the death of her husband. An exception was made if the woman became widowed before she bore a son to carry on the family name (see Deut. 25:5–10).

A key element and the governing presupposition of these rules is that the Israelites would not intermarry with the inhabitants of the surrounding nations. Elsewhere the Lord forbade them (see Deut. 7:3–4; Ezra 10:2–4). The motive behind this was purely spiritual.

F Foreign Practices Forbidden (18:19–30)

SUPPORTING IDEA: *The Lord provided safeguards from defilement by heathen practices.*

18:19–23. The Bible forbids any form of adultery, a sin specifically defined as sexual intercourse between a man and either a married or betrothed woman. If a married man had intercourse with a single woman not betrothed to another, he would not suffer the death penalty (see Deut. 22:22 for the penalty for simple adultery and Deut. 22:28–29 for the latter example).

The Lord next prohibited certain practices considered detestable in any civilized society. One such practice was offering a sacrifice to Molech (see "Deeper Discoveries"). Although this was abominable on its own merits and repulsive to even unprincipled people, child sacrifice was practiced in pagan settings (see Deut. 12:31). Such evil practices would defile the nation and profane the name of the Lord. The Bible prohibited homosexuality and bestiality, admitting of no exceptions (see "Deeper Discoveries"). God regarded such evil as an "abomination," or something hated by him (Prov. 6:16). Not only did such perversions threaten the nation, but they also violated the natural order (see Rom. 1:24–28).

18:24–30. Leviticus 26 and Deuteronomy 28 form a close parallel to this passage. They pronounce blessings on the obedient nation while raining down curses on flagrant disobedience. God never promised Israel global domination, only complete deliverance from their enemies as a reward for obedience. The Lord would soon exterminate the Canaanites for their sacrilegious and detestable practices, but Israel could face a similar fate if she should fall into the same sort of sins.

G Conduct Toward God (19:1–8)

SUPPORTING IDEA: *The Lord told the Israelites to express love toward him and his institutions.*

19:1–2. The Lord placed Israel in a unique relationship to him not because Israel adopted the Lord to be her God but because the Lord set his love on Israel and adopted the nation to be his own (Hos. 11:1). Because the Lord was holy, Israel was to reflect this quality in individuals as well as its national character. The bond between the Lord and Israel began in relational terms from the outset—a personal God leading his children who were to mirror his character in their lives.

19:3–8. The Lord established two fundamental "pillars of the moral government" (Keil, 419)—respect toward parents and a meaningful observance of the Sabbath. One owes allegiance to the supreme human institution—the family—the other to God directly.

The Lord next repeated the two opening commands in the Ten Commandments, telling the nation not to **turn to idols or make gods of cast metal**. The first part speaks to Israel's attitude toward the Lord. If they should **turn** toward another god, although it does not exist, they would be turning away from the Lord. This, in turn, would bring on a jealous response from the Lord as a reflection of his own possessive and holy love toward the adopted nation.

The Lord repeated the command from 7:15–18, prohibiting worshipers from eating the sacrificial fellowship offerings on the third day. Here the Lord attached a capital penalty for any violators.

Ⓗ Conduct Toward One's Neighbor (19:9–18)

SUPPORTING IDEA: *The Lord instructed the Israelites in expressing love in relationships toward one's neighbor.*

19:9–10. The kind of welfare system envisioned here will only work in an unselfish nation that does not hoard and gobble up land in crass colonialism. The land belonged to the Lord, and it was his to give and take away. Accordingly, the Israelites were not to reap the edges of their fields or glean the vineyard a second time. They were to leave remnants of food for the poor. With these laws in mind, Amos thundered against the rich heartless "cows" (Amos 4:1). But again the Lord suspended these laws on a nation that was to show due regard to the poor and distressed.

19:11–18. The Lord next introduced various laws related to national life, most of which were found elsewhere. He prohibited the Israelites from stealing, lying, or otherwise deceiving and slandering their neighbors. He also forbade them from robbing others, either by force or by withholding wages for work performed. They were to maintain a just relation toward justice in general and compassion toward the unfortunate in particular.

But all this once depended on a people who loved both God and neighbor, something that was clearly a heart issue. Therefore the Lord commanded the Israelites not to **hate** or seek revenge against their neighbors, possibly by slandering them. Instead, they were to **rebuke** their neighbors **frankly**, thereby avoiding slander and even preventing their neighbors from sinning. Since love is the fulfillment of the law (Rom. 13:8), no law related to community living could be obeyed without a governing attitude that proceeded from a loving heart. Here is a glimpse at the anticipated New Testament themes that God would announce with the arrival of his Son (Heb. 1:2).

▌ Various Laws (19:19–37)

SUPPORTING IDEA: *The Lord established laws about an orderly and natural creation.*

19:19. Although the Lord did not provide us with a rationale for these commands, he did emphasize their importance, and we can see the reasoning behind them. The people were not to mix things separated by God in the created order. They were not to **mate different kinds of animals**, or mix different kinds of seed when planting their fields, or even wear clothing made of mixed material (see also Deut. 22:9–10). Scholars have tried to explain these laws in mystical or symbolic terms, but they miss the point. God wanted them to maintain the natural order of things.

19:20–22. The Lord protected the rights of slaves, or servants, by not allowing the Israelites to treat them as though they were personal property. If a man had sexual relations with a slave who was pledged to another, he was to be punished, and he had to bring a guilt offering to atone for his sin.

19:23–25. When the Israelites arrived in the land of Canaan and planted fruit trees, they were not to eat from it for a full three years. Some cite common horticultural practices as the reason behind this command. The argument states that picking from an immature tree would prevent its future fruitfulness. But the Lord probably wanted the Israelites to set apart such trees as gifts from God and to be so acknowledged.

19:26–32. Israel would often fall prey to heathen practices in the years ahead, but it was not as though they lacked warning. God strictly prohibited heathen practices such as eating blood (see 17:10–12) or engaging in any kind of sorcery. They were not to disfigure their bodies in any manner or adorn their bodies with tattoos. The Lord commanded them not to prostitute their daughters for money lest they defile the entire nation. They were to honor both the Sabbath day and the aged who live in the land.

19:33–37. Finally, the Lord reminded the people to remember their own sojourn in the land of Egypt as a basis for proper treatment of foreigners in their own land. And whether they did business with foreigners or fellow Israelites, they were to conduct themselves honestly and use honest scales.

▌ Spiritual Sins (20:1–8)

SUPPORTING IDEA: *The Lord will punish all who engage in false worship.*

20:1–8. In chapter 18 the Lord forbade any worship of Molech. Here he decrees stoning as the punishment for such apostasy. The same punishment was required for blasphemy (Lev. 24:16), Sabbath-breaking (Num. 15:35–36), and idolatry (Deut. 13:6–11), among others. Furthermore, the community was responsible to enforce this law and not turn a blind eye to this or other evil practices.

The Lord also commanded the people not to engage in necromancy of any form. So defiling was this sin that the Lord himself said, **I will set my face against the person who turns to mediums and spiritists.**

The Israelites were to **consecrate** themselves and to consider themselves separate from the nations which sought to bring them down. By dabbling with the religions of the surrounding nations, Israel would bring trouble and inevitable judgment on herself. The Lord was the one who enabled Israel to obey him by his grace and strength. Never were the temptations so great as to make obedience to him impossible.

Ⓚ Family Sins (20:9–21)

SUPPORTING IDEA: *The Lord will punish those who defame the family unit.*

20:9–21. In the Ten Commandments the Lord reinforced the foundations of the family by commanding the Israelites to honor their father and mother. Here he makes cursing one's parents a capital crime. To curse involved more than uttering a profane word. If someone uttered a curse, he or she engaged in malice. When Shimei cursed David, he did so with venom in his heart and words. He sought David's harm and overthrow (2 Sam. 16:5–8). Since the family formed the foundation of society, God would always uphold parental authority in his law. The parents in a real sense represented God to the children. When children questioned their parents' authority, they would soon question God's.

This section also prescribes stiff punishments for assorted crimes against the family, including adultery (v. 10), incest (vv. 11–12,14,17,19–21), bestiality (vv. 15–16), and homosexuality (v. 13). The Lord also forbade sexual intercourse with a woman during her menstrual period (v. 18). For all these crimes the Lord decreed the death penalty, with the exception of the forms of incest mentioned in verses 20–21. For those the perpetrators would **die childless,** a fate considered the worst kind of curse (see 1 Sam. 1:8–17).

Ⓛ Final Exhortations (20:22–27)

SUPPORTING IDEA: *The Lord will punish serious infractions of a general nature.*

20:22–24. The land promised to Israel carried certain conditions. If Israel failed to keep these conditions, they would be expelled from the land, and the Lord would **vomit** them out. The Lord brought Israel into the land partly as a judgment against the natives who engaged in wickedness. Could Israel expect a different fate if she became a party to such behavior?

20:25–27. The Lord did not distinguish between civil and ceremonial law, although some interpreters attempt to read a division back into the Old Testament. The law was all one and Israel's close relationship with God depended on her keeping the law. As it was wrong not to **make a distinction between clean and unclean animals**, so it was wrong to engage in necromancy of any kind.

> **MAIN IDEA REVIEW:** *Instructions are given on offering and eating sacrifices, maintaining sexual purity, relating to God and others, and forsaking all false gods.*

III. CONCLUSION

Don't Miss the Real Thing

A little boy lived out in the country around the beginning of the twentieth century. He had never seen a traveling circus, and one was coming to town on Saturday. When he asked his father for permission to go, his dad said he could, providing his chores were done early. Saturday morning came. Chores finished, the little boy asked his father for some money to go to the circus. His dad reached down in his overalls and pulled out a dollar bill, the most money the boy had ever seen at one time. Off the wide-eyed boy went. As he approached the town, he saw people lining the streets. Peering through the line at one point, he got his first glimpse of the parade. There were animals in cages and marching bands. Finally, a clown was seen bringing up the rear of the parade. The little boy was so excited that when the clown passed, he reached in his pocket and handed him the precious dollar bill. Thinking he had seen the circus when he had only seen the parade, the little boy turned around and went home.

There is a lot of this little boy in every believer. So many Christians go through life as phonies, content on enjoying the "parade of church" and miss the "circus of life," where the real action is found. They peer through the pews to watch all the activity of others who are serving, others who are repenting, and others who are confessing and fail to enjoy the big event—a day-by-day walk of faith and obedience. This is where we find personal encounter with the true God and realize what our worship is all about.

PRINCIPLES

- Genuine followers of God want to obey his commandments and fulfill his expectations.
- We have little control over what happens in this world, so we must remain confident in God's sovereignty.

- Sex outside of the boundary of marriage is always harmful.
- Man is capable of great evil when left to his own devices.

APPLICATIONS

- Be a continual learner. Learn what you can from each nugget that God shares in his Word.
- If you are planning to be married or are now married, consider the seriousness of your vows.
- Choose to follow God's standards, not the world's.
- Become aware of satanic activity around you, and pray for God's intervention.

IV. LIFE APPLICATION

Learning by Doing

A young man came to the pastor's office and said he wanted to be a Christian but he didn't know what being a Christian was all about. The wise pastor told the young man to read the Book of Acts as preparation and then come back and they would talk about what he had learned and how to apply it. A week went by and then another week and then another. The preacher began to think that he had made a serious mistake in his suggestion to the man. Finally, almost a year later, the young man finally appeared. When the surprised pastor asked where he had been, the young man said, "You told me to read the Book of Acts. Every time I started to read it, it told me to do something. So I went and did it. I've just been too busy to come back."

This young man read the Bible expectantly. His example of obedience and activity is a model for all of us. Read the Bible with the same level of expectation and obedience, and you will never miss God's will for your life.

V. PRAYER

Gracious Father, thank you for the truths in these chapters. Your standards for my life are much higher than I ever dreamed. Strengthen me to walk in your will. In Jesus' name. Amen!

VI. DEEPER DISCOVERIES

A. The Bible and Sexuality

From the earliest times God acknowledged the existence of and controlled the conduct of human sexuality. The sexual motivation comes from the inner nature of man, and it forms the drive to populate the earth (Gen. 1:28). Men and women can fulfill this mandate with the utmost fulfillment, provided they follow the teachings of the Bible on sexual conduct. Sarah even used the term *pleasure* to describe the sexual act (Gen. 18:12). God intended the physical union between man and woman to represent a holy intimacy, at times describing the very act as "knowing" the partner (Num. 31:17). Such knowledge assumes a deep personal connection between the husband and wife that extends far beyond the physical realm but includes the entire person.

God himself describes the sexual partners as forming "one flesh" (Gen. 2:24; Mark 10:7–8; Eph. 5:31). The man who engages a prostitute in intercourse becomes "one with her in body" (1 Cor. 6:16), a practice God commands us to "flee" lest we sin against our own bodies (1 Cor. 6:18). God intended the normal sexual function to include a commitment and love that went beyond sexual fulfillment.

The Old Testament required young women to remain virgins until marriage on penalty of death (Deut. 22:13–24). While God did not repeat the same restrictions for males, he implied it by prohibiting fornication (Exod. 22:16–17) and punishing it with varying penalties. Adultery was strictly forbidden, and this comprised one of the Ten Commandments (Exod. 20:14). God forbade any species of incest, physical unions between family members, although some people in the Bible ignored such warnings. Lot, seduced by his daughters into a drunken stupor, lost his powers of judgment and impregnated them (Gen. 19:30–38). Reuben slept with his father Jacob's concubine (Gen. 35:22), and Judah had relations with his daughter-in-law Tamar (Gen. 38).

Jesus and the apostles shed the clearest light of all on this delicate issue. Jesus redefined popular notions of sin by discovering its origins: it resides in the human heart. Consequently, a man commits adultery not only by engaging in unlawful intercourse with his neighbor's wife but by harboring such desires in his heart (Matt. 5:27–30). Luke faithfully records the decrees of the early church that, among other things, prohibited sexual immorality (Acts 15:20). Paul constructed an elaborate theology of marriage, detailing both its positive privileges and strict parameters (1 Cor. 6:13–20; 7:1–40; Eph. 5:3–7; 1 Thess. 4:3).

Finally, the Bible forbids homosexuality of any sort (Lev. 18:22; 20:13; Rom. 1:26–27). The modern term *sodomy* derived its name from the failed attempts of the inhabitants of Sodom to rape the visiting angels (Gen. 19:4–11). The degree to which a society gives way to such practices is a good gauge to measure not only the nation's separation from God but also its prospects for long-term survival (see Lev. 18:24–25; cp. Gen. 15:16).

The only island of sanity we find in a sea without sexual standards is the comprehensive biblical instruction on sexual behavior. On a positive and hopeful note, many whom God saved from pagan and hedonistic lifestyles have found peace, purpose, and fulfillment in Christ. God did a marvelous work in their lives and renewed them in the way they approach these matters. God leaves no one outside of the reach of his gracious provision in Christ, and many who once sought meaning in the empty relationships now find complete fulfillment in following the Bible's prescription for healthy and satisfying sexual behavior.

B. Molech

In the middle of this lengthy discussion on sexual standards, the Lord inserts a warning against sacrificing children to *Molech* (18:21). Because he mentions it within a context exclusively devoted to sexuality, we can conclude it had some reference to that discussion. Kiel thinks the placement here was suitable because the practice involved "spiritual whoredom" (416).

Scholars have wrestled with two primary issues concerning Molech: its identity and whether worship of Molech involved child sacrifice.

Most of the Old Testament references to Molech allude to the Ammonite god to which Solomon later erected a shrine (1 Kgs. 11:7). The consonants used to form its root are also used with "king." Some have identified this god with "Milcom" used in some versions, but other scholars are not so sure. The Bible sometimes associates Molech with Baal (Jer. 32:35).

Kiel, while admitting that children were indeed offered to Molech (Ezek. 16:21; Jer. 7:31), does not think this necessarily involved child sacrifice (416–17). He compared the expression "passing through to Molech" to a ritual of consecrating children to Molech without actually offering them up in sacrifice. But even Kiel admits that later kings performed such offerings. Kiel thinks that if children were offered or burned in sacrifice, it would have been mentioned unambiguously. Wenham concludes, however, "it is now fairly certain that it involved child sacrifice" (259). Some evidence exists from the remains of these sacrifices that children were actually thrown into the fire. King Ahaz burned his own children to a Molech shrine in the Valley of Hinnom (2 Chr. 28:3), and Manasseh sacrificed one of his own sons in the fire (2 Kgs. 21:6). Later godly King Josiah destroyed this hideous high place (2 Kgs. 23:10,13).

C. Identification and Treatment of the Poor

When God spoke of the blessings he would provide the Israelites once they took possession of the land, many of these blessings were material in nature (Deut. 1:25; 28:8–12). Still, not all Israelites would share equally in these blessings, and the poor would always be among them (Deut. 15:11).

The people would indeed participate in the blessings of Canaan. God established laws, such as the year of Jubilee, to protect those who fell on hard times (Lev. 25:8–13). But God, in his wise providence, did not allocate material goods uniformly. Of course, sometimes people, through their own laziness, neglect, or other personal character defects, brought poverty on their own heads (Prov. 5:7–10; 27:23–27). The only remedy for them was personal repentance.

The Lord did make some special provisions in the law to care for the poor. The poor had the right to gather scraps and other food items in the vineyard or grain field of another (Deut. 23:24–25). They could glean the fields after the reaper did a once-through and may have left some sheaves behind (Lev. 19:9–10; 23:22; Deut. 24:19–21). Israelites who did not turn away the poor as they gleaned their fields became objects of God's special blessings (Deut. 24:19). Even those who became so poor that they had to resort to selling their services as servants to others were allowed to go free in a special year of release (Lev. 25:39–43).

In a unique show of special care for the poor not seen in virtually any other nation in ancient or modern times, the Lord required people of means to grant loans to the poor upon request (Deut. 15:7–10). The Lord also warned the people against taking advantage of the poor through oppression (Exod. 22:21–27), a sin Israel proved not to be immune to (Amos 2:6–7; Mal. 3:5).

In addition to the laws protecting the poor, the Lord also vowed to protect the poor when they cried out to him, particularly when someone oppressed them (Exod. 22:27). He created all people equal in his sight, including the poor.

Today many people in the Western nations attribute their wealth to the Protestant work ethic. At least in part they are quite correct. But the presence of wealth does not imply that God's favor rests upon the wealthy. In fact, Israel first began to drift from God when they "grew fat" (Deut. 32:15), and they ultimately self-destructed through their callous treatment of the poor, among other sins (Ezek. 16:49). Many today erect aberrant theologies that equate a faithful walk with material wealth. But the apostle Paul argued against this notion, attributing such teachings to corrupt minds (1 Tim. 6:5). God is compassionate (Exod. 22:27), and he expects his people to exercise mercy toward the poor.

D. Necromancy

The practice of necromancy, or communication with a "familiar spirit," involved attempts to contact the dead, often with a desire to glimpse into the future (see Deut. 18:11). Those who practiced necromancy were called mediums (Isa. 8:19). The medium allegedly had the power to contact the departed spirit of a deceased soul and call it up during a ritual such as a séance. Some felt they could call up any spirit. The medium of Endor tried to bring up the departed spirit of Samuel (1 Sam. 28:8–19).

The Bible pronounced anathema on those who practiced such divination (Lev. 19:31; Isa. 8:19). They should have consulted the "law" and "testimony" instead (Isa. 8:20). The Lord cautioned Israel about consulting the dead and decreed the death penalty for those who did (Lev. 20:6,27).

VII. TEACHING OUTLINE

A. INTRODUCTION

1. Lead Story: Who Are the Phonies?
2. Context: God is holy and has redeemed his people so they can be holy. They are to be different from people who don't know God.
3. Transition: Ceremonial and moral command weren't distinguished in Israel. Chapter 17 shows the way in which blood was to be viewed and treated. Chapters 18–20 set forth standards for ethical behavior.

B. COMMENTARY

1. The Place of Sacrifice (17:1–9)
2. Eating Blood (17:10–12)
3. Hunting Game (17:13–16)
4. Foundations for Sexual Morality (18:1–5)
5. Specific Unions Forbidden (18:6–18)
6. Foreign Practices Forbidden (18:19–30)
7. Conduct Toward God (19:1–8)
8. Conduct Toward One's Neighbor (19:9–18)
9. Various Laws (19:19–37)
10. Spiritual Sins (20:1–8)
11. Family Sins (20:9–21)
12. Final Exhortations (20:22–27)

C. CONCLUSION: LEARNING BY DOING

VIII. ISSUES FOR DISCUSSION

1. As you read chapter 17, you most likely became aware of God's high standards for the sacrificial process. What problems could occur if these sacrifices were done incorrectly?
2. If God spent so much time providing the people of Israel with prohibitions for sexual intimacy, what must have been going on in the

surrounding nations? How is the obedience of 18:5 related to God's blessing on purity in relationships?

3. What did these expectations from God have to do with maintaining a right relationship with their Master? Review chapter 19 and see what laws apply to you at work, home, and school this week.

4. A great debate in the judicial system today revolves around the idea of punishment being either a deterrent to breaking the law or a motivation to right behavior. Chapter 20 contains not only a listing of various regulations for living but also their accompanying punishments. Is God motivating his people to live lives that honor him? Or is God saying, "Better watch out, or I will get you if you do these things"?

Leviticus 21–24

Servants, Standards, and Structures

"*A* Christian man is the most free lord of all, and subject to none; a Christian man is the most dutiful servant of all, and subject to everyone."

M a r t i n L u t h e r

Leviticus 21–24

IN A NUTSHELL

*L*eviticus 21–24 is a further examination of the priesthood from three perspectives. First they are to be servants and represent God to the people as priests. Second, the standards for the life of a priest are to be very high. Third, they will take on a major responsibility in ordering the seven major feasts of Israel and maintain significant involvement in the tabernacle, representing God's presence in the world.

Servants, Standards, and Structures

I. INTRODUCTION

A Valentine's Day Revelation

*L*ittle Chad was a shy, quiet young lad, who always seemed to be alone. One day he came home and told his mother that Valentine's Day was only a week away and he wanted to make a valentine for everyone in his class at school. Mom's heart sank. She thought, "I wish he wouldn't do that. He is only going to be hurt again." Mom had spent many hours with tears running down her weary cheeks, watching the little children make their way home from school. Chad was never with the "inner group," so he always walked behind the rest of the kids. As they laughed and joked around, Chad was never included. Nevertheless, she decided she would go along with her good-hearted son and purchase the paper, glue, and crayons for his artistic endeavor.

For the better part of the next week, Chad worked every night to make thirty-five of the best valentines you would ever see. When Valentine's Day arrived, so did the excitement in Chad's heart. He carefully stacked the cards up, put them in a bag, and bolted out the door. Mom stood there watching her son run down the sidewalk, knowing how sad he would be if he received no valentines of his own. Mom decided to bake Chad some of his favorite cookies so when he arrived home, she would be ready to cheer him up with his favorite cookies and milk. She thought, "Maybe this will ease the pain a little."

That afternoon she had the cookies and milk on the table, all ready for her generous son. When she heard the children outside, she went to the window. Sure enough, here they came, laughing and having the best of time. And, as always, there was Chad in the rear. But Chad was walking a little faster than usual. "Maybe he will burst into tears when he gets home. I'm sure glad I have the cookies ready," she thought. When he entered the door, she noticed that his arms were empty and ran to him saying, "Mommy has some warm cookies and a glass of milk for you. Your favorite!" But Chad hardly heard her words. He just looked at his mother and told her, "Not a one . . . not a one!" Her heart sank. Then little Chad added with a huge smile, "Mommy, I didn't forget one, not a single one!"

What a little servant! Here was a child demonstrating the life God intends for all who will seek him, all who take on the responsibility of being a "priest," a person who has invited Christ into his life. When God is in control of his servants, he is also in control of the servant's attitude and perspectives. A servant understands that life's greatest joy is to serve others, to give away what God has given him. This perspective is a common thread through Leviticus 21–24. Read carefully concerning the servants of God and their standards for ministry. Read about the wonderful symbolism in the feasts God ordained for Israel. Enjoy remembering God's valentine to you in the tabernacle. By the way, God hasn't forgotten one of us . . . not one!

II. COMMENTARY

Servants, Standards, and Structures

> **MAIN IDEA:** *Mediating God's grace and forgiveness through a properly functioning priesthood and instructions on observation of the major feasts of Israel.*

A Priestly Standards (21:1–24)

> **SUPPORTING IDEA:** *Higher standards are expected for leaders.*

21:1–4. The Lord forbade priests to become ceremonially unclean through touching a dead body. Hence they were not allowed to participate directly in funerals when it called for coming in contact with a dead body. The Lord made an exception for close family members. Although the text does not mention the priests' wives, they would be included among the exceptions.

21:5–9. The Lord also forbade facial disfigurement, such as shaving **their heads** or **the edges of their beards** or cutting their bodies in any way. The only place the priests would learn such practices was from the neighboring nations around them who incorporated such things in heathen rituals. The priests were to **present the offerings made to the LORD by fire** and hence must remain fully consecrated in both body and soul.

The priests were forbidden to marry women who either engaged in prostitution or who were divorced. Their wives must be of high character, a trait that transferred over to the New Testament church (1 Tim. 3:11). The priests (but not the high priest) could, however, marry widows. Although the text does not supply the reason for the prohibition against marrying a divorcee—who may have been an innocent party—sometimes it's difficult to determine the guilty party. The wife's reputation was to be blameless.

The priest's family must uphold certain standards because eyes would also be watching them. For example, if a priest's daughter turned to prostitution, she was not to be spared the highest penalty. In this case, it was death by burning. Such a punishment not only fit the crime, but this was a way to discourage such sin, often associated with ritualistic and cultic worship. The priest's family was not exempt from temptation as we later learn from the example of both Eli and Samuel, whose children did not live up to expectations.

21:10–12. The officiating priest, or high priest, must maintain even the highest grooming standards. An unkempt appearance would be in direct contradiction to the beautiful and elaborate priestly clothing designed by God himself. He was not to participate in funerals even of close relatives (allowed for normal priests, see vv. 2–3). The priest was to confine himself, for the most part, to the **sanctuary of his God**, where he would offer sacrifices and represent the people before God.

21:13–15. As in the case of priests, the wife of the high priest must exemplify the highest character. She must be a virgin, which necessarily excluded a priest from marrying even a widow. Since both father and mother contributed to the rearing of a wholesome family, the priest was to take great care in choosing a suitable wife. Wenham notes that another reason for the above restrictions might have been as a means of proving the high priest's children—who often stood to succeed him in office—really belonged to him (Wenham, 292).

21:16–24. The Lord did not allow any priest who had a physical defect or deformity to officiate in the sanctuary. Just as the Lord required the animals destined for sacrifice to be without blemish, so he required the same for priests who represented him.

B Rules for Officiating and Consuming Sacrifices (22:1–33)

SUPPORTING IDEA: *The Lord establishes proper procedures for officiating at the altar.*

22:1–9. No priest could participate in the formal duties of the priesthood while in an unclean condition. This restriction was quite broad and covered all circumstances that fell under the wide umbrella of ceremonial uncleanness. The Lord required the life of any priest who so defiled himself while performing priestly functions. The restrictions included any skin disease, ceremonial uncleanness, and all other forms of personal defilement otherwise mentioned in the Law of Moses. If he should become defiled, the priest must exempt himself from official duties until he became clean.

22:10–16. The priests lived on the tithes and offerings of the people and had no land of their own to work. Accordingly, their families were to partake also of priestly food. This section describes what constituted the priest's family and could thus be allowed to eat the assigned food. Visitors in his home who were not part of his family could not partake of sacred food. The slaves, however, and their families could partake.

When a priest's daughter married a man who was not a priest, neither she nor her new family could eat the consecrated food. If she became widowed or divorced and remained childless, she could once again become incorporated into her father's household and his food.

If someone not of the priest's household ate the priestly food, he must replace it and add 20 percent. But the priest was to regulate his table carefully and not allow an "outsider" who was not duly sanctioned to eat the food.

22:17–30. Since the priests could become disqualified because of physical defects, the sacrificial animals themselves must be perfect. The connection between priest and sacrifice becomes clearer in this section. Some of the same defects mentioned for the priests are repeated here for animal sacrifices.

The priests were to present an unblemished male from the **cattle, sheep or goats** as the normal offering from either the herd or flock. The only exception to this rule was an ox or sheep offered as a freewill offering as long as it was not offered in fulfillment of a vow (v. 23). The Lord even outlawed animals that had their reproductive organs damaged or removed, no doubt because they represented the reproductive creation of God.

22:31–33. The Lord always tied in his relationship with the Israelites with their obligation to maintain his laws strictly without compromise. The name of the Lord was holy, and the Israelites were not to profane his name. They owed their unique status to him as well as any claim to holiness. He was the one who made them holy and redeemed them from the slavery of Egypt.

The underlying principle of unblemished sacrifices and priesthood foreshadows the New Testament fulfillment where these two become one in Christ. The alert reader of the Book of Hebrews comes upon this truth from chapters 5–10. Christ's priesthood, although not stemming from the earthly stock of Aaron (ch. 7), functioned from a new covenant (ch. 8). His work was anticipated in the Old Testament tabernacle (ch. 9), which typified heaven itself (9:23–24). Most important was the merging of priest and sacrifice (9:26–10:18) in one person and one body, the Lord Jesus Christ, who appeared at the end of the ages to put away sin by sacrificing himself (9:26).

◖ The Feasts of Israel (23:1–44)

SUPPORTING IDEA: *The Lord appoints special times of meeting with his people.*

23:1–3. The chapter before us lists the **appointed feasts** of the Lord that were to be observed as regular features of the Hebrew year. The term *appointed* means "fixed" in the sense they were set by God himself and he would meet with the people as they observed these feasts. The appointed feasts reminded Israel of its own birthright and God's sovereign rule over the nation. They were a national call to come apart and remember him who gave birth to the nation.

The weekly Sabbath reminded Israel that they were a holy people who served a holy God (House, 146). The Sabbath provided the Israelites physical and mental rest from their daily labors. It also drew them closer to the Lord as they acknowledged him as their chief provider.

23:4–8. The Lord repeated to Moses the instructions he had given him earlier in Exodus 12:6–20 about the Passover and Feast of Unleavened Bread. The Passover opened the feast year much as the exodus marked Israel's birth as a nation (House, 146). At that time the Lord drew a distinction between Israel and Egypt and thus established his sovereign election of Israel, a theme the apostle Paul would later develop in Romans 9.

23:9–14. When Israel came into the land and began to reap a harvest, they were to **bring to the priest a sheaf of the first grain** (which was probably barley because it ripened before the wheat). The priest would wave the sheaf before the Lord. Then the people would offer a year-old lamb and two-tenths of an ephah of flour and oil. To that they would add a **quarter of a hin of wine**. This would be performed one day after the Sabbath, which could have been the weekly Sabbath or the first day of unleavened bread when work was forbidden.

When the Israelites observed this feast, they would be reminded that the land and its plentiful harvests came from God. Any claim they had to agricultural wealth was based on God's gift of the land to them. They depended on his favor for the harvest.

23:15–22. The Lord did not formally introduce this next feast, called the Feast of Weeks, because it was so closely connected with the Feast of Firstfruits just mentioned. The Israelites were to number fifty days after the first day of unleavened bread and then make a special offering before the Lord. This offering marked the end of the grain harvest. In New Testament times it was called the Feast of Pentecost (Acts 2). The Israelites were to offer two loaves and **seven male lambs**, plus a bull and two rams. The priest would wave the two fellowship offerings before the Lord as an acknowledgment of his gracious provision.

The Feast of Weeks reminded the Israelites that they owed their grain and, beyond that, their very existence to God's sovereign mercy. The God who redeemed them from the house of slavery would provide them with abundant bread so they could feed themselves as well as **the poor and the alien**.

23:23–25. The chapter closes with the special fall feasts, or festivals: Trumpets, Atonement, and the Feast of Tabernacles. The first, Trumpets, occurred on the very first day of the seventh month and was a special Sabbath. The only unique feature of this feast was the sounding of trumpets (see "Deeper Discoveries"). Perhaps the trumpet blasts formally summoned Israel to gather physically and spiritually before the Lord in solemn preparation for the Day of Atonement and a month of holy observance.

23:26–32. The second observance of the seventh month was the Day of Atonement, already described in chapter 16. This assembly involved fasting, community contrition, and abstaining from regular work. Violators of these restrictions were to be put to death.

23:33–44. The next feast was **the LORD's Feast of Tabernacles**. The name was derived from the special booths the Israelites lived in while observing this feast. These booths would be constructed from branches and would provide shelter for the Israelites during the feast time. On the first day of the feast, they would gather **choice fruit from the trees** along with branches and other tokens of the land's fruitfulness and then **rejoice before the LORD** for seven days. For seven days they were to present offerings to the Lord and then close on the eighth day by gathering in sacred assembly to **present an offering made to the LORD by fire**.

The chief characteristic of this feast was joy (Deut. 16:14–15). The Israelites were to celebrate joyfully the blessings the Lord had rained down on them.

D Oil and Bread (24:1–9)

SUPPORTING IDEA: *The Lord gives directions for the regular ministry of the tabernacle.*

24:1–4. These instructions had already been given in Exodus 27:20–21. But the Lord repeated them to emphasize that Aaron was to tend the lamps regularly.

24:5–9. The other routine ministry of the tabernacle was maintaining the bread of the presence (see Exod. 25:23–30 for the making of the table). The priests were to **take fine flour and bake twelve loaves of bread** and place them in two rows of six each. The number of loaves probably represented the twelve tribes of Israel. The bread was replaced each Sabbath day, along with incense placed on the table to be burned **as a memorial portion** to the Lord. The bread itself could only be eaten by the priests in a holy place.

E A Sobering Example (24:10–23)

SUPPORTING IDEA: *The Lord tests the Israelites about their faithfulness in enforcing the law.*

24:10–16. When the Bible reports that Israel failed to keep the law (e.g., 2 Kgs. 17:13–17), much of that failure can be attributed to not *enforcing* the laws themselves, particularly the penalties. We know from everyday life that this can be the most difficult aspect of maintaining order in any institution, yet the laws were designed to preserve order. In Israel's case, the law had a greater purpose, because it would ensure the nation's longevity in the land. Accordingly, the Lord provided an example to demonstrate his intention of having them enforce the entire law.

Here is what happened: **The son of an Israelite mother and an Egyptian father** got into a tussle with an Israelite. During the course of the fight, the half-Israelite **blasphemed the Name with a curse**. He may have used the name of the Lord to invoke a curse on his opponent. Because this man was a foreigner or at least a resident alien, Moses sought the Lord's will about how to deal with this situation.

The Lord commanded Moses to take the accused outside the camp, then gather all who witnessed the blasphemy. The witnesses who heard the man utter the curse were **to lay their hands on his head**, and the entire assembly was **to stone him**. In this way the entire congregation participated in the judgment and penalty and also witnessed the consequences of committing such a sin. The name of the Lord was to be revered and held in high esteem.

24:17–23. The Lord mentioned other capital crimes that required capital punishment, such as murder, and some others that required restitution of some sort. The point the Lord emphasized is that life is precious, and no one should take it away or injure it with impunity.

Finally, the Lord gave his judgment that the congregation was to make no distinction between foreigners and natives for such offenses. According to God's command, **they took the blasphemer outside the camp and stoned him.**

MAIN IDEA REVIEW: *Mediating God's grace and forgiveness through a properly functioning priesthood and instructions on observation of the major feasts of Israel.*

III. CONCLUSION

Shelter of His Wings

There was an article in *National Geographic* several years ago that provides a penetrating picture of God's wings. After a forest fire in Yellowstone

National Park, forest rangers began their trek up a mountain to assess the inferno's damage. One ranger found a bird literally petrified in ashes, perched statuesquely on the ground at the base of a tree. Somewhat sickened by the eerie sight, he knocked over the bird with a stick. When he struck it, three tiny chicks scurried from under their dead mother's scorched wings. The mother had carried her offspring to the base of a tree and had gathered them under her wings to protect them. She could have flown to safety but had refused to abandon her babies. When the blaze had arrived and the heat had singed her body, the mother had remained steadfast, dying that those under the cover of her wings had survived.

The psalmist writes, "He will cover you with his feathers, and under his wings you will find refuge; his faithfulness will be your shield and rampart" (Ps. 91:4). God is described throughout the Bible as compassionate, loving, and merciful. The New Testament student recognizes these traits in the truth of the cross of Jesus. The Old Testament student must look at the multiple ways God shelters his people from the pain of life. God knows his people need both a sacrifice and a priest. God has given us both. God knows how many reminders man would need to retain an understanding of his presence. God gave the people of Israel a series of feasts to do just that. In the New Testament, we have the indwelling of the Holy Spirit. In the Old Testament, God provided the tabernacle. How could anyone fail to see the security found in the shelter of God's wings?

PRINCIPLES

- God has established a certain criteria for those whom he has called to serve him.
- People need a weekly Sabbath.
- The Passover is God's graphic representation of our dependence upon God's salvation.
- God's plan will never be thwarted. But God may use someone else to accomplish his plans if his servant has been defiled or fails to follow his strict guidelines.

APPLICATIONS

- Establish a pattern of personal holiness as a virtue to live by.
- Avoid any alliance that will draw you away from God and his ways.
- As a priest of the Lord Jesus Christ, take every opportunity to minister to people around you.
- Take a day off each week to recharge your batteries physically and spiritually.

- Flood your mind with the truth of the Scripture so when temptation strikes or busyness sets in, you do not revert back to your natural way of thinking.

IV. LIFE APPLICATION

Put On Your Overalls

Henry Ward Beecher once said, "Religion means work; it means hard work; it means work in a dirty world. The world has to be cleaned by somebody and you are not really called of God unless you are prepared to scour and scrub." Put on your overalls!

This quote may represent the very heart of everything we have learned in this chapter. Through Christ, we are all servants—servants in a dirty world. Where are you investing your life? Whose life can you touch with the truth God has given to you? God has placed you strategically in the wilderness of this dirty world to reveal himself to people who need hope and forgiveness and cleansing. It's time to put on your overalls.

V. PRAYER

Lord, one day I will give an account of the services I have rendered while on this planet. I want to hear you say, "Well done, good and faithful servant." Servanthood has not always been easy for me, but my desire to hear those words from you compels me to serve you and fulfill my role as part of a royal priesthood on earth. Amen.

VI. DEEPER DISCOVERIES

A. The Biblical Meaning of Atonement

The Day of Atonement, or Yom Kippur, was the annual day of humiliation and forgiveness for Israel. But what does "atonement" really mean? Two ideas flow from this term—satisfaction and reconciliation.

To satisfy God meant to appease his response to man's sinfulness and sinful acts. Some call this propitiation. The uniform biblical teaching on the nature of atonement involved satisfying the demands of God's law and then reconciling us to him. The Old Testament used the term *kipper,* which means "to cover sin." When the priest offered the sacrifice on the Day of Atonement, he turned away the wrath of God from the sinner (or sinful nation). The Bible elsewhere teaches that Christ is the propitiation for the sins of the world (1 John 2:2; 4:10). God requires such a sacrifice to satisfy the demands of his holy nature. If we made no sacrifice, God would have to resort to wrath in order to satisfy those demands (see Heb. 10:26–31). In the sacrifice God appoints a vicar or substitute to take the sinner's place. Hence we get the expression "vicarious atonement."

The wider biblical teaching presents Jesus Christ as the only sufficient and acceptable sacrifice for sin. Without his sacrifice man would be subject to eternal ruin. Hence Christ "bore our sins in his body on the tree" (1 Pet. 2:24) as "the Lamb of God" (John 1:29), and really became "a curse for us" (Gal. 3:13). The effect of his sacrifice was both powerful and efficacious: our guilt was imputed to him (Berkhof, 377). The Bible portrays a God of perfect holiness and justice who cannot overlook sin. The only remedy he provided for man's dilemma was the sacrifice of his own Son on the cross.

The other idea portrayed in atonement is reconciliation. The sinner, alienated from God by evil deeds, becomes reconciled to God when he or she responds in faith to God's only provision in Christ (Col. 1:21–22). The earliest chapters of Genesis show man banished from the garden of Eden because of his sin. Christ came into the world to rescue sinners from such alienation by offering his own life as a ransom for ours. When sinners turn to Christ, they are brought back to God and no longer face eternal estrangement. One day the entire curse brought on by sin will be removed, and then God will forever dwell with men (Rev. 21:3). Until that time we can only turn to him who brought us this great salvation (Heb. 2:3) and then proclaim this same salvation—indeed, the only salvation—to others who have no hope.

B. What Is Blasphemy?

The idea of blasphemy includes pouring contempt on God's name by cursing it, using irreverent speech, or invoking his name in an improper manner. Of course, one may do this in a number of ways. A person could try to invoke the name of God in a curse on his enemies. Or one could simply pray in a loose, irreverent manner. The Israelites made light of God's name by practicing false worship (Ezek. 20:27–29). The Jews accused Jesus of blasphemy, especially when he associated himself or his mission with deity (John 10:33). Paul described his former manner of life as blasphemy when he sought to silence the early Christians (Acts 26:11).

The prophets who announced the gospel spoke with the power of the Holy Spirit, as did the apostles (1 Pet. 1:12; Acts 13:9). To make light of this message or to repudiate it with firm and permanent resolve is equivalent to blaspheming the Holy Spirit (Mark 3:28–29).

Our speech should be carefully guarded especially under the watchful eye of the world (Col. 4:6). Christians should also pray with reverence for God's dear name.

VII. TEACHING OUTLINE

A. INTRODUCTION

1. Lead Story: A Valentine's Day Revelation

2. Context: God is holy, and he calls his people to be holy.

3. Transition: God set apart a priesthood for which there were high standards. Priests were to give careful attention to God's prescriptions for leading worship.

B. COMMENTARY

1. Priestly Standards (21:1–24)

2. Rules for Officiating and Consuming Sacrifices (22:1–33)

3. The Feasts of Israel (23:1–44)

4. Oil and Bread (24:1–9)

5. A Sobering Example (24:10–23)

C. CONCLUSION: PUT ON YOUR OVERALLS

VIII. ISSUES FOR DISCUSSION

1. The standards for the priesthood were very high. Why do you believe God established these high standards of cleanliness and holiness? How does this relate to your acts of sacrifice and service?

2. God's listing of unacceptable sacrifices speaks volumes about the value of the gifts we offer him. How does this list impact your desire to worship God and grow in your intimacy with him? In what area of giving do you need to grow?

3. One common thread throughout God's teaching on the feast days was that the people of Israel were not supposed to work on these days. Why did God place this emphasis on each feast? How would this change your work habits?

4. What is blasphemy? Why is blasphemy such a serious violation in God's eyes?

Leviticus 25–27

Living the Good Life

Q u o t e

"*I*n simple trust like theirs who heard

Beside the Syrian sea

The gracious calling of the Lord,

Let us, like them, without a word,

Rise up and follow thee."

John Greenleaf Whittier

Leviticus 25–27

 IN A NUTSHELL

*I*t is not by accident that God concludes his instructions to his people in Leviticus by dealing with human behavior. Since a sacrifice has been made on your behalf and an advocate, a High Priest, has offered forgiveness for your sin, live the good life, a life worthy of your calling and redemption. Live a life sensitive to the physical and mental rest God wants you to have (Lev. 25); live a life aware of the idolatry permeating your world and God's discipline for those who are trapped in it (Lev. 26); and live a life of integrity where your resolutions and promises mean something (Lev. 27). With all you have received from God, enjoy the liberty of being his child as you walk in obedience to his leading.

Living the Good Life

I. INTRODUCTION

A Prison for Goldfish

*G*ladys was a little girl of about seven. One day at a county fair, she won a goldfish. She took it home in its little round bowl. Day by day, she fed and cared for the goldfish as it swam around and around in the bowl. The family decided to take a vacation at a nearby lake. Gladys took her goldfish along. When she saw all that beautiful blue water, she decided she wanted to set the goldfish free. She took the little round bowl to the dock and lowered it into the shallow waters without letting the goldfish leave the bowl. The goldfish still swam around and around. Gladys was called away for lunch. When she came back to get the bowl, the goldfish was still swimming around and around. Wading into the water, Gladys slowly turned the bowl over and set the goldfish free. But still the goldfish swam in circles. All afternoon, that evening, and even the next morning when she checked on her former pet, the goldfish continued to swim around and around in the same circle that had become its life—and its prison.

Our lives often take on the same picture, even though the Scriptures declare our freedom in Christ. Some past incident, a secret shame, or some haunting guilt can imprison us as surely as a little round goldfish bowl. This is why God gave us biblical guidelines for life and liberty. The final three chapters of Leviticus give us further insight into this liberty—what living the good life is all about. Chapter 25 looks at the freedom of the Sabbath and the year of Jubilee; chapter 26 examines the liberty found in overcoming the trap of idolatry; and chapter 27 reveals the freedom of keeping your vows before God.

II. COMMENTARY

Living the Good Life

MAIN IDEA: *The holy nation must remember to observe all of God's laws because they bring meaningful life and liberty.*

A The Sabbath Year and Jubilee (25:1–55)

SUPPORTING IDEA: *The Lord establishes rest and freedom in the holy nation.*

25:1–7. These special sabbatical laws begin with a reminder to give the land a rest every seven years (Exod. 23:10–11). The land was to be worked for six years, then allowed to rest for an entire year. During that year of rest, the Israelites were not allowed to sow their fields or prune their vineyards. They should not till or reap their fields. The idea was that the owner was not formally to reap and gather his crops during the seventh year, but to allow the field or vineyard to provide food for the common man or beast. The purpose of this law was to give the land itself rest much the same way the weekly Sabbath provided rest for the worker.

The regulations for observing the sabbatical year raised some questions. How could they expect to live off the crops while not tilling the land? To remedy this the Lord would provide an abundant harvest the sixth year to provide for their needs until the harvest of the ninth year was gathered in (since they wouldn't sow during the seventh year).

25:8–24. As the land Sabbath afforded the earth rest from cultivation, so the Jubilee granted those who fell upon tough times a fresh start. Following the seventh Sabbath (or forty-nine years), the Lord instituted a Jubilee year during which land that had been sold off reverted to its original owners. The passage assumes the main reason for selling the land in the first place was that people had been compelled through poverty to do so. The Jubilee would begin on the Day of Atonement of that year. On that day the blowing of the trumpet signaled a return of the land to its original owners and liberty to any who were enslaved. In this way the land was never permanently sold off. This would have upset the balance of land among the tribes.

The Lord did set up some parameters for administrating this principle. Those who sold off their land did not have to wait until the Jubilee celebration to regain their property. Assuming they or a close relative had the means and a willing heart, they could redeem or buy back their land from the new owners. They would determine the redemption price by calculating how many years remained until the Jubilee. Also, if someone sold land in a walled city, they lost it permanently and would not receive it back during the Jubilee year. If the Levites sold their land, however, it would revert back to them since they did not own any land outright and lived within designated cities.

25:25–38. The final effect of the Jubilee year related to the person who became **poor** and was **unable to support himself**. The Israelites were to provide him assistance by not charging him exorbitant interest. Their motive for obeying this regulation was the fear of God, who watched over the land and had brought them out of bondage in Egypt.

25:39–46. Furthermore, if someone became so impoverished that he sold himself to one of his countrymen as a slave, he was not to be treated **ruthlessly** but as a hired servant. Both he and his family were to be released during **the Year of Jubilee**. God did allow the Israelites to subjugate as servants some from the idolatrous nations that they conquered and some who lived among them as temporary residents.

25:47–55. If a foreigner should become rich while an Israelite became poor, and the former obtained the latter as a slave, the Israelite could redeem himself from slavery at any time, provided he had the means to do so. Again the terms specified that they count the remaining years up to the Jubilee and then determine the price according to the going price of a hired man. But if the Israelite could not redeem himself, he would still go free in the year of Jubilee.

🅱 Promises and Warnings (26:1–46)

SUPPORTING IDEA: *The Lord provides a formula for blessing and a warning against disobedience.*

26:1–2. These prominent commands form a summary of all the chief commands incumbent upon the Israelites if they were to reap the blessings of the covenant. They were to set the Lord apart as the covenant Lord and worship him exclusively without setting up images of false gods to worship. Neither were they to worship the land itself or to attribute its fruitfulness to any other deity other than Yahweh. To demonstrate this faithfulness, the Lord commanded the Israelites to observe his **Sabbaths** and respect his sanctuary.

26:3–13. First, the Lord stated positively what the Israelites could expect if they obeyed the Lord's commands. The Lord would reward their obedience by producing rich harvests that would be guaranteed by rain at regular intervals. Normally it rained in Palestine during the fall and winter seasons. The early rain usually occurred in October, with the heaviest rain coming in January. The later rain fell during April. One can only imagine how thirsty this parched land can be and what havoc a rainless season would produce. If they fully obeyed the Lord and the terms of his covenant, he would bless them with seasonal rain and rich harvests. God would also reward their faithfulness by protecting them against assault from predatory nations and wild beasts.

The chief blessing arising from their careful observance of his law would be the Lord's presence in their midst. He would look on them with favor and put his **dwelling place** among them. The other nations would eye Israel with envy and seek to plunder their wealth. But the covenant God who longed to dwell with them would protect them against all threats to their welfare if they obeyed his commands.

26:14–17. But the Lord went on to threaten Israel with catastrophic judgments if they failed to obey him. He did not base these threats on isolated violations of the law but for repeated, willful, and presumptuous infractions. The judgments would increase in degree, according to the levels of Israel's persistence in sin.

The first judgment would come in the form of **sudden terror**, manifested by diseases that would strike the nation's health. The terror would also affect the produce of the land by making it vulnerable to enemy subjugation. This opening judgment would serve as a gentler rebuke than what would come if they persisted in stubborn unbelief.

26:18–20. If Israel still did not turn back to God, he would punish them **seven times over.** Since seven was the number of God's ultimate perfection, God would punish them to the fullest measure as a chastisement for their pride and spiritual neglect. The expressions "iron sky" and "bronze earth" depict horrendous drought conditions that would affect their agriculture.

26:21–26. The next punishment God would send for their disobedience would be fierce wild animals. These beasts of prey would spare neither field nor child. People would be afraid to travel on open roads—a condition that would also have bitter economic fallout. If Israel still refused to return from the error of their ways, God would send the sword and severe plagues against them. These would affect their ability to make bread. Their rations would be so depleted that **ten women** would be able to bake their **bread in one oven,** then ration it so that no one would be satisfied (see Isa. 3:1).

26:27–35. If the people still continued in their sinful ways, God would intensify famine conditions so much that they would have to resort to cannibalism to ward off hunger. In the process God would destroy all the tokens of their false worship, including **incense altars** and **sanctuaries.** He would scatter them **among the nations** in captivity.

26:36–39. The psychological effect of judgment would be massive, causing widespread paranoia and fear. The nation would experience not only the removal of God's blessing but his very presence (Ezek. 10:1–22). Attempts to fight against their enemies would be futile. Finally, they would **waste away in the lands of their enemies because of their sins.**

26:40–46. But God would never punish them beyond total remedy. If in their extreme suffering they turned to him and confessed their sins, God would hear them once again. The basis of God restoring them was his covenant with Jacob and Isaac when God promised to multiply them and place them in the promised land.

C The Law of Vows (27:1–34)

SUPPORTING IDEA: *The Lord gives governing rules for individual vows.*

27:1–8. The vow, in the biblical sense, involved a voluntary obligation to God by a person, sometimes in an attempt to gain a favor from God (see Gen. 28:20–22; Judg. 11:30–31). Man's tendency is to promise God something in return for a favor granted, usually during severe affliction. Such vows demonstrate dependence on God and an acknowledgment that he alone can provide such a favor or blessing.

When a man devoted someone to the sanctuary service, he usually redeemed this vow. The price of such redemption varied with age and gender. The price of redemption for a devoted male between the age of twenty and sixty was **fifty shekels of silver**. For females the price was reduced to **thirty shekels**. The reason for the reduction was probably due to the physical strength of the male compared to the female and the kind of work such strength might produce. For children aged five to twenty, the value was set at twenty shekels for males and ten for females. Infants between one month and five years old were valued at five shekels for males and three for females. The elderly came in at fifteen for males and ten for females. A poor person who could not afford the usual price for any of these vows might have the value reduced at the discretion of the presiding priest.

27:9–15. A man could vow an animal to the Lord if it was free from defect and otherwise acceptable. He could not exchange one animal for another if the animal was fit for sacrifice. The expression **becomes holy** means it could not be redeemed. If, however, the animal was not fit for sacrifice (e.g., donkeys), the priest would determine whether the animal could be of use around the sanctuary and, if not, set its value and sell it for profit. If the man wanted to redeem these animals, he could do so by adding 20 percent to the valued cost. The laws for unclean animals also applied to houses vowed to the Lord. These houses did not involve tribal land but probably city dwellings that could be sold legally.

27:16–25. If a man dedicated to the Lord **part of his family land**, he was to value it according to how much it would produce in the years before the Jubilee. He could redeem this vow if he added 20 percent to its estimated value set by the priest. If he failed to redeem the field or sold it off, he could not redeem it, and it fell to the priests. Such a scenario might exist if the man vowed the land to the Lord and then simply paid the annual value of the crops to the priests. He then temporarily sold the land with the intention of redeeming it before the Jubilee but forgot to do so. In such cases the land would go to the priests. The standard of payment was **twenty gerahs to the shekel**. Should there be a dispute in scale weights, they were to weigh it by the sanctuary shekel.

27:26–27. The **firstborn of an animal** was already dedicated to the Lord and thus could not be redeemed. If the animal was unclean and therefore not suitable for sacrifice, the owner could either redeem it at cost plus 20 percent or sell it outright to the priests.

27:28–29. A man could irrevocably devote, or ban, something to the Lord under certain conditions. Such vows could include land, animals, and even people. Some situations called for this—for example, when Israel conquered an idolatrous land. When someone devoted a person to destruction, it involved someone who engaged in idolatry or false worship of some sort (see

Exod. 22:20). In all these cases the items devoted to destruction could not be redeemed.

27:30–34. People could not vow their tithes to the Lord because they, as in the case of the firstborn, already belonged to the Lord (see "Deeper Discoveries"). They could, however, redeem their tithes of produce by paying the valued price and adding 20 percent. The Israelites could not substitute one animal for another vowed animal, but if they did, both animals would go to the Lord.

> **MAIN IDEA REVIEW:** *The holy nation must remember to observe all of God's laws because they bring meaningful life and liberty.*

III. CONCLUSION

It All Tastes the Same

As a pastor, I have attended many potlucks with the people in my church. Each of these potlucks has a wide variety of contributions, some not necessarily complementing the other dishes. On one occasion I noticed some of the casseroles did not have serving utensils and people were using the same spoon to scoop out the onion dishes, the potato dishes, the beef stroganoff, and whatever moved them as they paraded past the table. The spoon was then passed back down the line for the next person to do the same.

One lady at my table made an interesting observation: "My, everything tastes a lot like everything else." Some of the beef stroganoff juices were in the onion dish, and both of their juices were now part of several other dishes. Each dish now began to taste the same.

As Christians, we arrive at church, click on our halos, and enter an auditorium filled with music. We sing "Onward Christian Soldier" at church and go AWOL during the week. And soon the "juices" of the world creep into our spiritual lives, and everything begins to look and feel the same. This is not God's design. When God says, "Take a day off," there is no need to hesitate. Take the day off to worship and recharge your batteries. When God reminds you of idolatry in your life, run! No need to ponder the different forms of idolatry; just get away from them. Our lives are to be much different from the "stroganoff" or other dishes of this world. We are not to taste the same, act the same, live the same, or speak the same.

PRINCIPLES

- God always provides what we need for life and security.

- Everything we think we own is God's; we are only stewards of what he has entrusted to us.
- When we follow God's commandments, life will be more fruitful and meaningful.
- God's disciple follows man's disobedience.

APPLICATIONS

- Care for the poor around you, realizing this is a part of God's call on our lives.
- Make yourself available for God's use.
- Avoid all forms of idolatry.
- Consider carefully each promise you make since vows and promises are important to God.

IV. LIFE APPLICATION

The Danger of Independence

In Lake County, Florida, two elderly sisters drove around for two and one-half days before their car finally bogged down in a muddy orange grove. The two women, one eighty and the other eighty-four, had been on a shopping trip into a town just twenty miles from their rural home where they lived together. But somewhere on the return trip, the driver took a wrong turn. In an attempt to get back on the right road, the women evidently drove around in circles for over sixty hours straight, not stopping to eat, never once asking for directions. The police, attempting to retrace their journey, estimated that the two had traveled over two hundred miles trying to reach their home only twenty miles away. Finally, a farmer discovered them; their car hopelessly stuck, one sister dead from exposure and the other lying under an orange tree in critical condition with a sweater covering her face to ward off mosquitoes.

When asked why they did not seek help or ask questions, the surviving sister said, "Oh, we didn't want to do that! We've always been so independent, we wouldn't have dreamed of admitting we needed help."

Do not think that life becomes any easier when you ignore your problems and hope they will disappear. Like the goldfish you may spend your remaining hours swimming around and around in a sea of guilt and continue to be unusable for the kingdom of God. Freedom is found in Jesus Christ alone. When you invite his forgiveness and presence into your life, continued growth in obedience leads to greater freedom and greater use for God. When you sense life in a fishbowl, stop, confess, get some peace and rest from the

Scriptures, and move toward obedience. Stubborn independence is never an option for a follower of Christ.

V. PRAYER

Lord, the end of Leviticus has been a great reminder of your longing for my obedience and the consequences of my lack of obedience. I long to please you, Lord. May your Spirit convict and guide me daily, more than I have ever experienced as I continue to break free from the prison of sin and discover the liberty of your love. Amen.

VI. DEEPER DISCOVERIES

A. The Old Testament Law of Tithing

Strictly defined, the tithe is one-tenth of one's income devoted to God. From antiquity various nations have practiced tithing in one form or another. Abraham, after defeating a large confederation of enemies, devoted one-tenth of all the spoils to Melchizedek, the priest-king of Salem (Gen. 14:20). In doing so, Abraham acknowledged God as Creator of heaven and earth and the one who gave them the victory (14:19). Jacob vowed to give God one-tenth of all he had if the Lord granted him a safe journey (Gen. 28:22). Some point to the "fifth" that Joseph exacted from the impoverished Egyptians (Gen. 41:34; 47:24,26) as the origin of the tithe concept, but Abraham tithed long years before this.

The Old Testament did not label the tithe as a tax but as a prescribed donation for spiritual purposes. The tithe was to be brought to the one place designated by God as the spiritual center of worship—the sanctuary (Deut. 12:5–6). There the people could eat their tithe (whether grain, wine, or animals) "before the Lord" (i.e., at the sanctuary). The remainder would go to the Levites (Deut. 12:12; 26:12–15). If they lived too far from the designated place and could not travel to it without great inconvenience, they could exchange money for this offering. Once they arrived at the sanctuary, however, they must purchase the prescribed offerings, then follow the proper procedures for giving the tithe (Deut. 14:23–27).

To provide for the Levites, the Lord commanded the Israelites every third year to lay their tithes in store (in the town) so the Levites and the unfortunate would be able to eat (Deut. 14:28–29). Large storehouses were later constructed to house the tithe (2 Chr. 31:11; Neh. 13:12).

The tithe is man's acknowledgment that he is a steward of God's creation (Bible Almanac, 334). The Lord alone is Creator and possessor of heaven and earth, and man is God's servant. Whatever material wealth man can lay claim to is the direct gift of God. Thus in the tithe man attributes to God his due by giving back a portion.

VII. TEACHING OUTLINE

A. INTRODUCTION

1. Lead Story: A Prison for Goldfish
2. Context: God's call to holiness is a call to freedom. The more we live within God's guidelines, the more freedom we experience.
3. Transition: God provides guidelines for the physical and mental rest we need for a full life (Lev. 25). Turning from idolatry to the living God is a path toward freedom (Lev. 26). Acting with integrity by keeping promises and vows brings a sense of well-being (Lev. 27).

B. COMMENTARY

1. The Sabbath Year and Jubilee (25:1–55)
2. Promises and Warnings (26:1–46)
3. The Law of Vows (27:1–34)

C. CONCLUSION: THE DANGER OF INDEPENDENCE

VIII. ISSUES FOR DISCUSSION

1. In what area of your life have you felt in bondage? What do you think God wants you to do about this?
2. Do you believe God should reward obedience? What evidence in chapter 26 supports your conclusion?
3. Have you ever experienced the discipline of God? What is the difference between God's discipline and times of suffering? How does God use both in a person's life?
4. What are the consequences of not being a person of your word? How does "keeping promises" or not keeping them reflect a person's value system?

Introduction to

Numbers

The English word *Numbers* comes from the Vulgate *Numeri,* itself a translation of *Arithmoi,* taken from the title in the Greek Septuagint. Some ancient Hebrew manuscripts title the book "In the Wilderness."

GENERAL SYNOPSIS

In Numbers the Lord prepared his people to take the promised land. Accordingly, he taught them how to set up and take down camp, travel together, and function as a covenant community. The Lord had Moses take a census and furnished him supplemental instructions not mentioned earlier (chs. 1–10). Numbers then records the nation's journey from Sinai to the Plains of Moab. When they reached the Paran Desert, they sent our spies to view the land and bring back a report. Upon their return the spies brought back a mixed report. The land was good, just as the Lord told them, but the residents of the land would offer formidable resistance. For their unbelief, the Lord judged them and sentenced them to a generation of wandering in the desert (chs. 13–14).

During these wanderings Moses recorded some fateful events that provide glimpses of life during these forty years. Finally, the Lord had Moses number a new generation of eligible fighting men who would prepare to enter the land under Joshua's leadership. Along the way, they engaged several enemies, such as the Midianites, whom they defeated in short order. Just before arriving at their destination, two and one-half tribes sought and gained permission from Moses to settle in the territory immediately east of Jordan. Gad, Reuben, and the half tribe of Manasseh cleared some land and settled their families in these territories, but they faithfully prepared to join their brothers in the fateful battle for Canaan. Around this time, Moses formally appointed Joshua as his successor (27:12–23). With this the book begins to close the door on this stage in Israel's life—one fraught with many difficulties that resulted from the peoples' disobedience. In spite of this, it was always in God's heart to guide Israel to the land of rest.

CHARACTERISTICS OF NUMBERS

Purpose. Moses wrote of order, direction, and consequences. The Lord prepared his people before escorting them into the land of their inheritance. He wanted to show them how he alone could infallibly guide them through dark and unknown terrain where they would encounter many enemies and temptations. He also showed them the futility of refusing to follow his commands and provided several sobering examples of some who chose not to follow him and were swiftly judged. He even taught Israel he was not a respecter of persons by bringing a series of judgments on the first family of Israel.

Moses, the lawgiver and spiritual leader of Israel and one who shared a unique relationship with God, would not himself go into the promised land because of his sin in not honoring God as holy at Meribah (20:1–13). Aaron, who was an accomplice with Moses in his sin and who earlier fell into gross idolatry, was also denied entrance into Canaan (20:22–29). Finally, when Miriam, herself a prophetess, challenged Moses' sole leadership, the Lord struck her with leprosy, although she did recover (12:1–15). When some chief leaders from the priestly tribe of Levi sought to wrest control from Moses, Aaron, and the priests, the Lord judged many of them severely, then clarified for all time Aaron's family as the priests of Israel (chs. 16–18).

As the covenant God of Israel, the Lord taught Israel to worship him alone and to stay clear of foreign religious influence. Throughout their history as a nation, Israel would never fully learn this lesson. Moses recorded a mysterious encounter with a heathen prophet named Balaam. Balak, the king of Moab, hired Balaam to curse Israel, something the seer tried to do. But time and time again God overruled him, leading him instead to bless Israel, his covenant people. God even accorded the seer the ability to prophesy of Israel's glorious future (see chs. 22–24).

The Lord showed Israel that he ruled them whether or not they had a permanent land possession. He related to them as their Lord and constant sustainer even during their endless wanderings in the desert.

Identification. Within this book Moses took two detailed censuses of the tribes and Levi and gave the latter precise instructions for the service they would render and which would constitute their separate identity. He set apart Aaron and his sons to officiate within the veil of the tabernacle and admitted no rivals to this office. He enumerated supplementary offerings and sacrifices not fully mentioned earlier and even provided two chapters to grapple with a special case involving the land rights of the daughters of Zelophehad (chs. 27; 36). Moses then detailed precise boundaries of the land the nation would inherit (ch. 34) plus specific cities of refuge where accused murderers could flee from pursuing avengers (ch. 35). Thus the Lord identified Israel as a separate and special nation. Within this nation functioned a separate tribe that would assist an official priesthood. He led them toward a land with specified boundaries where they would worship God in a carefully prescribed manner.

Author. Moses wrote the Book of Numbers as he did the rest of the Pentateuch. The expression "The Lord said to Moses" or a derivative occurs more than eighty times. The extended discourse about Balaam does not mention Moses as the author, but neither does it furnish any reason for us to doubt Mosaic authorship.

Date. The events of the Book of Numbers take us close to the time of Moses' death, although Numbers does not record Moses' death. Conservative scholars generally assign the exodus an early date of 1445 B.C. The events of Numbers take place from that time on, ending just before Moses' death (about 1406 B.C., see Archer, *EBC*, I, 367). Some have questioned this early date and doubted whether writing was even available during this time. But we now know that writing originated around 3300 B.C. (Harrison, 21). The Lord speaks often to Moses especially in this book (see above), and Moses must have written the bulk of the book or at least supervised its composition. No event described in Numbers is anachronistic or belongs to another era. The writing with its detailed descriptions of geographical locales and minute accounts of Israel's travels (see ch. 33) demand an early date written by an eyewitness. Some have ascribed a much later date for this book as they do the Pentateuch as a whole. But we have every reason to believe that a single eyewitness wrote these events soon after they happened.

Theology of the book. The truth we derive from the Book of Numbers is consistent with the message of the wider Pentateuch: God is establishing a special relationship with his people.

God. The God who led the nation from its inhospitable stay in Egypt made clear his will and character to the people. He dwelt among the people by means of the elaborately designed tabernacle (1:51–53). During the journeys he took pains to teach them his ways and to fight off evil influences. The Israelites clearly saw his love by the way he cared for them and provided for their every need. They also witnessed many instances of his justice as well, not sparing even men and leaders of notoriety. Yet he taught the people the value of prayer and that he was a prayer-hearing God. When he sought to destroy the people for their sin, Moses prayed on their behalf, and God listened to him (14:13–25). God revealed his sovereignty by toppling the Balak/Balaam conspiracy to curse Israel and thereby demonstrated that his immutable purpose would stand (Heb. 6:17–19). No man or nation can curse or overcome the nation that is protected by God.

Man. Numbers provides the reader with a microcosm of the biblical understanding of man. The reader sees the special care and provision of God toward his people but then discovers a corrupting tendency within the people themselves. The root cause of that evil tendency can be traced to unbelief, the reluctance to believe God and his Word. The people came to the edge of certain blessing when they peered into the fertile landscape of Palestine. But they refused to enter because they would not believe God and trust in his protecting providence to bring them into the land.

On the other hand, Moses wrote of faithful men and women who took God at his word and were thus rewarded. Caleb and Joshua were champions of faith when they went against the majority opinion and urged the trembling nation to discard its fears and seize the moment. We see two men who look beyond fear and act in faith. This is what God wants for all of his people. Joshua and Caleb trusted God and took his word and set out to run to their reward. Later God would reward them for their trust in him, but not until he removed the generation that rebelled at his Word.

Ecclesiology. Some might balk at even mentioning ecclesiology so early in the Bible, but an embryonic form of what later would emerge as the church does appear in this book. The writer assumes these people share a covenant relationship with God and one another. God's law binds them to a community ethic and singular purpose—to glorify God. The Lord gives them marching orders and assigns them specific portions of the land. He thereby establishs them as a community of called-out people living in separate tribes but governed by a uniform covenant. Although they would live far apart from one another, they worshiped the same God in the same manner. He separated one tribe from the rest and one family from that tribe to attend to the spiritual needs of the nation. He furthermore regulated their worship with prescribed ceremony and sacrificial observances. He pinpointed the tabernacle sanctuary as the spiritual center of the nation. Within its confines the people would seek God's forgiveness through priestly intercession and representation.

Eschatology. From Balaam's prophecies to the prediction of Moses' death, the Book of Numbers gives the observant reader a preview of final events, if only in seed form. None of the teachings or events describes final things with any detail, but they do give a glimpse into the world of ultimate destination. When Korah and his insurrectionists challenged Moses, the Lord sent them to an early exit when "the earth opened its mouth and swallowed them" (16:32). No one came by and buried these people, because their bodies were nowhere to be found. Again, Moses did not give details or explain the significance of their demise, but he did provide a picture of an ominous ending where families were swallowed by the ground they stood on.

Balaam predicted a glorious future for Israel, the people of God (24:15–19). He couched his words in types and figures, as did the true prophets of Israel. But he wrote of a leader who would emerge to defend Israel and destroy her enemies. But this community of God's people would continue to multiply. Later it would support another branch that also would bear fruit (Rom. 11:11–24).

Aaron would face an early death for his sin, but then "be gathered to his people" (Num. 20:24,26). He would not collapse one day and cease to exist and then atomize into nothingness. He would travel to a place where his fathers preceded him and where all the faithful would go one day. Such a passage breathes assurance into the heart of the careful and observant reader who sees shadows of a greater New Testament reality, even eternal life.

Finally, the Lord dwelt in the most holy place between the cherubim. He made his place near the people. As they camped and then set out to travel again, he remained nearby. He gave them visible tokens of his presence by the pillar of fire by night and the cloud by day. As the tribes ventured closer and closer to Canaan, they came closer to the time when God would reform the way people come into his presence. Would that veil ever bar their access to him? If only it were legitimately "torn in two" (Matt. 27:51). If only someone would announce, "Now the dwelling of God is with men, and he will live with them" (Rev. 21:3).

Numbers 1–4

God Knows Who You Are

Quote

"*G*od could have kept Daniel out of the lion's den. . . . He could have kept Paul and Silas out of jail—he could have kept the three Hebrew children out of the fiery furnace. . . . But God has never promised to keep us out of hard places. . . . What he has promised is to go with us through every hard place, and to bring us through victoriously."

Merv Rosell

Numbers 1–4

IN A NUTSHELL

*T*he people of Israel had grown numerically since their journey of freedom began, and now God wanted them to learn a great lesson through a census and some instructions on where each family belonged around the tabernacle and who was to serve in the tabernacle during their wilderness education.

God Knows Who You Are

I. INTRODUCTION

A Parent's Worst Nightmare

*E*very parent's worst nightmare is the loss of a child. We have friends at our church who were at the lake one afternoon and lost track of their five-year-old son. After searching for him for the next three to four minutes, the father found him submerged in four feet of water. After doing CPR on his son until the paramedics arrived, the boy was rushed to a local hospital and later airlifted to a children's specialty hospital near Los Angeles where he regained complete health and memory over the next week. It truly was a miracle from God. I have often wondered what it would have been like to be that father who found his son, in crisis, not breathing and the panic in his heart.

Both these parents realized, however, that no matter where their child was and what crisis they might face, God never loses sight of his children. The Bible supports this truth many times. In Mark 5 we meet a woman who had been bleeding for years and had spent all of her life savings on healing specialists. She had done everything she could to fight this ailment that made her ceremonially unclean and physically weak. She had one hope—just touch Jesus' robe and she would be healed. Remember the story? Jesus was on his way to Jairus's house and sensed someone with faith had touched him. He turned to pick out from the crowd this woman who was probably an outcast in society. God always knows where his true children are located and where they are supposed to be.

In Numbers 1–4, we are invited into a study of the first census prompted by God. Again we learn how God is interested in the individual person and how every person has a responsibility to serve God.

II. COMMENTARY

God Knows Who You Are

> **MAIN IDEA:** *Although the tribes comprised a unified nation, each had its own identity and unique function.*

A The Census (1:1–54)

> **SUPPORTING IDEA:** *The Lord sets apart men to serve in Israel's army.*

1:1–2. The underlying purpose for this and other similar censuses was military, but the result could be used for other reasons, such as land distribution (see Num. 26:55–56). Later Joshua distributed land to tribes according to their size. The present census is the first formal census recorded in the Bible. Later censuses include one thirty-eight years later (26:1–51), and the infamous Davidic census that led to God's displeasure (2 Sam. 24:1–9; 1 Chr. 21:1–7).

1:3–16. The procedure called for each tribe and family to be counted and named in the official enrollment. They were to count only those men who were twenty and older. To assist Moses the Lord chose **one man from each tribe** (who also was the head of the tribe).

1:17–46. On **first day of the second month** that the people of Israel fled Egypt, the count began **in the Desert of Sinai.** The results of the count were as follows:

Reuben	Simeon	Gad	Judah	Issachar	Zebulun
46,500	59,300	45,650	74,600	54,400	57,400
Ephraim	Manasseh	Benjamin	Dan	Asher-	Naphtali
40,500	32,200	35,400	62,700	41,500	53,400

The total number came to **603,550.**

1:47–54. The Lord exempted Levi from the census because to this tribe fell the service of the tabernacle. The Levites were to oversee all the ministry of the tabernacle worship and accompanying duties. Since the tabernacle accompanied the Israelites wherever they went, the Levites had to put it up and take it down. No other tribe could perform this ministry. This last rule was such an essential component of the divinely sanctioned plan that violators would **be put to death.** The Levites must set camp around the tabernacle lest God become displeased with the entire community.

B The Camp Arrangements of the Tribes (2:1–34)

SUPPORTING IDEA: *The tribes are designated specific campsites in relation to the tabernacle.*

2:1–2. Next in the order of travel organization came the camp arrangements around the tent of meeting. The tribes were to camp with raised standards or identifying banners. The result of this arrangement had the twelve tribes forming four large camps around the tabernacle.

2:3–34. **On the east** side of the tabernacle went three tribes. **Judah** would camp directly toward the east. Next to him went **Issachar** followed by **Zebulun.** The combined strength of this camp was **186,400.**

Next and **on the south** went **Reuben**, followed by **Simeon**, then **Gad**. This camp numbered **151,450**.

The **Levites** camped **in the middle** of all the camp divisions around the **Tent of Meeting**.

On the west went **Ephraim**, **Manasseh**, and **Benjamin**. The three tribes totaled **108,100**.

The final camp division came **on the north**, and included **Dan, Asher,** and **Naphtali**. The total of this camp division came to **157,600**.

During the wilderness journeys the camps would set up and depart in this order as arranged by God.

◨ The Order and Duties of the Levites (3:1–51)

SUPPORTING IDEA: *The Lord describes the origin and duties of the Levitical divisions.*

3:1–4. The Levites, sometimes called the thirteenth tribe, were descended from Moses and Aaron. When Jacob adopted Ephraim and Manasseh as official tribes of Israel, he allowed for an even tribal distribution of land allocations once they settled in the land of Palestine (see "Deeper Discoveries"). Of course, the Levites were also a fixed tribe in Israel, but because of their unique role they received no land inheritance. Instead, they presided over the tabernacle worship and sacrificial system.

God chose **Aaron** and his descendents to serve as priests, with the other Levitical tribes assisting them. Aaron's first sons who served as priests, Nadab and Abihu, both died when they offered **unauthorized fire** before the Lord **in the Desert of Sinai**. The Lord replaced them with Aaron's other sons, Eleazar and Ithamar. Determining just who qualified to serve as priest required scrupulous record-keeping on the part of the tribe.

3:5–39. The Lord delineated the specific duties of each tribe division, beginning with the priests. They were responsible for all the tabernacle duties, including the materials and transport. The Lord gave them the remaining tribal members to assist them, and from these members he created three separate divisions according to family origin to preside over different duties. But these other Levites who were not priests could not perform priestly functions as could Aaron's immediate descendents. Any Levite who did so was to be put to death.

The Levites represented the **first male offspring of every Israelite woman** and, as such, belonged to the Lord. The sanctification of the firstborn to the Lord corresponded to the killing of the Egyptian firstborn during the first Passover.

Although the Levites were not numbered among those ready for war, they were indeed numbered for service. Moses was commanded to number each male Levite more than one month old. The three primary families were

Gershon, Kohath, and Merari. From these families came the divisions that would perform the three primary responsibilities of the tabernacle when readying it for transport.

The number from Gershon totaled 7,500. They camped on the westerly section of the Levitical settlement, directly behind the tabernacle. Their duties consisted of caring for the tent proper, the various curtains, the coverings, and the courtyard curtains.

The family of Kohath numbered 8,600. The Lord assigned to them the **care of the sanctuary** including the altars, tables, ark, lampstand, and the other furniture used in the tabernacle service. They camped south of the tabernacle.

The third family, the Merarites, numbered 6,200, and they camped to the north. They were to care for the tabernacle frames, bars, bases, and **everything related to their use**.

Moses and Aaron camped to the east of the tabernacle in front of the tent of meeting. The priests officiated in the tent of meeting and performed all the prescribed priestly duties on behalf of Israel. The total number of Levites came to **22,000** (with 273 firstborn; see v. 46). The number seems disproportionately small but presents no real critical problem. Consider, for example, the large number from Judah as compared to the other tribes. Still, no reason is given for the smaller numbers of this tribe.

3:40–51. The Lord next commanded Moses to total the number of firstborn from the tribes and to exchange them for the Levites. He also had them exchange the firstborn of all livestock. The redemption price for the exchange of the 273 remaining firstborn came to **five shekels** for each one. Again the standard weight was the **sanctuary shekel**.

Ⅾ The Threefold Division of Levitical Families and Their Duties (4:1–49)

SUPPORTING IDEA: *The Lord gives the Levites specific assignments pertaining to their tabernacle service.*

4:1–6. The Lord did not delegate to Moses or Israel the privilege of self-organization, at least in broader terms. Although the two brothers, Moses and Aaron, do figure prominently as servants and spokesmen for Yahweh, they were to enact only what the Lord said. Here they are to **take a census**. The census of the present chapter both complements and differs from the one in the preceding chapter. The first census pertained to general duties of the Levitical families, and it registered all males one month old and above. The present census enrolled all males from thirty to fifty years of age **who come to serve in the work in the Tent of Meeting**. Harrison describes these as "working Levites" (81).

We might describe the Kohathite family as the elite family among the Levitical families. To the Kohath tribe fell the responsibility of guarding, maintaining, and transporting the sacred furniture of the tabernacle, or **most holy things**.

The Lord first gave the Kohathites directions for transporting the furniture of the tabernacle. Only the priests (or **Aaron and his sons**) were to venture into the holy places of the tabernacle. Once there, they were first to cover the sacred vessels such as the **ark of the Testimony**. The cover was made out of an animal skin (less likely "porpoise" or **sea cows**, as in our translation; see the discussion in Harrison, 82–83) over which went another blue cloth. Apparently the carrying poles remained in the vessels at all times (see Exod. 25:15; 1 Kgs. 8:8).

4:7–20. The Kohathites were to employ a similar procedure for the **table of the Presence** with the special provision that the bread was to remain on the table even during transport. They were likewise to cover the **lampstand** and its accessories with a blue cloth and animal skin (leather).

Next the men were to place a similar cover over the **gold altar**, or altar of incense, along with any remaining articles used in the sanctuary service. To aid the transporting of the latter, they used a **carrying frame**.

Although the bread was to remain on the table during the journeys that followed, the Kohathites were allowed to clean the ashes from the **bronze altar** of sacrifice. The altar utensils went with the altar wherever it traveled and were wrapped in leather.

The final note to this family came as a reminder and a warning. Only the qualified Kohathite men could handle the sacred furniture of the tabernacle, but even they could neither touch nor even look upon those items if the priests did not first properly cover them. Should they violate this last injunction they would have to pay with their lives.

4:21–28. The next family from the Levitical tribe, the **Gershonites**, handled the various coverings, cords, and hangings that adorned the tabernacle. In keeping with the latest census, only those **thirty to fifty years of age** could actually serve in this capacity. The restriction came not because of some ceremonial reason or need for men in the full vigor of strength (for those in their twenties are, for the most part, stronger than those in their thirties), but because the margin of error was so small in these sacred undertakings. The prescribed age bracket provided a hedge against errors stemming from physical limitations (i.e., those above fifty) and those attributed to insufficient experience and maturation (those under thirty).

4:29–33. The final clan, the **Merarites**, were responsible for what remained—the supporting **frames of the tabernacle, its crossbars, posts and bases** as well as anything related to the courtyard. These items provided the physical framework for the tabernacle.

4:34–49. The leaders of Israel registered the tribal families as prescribed, then totaled their numbers. The total of the Kohathites stood at 2,750 eligible males who could perform the service. The Gershonites numbered 2,630 and the Merarites 3,200. The census came by direct command of the Lord and was done as commanded. The divine sanction of this census raises key questions about another census taken in Israel that fell under divine wrath (see "Deeper Discoveries"). But for now, they carried out this numbering as ordered by God and prepared to transport the tabernacle.

> **MAIN IDEA REVIEW:** *Although the tribes comprised a unified nation, each had its own identity and unique function.*

III. CONCLUSION

You Forgot to Look Up

The father of a small boy would often sneak into a nearby neighbor's orchard and pick some of the neighbor's finest apples. He evidently had done this for some time without being caught but always made sure the "coast was clear" before stepping onto the foreign property. One day the man's son was tagging along and asked if he could join his father. After carefully looking in every direction and seeing no one, the father began to creep through the fence. The father was just about ready to help himself to some of his neighbor's best when the youngster startled him by crying out, "Dad! Dad! You forgot to look up! You forgot to see if God is watching!"

In every area of life, we need this reminder. God knows where you are in your life right now and whether or not you are where you should be. He knows you have been called to do something special with your life. He knows if you have invited Christ into your life and if you have received forgiveness for your sins. He knows that an eternal census has been taken, and he knows whether your name has been written in the Lamb's Book of Life with a permanent marker.

PRINCIPLES

- God cares for the individual.
- God knows exactly where each one of his people belongs. His plan is perfect and is always to be trusted and followed.
- The initial census did not include the tribe of Levi because they were never to be included in warfare but to serve specifically in the tabernacle.
- Every child of God has a place to serve.

APPLICATIONS

- Take some time to reflect on the fact that God knows you thoroughly, knows your family of origin, and knows the joys and sorrows of your life.

- Ask God to show you not only where you've come from but where he wants you to go from this time forward.

- God is holy and wants us to treat his sacred things with respect and reverence.

IV. LIFE APPLICATION

Eternal Auction

Auctions have become a primary means of selling and buying. Internet sites like eBay have opened up the entire world of objects never before considered valuable. One can quickly tell the value of an object by the price that a qualified person places on the object.

Centuries ago mankind was on the auction block. We were all set to go to the highest bidder. Satan was offering this and that, and it looked as if we were all doomed to a life of sin and shame. All hope for redemption appeared to be gone. Just then the door of the auction house swung open and in walked the Son of God. The auctioneer was saying, "Going, going" and about to say "gone" when Jesus said, "I'll buy them!" The auctioneer said that this was highly irregular. "Why, you don't even know what the bid is, sir." Jesus responded, "It matters not . . . I will take them." Satan quickly upped his bid and offered pleasure. Jesus said that pleasure would last only a season. He said that he offered eternal joy in his presence. Satan then offered fame. Jesus then shared how fame was fleeting and offered the acceptance of the Father and adoption into the family of God.

But Satan was not done. He offered wealth as his next bid. Jesus responded with the truth of how wealth is so temporary and that the wealth he offered would survive even the grave. And so the bidding went until Jesus said that he would give his life for mankind. Satan fell silent. He would not make such a sacrifice. Only our Lord had that kind of love. Only he saw that kind of worth in man. He saw it in us because he had created it there in the form of his own image and likeness. And what is even more amazing is that God knew all this in eternity past. Before time began, God knew who you were and where you belonged. Your name was already on God's mind before you were created. Is there any doubt about his love and guidance in your life?

V. PRAYER

Lord God, Creator of heaven and earth, ruler of all nations, and Lord over all, I want to stop for a moment and be reminded of how much you love me. As you stationed each tribe around the tabernacle, station me in life at the precise place where I can serve you best. Remind me to be fruitful and faithful in the days you give me. In Jesus' name. Amen!

VI. DEEPER DISCOVERIES

A. What Makes a Census Proper or Improper?

A census was an administrative device that aided a government in everything from tax collection to a military draft. At the Lord's command Moses numbered the people and levied them for a sanctuary tax so he could construct the tabernacle (Exod. 30:11–16). He counted males twenty years old and above who could go to war. Later another census was taken following the Baal incident and other rebellions of Israel (see ch. 26). These censuses all seemed normal and even sanctioned by God and duly carried out.

Years later, however, David took a census that was severely judged by God (see 2 Sam. 24; 1 Chr. 21). In the Samuel passage, the Lord ordered David to take a census of Israel, but in the Chronicles passage Satan moved him to count Israel. David even felt remorse following the actual count, but the Lord still sent a terrible plague that was stayed only by David's sacrificial intercession. Scholars have considered the merits of arguments and counterarguments about why David's census was considered evil by God. Most conclude that David's arrogance led him to measure his military readiness, while some believe he didn't raise the prescribed census tax ordered earlier by God. Yet God did seem at some point to order the census. Perhaps David took a levy from the people which was excessive. Nearly all conclude that David's pride played a role in the census.

The earlier censuses involved some elements that David's did not and perhaps supply the key to their legitimacy. First of all, they were clearly *ordered by the Lord*. The Lord specifically told Moses what to do and how to do it. David might have disobeyed the Lord in some detail that the biblical account is silent about. Second, they had a *clear purpose*. Either they were raising revenues for a holy purpose, such as constructing the tabernacle or mustering the young men for a war ordained by God. Third, the order was carried out *precisely as the Lord required*. The Lord went to battle against Israel's enemies but used its army to win those wars. A census could be quite helpful. We also know the census helped Joshua and Eleazar determine how much land to allot the individual tribes, since land was distributed in accordance with each tribes' relative size.

B. Joseph's Adoption of Ephraim and Manasseh and Tribal Numbering

The nation of Israel consisted of twelve tribes who came from the names of Jacob's twelve sons. The number twelve was maintained, but the specific tribal names making up the twelve varied. When Joseph adopted Ephraim and Manasseh, he did so by divine command and divine necessity. With Levi excluded from land ownership, the actual number of tribes that settled into land ownership would have been eleven, not twelve. Yet God assigned a significance to the number twelve (see Matt. 11:1; cp. Acts 1:15–26 and the disciples' desire to maintain their number at twelve; Rev. 21:12–21; 22:2). He therefore split Joseph in two so that, when necessary, he could exclude Levi from their official number without compromising its legitimate place among the tribes. On the other hand, he could easily insert Levi among the tribes of the nations when it suited his purposes. When that occurred, the sacred record includes Joseph instead of his two sons Ephraim and Manasseh.

Jacob combined his adopted sons Ephraim and Manasseh into Joseph when he prophesized about the nation in days to come (Gen. 49:22–26). In one instance, the apostle John left out the tribe of Ephraim while leaving in Levi and Manasseh (Rev. 7:5–8). He didn't provide a reason for Ephraim's exclusion, and few have offered any plausible explanation. But God did maintain the number twelve there as in other passages. Many have speculated about the significance of the number twelve. We do know God considered it quite important in the divine economy of redemption.

VII. TEACHING OUTLINE

A. INTRODUCTION

1. Lead Story: A Parent's Worst Nightmare
2. Context: God had heard the cries of his people in Egypt. He called Moses to return to Egypt and lead them out of slavery and into a good land. This group of former slaves had much to learn in order to become the people through whom God would bless the nations. The discipline and order we see in these chapters of Numbers is a part of that educational process.
3. Transition: Today God continues to call people out of slavery to sin to the life of being his people. Having been redeemed by the sacrificial death of Christ, we are to live as people who have been purchased at an incalculable price.

B. COMMENTARY

1. The Census (1:1–54)
2. The Camp Arrangements of the Tribes (2:1–34)
3. The Order and Duties of the Levites (3:1–51)
4. The Threefold Division of Levitical Families and Their Duties (4:1–49)

C. CONCLUSION: ETERNAL AUCTION

VIII. ISSUES FOR DISCUSSION

1. What was God's intent for using all these man-hours and all this time to take a census of the people? What impact could these counts have in the future for the Hebrew people?
2. Who were the Levites? What was their calling from God? What opportunities to serve were given to them and not to the rest of the Israelites?
3. What was the significance of the arrangement of the tribes around the tabernacle, and how would this enhance or inhibit their traveling?
4. Why was the sin of Nadab and Abihu such a big deal? What lessons were the people of Israel to learn from this? What lessons should we learn from God's willingness to include this failure in the Bible?
5. Why were the temple furnishings treated so carefully during transport? What was God trying to teach the Israelites?

Numbers 5–8

Preparation for Holiness

I. INTRODUCTION
Holy, Holy, Holy

II. COMMENTARY
A verse-by-verse explanation of these chapters.

III. CONCLUSION
Tozer on God's Holiness

An overview of the principles and applications from these chapters.

IV. LIFE APPLICATION
Mr. Glory-Face

Melding these chapters to life.

V. PRAYER
Tying these chapters to life with God.

VI. DEEPER DISCOVERIES
Historical, geographical, and grammatical enrichment of the commentary.

VII. TEACHING OUTLINE
Suggested step-by-step group study of these chapters.

VIII. ISSUES FOR DISCUSSION
Zeroing these chapters in on daily life.

Numbers 5–8

I N   A   N U T S H E L L

*T*he people of Israel had received their marching orders from God and had some final preparations to make. Those who were considered defiled must be removed from the campsite. Restitution was required for all offenses, and a special offering was instituted. An offer of a closer, more obedient walk with God was offered the people through the Nazarite vow, and the Levitical servants were required to go through a cleansing process. This was all to take place in preparation for God's presence and God's holiness among them.

Preparation for Holiness

I. INTRODUCTION

Holy, Holy, Holy

*P*hiladelphia pastor James Montgomery Boice once spoke to a discipleship group on the attributes of God. He began by asking them to list God's qualities in order of importance. They put love first, followed by wisdom, power, mercy, omniscience, and truth. At the end of the list they put holiness. "That did surprise me," Boice later wrote in an article in *Moody* magazine, "because the Bible refers to God's holiness more than any other attribute. The Bible doesn't generally refer to God as *Loving, Loving, Loving* or *Wise, Wise, Wise* or *Omniscient, Omniscient, Omniscient!* But over and over we read the cry of the angels, *Holy, Holy, Holy!*"

We serve a holy God, a God who cannot tolerate the presence of sin. This is why heaven will be a perfect place. But most believers spend little time contemplating and appreciating the holiness of God. In his *Systematic Theology,* Louis Berkhof wrote, "It does not seem proper to speak of one attribute of God as being more central and fundamental than another; but if this were permissible, the scriptural emphasis on the holiness of God would seem to justify its selection." The people of Israel were now in a position of preparation. Their focus must temporarily change to cleanse the camp and make it holy for both the journey and God's presence.

II. COMMENTARY

Preparation for Holiness

> **MAIN IDEA:** *Just before Israel marched forward, the Lord assigned them some final preparations, including cleansing directions and provision for special commitments.*

The Purity of the Tribes (5:1–31)

> **SUPPORTING IDEA:** *To ensure the purity of the camp, the Lord gave the Israelites directions for restitution and a special purity test.*

5:1–4. The Lord reminded Moses to comply with the prohibitions and regulations governing **infectious skin disease** (see Lev. 13–14) or other contaminating defilement that threatened the purity of the camp. Once reminded that they needed to quarantine those infected from the community, **the Israelites did this**—they obeyed—and sent them away **just as the LORD had instructed Moses.**

5:5–10. The Lord reintroduced a summary of the laws of restitution he had given in Leviticus 6:1–7 that deal with offenses resulting in loss. The laws linked such offenses to another with one's faithfulness to the Lord, a truth that New Testament writers would later bring to light (Matt. 25:44–46; Mark 12:28–34; Luke 10:16; Acts 9:4; 1 Thess. 4:8). When such wrongs went ignored or due reparations were not forthcoming, the Lord himself would take up the cause. But the scope of such truths brings us back to the law of love to one's neighbor (Lev. 19:18).

But the Lord added a new feature to this law in case the wronged party had since died, perhaps due to the wrong inflicted. If the victim died without leaving a close relative to realize the benefit of the required restitution, the perpetrator might walk away unpunished. The new supplemental law left the amount of the loss plus the required 20 percent to the priest. The offender must also offer the prescribed ram of atonement as a guilt offering (Lev. 6:6). The gifts contributed to the maintenance of the tabernacle and priestly families.

With such regulations came a reminder of the heinousness of sin that always carried painful and costly consequences. The course of sin, however, had already spun out of control so much that these legal stipulations could not serve as a permanent remedy. So in the act of restitution we see pain and consequences. But in the offering we obtain a glimpse of a better solution, looking forward to him who would appear "once for all at the end of the ages to do away with sin by the sacrifice of himself" (Heb. 9:26).

5:11–14. But what of crimes that were done in secret and provided no willing eyewitnesses, a characteristic of most sexual sins? Or how would a faithful wife, suspected and possibly slandered by a distrustful husband, vindicate her good name? For such hard-to-adjudicate cases the Lord introduced the law of **jealousy**. The words here indicate the husband's feelings of suspicion may or may not have had validity. When his feelings later proved true, we could entertain the possibility that these feelings were sent by the Lord as an incentive to inquire further into the matter. But then again the feelings may have come from an overexercised suspicion or distrustful nature on the part of the husband. The rationale for this law is not hard to see. The Lord required purity in the relationships he established in the community. In this sense the present narrative connects naturally with the preceding discussion on wrongs committed on another (vv. 1–10).

5:15–17. The test required both husband and wife to appear before the priest, presenting him an offering of barley flour. The grain offering in Leviticus 6:20 came with oil, but the present offering required neither oil nor frankincense. It resembled the sin offering (Lev. 5:11), "but this should not be understood as a presumption of guilt" (Harrison, 108). The offering is a special case gift to the Lord, one unique to its own circumstances.

The priest would have the woman **stand before the LORD**, the true decider of guilt or innocence. The priest would then take some dust from the tabernacle floor—dust containing potential contaminants, no doubt—and put the dust into a jar of holy water.

5:18–22. The woman would next loose her hair in such a way that it would fall freely (required also of those who had leprosy; see Lev. 13:45). The priest placed the offering in her hands while he held on to the jar of water. The test involved the priest reciting a curse, which, if the accused was proved guilty, would come to pass. If the woman had committed adultery, the bitter water would cause her **thigh to waste away** and her **abdomen to swell**. The woman, if she hadn't confessed to this point, was supposed to show consent to this test by saying, **Amen. So be it.**

5:23–31. The priest would next inscribe the curses on a scroll, then stir them into the bitter water. The onlookers, including the terrified accused, may have supposed some transference of the curse took place at that point. The woman next drank from the jar, consuming the contents. The priest next took the grain offering from her hands and waved **it before the LORD** before placing it on the altar as a memorial offering. This act symbolized the Lord's involvement in arbitrating this case.

The guilt or innocence of the accused would be determined by the effect the water had on her. If she drank the bitter water without contracting the awful effects pronounced on guilty parties, she would be pronounced clean and would be free to have children. But if she went astray and broke her marriage vows, the water would produce the curse with attendant effects on her physical body.

Probably some guilty parties died from this ritual, while others suffered severe physical effects resulting in the inability to bear children. Not to be able to bear children was a severe judgment in a culture that lauded motherhood.

🅱 The Nazirite Vow (6:1–27)

SUPPORTING IDEA: *A special vow of separation is regulated by divine legislation.*

The nation of Israel stood unique among the nations of the world because of its relationship with God. No Israelite could lay claim to God apart from the community, although there were individuals, like Abraham or Moses, who had a special relationship with the Lord. The Nazirite vow could be taken by people who wanted to commit themselves totally to God.

6:1–8. The vow was one of consecration or separation to God, and it involved a protracted time frame and strict regulation. Male or female could take this vow, but they must abstain from fermented beverages of any kind including vinegar, itself a by-product of the vine. The latter requirement was similar to the restrictions put on functioning priests (Lev. 10:8–11). This vow required scrupulous attention to detail and strict attention to all governing regulations. Hence it was one of the few acts of personal devotion brought under Levitical legislation.

The stipulation that required the Nazirite never to shave his or her hair differed from some pagan rituals that required shaved heads (Harrison, 125). The unshaven hair, a unique symbol (vv. 5–6), was perhaps, as Keil notes, "an ornament in which the whole strength and fullness of vitality were exhibited and which the Nazirite wore in honor of the Lord" (36). We hear much of this feature of the vow in the case of Samson (Judg. 13–16).

6:9–12. Another element of the vow was avoiding contact with the dead, something not always under the direct control of the Nazirite. But coming into contact with a corpse nullified the vow. In such cases the Nazirite must submit himself or herself to the required ritual cleansing. Following a seven-day waiting period, the Nazirite was to have his or her head completely shaved, followed by an offering of **two doves or two young pigeons** to the priest at the entrance to the tent of meeting. One of the birds would be offered as a sin offering and the other as a burnt offering. The Nazirite also offered up a one-year-old male lamb as a guilt offering.

6:13–21. To conclude the vow the Nazirite brought to the entrance to the tent of meeting a prescribed offering that included the one-year-old male lamb for a burnt offering, a one-year-old ewe lamb for a sin offering, followed by an unblemished ram for a fellowship offering. To cap the ritual the Nazirite brought grain and drink offerings plus a basket containing cakes made from unleavened bread with oiled wafers. The closing ritual contrasted with the somber nature of the vow itself in that the tone was celebrative. The vow was discharged, and now the consecrated Nazirite testified to the community of God's goodness and worthiness to be so honored by a special vow of separation. Harrison notes that all the ingredients to this closing ritual amounted to a great deal of expense. This indicates that short-term Nazirites probably came from wealthier families.

The priest conducted the closing ceremony **before the LORD** (offering the sacrifices in the normal prescribed fashion), followed by the Nazirite publicly shaving his or her hair and discarding the hair in the fire underneath the **sacrifice of the fellowship offering**. Finally, the priest waved before the Lord the boiled shoulder of the ram and one unleavened cake and wafer. With this the vow ended, and the Nazirite could resume a normal diet that included wine.

6:22–27. This chapter concludes with a beautiful blessing pronounced on Israel by the priests. Although God retained the privilege of *immediately* blessing the Israelites when and where he deemed wise, he chooses to bless them *mediately,* through priestly hands.

C The Dedicatory Offerings (7:1–89)

SUPPORTING IDEA: *The tabernacle is dedicated with special offerings.*

Before the nation could realize the glorious presence of God in and through his dwelling in the tabernacle, Moses, through the Lord's command, consecrated this sacred tent. Later King Solomon set apart the temple for special consecration in an elaborate ceremony (see 1 Kgs. 8–9; 2 Chr. 5–7). The tabernacle represented the presence of God among the nation, and, as such, it was the object of perpetual reverence. Israel's later history did not accord the sanctuary the sacred respect it deserved, and the nation suffered for this neglect.

Ezekiel's final extended prophecy included a protracted and elaborate description of an ideal sanctuary and attendant worship. The prophet Haggai sought to bring Israel back to God by drawing their attention once again to the sacred edifice instead of occupying their waking hours building and decorating their own houses (Hag. 1:2–15). The final word from God before the Messiah's first appearance warned the people that Messiah would come to his temple (Mal. 3:1), and when he did, he found it in a sad state (John 2:12–17). The Lord encouraged the people to start off on their best foot by offering gifts and sacrifices to the Lord at this dedication.

7:1–9. Once Moses set up the tabernacle, **he anointed it and consecrated it and all its furnishings**. This act by Moses moved the various leaders of Israel (heads of families) to bring to the tabernacle **six covered carts and twelve oxen**. The offering was not required by God and seemed to be quite spontaneous, although its organized character "indicates it to have been the result of concerted and previous arrangement" (JFB, 114). Apparently the leaders, aware of the pending dedication, voluntarily agreed to make an equal and collective contribution to the Lord's work.

That the Lord told Moses to accept these offerings may indicate initial reluctance on the part of Moses to do so. Moses had received specific instructions from the Lord about the arrangement of the tabernacle furniture and priestly service. He may have established a rule limiting all offerings and procedures to God's spoken command. But God continued to speak, and he instructed Moses to accept the offering of the people.

Churches today should not consider monetary gifts the only acceptable offerings. People have much more to give. God's cause is worthy of all the talents people are willing to share. The biblical heroes, including Nehemiah and the apostle Paul, never shied away from employing God's people in all manner of service, whether special or mundane. But Moses took the **carts and oxen** and **gave them to the Levites**. He divvied out two carts and four oxen to the Gershonites and four carts and eight carts to the Merarites. The

Kohathites received no such help because they were charged with carrying the sacred furniture on their shoulders.

7:10–83. Once Moses anointed the altar, the leaders **brought their offerings for its dedication** and presented them before the altar. The leaders would be assigned a day on which they would bring their offerings. The actual offerings consisted of a silver plate and a sprinkling bowl, each filled with fine flour mixed with oil. They also brought a gold dish filled with incense, a young bull, a ram, and a male lamb for a burnt offering, followed by **one male goat** for a sin offering. To conclude the offerings they also brought **two oxen, five rams, five male goats and five male lambs** for fellowship offerings. This series of offerings proceeded through the various tribes and concluded with the offering of **Ahira son of Enan**.

7:84–89. Moses summed up the collective offerings by the representative leaders of Israel. The gifts totaled as follows: twelve silver plates, each amounting to one hundred and thirty shekels; twelve silver bowls, each amounting to seventy shekels; and twelve golden dishes, totaling ten shekels apiece. The animals used for the burnt, sin, and fellowship offerings also were totaled equally across each tribal family. The offerings themselves do not seem too impressive at least in quantity, especially when compared to Solomon's massive and lavish ceremony, but they were accepted by God. Apparently they accorded well with the means of the people.

The careful obedience of Moses issued in God fulfilling his promise to dwell with his people. Although God cannot be confined to one locale, his special redemptive/covenant presence always resided where man could find forgiveness—on the mercy seat that crowned the **ark of the Testimony**. Moses alone was granted a special dispensation to enter the **Tent of Meeting** to speak with God. As God would affirm, "With him I speak face to face, clearly and not in riddles; he sees the form of the LORD" (12:8). The expression "face to face" is "an adverbial phrase synonymous with 'mouth to mouth,' and by no means equivalent to a vision of the divine face" (Vos, 105).

Ⅾ Other Dedicatory Offerings (8:1–26)

SUPPORTING IDEA: *Moses prepares the lamps and the Levites for sacred service.*

8:1–4. The lampstand provided light for the priests so they could move freely and safely within the darkened tabernacle. The lamps on the lampstand provided light to illuminate the **area in front of the lampstand**. These instructions supplemented the general instructions which had already been given in Exodus 25:37; 27:21.

8:5–14. The Lord had already consecrated the priests who would serve in the tabernacle (see Lev. 8). He now set apart their assistants, the Levites, for their service. The first step was to sprinkle on them **the water of cleansing**, water probably taken from the laver in the courtyard (Harrison, 152; Kiel, 47). Then the Levites shaved the hair from their bodies and washed their clothes.

For their offering the Levites presented a young bull with a grain offering followed by a second bull for a sin offering. Then they were to assemble in front of the Lord (i.e., the tabernacle) where the community would lay their hands on them. The Levites were thus presented before the Lord as a **wave offering from the Israelites** in order to commission them for service. The wave offering concept came from the fellowship offering as the priest's portion to be waved before the Lord (Lev. 7:28–34). In a sense, the Israelites were waving before the Lord the Levites as ones who would serve them throughout the year in the sacred service. The Lord set aside the tribe of Levites as his own possession to be continually employed in his service. The Levites next offered one bull for a sin offering followed by another bull for a burnt offering.

8:15–22. Once the Levites were ordained for their service, they could enter into their duties. They stood in close relation to the Lord by calling, and hence the Lord himself was their inheritance. The Lord required the entire firstborn of all the Israelites and accepted this tribe in their stead (see Exod. 13:2,12; Num. 3:12–13). Any violation of this decree would result in a judgment of **plague**.

Moses and all the people did with the Levites **just as the LORD commanded Moses**. The Levites then began their service under the supervision of Aaron and his sons, the priests.

8:23–26. Eligibility for Levitical service was limited to men between the ages of **twenty-five years old** and **the age of fifty**, at which time they must retire from active service. Those beyond fifty years of age could assist their younger brothers in the service of the tabernacle, but they could not engage directly in the actual assigned duties. Earlier the Lord had the Israelites take a census of the Levites who were between thirty and fifty years old, but this probably referred to the specific duty of transporting the tabernacle (Keil, 49). Here younger men could perhaps be employed in helping to erect it and take it down. King David later lowered the Levitical age to twenty (1 Chr. 23:24–25) because the Lord as represented by the tabernacle had come to dwell in Jerusalem forever and was no longer transported from place to place.

MAIN IDEA REVIEW: *Just before Israel marched forward, the Lord assigned them some final preparations, including cleansing directions and provision for special commitments.*

III. CONCLUSION

Tozer on God's Holiness

In his book *The Knowledge of the Holy,* A. W. Tozer wrote:

> Neither the writer nor the reader of these words is qualified to appreciate the holiness of God. Quite literally a new channel must be cut through the desert of our minds to allow the sweet waters of truth that will heal our great sickness to flow in. We cannot grasp the true meaning of the divine holiness by thinking of someone or something very pure and then raising the concept to the highest degree we are capable of. God's holiness is not simply the best we know infinitely bettered. We know nothing like the divine holiness. It stands apart, unique, unapproachable, incomprehensible and unattainable. The natural man is blind to it. He may fear God's power and admire his wisdom, but his holiness he cannot even imagine (11).

The campsite of the Hebrew people needed cleansing, and people were offered opportunities for greater intimacy with their sovereign God. But they still had a lot to learn about the depth and breadth of God's holiness.

PRINCIPLES

- Personal cleansing is vital before people can have fellowship with a holy God.
- Fidelity to marriage vows has always been a high priority with God.
- All people have opportunities throughout their lives to make deeper commitments to God.
- God takes careful note of our gifts to him.
- The people whom God uses must allow God to cleanse them.
- Love for God will always be demonstrated in service for God.
- Accountability is required of God's people.

APPLICATIONS

- What do we learn about God's nature from his commandments about dealing with communicable diseases?
- Are there broken relationships in your life which God would have you take the initiative in restoring?
- Make a list of the priorities in your life. Where is God on that list? How would your life change if God were in first place?

- What promises have you made to God? How are you doing in keeping them?
- What difference does it make in a person's life when he or she realizes that God is holy?

IV. LIFE APPLICATION

Mr. Glory-Face

Adoniram Judson was so filled with the desire to preach the gospel that, when he arrived as a missionary in Burma, he walked up to a Burman and embraced him. The man went home and reported that he had seen an angel. The living Christ was so radiant in Judson's face that people called him Mr. Glory-Face.

Can people see a difference in your life as a result of the presence of God in your life? What do people see when they watch you at church, home, and school?

When we make the commitment to get closer to the Lord, a series of additional commitments is needed: a commitment to flood our minds with God's Word; a commitment to seek personal cleansing through confession, repentance, and restitution; a commitment to be "set apart" from those things of the world that will contaminate and inhibit our intimacy with God; and a commitment to do whatever it takes to maintain our intimacy with the Lord.

V. PRAYER

Lord Jesus, I want to know you and the power of your resurrection. I want to get closer to you. I am willing to make those changes that are necessary to be nearer your love and care. Please bring to mind those areas of my life that keep me from drawing close to you. Amen.

VI. DEEPER DISCOVERIES

A. The Jealousy of God and Man

The law of the jealousy offering showed the priests what to do in case a husband grew jealous over his wife and suspected her of cheating. But it offered no comment on the propriety of such jealousy in general. To discover whether such jealousy is ever in order, we need to look at the meaning of jealousy in the Bible. God commanded Israel:

You shall not make for yourself an idol in the form of anything in heaven above or on the earth beneath or in the waters below. You shall not bow down to them or worship them for I, the LORD your God, am a jealous God, punishing the children for the sin of the fathers to the third and fourth generation of those who hate me, but showing love to a thousand generations of those who love me and keep my commandments (Exod. 20:4–5).

When the covenant people of God make or worship idols they awaken the jealousy of God. The word describes "conjugal zeal," particularly in the marriage relationship (Vos, 136). Here man brings God down to a visible representation that man finds acceptable. But God, in order to be worshiped in a pure manner, must be approached for who he is and as the exclusive object of our singular love and devotion. Likewise, the marital union must allow no rivals. When husbands and wives make themselves available to competing suitors, they threaten the foundation of holy love. God draws a close analogy between the spiritual union between himself and his people and the human marital relationship.

Such close intimate relationships imply a sense of ownership. Of course, men should never view their wives as mere property, nor should the wife view her husband that way. But even Paul grew jealous when his spiritual children strayed from Christ (2 Cor. 11:2). James notes in his epistle that the Spirit yearns jealously (NKJV), envies intensely, or God himself desires the Spirit who dwells in us (Jas. 4:5 NASB). God has an exclusive claim to our lives.

Sometimes a husband might grow jealous of his wife for no good reason. In such cases, the woman who followed the procedures described in the law of the jealously offering would be cleared of any wrongdoing. Likewise, we should understand that the Bible frowns upon jealousy. James reminds his readers that where "you have envy and selfish ambition, there you find disorder and every evil practice" (Jas. 3:16). Fits of jealousy lead to slander—something God tells us to rid ourselves of (Col. 3:8) and something that God designed the jealousy offering to muzzle.

Husbands and wives should commit themselves to each other in marital faithfulness and establish such a track record of trust and fidelity that suspicions would find no footing. On the other hand, we shouldn't frown on those who have legitimate grounds for protecting the honor of their marriage and whose spouses have provided sufficient reasons for healthy suspicion.

B. Moses' Unique Relationship with God

During the period of the Old Testament, God spoke to the "forefathers through the prophets at many times and in various ways" (Heb. 1:1). He spoke to Moses and used Moses to speak to the people in a unique manner. In fact, nowhere else do we see the kind of permanent face-to-face, God-to-man encounter between God and man. To be sure, sometimes God spoke to others more or less face-to-face. But he would rarely do so and would also speak to them through dreams, visions, and, in at least one time with Samuel, audibly (1 Sam. 3:2–14). David at times appeared to share an unusually close relationship with God, but he used various media to consult him, such as an ephod, or a prophet. At other times he may have spoken to God directly, but the text does not always make that clear (see 1 Sam. 23:1–4, where David may have spoken to God directly or through some other legitimate media).

Joshua, who succeeded Moses, did not succeed him in every particular. God did apparently speak to Joshua directly on the eve of his conquest of Canaan, but thereafter he committed him to the inscripturated Word of God to guide him all the days of his life and to provide sound counsel during his difficult conquests (Josh. 1:1–8). The apostle Paul spoke directly to the glorified Savior on the road to Damascus, but he also went "on to visions and revelations from the Lord" (2 Cor. 12:1).

Scholars and ordinary readers sometimes don't know what to call Moses. Was he a prophet? If he was, we know "there was no prophet who was honored with the direct and continuous access to Jehovah that Moses enjoyed" (Vos, 105). We know he wasn't a priest like his brother Aaron, although he did have close access to God. He lived before the Lord established a monarchy, but he couldn't have been a legitimate king because he did not originate from the tribe of Judah. Perhaps we should simply acknowledge Moses as a unique and privileged mouthpiece of God and as one who spoke and communed with God in a unique way.

VII. TEACHING OUTLINE

A. INTRODUCTION

1. Lead Story: Holy, Holy, Holy
2. Context: As God prepared his people to move from slavery to receiving the gift of a good land, he gave them guidelines for physical health, for resolving conflicts, and for setting apart people for special service to him.
3. Transition: In a very different time and circumstance, God called his people to be holy, to be set apart for his service.

B. COMMENTARY

1. The Purity of the Tribes (5:1–31)
2. The Nazirite Vow (6:1–27)
3. The Dedicatory Offerings (7:1–89)
4. Other Dedicatory Offerings (8:1–26)

C. CONCLUSION: MR. GLORY-FACE

VIII. ISSUES FOR DISCUSSION

1. The opening verses of Numbers 5 appear a little harsh. What do you think God was trying to teach the Israelites, and how would this lesson impact their wilderness journey?

2. What impact would the testing for unfaithfulness outlined in 5:11–29 have on those contemplating adultery? What principles can be drawn into our twenty-first-century mind-set?

3. What is the significance of each of the prohibitions of the Nazirite vow?

4. What was the last gift you gave sacrificially to God? What was your motivation in giving this gift?

5. Why do you think each tribe gave an identical gift to God? How would this help build unity?

6. What does it means "to be set apart"? After examining Numbers 8, what has God said to you about your lifestyle?

Numbers 9–12

The Guidance of God

| Q u o t e |

"*G*od generally guides me by presenting reasons to

my mind for acting in a certain way."

J o h n   W e s l e y

Numbers 9–12

I N   A   N U T S H E L L

*I*n Numbers 9–12, the people of Israel are preparing for the journey and begin their march. As God was guiding them with a pillar of cloud and fire in their journey, they were expected to follow certain rituals. They were expected to observe the Passover feast (Num. 9); they were required to march in a specific order (Num. 10); they watched God overcome their complaining by providing the quail (Num. 11); and they saw how God deals with rebellion among his leaders (Num. 12).

The Guidance of God

I. INTRODUCTION

God's GPS

*W*hen in flight, an airplane is typically off course 90 percent of the time. However, commercial planes are equipped with a Global Positioning System (GPS) to keep them on course. Every plane's system is constantly making midair corrections to adjust to wind currents, up drafts and down drafts, and other planes in their airspace so they can get back on course.

God also has a GPS. On autumn nights as we sleep peacefully in our beds, millions of songbirds are quietly traveling under darkness, heading south for warmer climates. Take the orioles, for example. Every fall they pack their bags, close up their homes, and head south. The weather patterns tell the birds it is time to move. "As cold fronts move across eastern North America," one expert writes, "they're sending waves of orioles, along with warblers and other songbirds, on their way to wintering grounds in Mexico and Latin America." As cold fronts pass, clear skies and north winds usually follow. These conditions are ideal for migration, allowing the birds to travel with no risk of storms, the wind at their backs, and a clear view of the stars to help them find their way.

They fly over thousands of houses, highways, shopping centers, and parking lots, passing state after state. If a particular oriole opts for a direct flight home, it will fly over the Gulf of Mexico in a single night, crossing six hundred miles of open water. The trip to Mexico, Panama, or Costa Rica takes about two weeks. But the oriole knows exactly where it is going. God planted within its brain a perfect guidance system that tells it exactly where to go, and when, and how.

The people of Israel would have enjoyed an internal GPS. But God had other plans. God taught the people to trust him in the journey. God would provide necessary training for the needs of the promised land when they arrived. So, as a part of the first global positioning system for the Israelites, chapters 9–12 provide the marching orders to avoid drifting off course.

II. COMMENTARY

The Guidance of God

> **MAIN IDEA:** *As the Lord miraculously led Israel, he required them to obey him fully by observing the established feasts, blowing the prescribed trumpets in an orderly manner, trusting in his provision, and respecting his chosen leaders.*

A Supplemental Instructions on the Passover and the Appearance of the Cloud (9:1–23)

> **SUPPORTING IDEA:** *The people enjoyed both the Passover and presence of God.*

9:1–5. The first Passover was celebrated as the people of Israel prepared to make their escape from Egypt ahead of the pursuing pharaoh. But they were to observe this ordinance in perpetuity once they reached the land of Canaan (Exod. 12:24–25). But lest they postpone it in the intermediate years before their arrival in the land, the Lord commanded them to observe it while they were at Sinai. But the time of celebration did not change. They were to observe it at twilight on the **fourteenth day of this month** (Abib). In observing the feast, they were to maintain scrupulously all the previous requirements except perhaps smearing the blood on the door frames (Exod. 12:22–23). That element was unique to their circumstances and a means of protection from the avenging angel.

9:6–14. But a special provision had to be made for some people who became **ceremonially unclean** because of a dead body. The Lord had commanded the Israelites earlier to expel from the camp anyone who came into contact with a corpse (Num. 5:1–3). But these unclean people wanted to observe the Passover as well. The problem was new and had not been previously addressed by the Lord. So Moses sought the Lord's guidance and told the inquirers to wait until he found out **what the LORD commands concerning you**.

The Lord responded to Moses' inquiry by allowing those Israelites to celebrate the feast on the following month. The intervening month probably allowed the defiled individuals time to observe ritual cleansing. In one final perilous reminder, the Lord warned the community to observe the feast without excuse. Failure to do so would result in death. Foreigners could observe the feast at the regular time.

9:15–23. Moses had concluded the Book of Exodus with an account of the guiding cloud that covered the tent of meeting and how the "glory of the LORD filled the tabernacle" (Exod. 40:34–38). Here he supplied more details about the cloud and its role in directing the Israelites from place to place.

"God himself conducted the march" (Keil, 52). In all likelihood the cloud "was centered over the Holy Place and the Most Holy Place" in the tabernacle (Harrison, 161–62). At night the cloud **looked like fire**. The fiery appearance did not, as Harrison supposes, proclaim God's sovereignty as opposed to the daytime cloud that concealed his majesty. It simply provided "a visible sign and vehicle of his gracious presence" (Keil, 52).

Accordingly, the cloud brought comfort to the traveling nation and also reminded them of their obligation to obey the Lord. The routine was simple enough: **Whenever the cloud lifted from above the Tent, the Israelites set out; whenever the cloud settled, the Israelites encamped.**

These verses reminded the nation to depend totally on God and not attempt to travel apart from his direct leading. The people were not to set out unless they first witnessed the cloud moving out ahead of them. At times they would travel quickly with many short stays in several different places. At other times they would remain camped at the same place for a long time. Whether **two days or a month or a year**, the Israelites were to remain in place until they saw the cloud lift; only then should they set out. The Levites probably appointed "watchers" who stood guard over the cloud to see if it lifted during the night.

B The Silver Trumpets and God's Guidance (10:1–36)

SUPPORTING IDEA: *The people assemble at the call of trumpets and leave Sinai.*

10:1–10. To help muster the nation quickly, the Lord directed Moses to **make two trumpets of hammered silver**. These were to be used for calling the community together and for having the camps set out. These trumpets could be used as signals to alert the tribes that the Lord had lifted his cloud and they would soon move on.

Whenever both trumpets sounded, the entire community would assemble before Moses at the tent of meeting. But if one trumpet sounded, only the leaders would be summoned to appear before Moses. When the tribes were to break camp and move on, the signal was a **blast**, evidently a different sound than the signal for gathering them together, which required a **blow**. The latter was probably a longer sound.

Aaron and his sons were **to blow the trumpets**. The Lord directed them to observe this procedure as **a lasting ordinance**. He also provided two other uses of the trumpet—a battle cry to arms when attacked by an enemy and a summons to feast days. The first alarm looked forward to the nation residing in the land. Before they drew arms, they would sound the trumpets as a means of asking for God's help in engaging their enemies. The other use of the trumpet came during the observance of important feast days. The priests were to sound a trumpet blast over their **burnt offerings and fellowship offerings** as a remembrance before the Lord forever.

10:11–13. Now that the Lord had given the nation its spiritual foundation—regulations for tabernacle worship and related procedures—he directed the people toward the promised land. He led them toward their destination with the promise of his abiding presence. But they must keep short accounts with him and heed all the precepts he had issued. The Lord conditioned his own presence among them on their obedience.

Their first major destination was the **Desert of Paran**, probably located southwest of Palestine. This was the home of the family of Ishmael (Gen. 21:21). Scholars continue to debate the precise locations of Paran and other places in the narrative. Between Sinai and Paran, however, they stopped at various places for shorter rest periods (Num. 11:34–35). The **cloud** led them along, then rested at their next appointed destination. The Lord guided them through Moses.

10:14–28. Judah led the initial march toward Paran under the command of Nahshon, the son of Amminadab. The tribe followed behind their standard, a symbol that identified it. Following Judah was the tribe of Issachar, led by Nethanel, and Zebulun, headed by Eliab. The appointed Levites also began their work of dismantling the tabernacle and transporting it behind the tribe of Judah.

The tribes of Reuben, Simeon, and Gad next headed out under the commands of Elizur, Shelumiel, and Eliasaph, respectively, each tribe with its own standard. The tribes of Ephraim, Manasseh, and Benjamin, in turn, followed them. Bringing up the rear were the tribes of Dan, Asher, and Naphtali.

10:29–32. Scholars have debated the identification of **Hobab son of Reuel**, the debate coming from some texts that, at first glance, seem out of harmony. Our present text identifies Hobab as the son of Moses' father-in-law. Judges 4:11 in the KJV, NASB, NJKV, and RSV and some other versions indicate that the Kenites descended from a Hobab, Moses' "father-in-law." But in Exodus 3:1, Jethro, whom we know from our present text to be Reuel (see also the explicit reference in Exod. 2:18), was Moses' father-in-law. Islamic teachings identify Hobab with Jethro, as do some Christian scholars, a quite untenable solution. They try to justify this by making Reuel a tribal name of sorts, such as Jeroboam, repeated many times within a family tribe.

The NIV renders the term as "brother-in-law" in Judges 4:11, and probably translated it more as a "marriage relation" than anything specific (Winterbotham, 92). In that case Judges 4:11 meant to identify the precise Kenite group that Heber belonged to, namely, Hobab, and that this group related to Moses by marriage. Thus Hobab was Moses' brother-in-law and also the son of Reuel (Jethro).

Moses asked Hobab to guide Moses and the tribes on their journey. At first Hobab declined, desiring to return to his own land and people. But with some persuading Moses prevailed, and they set out from Sinai.

10:33–36. The nation marched on for three days with the **ark of the covenant** leading the way. When the ark set out Moses prayed in militaristic language for God to protect them by routing the Lord's enemies. But when the ark came to rest, Moses cried out, **Return, O LORD, to the countless thousands of Israel**. The same Lord who became his people's chief ally would strike terror in all who opposed his purposes (cp. 2 Cor. 2:14–16).

C Fire, Quail, and Testing (11:1–35)

SUPPORTING IDEA: *The Israelites learned to trust God's abundant provision.*

11:1–3. Following their first extended march, the people **complained about their hardships** before Moses and the Lord. We can connect the two and trace their lack of restraint to fatigue, although this does not excuse them from whining in the ears of the Lord. The Lord, in turn, responded in **anger** (see "Deeper Discoveries"). The Lord responded to their complaints by sending fire that **consumed some of the outskirts of the camp** but did not, apparently, injure anyone. The fire struck terror in their minds and awoke many from their spiritual slumber. The people cried to Moses who himself **prayed to the LORD** to remove the fire. The Lord then answered Moses' prayer, and the fire began to die.

The name **Taberah** means "to burn" or "burning" (cp. NIV margin) and, as Harrison notes (182), is not mentioned in the journey summary in Numbers 33, but Moses did record it in Deuteronomy 9:22.

11:4–9. The people next complained of their monotonous diet of manna, longing for the food they had in Egypt. Here they had consumed fresh vegetables and fish.

11:10–15. How could Moses endure the incessant complaints of so large a throng? Here Moses indulged in a bit of self-pity. Did Moses himself forget the horrid conditions in Egypt? Did he not recall his own deliverance so many decades ago when he fled to Midian after killing an Egyptian? And how could he not remember and appreciate the Lord's deliverance from Egypt through signs and wonders? Moses then sought to excuse himself from caring for these people because they were not his problem. He didn't create this nation, nor had he sought to lead them in the first place. Furthermore, how could he provide for them with the scant resources of such an arid place? Moses saw only personal **ruin** ahead and even requested his own death.

11:16–17. The Lord saw things in a different light, and he used this situation to teach Moses about shared leadership. The Lord divided some of Moses' leadership among **seventy of Israel's elders** by giving them the same

Spirit that rested on Moses and enabling them to **carry the burden of the people**.

11:18–25. The Lord told Moses to have the people prepare themselves for the Lord's next visitation—one that would give them meat to eat. But the Lord would also punish them for their unbelief and perhaps cause them to understand that any food can become monotonous if eaten long enough. Moses questioned the Lord about how he could do all this. The Lord asked Moses a question himself: **Is the LORD's arm too short?** With these words Moses shared with the people the Lord's words and also gathered the seventy elders who would assume greater leadership responsibility.

11:26–30. We now see a glimpse of Moses' true character and also a trait necessary for anyone who would be used of the Lord: humility. Apparently two people who had been absent when the seventy received their spiritual endowment from God now also received this same grace and were **prophesying in the camp**. Evidently the Lord had given them these gifts without informing anyone else. This activity alerted the loyal Joshua, who told Moses to **stop them**. Moses responded by voicing approval for these two servants, **Eldad and Medad**. He stated that he wished **all the LORD's people were prophets** and would display similar gifts. He reasoned that God's influence would spread with more prophets such as them.

11:31–35. The Lord brought the promised quail through a strong wind. These birds may have been migrating in that direction from Africa (Harrison, 191). The wind may have made the quail too weak to escape the clutches of the people. They gathered liberal quantities of these quail—**no one gathered less than homers**—and spread out their bounty throughout the camp. But even while they consumed the quail, the Lord struck them with a severe plague. Moses called the place **Kibroth Hattaavah** ("graves of lust"), possibly hinting that only those who gorged on the meat perished (JFB, 120).

Ⅾ Miriam and Aaron Challenge Moses' Leadership (12:1–16)

> **SUPPORTING IDEA:** *Blind ambition has its limits and consequences.*

12:1–2. Some time after Israel's arrival at Hazeroth, Moses faced a trial perhaps more personal than any he had experienced up to this time. His own flesh and blood rose up to contest his authority. Miriam and Aaron began to talk against Moses **because of his Cushite wife**. We can assume Miriam took the lead for several reasons. She is mentioned first in the account, followed by Aaron. In addition, she alone incurred the direct judgment of the Lord. Finally, Aaron had already established himself as a weak-willed follower and probably fell prey to the pressure from Miriam as he had to that of the idolaters (see Exod. 32).

Miriam criticized Moses by finding fault with his choice of a wife, a **Cushite**. In all likelihood, Zipporah had died (since she is nowhere mentioned), and Moses remarried. He may have met the Cushite somewhere along the journey, or possibly she accompanied Israel all the way from Egypt. But Miriam's argument was shortsighted. The Lord had prohibited Israel from intermarrying foreign women from the land of Canaan (Exod. 34:15–16), but he did not expressly forbid all foreign marriages. Miriam pointed to Moses' marriage to the Cushite as a reason not to trust his leadership.

Miriam and Aaron began to drop the line, **Hasn't he also spoken through us?** But the Lord heard their words and would not delay his response. Were not Aaron and Miriam already exalted in the eyes of Israel? Aaron headed not only the Levitical family but the priestly line as well. He and his descendants alone would offer the Lord's sacrifice. And Miriam already held the title of prophetess—no doubt the most celebrated one in Israel because of her affiliation with Moses (Exod. 15:20–21).

12:3. Moses never thought so highly of himself as to be offended by these remarks. They may have even made sense to Moses! The reason for this came from the character he embodied. He was a very humble man, **more humble than anyone else on the face of the earth**. Moses reflected the spirit of Christ, who "did not consider equality with God something to be grasped" (Phil. 2:6), but took on the form of a servant. Moses did not cling to his position and rank, but apparently stood silent.

12:4–9. The Lord would not delay his response and would decide the matter by summoning the principals to the **Tent of Meeting**. There the Lord descended in the **pillar of cloud**. The Lord would leave no doubt who was speaking. He would speak to ordinary prophets through a variety of media, such as **visions** or **dreams**. But Moses alone enjoyed a **face to face** relationship. Virtually all the instances of God communicating to Moses bear this out. He spoke to Moses as one person would speak to another. Moreover, Moses saw **the form of the LORD**—a reference to some visible phenomena that the Lord accorded to Moses when he spoke with him. Since "God is spirit" (John 4:24) and does not have a body, we know Moses witnessed some visible manifestation of God's presence similar to the experience of Isaiah (Isa. 6:1–5). The Lord now responded in anger at Moses' two siblings.

12:10–16. The Lord's presence does not always come to deliver, as Miriam found out. When the cloud lifted from above the tent, **there stood Miriam—leprous, like snow**. When Aaron beheld Miriam, he immediately recognized God's role in this and the consequences for their sin. He asked Moses to do something about Miriam's condition. Then Moses asked God to heal her leprous condition.

The Lord replied with puzzling words: **If her father had spit in her face, would she not have been in disgrace for seven days?** Such an occurrence would indeed prove humiliating to Miriam. The Lord showed her that he would inflict no more punishment than what that family shame would involve. Miriam would be kept out of the camp for seven days for purification, then be allowed to return. With that the people resumed their journey and next came to rest in **Paran**.

> **MAIN IDEA REVIEW:** *As the Lord miraculously led Israel, he required them to obey him fully by observing the established feasts, blowing the prescribed trumpets in an orderly manner, trusting in his provision, and respecting his chosen leaders.*

III. CONCLUSION

Being Where God Wants You

Sometimes when our plans don't work out as hoped, it's because God is detouring us, leading us elsewhere, in his overruling providence. In his book *On This Day*, Robert J. Morgan tells about Thomas Coke, a sophisticated Oxford-educated Welshman, who left his ministry in the Anglican Church in 1777 to become John Wesley's chief assistant in the new and quickly growing Methodist movement. On September 24, 1785, he packed his books and bags and sailed out of England, down the Channel, and into the Atlantic, leaving for Nova Scotia where he wanted to establish a group of missionaries who accompanied him. But the voyage was ill-fated and grew more perilous by the day, the ship being caught in mountainous waves and mast-splitting winds. The ship's captain determined that Coke and his missionaries, like biblical Jonah, were bringing misfortune on his ship, and he considered throwing them overboard. He did, in fact, gather up some of Coke's papers and tossed them into the raging ocean. The voyage took three months rather than the expected one, and instead of landing in Nova Scotia, the damaged ship ended up in the Caribbean, limping into St. John's harbor on the island of Antigua on Christmas Day.

Coke knew that at least one Methodist lived somewhere on Antigua, a missionary named John Baxter. Hoping to find him, Coke and his three missionaries asked to be rowed ashore from their shattered ship in the predawn morning. They started down the street in St. John's and stopped the first person they found, a fellow swinging a lantern in his hand, to inquire of Baxter.

It was John Baxter himself. He was on his way to special Christmas morning services he had planned for the island, and the sudden appearance of Coke and his missionaries out of the darkness—out of nowhere—seemed too good to be true. It took three services that day to accommodate the crowds.

After it was over, Coke and his associates abandoned any idea of going to Nova Scotia. They planted the missionary team instead on Antigua and on the neighboring islands, and by the time of Coke's death in 1814, there were over 17,000 believers in the Methodist churches there.

The story of the Israelite journey was not always one filled with blessings and immediate deliverance. But the travel was always designed to grow God's people in faith and endurance, so they would be the people God wanted them to be, and they would go where God wanted them to go. In God's will, there is no "off course."

PRINCIPLES

- God desires to guide you in the process of decision-making through the Scriptures.
- God is a God of order.
- God always uses his chosen leaders to rally the people and to create vision and direction.
- Criticizing and complaining, if left unchecked, has a way of spreading through the camp.
- Leaders are just as susceptible to complaining as followers.
- God is very patient when we complain about not getting our way.
- God never asks any person to do more than God empowers him or her to do.

APPLICATIONS

- Appeal to the Bible for everything. God's Word is inerrant and infallible and will never let you down.
- Take time every day to sense God's direction in your life.
- Every believer enjoys the presence of the Holy Spirit as a tangible indication of his care and leading.
- Any time you take on leadership responsibilities for God, trust that God will go before you in your journey.
- When offended, pray for those who have mistreated you. God will honor your mercy and grace and forgiveness.

IV. LIFE APPLICATION

A Wise Captain

The ship was nearing land. Famous Bible teacher F. B. Meyer stood in the cool of the day, wondering how the captain and his crew were going to steer the ship to the safety of the dock. It was a stormy night, and visibility was poor. Meyer approached the captain to ask, "How do you know when to turn this ship into that narrow harbor?"

"Do you see those three red lights on the shore?" the Captain replied. "When they're all in a straight line, I go right in."

Later Meyer said, "When we want to know God's will, there are three things that always occur: the inward impulse, the Word of God, and the trend of circumstances. . . . Never act until these three things agree."

These are words from both a wise captain and a wise Christian. Events of life always happen for a reason when understood in light of the sovereignty of God. The people of Israel had to learn to trust and obey. Seek to align the light of the Word, the light of God's quiet voice, and the light of the open and closed doors before you—and go right in!

V. PRAYER

Lord, I wish you would guide me with more clarity than you do. Help me to tune in to your GPS and stay on course. Grant wisdom when I come to a fork in the road, to choose your road. Grant wisdom to associate with others who will journey with me. And grant courage to trust you when the road seems to take a different direction. In Jesus' name. Amen.

VI. DEEPER DISCOVERIES

A. How Does God Lead Us Today? A Theology of Guidance

The pillar of cloud and fire led Israel for forty years in the desert, providing the nation with a visible reminder of God's protection. Throughout our study we've seen other examples of divine guidance, such as consulting the urim and thummim or casting lots. But should we expect such guidance today and resort to similar means to determine God's will for our life's decisions?

These methods were for a specific time in Israel's history, and we should not consider them normative for us today. Nevertheless, God can lead us today just as he led them. How do we determine God's will? First of all, we must acknowledge God's sovereign will in everything we do. We must not simply acknowledge that our God is a powerful God but go one step further. We must yield ourselves to his governing purpose for our lives: our holiness (1 Thess. 4:3). Truly, "the glory of God is a determining factor in the Christian's life, or ought to be" (Ferguson, 20).

The Christian must follow the Word of God for his or her life. Sometimes we refer to this as the *moral* will of God. The Word of God teaches us God's purpose for our lives and the commands we are to follow. Only as we gaze through the lens of Scripture can we free ourselves of the sin that blurs our spiritual vision. Here we will find certain general boundaries that will direct our way through life. But the Christian must pay close attention to the Word of God and meditate on its precepts.

God will lead us as he chooses and will give us directions on how to follow his leading. For example, when we consider a life's calling, we should consider those spiritual endowments God has given us (Rom. 12:4–8; 1 Cor. 12:1–31). God would never lead us into something he didn't equip us for. We should examine our present and future opportunities. Paul longed to visit Thessalonica again, "but Satan stopped" him (1 Thess. 2:18). In looking at our possible opportunities, we should note that our own laziness can limit our possibilities (Prov. 6:6–11). For example, let's suppose that we want to explore medicine but don't want to bother with the necessary education that would qualify us for that position. We in essence cut ourselves off from a possible opportunity by never qualifying for it in the first place. But all in all, God will open the necessary doors (and close some too) to ensure that we find his will for our lives.

B. Is All Complaining Sin?

Time and again the people of Israel tested God and wore out Moses with their incessant complaining about virtually everything. They ranted about the conditions of their journeys and railed against Moses for their monotonous diet of manna. Although God put up with their complaining with remarkable patience, he punished them when it became too much.

Still, could God ever make allowance for complaining, even delight in it? The psalmists and other sacred writers seem to prove that not all complaining is bad. In Psalms 77 and 88 the writer pours out his soul to God about his many woes and travails, finding confidence in God's ability to deliver him. Hannah poured out her heart in bitter complaint and even refused to eat because of the heavy burden she felt over her childless state. But God answered her complaint and gave her a son named Samuel. Job complained throughout most of the book that bears his name, and briefly the Lord reproved him for his unbelief. But the Lord also blessed him with a huge bounty, partly in answer to prayer that may have sounded to some as complaining.

When we offer our complaint to God, we must steer clear of blaming him for what happened in our lives. He clearly allowed what happened in our lives. But we can offer our wails before the Lord and pour out our heart to him. Once we submit our lives to his will, our very complaints will translate to prayer before the throne of grace.

VII. TEACHING OUTLINE

A. INTRODUCTION

1. Lead Story: God's GPS
2. Context: Being God's people means being attentive to his guidance in our lives. Although they had been delivered from slavery in Egypt, Israel faced choices every day about whether they would be slaves to sin and rebellion or whether they would hear and follow the voice of the Lord.
3. Transition: As we read the Acts of the Apostles, we see that God desires to lead his people and that remarkable results follow obedience. God's modern methods of guidance are different than they were for Israel, but the reality of his leadership has not changed.

B. COMMENTARY

1. Supplemental Instructions on the Passover and the Appearance of the Cloud (9:1–23)
2. The Silver Trumpets and God's Guidance (10:1–36)
3. Fire, Quail, and Testing (11:1–35)
4. Miriam and Aaron Challenge Moses' Leadership (12:1–16)

C. CONCLUSION: A WISE CAPTAIN

VIII. ISSUES FOR DISCUSSION

1. Exclusion is a powerful punishment. However, some people were excluded from the Passover for what appears to be "no big deal." Why was God so stern in his requirements, and why was the Passover feast so important anyway?
2. Where else in the Bible do you read about trumpets? What significance seems to accompany their sounding?
3. Take a moment to reflect on Numbers 9:15–23. What has happened to the Hebrew perspective in such a short time? What do you believe has caused such a rapid decline in the morale of the people?
4. Have you ever been discouraged? Share the circumstances of the last battle you had with discouragement and frustration. What caused your pain? Compare your situation with that of Moses and see if there are any similarities between lessons that both of you need to learn.
5. Describe Moses' leadership while dealing with his family situation in Numbers 12. What lessons can we learn from Moses' and God's expectations?

Numbers 13–14

Time to Have Faith Tested

I. INTRODUCTION
Looking Unbeatable

II. COMMENTARY
A verse-by-verse explanation of these chapters.

III. CONCLUSION
Why God Responds to Faith

An overview of the principles and applications from these chapters.

IV. LIFE APPLICATION
An Oldie but a Goodie

Melding these chapters to life.

V. PRAYER
Tying these chapters to life with God.

VI. DEEPER DISCOVERIES
Historical, geographical, and grammatical enrichment of the commentary.

VII. TEACHING OUTLINE
Suggested step-by-step group study of these chapters.

VIII. ISSUES FOR DISCUSSION
Zeroing these chapters in on daily life.

Q u o t e

"*F*aith is like a muscle which grows stronger and stronger with use, rather than rubber, which weakens when it is stretched."

J .   O .   F r a s e r

Numbers 13–14

IN A NUTSHELL

*A*s the people of Israel near the end of their journey, they come to Kadesh Barnea, a place where their faith is to be tested. The leadership decides to send twelve spies into the promised land to investigate the land. Israel refuses to enter the land promised them by God, so God's anger is kindled. Despite the pleas of Moses, the personal desires of the people, not faith, lead them into a battle they lose with the Amalekites and the Canaanites.

Time to Have Faith Tested

I. INTRODUCTION

Looking Unbeatable

There have been many stories over the years about the legendary Knute Rockne of Notre Dame. One story may be of particular interest in our study of the Book of Numbers. It seems Knute Rockne was about to face the USC football team. He knew that USC had a far superior team and wondered if there was any way he could defeat them. Then he hit on an idea. He scoured the city of South Bend, Indiana, for the biggest men he could find. When he had found about one hundred men, each at least 6'5" or more and weighing in at three hundred pounds or more, he put them all in Notre Dame uniforms. With their shoulder pads and helmets, this group of "recruits" looked huge and unbeatable.

Then, when it was time for the game to begin, Rockne sent these men out of the locker room first. As the USC football team watched, they just kept coming, and coming, and coming until these hundred men were all the USC team saw. The USC coach kept telling his team, "They can only field eleven men at a time." But the damage was done. USC had become so intimidated at the sight of these "giants" that they played poorly, and Notre Dame won the game.

This story has an Old Testament equivalent. One day twelve new recruits were sent into a foreign stadium to scout the land and the opposition. When they viewed the new land, it was beautiful—everything they ever dreamed a "promised land" would be. One problem: This land was inhabited by a large enemy team which looked like unbeatable giants. This section of Scripture provides insights into what can happen when people allow themselves to focus on the enemy and lose sight of God.

II. COMMENTARY

Time to Have Faith Tested

> **MAIN IDEA:** *God guided Israel to view and take the land, but their fear replaced their faith and smothered their spirit.*

Exploring the Promised Land (13:1–33)

> **SUPPORTING IDEA:** *God sends out spies who view the land and return with a bad report.*

13:1–16. The journeys of Israel took on a more targeted approach to the promised inheritance. The Lord sought to bolster the confidence of the troops by having them see, observe, and even taste of the luscious land ahead. Deuteronomy 1:22 indicates the people themselves asked Moses to let them spy out the land. Apparently, the Lord moved in the people's hearts to make such a request. Moses selected some men to explore the land and bring back a report to the people. Evidently Moses selected the men from every tribe as the Lord commanded. The actual names did not comprise the elders of Numbers 1.

13:17–25. Moses instructed the spies to go to Canaan and learn the layout of the land. He was particularly concerned with the hilly **Negev** in southern Canaan. He also told them to observe the people of the land to see how many they were and what kind of resistance they might offer. Were the cities walled or unprotected, and was the land fertile? He told them to bring back some samples of the fruit of the land. The Lord's instructions served both to motivate and to challenge the tribes. The beauty and richness of the land would motivate them to forge ahead, but the strength and magnitude of the opposition they would face would try their faith. But they would need only to remember the ominous shores of the Red Sea and the approaching Egyptian army to fortify their hearts.

The spies traveled north all the way to Hebron. At the **Valley of Eshcol**, they cut off a branch of grapes in accordance with Moses' instructions, and transported it by pole on the shoulders of two men. They also took some **pomegranates and figs**. They explored and observed the land for forty days and then returned to the awaiting tribes.

13:26–33. Upon their arrival **at Kadesh**, the spies reported that the land was indeed good, and they offered their samples as proof. Their own eyes confirmed the words of the Lord that the land did flow with **milk and honey**. But they also spoke of the resistance they would meet if they attacked the land. The people of the land were **powerful**, living in large spacious cities. There they saw **descendants of Anak** (see "Deeper Discoveries"). Furthermore, they would have to fight other warlike people, such as the **Amalekites** . . . **Hittites, Jebusites and Amorites** in addition to the **Canaanites**. The latter group inhabited regions along the Mediterranean coast as well as Jordan.

The report must have struck paralyzing fear in the tribes that stood and listened. Terror seized their hearts, and **Caleb** must have immediately sized up the situation. He replied with a swift conclusion without taking the time to build up his case: They should take possession of the land, he said, **for we can certainly do it**. Caleb's response was the response of faith. God's words stirred up his heart in believing faith, and the empirical evidence he had gained by witnessing the land for himself corroborated this conclusion.

We can imagine a heated debate took place because faith and fear can never meet together except in animosity. Before the Israelites was a rich and plentiful land worth taking. But they would meet fierce resistance. What they had experienced in Egypt was minimal in comparison to the opposition they would face in Canaan. But the fearful report of the other leaders provided enough psychological fodder to turn the tide in favor of retreat. Now was not the time for brainstorming and "thinking out of the box." Now was the time for believing faith and action.

B A Nation Rebels (14:1–45)

SUPPORTING IDEA: *An entire generation fails the test of faith and will not see the promised land.*

14:1–4. The majority report, called "a bad report" by the narrator (13:32), appealed to the people and soon grew into public revolt. Fear turned to despair and pessimism. All that night the people of the community **raised their voices and wept aloud.** They grumbled against Moses and Aaron and even spoke of appointing a new leader who would guide them back to Egypt.

14:5–9. Moses and Aaron fell **facedown** on the ground in shame and contempt, knowing the Lord would respond to the growing revolt. **Joshua** and **Caleb** joined them and even tore their clothes and tried to rally the nation to arms. Their chief argument was that the Lord was with them and that the land was as good as the Lord had promised. They cautioned the cowering nation not to **rebel against the LORD** or fear the inhabitants of the land. The two champions again spoke of the Lord's presence among them and the certainty of victory. The people who lived in Canaan did not enjoy the protection of God as Israel did; therefore, they could not defeat Israel.

14:10–12. But the people refused to hear the words of Caleb and Joshua. Moses and Aaron apparently remained silent for a time. Their younger disciples had already presented a good case for entering the land. But the people **talked about stoning them.** Before they could utter another word, the Lord appeared in glory **at the Tent of Meeting** and took control of the proceedings. He put the blame on the people and identified himself as the true target of their contempt and unbelief. He reminded them of the miraculous wonders he had performed for them in Egypt. He announced that he would **strike them down with a plague,** then make from the believing remnant a greater nation.

14:13–19. Moses appealed to the compassion of God and to reason as he prayed that the Lord would adopt another course of action. He also appealed to God's glory. If the Egyptians heard about God's destruction of the Israelites, they would exploit it and draw untruthful conclusions that they would proclaim to the surrounding nations. Indeed, the whole world would hear of it and conclude that God **was not able to bring these people into the land he promised them.** It would become a contest of gods, and the stakes were high.

Moses appealed to God's glory as a motive to forgive the erring Israelites and remit their strict sentence. He did not appeal to the nation's merit, because it had none. What effect would such a sentence have on God's name? The nations would arrive at false theological conclusions about the nature of

God, particularly his omnipotence. The Lord, for whom nothing is too hard (Gen. 18:14), had guided the nation by **pillar of cloud by day and a pillar of fire by night**. The nations already knew that God identified himself with these people. Now what would happen if the promise of God failed, at least in the eyes of these people? Moses' prayer sought to honor God's name and bolster his image even in the eyes of enemies.

Moses also mentioned God's gracious and compassionate nature. He abounded in love yet did not compromise his justice. The wicked would be judged with a sentence that would ring in the ears of the children of the guilty until the **third and fourth generation** (see "Deeper Discoveries"). Moses asked God to **forgive the sin of these people** as he had several times since they had left Egypt.

14:20–25. The Lord responded by pardoning the Israelites but not without consequences. Even though nations and spiritual entities, hidden from mortal eyes, seek to eclipse God's influence in the world, his glory **fills the whole earth**. And the glory of the Lord comes in both salvation and judgment. The rebels who, by their unbelief and fear, had kept a nation from entering the land of promise would never **see the land**. On the other hand, **Caleb**, who valiantly stood up and declared his belief in God's promise and who stood against the panic-stricken revolt, would enter the land. His descendants would also share in the inheritance because of their father's bold faith. But the others would not see the land. From this point on, the Lord would not support them in any attempt to enter the land. He told them to turn back and set out toward the desert **along the route to the Red Sea**.

14:26–35. Evidently the Lord's sentence did not stop the people from complaining. Previously, they had voiced a desire to perish in the desert (Num. 14:2), and now the Lord would grant their request. They would indeed die in the desert without setting foot in the land of promise. All the people who were **twenty years old or more** would share that fate, with the exception of Caleb and Joshua. The children of this rebellious generation would possess the land but not until they had wandered in the desert for forty years—one year for every day they had explored the land. Those days of exploration were designed to instill faith not fear, and the people's contempt of God's word would now prove fatal to most of them.

14:36–45. The actual perpetrators were struck down by a plague, the exact nature of which is uncertain. It could have been lightening or fire (Harrison, 218).

Stricken with the reality of their plight, the Israelites who did not die in the plague sought to remedy their situation by turning again toward Canaan and attempting to take it. But God was not with them. Moses confronted them and warned them not to attempt such a foolish act. They would be **disobeying the LORD's command**—his new command to wander in the desert.

But they would not listen and **went up toward the high hill country**, where they were defeated by the Amalekites and the Canaanites.

> **MAIN IDEA REVIEW:** *God guided Israel to view and take the land, but their fear replaced their faith and smothered their spirit.*

III. CONCLUSION

Why God Responds to Faith

In his book *The Power of Positive Praying*, Houston pastor John Bisango describes a time when his daughter Melodye Jan, age five, came to him and asked for a dollhouse. John promised to build her one, and then he went back to reading his book. Soon he glanced out the study window and saw her arms filled with dishes, toys, and dolls, making trip after trip until she had a great pile of toys in the yard. He asked his wife what Melodye Jan was doing. "You promised to build her a doll house, and she believes you. She's just getting ready for it."

"You would have thought I'd been hit by an atom bomb," John said. "I threw aside that book, raced to the lumber yard for supplies, and quickly built that little girl a dollhouse. Now why did I respond? Because I wanted to? No. Because she deserved it? No. Her daddy had given his word, and she believed it and acted upon it. When I saw her faith, nothing could keep me from carrying out my word."

If you have been watching the events in the lives of the Israelites unfold, you have detected the leading of God based upon his promises to guide and bless. The same God, who provided deliverance from the tyranny of the Egyptians and parted the Red Sea, has now brought them to the brink of the land of milk and honey. Their job was to have faith and enter the land. But they failed the test of faith and suffered the consequences.

PRINCIPLES

- God wants his people to walk by faith and in obedience to his Word.
- God provides above and beyond what we could ever dream.
- Unbelief will prevent us from enjoying God's blessing in our lives.
- God can see past our excuses to the reality of our unbelief or lack of faith.

APPLICATIONS

- Always confirm information gathered through the authority of the Bible.

- Because the majority is not always right, vote your heart and vote based upon revelation from God.
- God wants you to have faith in spite of the data. He is greater than your greatest problem and bigger than your biggest failure.

IV. LIFE APPLICATION

An Oldie but a Goodie

One of the oldest sermon illustrations in most pastors' files is a powerful picture of the lives of many believers. A famous tightrope walker came to Niagara Falls and stretched his rope across the thunderous currents from Canada to the United States. Before the breathless multitudes, he walked, then ran, across the falls. He did the same blindfolded, with drums rolling. Then, still blindfolded, he pushed a wheelbarrow across the falls. The crowds went wild, and the aerialist shouted to them, "Who believes I can push a man in this wheelbarrow across these falls?" A gentleman in the front waved his hands, shouting, "I do! I believe!" "Then," said the walker, "come and get in the wheelbarrow." But the man's intellectual assent failed to translate into personal belief.

God tells us that the moment we close our eyes for the last time, we immediately open them in the presence of the Lord Jesus Christ. Do you really believe that? Then climb in the wheelbarrow!

Surrender your family to the Lord and accept his leading. Surrender your debilitating habits to God, who will forgive your sins and purify you from all unrighteousness (1 John 1:9). Surrender your life to the Lordship of Jesus, knowing and trusting that he alone knows what is best for you and that he desires to use you in the future. Come on, climb in!

V. PRAYER

Lord, grant me courage to claim your promises. Grant me strength to move in the direction you are leading. And grant me the faith to take each day one step at a time in thanking you for promises fulfilled in my life. Amen.

VI. DEEPER DISCOVERIES

A. The Descendants of Anak

The people of Israel heard from the spies of a warlike people who lived in the land of Canaan, the descendants of Anak. The Arabic word means "neck," and the nearest Hebrew rendering is something like "necklace." The term may mean "long-necked people," or tall people. Anak was the generic name for the Anakim, who possibly descended from Arba (Josh. 14:15). Anak was probably the name of a distinct people since it is most often used with the article. They settled in Hebron and other neighboring towns in the surrounding hill country. Later Joshua would all but destroy them during the fight for Palestine (Josh. 10:36–39; 11:21). A small remnant remained in and near Gaza, Ashod, and Gath, notable Philistine towns, the last of which the celebrated Goliath came from. Some have concluded Goliath was indeed descended from Anakim stock.

The Jews regarded the Anakites as formidable warriors (Deut. 2:10,21; 9:2), who may have descended from the Nephilim (Gen. 6:4). Certain eighteenth-century Egyptian texts mention a tribe called Anak with leaders having Semitic names. The name, however, does not reappear in any extrabiblical literature.

B. Does God Judge Children for the Sins of Their Fathers?

Sometimes the Bible indicates that children somehow pay for the sins of the fathers (and mothers). Yet the Bible instructed the authorities not to specifically punish the children for the sins of their fathers (see Ezek. 18:14–20). How then can we reconcile these apparent contradictory statements? We run into a similar problem when we read about Noah cursing Canaan for the sins of his father, Ham (Gen. 9:20–27). What role did Canaan have in Ham's sin and, if none, why did he receive this curse? Saul put to death certain Gibeonites whom Israel swore not to kill. But God exacted the punishment from Saul's sons, not Saul himself (2 Sam. 21:1–14). We cannot pretend to know all the reasons for such curses and punishments, but we can briefly explore a possibility.

Perhaps both the sins and punishments passed from generation to generation and in that order. In addition, sins and their attending punishments did not necessarily pass on to another generation, in which case the latter generation did not get punished. We know that national characteristics can pass down through generations with little interruption. Some sins and evil characteristics seem to make up a people, almost giving it definition. Some groups, for example, have engaged in aggressive war from generation to generation. Others maintain extended lists of families plagued by alcoholism. In that sense they may well sow the wind and reap the whirlwind. Sin can weave its way into the economic fabric of a people and thus easily pass on to succeeding generations. The children in that sense inherit their fathers' sins. New generations can break that mold only with the greatest of determination.

We do know that God is just and that he does only what is righteous and pure. For many of these judgments we don't have all the answers. We will have to wait until glory before we obtain good answers to some of these puzzles. Some of the pieces may never fit from our perspective. But God is God, and he always does the right and proper thing.

VII. TEACHING OUTLINE

A. INTRODUCTION

1. Lead Story: Looking Unbeatable
2. Context: Preparation and education are for a purpose. They are to be used. God had freed his people from slavery in Egypt. He had given them his law at Sinai and had prepared them to take possession of the good land he had promised. Before he sent them into the land, he had twelve of them go on a reconnaissance mission into Canaan. Ten of the spies saw the glass half empty. Two, Joshua and Caleb, saw the glass half full. The consequences of unbelief on the part of Israel were severe.
3. Transition: Today God works through people as he did over three thousand years ago. People make choices to trust God or to be let fear triumph over trust. The consequences of these kinds of choices are the same as they were when Israel refused to move ahead and take the land.

B. COMMENTARY

1. Exploring the promised land (13:1–33)
2. A Nation Rebels (14:1–45)

C. CONCLUSION: AN OLDIE BUT A GOODIE

VIII. ISSUES FOR DISCUSSION

1. Who was your favorite explorer in your high school world history class? What made you so interested in this explorer, and what was he trying to find?
2. Why do you think Israel sent the spies into the promised land? Were they necessary? Read Deuteronomy 1:20–23. What was the purpose of the spy mission?
3. What were the people of Israel expecting upon the return of the spies? How did they respond to the bad news? How do you respond to bad news?
4. Were the fears of the people normal? Why did God show his glory in Numbers 14 to the people? Why is Numbers 14:18 quoted so often, and why is this verse important to you?
5. What is the difference between faith and presumption? Share some ways in which you have demonstrated both in your life.

Numbers 15–18

God Knows What He's Doing

"*W*ith the goodness of God to desire our highest welfare, the wisdom of God to plan it, and the power of God to achieve it, what do we lack?"

A . W .   T o z e r

Numbers 15–18

IN A NUTSHELL

*A*t Kadesh Barnea, the Hebrews choose to turn away from God's blessing and are sent back into the wilderness. The people of Israel are going to learn that God's purpose cannot be thwarted. So God gives them some directions on what life will be like when they finally enter the promised land (Num. 15). God demonstrates how he deals with those who attempt to undermine his authority (Num. 16). God validates the priesthood of Aaron with the budded rod (Num. 17). God confirms the priestly system (Num. 18).

God Knows What He's Doing

I. INTRODUCTION

God Controls the Traffic

In his book *The Light in the Lantern,* James L. Henderschedt tells about the experience of a man named Michael Thomas. He was driving to a business appointment in a hurry one day when he became very annoyed with the traffic. He was stopped at a busy intersection where the light had just turned red. "All right," Michael thought to himself, "I can beat the next light if I race ahead of the pack." He was ready to take off the instant the light turned green. But then he noticed a young couple—both blind—crossing the street. The woman had a baby in her arms. Both the man and the woman were using white canes to help them navigate across the busy intersection. With horror, Michael realized that the couple were not walking in the cross-walk but were instead veering diagonally, directly into the intersection and the cross traffic. The couple were walking right into the path of oncoming cars.

"As I watched," Michael recalls, "I saw a miracle unfold before my eyes; every car in every direction came to a simultaneous stop." He never heard the screech of brakes or even the beep of a car horn. Nobody even yelled, "Get out of the way!" The traffic just stopped. In that moment time seemed to stand still for this family as they made their way safely across the busy inter-section. It was as if God were telling Michael to look around, to be conscious of God's presence in the world.

The next ten chapters of Numbers are filled with examples of God's peo-ple lacking faith, making poor choices, and complaining about their position in life. They have been turned back toward the wilderness from which they came, and their sense of destiny has become a sense of discouragement. But God's purpose is still for the people to enter the promised land. God still intends to bless his people. The people may have delayed God's leading, but their actions will not prevent God's plan. Perhaps he will have to "stop the traffic" to see his will fulfilled.

II. COMMENTARY

God Knows What He's Doing

MAIN IDEA: *The Lord works through legitimate lines of authority.*

A Additional Rules for Offerings (15:1–41)

SUPPORTING IDEA: *The Lord gives guidance on further offerings and a test of obedience.*

The narrative now records the events that took place during the nearly forty years that intervened between the refusal to enter the land the first time and the arrival at Kadesh (20:1). The most significant event recorded is the rebellion of Korah and the divine certification of the Aaronic priesthood (chs. 16–18). The Israel that came out of Egypt would now begin to lose its identity because of their sin in not taking the land. In short, the Lord dropped them from the sacred history (Keil, 99–100). From the reader's point of view, their purpose now was to die! The history would resume with the next generation—the one God would bring into the land. Before that, the Lord would supplement some earlier laws with additional regulations that would help the tribes upon their arrival in the land.

15:1–16. Whenever anyone offered a burnt offering, he or she must accompany it with a **grain offering of a tenth of an ephah of fine flour** mixed with a quarter of a hin of oil. This supplements previous instructions for burnt offerings given in Leviticus 1, a supplement also required for fellowship offerings (Lev. 3:1–17). The Lord required this of the Israelites only upon their arrival in the land because the ingredients in the grain offering, grain and oil, would be scarce in the desert.

A lamb offering must be accompanied with **a quarter of a hin of wine as a drink offering**. The **ram** offering required more because it was larger (Harrison, 222), and the amount was also raised for the bull offering. The Lord made no distinction between the native Israelite and the foreigner, perhaps for a couple of reasons.

The first was to prevent foreign religious influence from entering the sacrificial system. If the priests and Levites guarded the prescribed laws and enforced penalties for each infringement, they need not worry about foreign influence. As time would prove, that was easier said than done. The second and perhaps obvious reason the Lord prescribed the same rules for native and alien was to anticipate that time when no distinction would exist between Jew or Gentile, male or female, slave or free (Gal. 3:28).

15:17–21. The Lord also instructed Israel to offer a special "land" offering once they arrived in Canaan. They were to take some of the food they found there and **present a portion as an offering to the LORD**. This offering was to be lifted or heaved (KJV) to the Lord in the form of a cake. Raised offerings differed slightly from the wave offering and carried symbolic significance. This token would remind the people that the land belonged to the Lord and was a gift to them.

15:22–26. These supplemental laws for the sin offering (see Lev. 4:13–21) add a new feature: provision for sins of omission. Here the sin is not described, but it involved cases when they failed to keep any of these **commands the LORD gave Moses**. Ignorance of known commands provided no excuse for priest, individual, or community. Now the community would have to pull together and work in unison. The priests would have to instruct the people, and the people, in turn, must comply. The subsequent history of Israel proved that the nation failed in this regard.

15:27–31. Moses reintroduced the law for the sin offering (Lev. 5), but now it included foreigners. But for any who sinned **defiantly** ("with an uplifted hand"), the law made no provision at all (Heb. 10:26–27). Such an attitude constituted an arrogant disregard for God's revealed will and could only be met with death. The ruling authorities were to make no distinction between native or foreigner.

15:32–36. Moses provided an instance of sinning defiantly as both an illustration and an example. We don't know when this event took place, but it involved a man **gathering wood** on the Sabbath day. The Lord had previously given the law of the Sabbath as a primary command (Exod. 20:8–11). The death penalty was prescribed for violators (Exod. 31:14–15). But the mode of death was never prescribed, and for that Moses had to seek God's counsel. The Lord indicated that the entire community was to **stone him outside the camp**. Why did the Lord require all the people to participate? Because he would not allow minority opinions on matters that he had clearly spelled out. The whole nation needed to abide by and enforce the commands of the Lord.

15:37–41. The chapter concludes with a reminder of the covenant laws that would govern the nation for generations to come. The Lord commanded Moses to instruct the people to wear tassels on the corners of their garments (see also Deut. 22:12). The tassels were a reminder to the people to keep the commands of the Lord all their days and to remember the Lord's words: **I am the LORD your God, who brought you out of Egypt.**

𝔹 Korah's Rebellion (16:1–50)

SUPPORTING IDEA: *Attempts to override God's authority will meet with his judgment.*

The next section (chs. 16–18) is the only detailed account of anything of merit that took place during the wilderness wandering years. Chapter 16 describes a major rebellion against the legitimate priesthood, and then the Lord's certification of the Aaronic priesthood as the sole functioning priesthood in Israel. The attempt to overthrow Moses and Aaron was the most serious on record, as was the judgment inflicted on the rebels.

16:1–3. The principal culprit in the rebellion was **Korah son of Izhar**, a Kohathite from the tribe of Levi. Two Reubenites also affiliated with him, Dathan and Abiram, in addition to 250 **well-known community leaders**. The **council** was probably the structure Moses had set up to assist him in governing the nation. They approached Moses and Aaron and questioned their authority. Evidently they did not recognize God's appointment of Moses to his special position and adopted an egalitarian view that extended equally to all Levites. Perhaps the ringleaders were jealous for being excluded from the priesthood, or maybe they had grown tired of the wanderings. Harrison suggests the Reubenites joined the conspiracy because they felt robbed of their birthright (Gen. 49:3–4; cp. 1 Chr. 5:1–2).

16:4–17. Moses fell to the ground in astonishment, knowing how the Lord would react to this public revolt. He refused to listen to any of the complaints of the group and announced that the Lord would adjudicate the matter the next day. The Lord had them **take censers** and, the next day, light them with fire as a test to determine who the Lord approved.

Then Moses addressed the ringleader, Korah. He scolded him not only for leading an insurrection but for not appreciating his privileged position of serving in the tabernacle. Apparently one of the issues revolved around the priesthood and not just over Moses' and Aaron's unique authority. Two of those whom Moses summoned, Dathan and Abiram, would not come. Instead they reproached Moses for his part in leading them by false promises into a virtual wasteland.

Moses became very angry because of these words and pleaded with the Lord not to acknowledge their offering. At least one of the indictments appeared to be an accusation that Moses tried to profit from his position. Either that or Moses was showing the irony of assuming both a dictatorship and a modest lifestyle. In truth Moses did none of these things nor, as he notes, did he knowingly wrong anyone. He demanded that Korah and his group appear the next day at the tent of meeting to present their censers before the Lord.

16:18–35. The next day they did as Moses instructed, and the glory of the Lord **appeared to the entire assembly.** The Lord was angry at their repeated grumbling and again pronounced judgment on them. But Moses and Aaron fell down and prayed to the Lord not to wipe out the entire congregation. They argued that only a relatively few leaders joined the conspiracy. Why should the entire nation suffer? The Lord responded by instructing Moses to tell the people to separate themselves from the **tents of Korah, Dathan and Abiram.** The congregation obeyed, and the three principal rebels with their wives and children stood outside in plain view.

Moses then uttered a prophecy that set his own authority over against that of the rebels. If no calamity occurred that destroyed these men, then the Lord had not spoken by Moses. But if an unprecedented judgment took place, then they would know that these rebels did not speak for God. At Moses' words the ground under them split open and the earth swallowed the rebels, **with their households and all Korah's men and all their possessions.** Thus the rebels perished in their sin before the eyes of the community. But the Lord was not done. **Fire came out** and destroyed the **250 men** who joined in the revolt as they offered their incense.

16:36–40. But the censers were still holy and needed to be retrieved. To prevent another disaster like the one that befell Nadab and Abihu (Lev. 10) for burning unauthorized fire, Eleazar at Moses' command took the censers out of the fire and scattered the burning coals. He then hammered the censers into sheets that covered the altar of sacrifice. This covering was no mere ornamentation but a memorial establishing the Aaronic priesthood as the only legitimate priesthood in Israel. Usurpers should consider themselves duly warned against challenging this authority.

16:41–50. But the next day the people blamed the deaths of these men on Moses and Aaron. As the revolt began to gather steam near the tent of meeting, **the cloud covered it and the glory of the Lord appeared.** The Lord again told Moses and Aaron to remove themselves from this assembly so he could destroy them. Moses told Aaron to recover his censer and light some incense to make atonement for them. The plague, which by this time had already broken out, was now averted, but not before **14,700 people died from the plague.**

Aaron's Priesthood Confirmed (17:1–13)

> **SUPPORTING IDEA:** *Aaron's family is established as the true priesthood.*

The Lord had already confirmed Aaron's right and that of his descendants to the priesthood by honoring his incense and prayer and staying the plague. He further authenticated this priesthood by offering an additional sign that would silence the congregation.

17:1–5. The Lord instructed Moses to speak to the Israelites and get **twelve staffs** from them, one from each tribal leader. The staff or rod was an indication of leadership in the home and tribe. Each man needed to write his name on the staff. This included Aaron, who would write his name on the staff from the tribe of Levi. Each staff would be placed inside the tent of meeting before the sacred ark and remain there overnight. A branch detached from a tree loses its connection with life and will die. But God would provide nourishment to the staff he would choose to represent Israel through the priesthood.

17:6–9. The next day Aaron's staff had not only sprouted but had **budded, blossomed and produced almonds.** The Lord performed this miracle through divine omnipotence and silenced the opponents. The budded staff also represented a fruit-bearing priesthood, one appointed by God. Later God would appointed another priesthood, that of Melchizedek (see "Deeper Discoveries"). The almond tree bears fruit the earliest of all other trees in Israel (see Keil, 114). The people could not answer a word, because anything that could be said the Lord had spoken through this miraculous sign.

17:10–13. The Lord commanded the people to put Aaron's staff **in front of the Testimony** as a reminder to the **rebellious**. The series of events associated with Korah's rebellion now settled into the hearts of the people. They anguished over what had happened and even despaired of their own lives. But they were taught a vital lesson. Although they would engage in other forms of rebellion, they would never again question Aaron's priesthood.

Ⅾ The Ministry of Priests and Levites (18:1–32)

SUPPORTING IDEA: *The Lord again established the primary duties of the Levites.*

18:1–7. The Lord addressed Aaron because to him fell the responsibility of the priesthood. God would mediate his forgiveness of the nation and its individuals through the priesthood of Aaron's family. Future aspirants to this office would be dealt with as severely as Korah and his cohorts. Aaron's **fellow Levites**, to whom God granted an exalted position, could **assist** Aaron and his sons in the work of the tabernacle service. But the Levites could not go near the sacred altar. Worship and the sacrificial system constituted the heart of Israel's existence. The Levites risked their own lives if they broke this law.

18:8–19. The Lord would sustain the priests through the sacrificial offerings of the people. When the people offered certain sacrifices, the priests could eat the proper portions of these offerings as their **regular share**. The male priests could partake of the grain, sin, and guilt offerings (see Lev. 2:1–16; 4:1–5:19). The priests could also eat the wave offerings as long as they were **ceremonially clean**. When the people came and offered the firstfruits of their **finest olive oil and all the finest new wine and grain**, they also sustained the priests through these offerings. If Israel followed these precepts, the priests would always receive an adequate living and not have to resort to outside work to support their families.

In addition to the regular offerings, the priests also received support from those things the people **devoted** to the Lord, or was otherwise under the "ban" (Lev. 27:28). All of the firstborn belonged to the priests, but the people must redeem every firstborn son and every unclean animal that could not be eaten. However, ceremonially clean animals, such as **an ox, a sheep or a goat**, must not be redeemed since they would be sacrificed. These animals served as food for the priests and their families.

18:20–24. The priests and Levites were forbidden from owning land. Accordingly, they received no allotment from Joshua when they entered the promised land. They did receive cities to live in, but no permanent land. The Lord himself was their inheritance, and they were to serve him exclusively. The people tithed their produce and livestock in order to support the Levites. The Lord again warned the Levites not to get close to **the Tent of Meeting** or they would die.

18:25–32. Since the Levites received their support directly from the people, we might think that they did not tithe. But they did. They received their support from *God* and were not to forget that. They offered the finest portion of the people's tithes as if they produced it themselves and gave it to Aaron and his sons.

MAIN IDEA REVIEW: *The Lord works through legitimate lines of authority.*

III. CONCLUSION

The Wrong Horse Won

Herb Miller has an amusing story in his book *Actions Speak Louder Than Verbs*. It seems that two Kentucky farmers who owned racing stables had developed a keen rivalry. One spring each of them entered a horse in a local steeplechase. Thinking that a professional rider might help him outdo his friend, one of the farmers hired a jockey with a winning record. The two horses were leading the race at the last fence, but it proved too tough for them. Both horses fell, unseating their riders. But his calamity did not stop the professional jockey. He quickly remounted and won the race. Returning triumphant to the paddock, the jockey found the farmer who had hired him fuming with rage.

"What's the matter?" the jockey asked. "I won, didn't I?"

"Oh yes," roared the farmer. "You won all right, but you still don't know, do you?"

"Know what?" asked the jockey.

"You won the race on the wrong horse."

God always wins. The people of Israel lacked faith, but God provided further training and won. The people rebelled, and God won by validating Moses' leadership and judging Moses' jealous rivals. The people of Israel needed a fully devoted priesthood when they entered Canaan, and God again won by validating Aaron and the priesthood. Satan may try everything to get the horse to fall, but God always remounts his leader to complete the race.

PRINCIPLES

- Faith is not always based on experience.

- God's purpose can be delayed but not destroyed.
- Leaders will face opposition.
- Jealousy and pride have caused many people to disregard God's leading and rebel against leadership.
- God protects his anointed leaders.
- Leaders must learn the art of managing conflict.
- Rebellion against God's leaders is actually rebellion against God.

APPLICATIONS

- When faced with a chance to follow a leader or become jealous, remember who has placed the authority in your life.
- If you are a leader, be patient and allow God to fight for you.
- God's Word provides clarity about the responsibilities of God's people.
- If you want God's blessing, you must learn to walk by faith.

IV. LIFE APPLICATION

Rings of Fire

Each year many visitors stand before a cross-section of the Sequoia trees near Yosemite National Park and count the rings. Each ring represents a year of growth; often these trees survive for hundreds of years. Some of the rings are thicker, due to the abundance of water that year, while in the years of less rainfall, the rings are thinner. Occasionally a ring may look dark or even damaged because of a fire that made its way through the forest that year. The growth of the tree may have been affected for several years after the blaze. These "trial by fire" years were painful for the tree, but they represent only a minor problem when compared to the numerous rings that show healthy growth and development.

A cross-section of your life can be equally mapped. Some lean years were caused by a lack of nourishment in the Word. Other abundant growth years are reminders of your growth in prayer and service for the kingdom. But like the purpose of God for the people of Israel, God's purpose can be delayed but never destroyed. You may be in a time of "trial by fire," but these events fit into the rings of life God has for you. Remain obedient and grow in your faith. God is not finished with you yet.

V. PRAYER

Heavenly Father, as I look back over my life, I am reminded of your loving guidance throughout the good, the bad, and even the ugly. You have stopped traffic for me when I was defiant; you have caused growth rings when I was obedient. But I want to grow in my faith and learn to make good decisions for your blessings and your leading. And when I complain, remind me of your faithfulness and show me how each day is another opportunity to love you and serve you. In Jesus' name. Amen.

VI. DEEPER DISCOVERIES

The Aaronic Versus the Melchizedek Priesthood

The incidents recorded in these chapters reminded the Israelites that the only legitimate priesthood was one established by God. But that does not exclude any priesthood other than Aaron's; it merely bars illegitimate claims to the priesthood. The Bible does speak of another priesthood—Melchizedek's. When Abraham returned from the slaughter of the kings, he was blessed by the king of Salem, who also held the title of "priest of God Most High" (Gen. 14:18–20). The psalmist briefly mentioned him years later (Ps. 110:4), but we had to wait until the author of Hebrews developed the Melchizedek theme at length before we could arrive at any satisfactory answer about who this person was. The Book of Hebrews concluded that Melchizedek's priesthood was superior to Aaron's (Heb. 6:20–7:28).

We can summarize the teaching in Hebrews about Melchizedek's priesthood as follows: Jesus was a priest "in the order of Melchizedek" (Heb. 5:6), a name that also means "king of peace" (7:2). He had no recorded genealogy and therefore in typological fashion resembled "the Son of God." We conclude with Hughes that he "was no more than a man, a type of the perfection of Christ" (242), but not, as some suppose, Christ himself. After all, "if Melchizedek resembles the Son of God he cannot at the same time be the same as the Son of God" (243). The same Melchizedek "blessed him who had the promises" (Heb. 7:6), indicating he was greater than Abraham (7:7).

In fact, Levi, who was not yet born but who descended from Abraham, in that sense "was still in the body of his ancestor" (7:10). The Aaronic priesthood, so necessary for the moment, looked forward to a time of reformation that included both "a change of the priesthood" and also "a change of the law" (7:12). In Christ God combined the offices of king, priest, and prophet.

VII. TEACHING OUTLINE

A. INTRODUCTION
1. Lead Story: God Controls the Traffic

2. Context: Israel disobeyed God at Kadesh Barnea by refusing to move forward and take the promised land. None of those people over twenty years old, except Joshua and Caleb, would enter the promised land. During this period of waiting for the older generation to die, Korah and others challenged Moses' and Aaron's leadership. God demonstrated in unmistakable ways whom he had appointed as leaders. This judgment against Korah and his followers was a vivid lesson of the integrity of God's Word.

3. Transition: In our modern culture, although it is very different from ancient Israel's, God still chooses leaders. God expects his leaders to rely on him and to be accountable to him for their actions. God expects those who are followers to respect those who are appointed to leadership, recognizing that all authority is from God.

B. COMMENTARY

1. Additional Rules for Offerings (15:1–41)

2. Korah's Rebellion (16:1–50)

3. Aaron's Priesthood Confirmed (17:1–13)

4. The Ministry of Priests and Levites (18:1–32)

C. CONCLUSION: RINGS OF FIRE

VIII. ISSUES FOR DISCUSSION

1. What significance does Numbers 15:14–16 have for the church? Why do you think God sees no difference between the native-born and the alien?

2. Explain the difference between an intentional sin and an unintentional sin. What does God's Word seem to indicate about God's view of sins in general?

3. What complaints did the people have about Moses? Do you think these complaints had any foundation? What causes a person to develop this kind of bitterness about others?

4. When Israel finally entered Canaan, leadership decisions would be vital to their success and safety. Why did God need to address the rebellion of Korah at this point in time? Why such a severe punishment?

5. What responsibility did the Levites have for the spiritual health of Israel? What responsibility do you have in the lives of the people whom you influence?

Numbers 19–21

God's Provision in the Journey

I. **INTRODUCTION**
These Forty Years

II. **COMMENTARY**
A verse-by-verse explanation of these chapters.

III. **CONCLUSION**
Spiders over the Fire

An overview of the principles and applications from these chapters.

IV. **LIFE APPLICATION**
Wrong Clocks

Melding these chapters to life.

V. **PRAYER**
Tying these chapters to life with God.

VI. **DEEPER DISCOVERIES**
Historical, geographical, and grammatical enrichment of the commentary.

VII. **TEACHING OUTLINE**
Suggested step-by-step group study of these chapters.

VIII. **ISSUES FOR DISCUSSION**
Zeroing these chapters in on daily life.

"*Y*ou have not really learned a commandment until you have obeyed it. . . . The church suffers today from Christians who know volumes more than they practice."

Vance Havner

Numbers 19–21

IN A NUTSHELL

*N*umbers 14–20 gives us snapshots into the wilderness experience of Israel. How did they deal with the sin of God's people while they were marching? A special offering was needed, and it is described in Numbers 19. Then the Israelites, thirty-seven years later, arrive at Kadesh Barnea—again—and God must deal with the same disobedience, but this time with Moses. The time arrives for their first battle. Great lessons are learned from further complaining and a serpent of brass.

God's Provision in the Journey

I. INTRODUCTION

These Forty Years

*S*olomon Ginsburg, a Polish Jew, became a flaming evangelist across Europe and South America. In 1911, needing rest, he decided to head to America on furlough. His route took him to Lisbon, where he planned to cross the Bay of Biscay to London, then on to the United States. Arriving in Lisbon, Ginsburg found the bulletin boards plastered with weather telegrams warning of terrible storms on the Bay of Biscay. It was dangerous sailing, and he was advised to delay his trip a week. His ticket allowed him to do that, and he prayed about it earnestly.

But as he prayed, he turned to his WMU prayer calendar and found the text for that day was Deuteronomy 2:7: "For the LORD your God has blessed you in all the work of your hand. He knows your trudging through this great wilderness. These forty years the LORD your God has been with you; you have lacked nothing" (NKJV). The Lord seemed to assure him that his long, world-wide travels were under divine protection. Ginsburg boarded the ship at once, crossed without incident, and caught the *Majestic* in London. His transatlantic voyage was smooth and restful.

Only after arriving in the United States did Solomon learn that if he had delayed his trip to Lisbon, he would have arrived in London just in time—just in time to board the *Titanic*.

Too bad Ginsburg's prayer calendar wasn't part of the baggage being carried by the people of Israel. God had been so faithful, so powerful, and so merciful every step of the way through their wilderness experience. And to show us still other ways God supplied every need for the Hebrew people, God allows us to study three more chapters dedicated to Israel's blessing and God's glory.

II. COMMENTARY

God's Provision in the Journey

MAIN IDEA: *The Lord brought his people closer to Canaan and taught them lessons on faith and conflict.*

A The Water of Purification (19:1–22)

SUPPORTING IDEA: *A red heifer ritual cleansed the Israelites from ceremonial defilement.*

19:1–10. The cleansing instrument God would use in purifying the Israelites from defilement began with a **red heifer**. A heifer was a young cow somewhere between a calf and a full-grown cow. They were to select a red heifer probably because of its resemblance to blood. They were to give the heifer to Eleazar the son of Aaron who would have it slaughtered outside the camp. He then would take some of the blood and **sprinkle it seven times** toward the front of the tent of meeting. They were to burn the heifer in Eleazar's sight and then he would toss into the fire **some cedar wood, hyssop and scarlet wool**.

We don't know precisely why he used cedar wood; perhaps it emitted an aroma (Harrison, 256). The red wool may have symbolized blood, as did the red heifer itself, or it may have served as a container of sorts for the hyssop (Harrison, 256). Keil notes that hyssop symbolized purification from death (124). The common hyssop plant is actually a sweet-smelling plant from the mint family (Packer, 252). It normally grows to a height a little over a foot and contains pointed leaves and colored flowers. It thrived in Egypt and Palestine and was used in several Jewish rituals (see also Lev. 14:4,6; Heb. 9:19).

The priest then washed his clothes and bathed with water, as did the man who actually burned the heifer. A man who was ceremonially clean then gathered up the ashes of the heifer and put them in a clean place outside the camp. Thereafter they would be kept as **the water of cleansing**, applied to those who became defiled by touching a corpse.

19:11–22. Whoever touched a dead body would be unclean for seven days. On the third and seventh days, he must purify himself with the water of cleansing (the ashes of the heifer) and he would be clean. Otherwise he would remain unclean. Because the tabernacle represented the life of the nation and the rituals provided for the cleansing of the people, whoever failed **to purify himself** would defile the Lord's tabernacle. Such an offense required the offender's life, and he would be put to death.

Whenever someone died in a tent, anyone in the tent at the time of death or anyone who entered it while the body was still present became unclean for seven days. Even open containers became unclean. Whoever touched a dead body in an open field, whether the person had been killed or had died a natural death, became unclean and had to go through this cleansing ritual.

The process of cleansing involved taking some of the ashes and mixing them with fresh water in a jar. Then a man who was ceremonially clean was **to take some hyssop**, dip it in the water and sprinkle the tent, its furniture, and anyone who was in the tent. This ceremonially clean man must then apply the water of cleansing to the defiled person on the prescribed third and seventh days. The man who cleansed the unclean man must also wash his clothes. If someone came into contact with this water of cleansing, he would be unclean until evening.

ⓑ Miraculous Water, Conflict, and the Death of Aaron (20:1–29)

SUPPORTING IDEA: *Tough times continued as Israel learned to trust in God's provision even as they lost a trusted leader.*

20:1–8. The journeys of the nation were now drawing to a close. In the **first month** of about the fortieth year following the exodus, the Israelites **arrived at the Desert of Zin** and camped at Kadesh. Here **Miriam died and was buried.** She was well advanced in years, and the people probably observed an extended period of mourning for her, as was their custom.

Some time after their arrival at Kadesh, the people ran out of water. This led them to complain again to Moses, wishing they had never left Egypt and had died in the desert. Where was this beautiful land with its rich and fruitful soil that Moses had spoken of? Where were the promised **grain or figs, grapevines or pomegranates?** By this time Moses may have thought that the people learned the painful lessons of the past. Did not God send an awful plague that silenced the rebel community? Thus the outburst must have pushed Moses to the brink.

He also knew that God's patience would wear thin and result in another punishment. Therefore, Moses and Aaron went to the entrance of the tent of meeting **and fell facedown.** The Lord and his glory then appeared. God told Moses to take his staff and **speak to that rock** so it would open up and provide the thirsty community and their livestock with needed water.

20:9–13. Instead of speaking to the rock as God had instructed him, Moses **struck the rock twice with his staff.** He thundered at them for their wrangling: **Listen, you rebels, must we bring you water out of this rock?** He uncharacteristically disobeyed the clear instructions of the Lord. Moses, it appeared, was angrier than God with the complaining throngs. Water flowed from the rock and the people drank, but the damage was done. The Lord pronounced a sentence on Moses and told him he would not enter the promised land with the people. The place was therefore named **Meribah,** meaning "to strive." This is not to be confused with an earlier Meribah near Mount Horeb (Exod. 17:7). Aaron, by virtue of his agreement with Moses, shared his guilt and was also judged (see Num. 20:24).

20:14–21. The endless years of wandering now drew to a close. Israel, perhaps now equipped with a growing resolve, made a beeline toward the eastern regions of Canaan with a view toward taking the land. To accomplish this, they must pass through the land of their ancient brother Edom. Moses followed diplomatic protocol when he dispatched messengers to the Edomite rulers, requesting permission to pass through. They would travel through Edom on the **king's highway,** an ancient route that linked Arabia with Ammon and Damascus (Harrison, 270).

Edom, however, refused passage and strictly warned them against any attempt to pass through lest they come out **and attack** them with the sword. Moses offered to pay them for water, but the Edomites again refused passage. Later Israel would purchase water from them, or probably containers to pull water out of small wells that Israel would dig (Deut. 2:6; see Keil, *Deut.*, 292). Edom then came out in a show of force, compelling Israel to turn away from them.

20:22–29. The community left Kadesh and traveled to Mount Hor, where the Lord informed Aaron he would now die. Aaron and Moses' sin at Meribah and Aaron's many other sins would now close his eyes permanently. The Lord instructed Moses to **get Aaron and his son Eleazar** and to remove Aaron's priestly garments and put them on Eleazar. So Moses did as the Lord commanded, and Aaron died just as the Lord said. Upon his return Moses and the whole congregation mourned Aaron for thirty days.

Conquests on the Way to Moab (21:1–35)

SUPPORTING IDEA: *The Lord primes Israel for future battle by engaging Og and Sihon.*

21:1–3. Before Israel embarked on its main military objective, the conquest of Canaan, the Lord prepared them with several lesser battles along the way. When the king of Arad heard that Israel drew close to them, **he attacked the Israelites** and captured some of them. Arad was a town in the Negev near the wilderness of Judah. But the people of Israel vowed to destroy the cities if the Lord gave them victory. **The LORD listened to Israel's plea** and gave them victory over the Canaanites. Israel thoroughly destroyed their cities and the people. Consequently, that place was named **Hormah**, or "devoted to destruction."

21:4–9. Israel moved into the wilderness of Zin to avoid land occupied by the Edomites. They ventured southwest and probably avoided further military conflicts (Harrison, 275). But along the way, **the people grew impatient.** They once again spoke against Moses who, as God's spokesman, represented God to the people. They therefore also spoke **against God.** Again they railed against him with old complaints of leaving the land of Egypt where they at least had enjoyed relative security. They complained of the manna and scarcity of water or other food. The Lord sent **venomous snakes among them,** killing many Israelites.

The people sought relief and confessed their sin to Moses, asking him to pray to remove the snakes. Moses prayed for them, and God answered by instructing Moses to **make a snake and put it up on a pole.** Whoever looked at the pole would recover from the snakebite. The Lord had them construct the bronze snake as "an emblem of healing rather than an object of veneration" (Harrison, 278). But later the Israelites, probably under the influence of Canaanite religion, worshiped and burned incense to this object. Still later, godly King Hezekiah destroyed the serpent (2 Kgs. 18:4).

Jesus provided apt symbolism for this bronze serpent in one of the major salvation passages in the entire Bible: "Just as Moses lifted up the snake in the desert, so the Son of Man must be lifted up, that everyone who believes in him may have eternal life" (John 3:14–15). The bronze serpent provided physical recovery from a poisonous snakebite, but the suffering Messiah brought a lasting healing of a spiritual nature, and "by his wounds we are healed" (Isa. 53:5).

21:10–20. Israel next traveled to **Oboth**, a city on the way to Moab. The name meant "water skins," and they probably found a spring or well in the area. From there they came to **Iye Abarim**, situated on the southeastern region of Moab. Mount Nebo was located here—the place from which Moses would later view the promised land. They journeyed to the **Arnon . . . between Moab and the Amorites**. One ancient account, called **the Book of the Wars** (see "Deeper Discoveries"), described some of the geography of the area, with its sloping ravines. Upon their arrival at **Beer** ("well"), the Lord graciously provided them water. In gratitude, Israel sang a song of thanks and joy. The water came from some underground source, and the Lord had them dig for it.

Just before their arrival at Moab they went through several areas that cannot be located with certainty. The **top of Pisgah** probably stood in the local mountain range where Mount Nebo was located.

21:21–35. Israel sent this message to King Sihon of the Amorites: **Let us pass through your country**. The capital city of the Amorites was Heshbon. In addition to his own people, Sihon ruled (or possibly allied himself with) five vassal tribes from Midian (Josh. 13:21). When Sihon refused Moses passage, Israel defeated them all the way to the Jordan River. Israel captured all these lands that would later fall to the tribes of Reuben and Gad (Num. 32:1–4,33–38).

In Jazer, the Israelites drove out the Amorite inhabitants. This land would later fall to Gad (Josh. 13:25) and to the Merarite Levites (Josh. 21:39). When they drew near Bashan, King Og came out against them. The Lord provided Moses with assurance of final victory, including possession of his land. With this, Moses crushed their armies with brute force, leaving no survivors. Israel now enjoyed a series of victories and a growing reputation among the surrounding nations.

MAIN IDEA REVIEW: *The Lord brought his people closer to Canaan and taught them lessons on faith and conflict.*

III. CONCLUSION

Spiders over the Fire

Jonathan Edwards was one of America's most brilliant theologians. At age six he studied Latin. He entered Yale when not quite thirteen and graduated when barely fifteen. He was ordained at age nineteen, taught at Yale by twenty, and later became president of Princeton. Harvard granted him both a bachelor's and a master's degree on the same day.

But Edwards is best known for his sermon, "Sinners in the Hands of an Angry God." He preached it on Sunday, July 8, 1741, while ministering in tiny Enfield, Connecticut. A group of women had spent the previous night praying for revival. When Edwards rose to speak, he quietly announced that his text was Deuteronomy 32:35: "Their foot shall slide in due time" (KJV). This "hellfire and brimstone" approach was a departure for Edwards. Of his one thousand written sermons, fewer than a dozen are of this type.

Edwards never gestured or raised his voice. He spoke softly and simply, warning the unconverted that they were dangling over hell like a spider over the fire. "O Sinner! Consider the fearful danger. The unconverted are now walking over the pit of hell on a rotten covering, and there are innumerable places in this covering so weak that it will not bear their weight, and these places are not seen."

Edwards's voice was suddenly lost amid cries and commotion from the crowd. He paused, appealing for calm. Then he concluded, "Let everyone that is out of Christ, now awake and fly from the wrath to come. The wrath of Almighty God is now undoubtedly hanging over a great part of this congregation. Let every one fly out of Sodom."

Strong men held to pews and posts, feeling they were sliding into hell. Others shook uncontrollably and rolled on the floor. During the night, cries of men and women throughout the village were heard, begging God to save them. Five hundred were converted that evening, sparking a revival that swept thousands into the kingdom. The Great Awakening had come (Morgan, *On This Day*).

By now the people of Israel had seen miracle after miracle, sign after sign, God's leading, and God's judgment. You would think a "Great Awakening" would be occurring among the people of Israel, but they still had a lot to learn. They needed to learn to quit complaining and start trusting. They needed to learn to quit wandering off and start staying in line. And they needed to learn there are consequences to rebellion and disobedience. There were "innumerable places" in their faith so weak they would not bear their weight.

PRINCIPLES

- In spite of your sin, God wants you to keep walking by faith.
- When we disobey God, we will pay the consequences.
- People are never satisfied and have a short memory.

APPLICATIONS

- God expects instant recognition and confession of our sin.
- Never take credit for the blessings that God brings into your life.

- The bronze serpent is a wonderful picture of Christ who was lifted up for your sin. You will either look to Christ and live or look away and perish—eternally.

IV. LIFE APPLICATION

Wrong Clocks

In September 1991, government officials of the Soviet Union admitted something it had denied for nearly sixty years. During the Stalin era, officials once forgot to set the national clocks back one hour when they came off daylight saving time. They were so embarrassed by the gaffe that the Soviet government stayed on the wrong time and denied the whole thing for nearly six decades.

People make this same mistake when they fail to see God's leading. Instead of accepting his deliverance, they gripe and complain, remaining entrenched in their wilderness experience. You have to appreciate the response to the snakes in the Hebrew camp: "We have sinned" (Num. 21:6–7). These people finally admitted they were living their lives by the wrong clock—their clock—and God wanted them to live by faith. And thousands of years later we are reminded of Jesus' discussion with Nicodemus. John 3:14–16 says, "Just as Moses lifted up the snake in the desert, so the Son of Man must be lifted up, that everyone who believes in him may have eternal life. 'For God so loved the world that he gave his one and only Son, that whoever believes in him shall not perish but have eternal life.'" No more denial; no more embarrassment; no more looking to yourself and your own abilities or righteousness. Admit it! You need a Savior.

V. PRAYER

Lord, help me to accept your leading and not insist on going my own way. Help me learn the lesson from the faithless Israelites to trust you and obey you. Amen!

VI. DEEPER DISCOVERIES

A. Moses' Severe Punishment

Moses disobeyed the Lord's command by striking the rock twice instead of speaking to it as God commanded. In striking the rock, Moses substituted human activity for God's direct provision (Harrison, 267). But when we review Moses' life, we notice this wasn't his first act of disobedience; yet his punishment here seems quite severe.

Moses was ending his long and illustrious life and was clearly an instrument of God in blessing Israel. While the Lord condemned Moses for his disobedience in not setting apart his holy name at this time, he did not reject his servant. It was time for Moses to go to his reward and for the younger Joshua to assume Moses' duties.

VII. TEACHING OUTLINE

A. INTRODUCTION

1. Lead Story: These Forty Years
2. Context: The Lord led Israel toward the promised land, awaiting the time when the older generation would die and the younger generation would take the land. Even though they had been corrected many times, Israel continued to be a complaining people. They had doubts that God would provide them water. Moses became so frustrated with the people that he disobeyed a direct order of God. As a result, he would not enter the promised land.
3. Transition: God's people today exemplify many of the attitudes of Israel as they traveled to the promised land. God still disciplines and provides a remedy for his wayward people if they will look to him in faith.

B. COMMENTARY

1. The Water of Purification (19:1–22)
2. Miraculous Water, Conflict, and the Death of Aaron (20:1–29)
3. Conquests on the Way to Moab (21:1–35)

C. CONCLUSION: WRONG CLOCKS

VIII. ISSUES FOR DISCUSSION

1. The offering of the red heifer is unique in the Old Testament. Why?
2. Can you live in your culture without touching sin? What process does God use to cleanse you from your sin?
3. Can you relate to Moses' frustration? Do you feel that God was a little harsh with Moses, considering everything Moses had to endure?
4. Explain the process God used to free the Israelites from the snakes. Read John 3:14–15; 6:32–35. How do these New Testament verses relate to your life in light of the deliverance you have received through Christ?

Numbers 22–25

The Story of Balaam

"*G*etting riches brings care;

keeping them brings trouble; abusing them brings guilt;

and losing them brings sorrow.

It is a great mistake to make so much of riches as we do."

D .   L .   M o o d y

Numbers 22–25

IN A NUTSHELL

*Y*ou are about to meet one of the most mysterious and compelling characters in the Old Testament. Balaam is a prophet called upon by Balak, the king of the Moabites, to curse Israel. God tells Balaam not to meet with Balak, but he does anyway and proceeds to offer three prophecies. Each prophecy is a blessing to God's people instead of a curse, and Balak becomes very angry. In the concluding score, Balaam demonstrates his lack of personal integrity by teaching Balak how to bring Israel down through idolatry. These are dark days for Israel, and God's judgment falls.

The Story of Balaam

I. INTRODUCTION

Talk's Cheap

*Y*ears ago, on late-night television, actor Adolph Menjou appeared on the Jack Paar show. Here was an actor who was known for playing the suave and confident role and who made a great maitre d'. Menjou was known for dressing with great care. This particular night Paar led a discussion on proper dress and what to wear after five. Menjou presented himself as both knowledgeable and smug in his understanding of appropriate dress decorum. He even stood to show off his "taste" in clothing. Then Paar told Menjou that his trousers were unzipped.

It's one thing to know and quite another to do. Menjou's mistake illustrates that just because we are unaware of our situation, our pride, and our sin, this doesn't mean that others aren't.

Meet Balaam, a prophet for hire. His focus on the almighty dollar, metaphorically speaking, was known by God and by the king of the Moabites, Balak. Would Balaam compromise principle to gain wealth? Was Balaam's conscience so seared that he would sell out God's people for advancement? And what would God think of all this? The story of Balaam is a picture of many people in this world who are caught between desire and faithfulness to God.

II. COMMENTARY

The Story of Balaam

> **MAIN IDEA:** *Not all prophets who talk religious talk are God's prophets.*

Balaam the Soothsayer (22:1–41)

> **SUPPORTING IDEA:** *God tests Israel and confronts a false prophet.*

22:1–6. As the people of Israel traveled to the **plains of Moab**, Balak, the king of Moab, became afraid of the countless throngs of Israelites coming his way. The people of Moab also feared what might happen and appealed to their leaders to do something. Balak summoned Balaam, son of Beor, who resided at Pethor. He told him of a people who came from Egypt and who now threatened Balak's kingdom. Balak asked Balaam to utter a curse over them since Balak could not hope to conquer them on his own. Word of Israel's recent conquests over Sihon and Og had probably reached the ears of the fearful king, and he now stood in peril.

Just why Balak selected Balaam to curse the Israelites is not known, except that he must have established a name for himself as a soothsayer. This diviner, who according to 23:21 apparently recognized Yahweh as the God of Israel (without himself giving allegiance to Yahweh), is mentioned in several passages throughout the Bible as one whom the Lord singled out for particular judgment (Deut. 23:4–5; Josh. 24:9–10; Neh. 13:2; Mic. 6:5; Jude 11; Rev. 2:14). Some of the language in this narrative might lead some readers to conclude that Balaam was a true prophet of the Lord. But nothing could be further from the truth. The verdict on Balaam is in (see "Deeper Discoveries"). The Bible assigns him the tag of false prophet, although God talked with him.

22:7–20. The elders of Moab approached Balaam with **the fee for divination**, which was no doubt customary. This provides us with a clue to Balaam's motives and character. The elders repeated the proposal to Balaam, and he asked them to wait until he heard from God. The Lord indeed appeared to Balaam and asked him what all this was about. Balaam repeated Balak's request that he curse Israel without so much as offering an opinion on whether he felt such a curse was the right thing to do. But God responded by telling Balaam these people were **blessed**. With this, Balaam returned to the awaiting leaders and sent them away, saying the Lord would not permit such a request.

But Balak refused to yield to Balaam's first response. He sent **other princes** to talk with Balaam. These were **more numerous and more distinguished than the first**. These leaders again asked Balaam if he would curse Israel for them. Balaam responded that no amount of money could turn God's hand if God had no intention of cursing them. The princes probably came armed with abundant bribe money, and Balaam, we must conclude, was not immune to the temptation (Jude 11). But he again asked them to remain while he made request to God on their behalf. God responded by allowing Balaam to go with the men, but he could only do what God told him. This last instruction provides a clue to interpreting the entire narrative and yields insight into the nature of Balaam's disobedience. He was only to say and do what God told him—and no more.

22:21–35. When Balaam awoke the next morning, he saddled his donkey and **went with the princes of Moab**. But God was angry about this, and the angel of the Lord stood in the road to oppose him. To understand this verse we must read what it says and *read nothing into it*. The passage does not say that Balaam sinned in going—only that God became angry when he went. Apparently Balaam uttered some words along the way that were unauthorized by God, thus disobeying God's command to do only what he told him to do or say.

To prevent Balaam from going any further, God sent his angel to stand in the road **to oppose him**. The Lord afforded the donkey the ability to see what Balaam could not. The donkey witnessed the angel of the Lord in the road with a drawn sword, indicating resistance, so he turned aside into an adjacent field. Balaam struck the donkey in an attempt to steer him back on course. As they rode on, the angel stood in a narrow path between two vineyards, **with walls on both sides**, thus preventing passage. The donkey, seeing the angel, hit the wall, **crushing Balaam's foot against it**. Angered by the donkey's apparent stubbornness, Balaam struck him again. The two headed out on the road but again confronted the angel, who stood in a narrow place where they could not get by.

The donkey suddenly **lay down under Balaam**, for which he received another thrashing. But **the LORD opened the donkey's mouth** and allowed it to speak to Balaam, protesting his cruel treatment. Curiously, the donkey's response did not alarm Balaam.

Finally, the Lord opened the eyes of Balaam and rebuked him for beating the donkey three times and for recklessly disobeying God. He also told Balaam that he came close to losing his life because of his sin. The angel then allowed Balaam to proceed to the awaiting king, but on the condition that he must speak only what God told him.

22:36-41. Balak went out to meet the approaching prophet and scolded him for not coming sooner. Balak reminded Balaam that he stood to receive a handsome reward for cursing God's people. But the chastened soothsayer could only reply that his future words would be constrained by God's instructions. The two then came to **Kiriath Huzoth** where they offered sacrifices. The next day Balak took Balaam to the top of **Bamoth Baal**, about two and one-half miles south of Mount Nebo. There they viewed **part of the people**.

B Balaam's Prophecies (23:1-30)

SUPPORTING IDEA: *Balaam unwittingly prophesies of great blessing for Israel.*

23:1-12. Balaam asked Balak to build him **seven altars** and to prepare **seven bulls and seven rams**. They offered a bull and ram on each altar. Then Balaam told Balak to remain by the altars while he stepped aside to consult with God. The Lord gave him an oracle and told him to return to the waiting king and speak the oracle to him.

In the oracle Balaam restated Balak's desire to **denounce Israel**. But he made it clear that he could not curse **those whom God has not cursed**. Balak thought that Balaam had the power to bless and curse at will. But Balaam attributed that power to God alone. Balaam looked upon the multitudes of

Israelites and recognized that God gave birth to them and multiplied them as the sand on the shore. Balaam even wished that blessing for himself and recognized that nation whom God pronounced **righteous**. But "not all who are descended from Israel are Israel" (Rom. 9:6). Balaam probably spoke of the faith of Abraham or those Jews who found favor with God. The narrative repeatedly corroborates the words just quoted from the apostle Paul. Israel as a nation time and again struggled with God and disobeyed him many times. But always God kept "a remnant chosen by grace" (Rom. 11:5).

Balak scolded Balaam for refusing to curse Israel. Balak only wanted to use Balaam to pray down a curse on Israel so Moab might not suffer from the inevitable conflict with that nation. But Balaam replied that he was constrained to utter only what God put in his mouth.

23:13–26. Balak took Balaam to another place where they could see just a part of the people of Israel. He may have concluded that Balaam was reluctant to curse Israel because of their number, so he showed him only a portion of the nation. They came to the **field of Zophim** on Mount Pisgah where they again built seven altars and sacrificed as before. Balaam repeated the words he had spoken to Balak before and went off a distance to consult with God. Again the Lord sent him back to Balak with new words but the same message.

Balak was probably accustomed to convincing people to change their minds. As king he could employ any methods he chose, such as bribery or threat of force, to achieve his sinful aims. But now he sought to move the hand of God. But with God, "who does not change" (Jas. 1:17) and "who does not lie" (Titus 1:2), no amount of human persuasion can force his hand. And God did constrain Balaam to speak and act accordingly. Other nations, such as **Egypt**, mounted great offenses against Israel to no avail. Furthermore, no amount of **sorcery against Jacob** could succeed. Balaam compared Israel to a lion known for its courage and strength. He knew God's protecting hand was on the nation.

23:27–30. In still another attempt to undermine the Israelites, Balak took Balaam **to the top of Peor**, a summit of the Abarim ranges. Balaam told Balak to build the seven altars on this site and to prepare a bull and ram to sacrifice on each of the altars.

Ⅽ Balaam's Concluding Oracles (24:1–25)

> **SUPPORTING IDEA:** *Balaam fails to curse Israel.*

24:1–4. Once Balaam knew that God would not curse Israel, he abandoned all attempts to cooperate with Balak's scheme. Instead he turned his eyes **toward the desert** where he saw the nation of God in their tribal formations. He then uttered another oracle prompted by the **Spirit of God**, who granted the soothsaying prophet a measure of spiritual sight. Balaam simply uttered what God constrained him to speak without internalizing the message. God gave him the facts, and Balaam repeated them.

24:5–9. As Balaam viewed the Israelite settlement below, he praised their dwelling places and acknowledged God's blessing on their tents. He foresaw the future of these people as they basked in God's bounty surrounded by his grace. Balaam compared Israel to **gardens beside a river**—a picture that Jeremiah would later compare to a man who trusts in the Lord (Jer. 17:7–8).

Furthermore, Israel would become powerful and subdue great nations. Balaam envisioned a king **greater than Agag**, probably a king known to locals at the time of this writing. Of course, Israel found her strength in God's omnipotent favor that brought her out of Egypt. Israel would pursue other nations and overcome them. The language Balaam used spoke of the crushing and painful defeat that Israel would unleash on her enemies. Balaam repeated an earlier thought that Israel, much like a resting lion, would carry such a formidable reputation that none would dare **rouse them** (see 23:24). Those who blessed Israel would themselves **be blessed**, while those who cursed her would **be cursed**. (For more on this conditional promise, see "Deeper Discoveries.")

24:10–14. Frustrated by Balaam's refusal to curse Israel, Balak reproached the diviner and asked him to leave his presence. Balak blamed the God of whom Balaam spoke for losing his diviner's fee. Balaam replied that his message from the very beginning was he could only go as far as God allowed him. God did not allow him to curse his inheritance, and he would not allow Balaam to direct any words toward Israel except blessing. But before he returned to his own people, Balaam had still another prophecy of warning for the frazzled king.

24:15–19. The next oracle of the seer was considerably shorter than the others, and he repeated his common introduction. Balaam described the bleak fortunes of Moab and Edom going against Israel. From Jacob would come a star and a scepter. The star (Heb. *Kokab*), once used by Isaiah to describe the king of Babylon whom some say represented Satan (Isa. 14:12), also depicted the "Root and the Offspring of David" (Rev. 22:16). Such a "ruler will come out of Jacob" and "rule in the midst of" her enemies (Ps. 110:2).

24:20–25. The fate of Amalek had been determined by God long before. By divine decree the Amalekites were never to enter the courts of God, and Israel would ultimately destroy them. Amalek was the first heathen nation to come out against Israel (Exod. 17:8–16), at which time God uttered her fate. Later King Saul would deal them a severe blow, but they did survive by a thread until the Simeonites finally drove them out in the days of King Hezekiah (1 Chr. 4:43).

Balaam then turned toward the Kenites, an ancient tribe, and spoke of their secure dwelling place. But Asshur, an obscure north Arabian group descended from Abraham (Harrison, 326), would capture and defeat them. Asshur itself would be defeated by seagoing invaders, as would Eber, another nomadic tribe that descended from Eber of Shem (Gen. 10:1, cp. 24–25).

Ⅾ Moab Seduces Israel (25:1–18)

SUPPORTING IDEA: *Although Balaam could not curse the Israelites, he did seduce them into idolatry.*

25:1–3. The Lord protected Israel from direct attack from Moab by stopping Balaam from cursing them. But they could not resist the sordid influence of the heathen nation. While at Shittim, the Israelite men began to indulge in sexual immorality with **Moabite women**. These women brought the men to their idolatrous sacrifices, and Israel soon bowed before them. Israel sacrificed to **Baal of Peor**, a fertility god who was "venerated by means of the most sensuous, orgiastic practices known to humanity" (Harrison, 336). Moab's local Baal was Chemosh to whom they offered their worship in all kinds of profligate expressions. History informs us of the close connection between sexual immorality and false religion. Moab's seduction of Israel was probably a strategic ploy by the persistent Balak, who was not a quitter. Balaam, now out of favor with Balak but no doubt eyeing the rewards the king dangled before his eyes, advised Moab about how to go about this (31:16). This idolatry incited the Lord to anger, which burned against the Israelites.

25:4–9. The Lord told Moses to destroy all the leaders who engaged in this practice and to **expose them in broad daylight**. Moses told the leaders, who should have policed their comrades better, to put them to death and publicly expose them.

Then an Israelite man took a Midianite woman into his tent as Moses and Israel looked on. Such arrogance and disregard for law and the tragic consequences of Israel's failure drew an immediate response from **Phinehas son of Eleazar**. He followed the Israelite man into his tent and drove a spear through both of them. The man and his companion died, and the Lord stopped a plague that had broken out among the violators. The plague, of unknown character, killed **24,000** of the Israelites.

25:10–18. The Lord commended Phinehas for his speedy action in killing the offending party and staying the plague. He enacted with Phinehas his **covenant of peace** that assured his descendants a lasting priesthood. Indeed, the high priesthood passed from Eleazar to Phinehas (Judg. 20:27–28) except for a brief time in the days of Eli (1 Sam. 1–3).

Moses mentioned the names of the two offenders, **Zimri son of Salu** and **Cozbi daughter of Zur**, a Midianite leader. Zur may have persuaded Cozbi to seduce Zimri, who was from a prestigious family, into spiritual compromise with the promise of greater reward. The Lord showed no mercy toward the Midianite nation and commanded Moses to oppose them to the death. At times the Lord does inflict justice on the enemies of God's people. Yet God alone reserves the right to pay back those who stray (2 Thess. 1:6–7).

> **MAIN IDEA REVIEW:** *Not all prophets who talk religious talk are God's prophets.*

III. CONCLUSION

A Helpless Feeling

In October 1999, professional golfer Payne Stewart was flying to a tournament in a small chartered jet when, somehow, the pilots lost consciousness after what appeared to be a routine take off. Air traffic controllers attempted to contact the plane when it failed to make the necessary turn toward Dallas, but there was no answer. Two Air Force jets were summoned to investigate the runaway plane, only to discover that no one was at the controls of the jet. The windows of the cockpit appeared to be fogged over, suggesting that the plane had depressurized at 45,000 feet, killing all the passengers. The only thing keeping the plane aloft was the autopilot system. One Air Force pilot said, "It's a helpless feeling to pull alongside another aircraft and realize the people inside are unconscious or in some other way incapacitated. And there's nothing I can do physically from my aircraft even though I'm fifty to one hundred feet away, to help them at all." You remember the story: One of the jet's engines ran out of fuel, and the plane crashed. Numerous news stories followed. Air traffic controllers were interviewed, golfers shared their loss, and pilots speculated on the plight of the passengers during depressurization.

Evidently the loss of oxygen and pressure can leave a person oblivious to what is happening. You may think everything is wonderful but be heading to the end of your life. Fortunately, Payne Stewart was a Christian and was loved and respected by all, but this incident has monumental implications. Humanity, like Balaam, Balak, and everyone else who does not follow and trust God, is on a collision course and apparently thinks the flight is going well. We can become so caught up in our own pleasures and pursuits that we fail to have any sense of urgency about our life's direction. The way of Balaam (2 Pet. 2:15) is the way of many—speeding along, unaware of our plight, with nothing but judgment ahead.

PRINCIPLES

- A good reputation is not the same as godliness or obedience.

- Greed will always get you into trouble.
- Sin is evidence of evil in a person's life.
- Compromise can bring us face-to-face with the wrath of God.

APPLICATIONS

- Be careful who you ask for advice.
- God gives us the freedom to make decisions, whether good or bad.
- When a Christian falls into sin, God's discipline is the natural consequence.

IV. LIFE APPLICATION

An Invisible Fence

It used to be that if one wanted his dog to run free in his yard, he had to fence in his property. Now, however, one can do the same with an invisible fence, which is a wire buried just beneath the topsoil around the edge of one's property. The dog wears a special electronic collar, so when it approaches the wire, it is stopped by an electrical jolt.

God has given each of us an invisible fence. We are privileged to experience an inner voice called the conscience that warns us when we are approaching forbidden territory. To cross these boundaries will cause heartache and grief, so God gives us ample warnings. But like Balaam, we can become so numb to God's voice that we tune out his warnings and his guidance. We may even get to the point where we no longer feel the occasional, loving jolt of his discipline.

Do not become so desensitized and seared in conscience that you cannot hear God. If you are his child, remember what J. Oswald Sanders wrote in his book *A Spiritual Clinic:* "Every conscience needs instruction. Its delicate mechanism has been thrown off balance by the Fall. Just as a bullet will reach the bull's-eye only if the two sights are in correct alignment, so correct moral judgments are delivered only when the conscience is correctly aligned with the Scriptures."

V. PRAYER

Lord, help me to remain faithful to your call and to resist compromise. And help me to resist Satan's deception. Grant me contentment in this life the world may never understand. Remind me to be grateful for all you have blessed me with. And remind me when I get too close to the flames of judgment and the way of Balaam to repent, step back, and move quickly toward your forgiveness. In Jesus' name. Amen.

VI. DEEPER DISCOVERIES

A. Balaam's Relationship with God

Some of the words in the extended Balaam narrative may lead the reader to believe that Balaam had some sort of relationship with God. Tertullian and Jerome were among some of the early church fathers who joined some modern thinkers in including Balaam among the true Hebrew prophets. Yet the reader will also note the position taken in this commentary that Balaam was a soothsayer and a false prophet. Scripture must govern all interpretation; when Scripture provides a clear conclusion, we must accept it. Some interpreters have concluded that we simply cannot determine Balaam's true character (see House, 164), but the Bible concludes differently.

Balaam clearly advised the Israelites to turn away from the Lord (Num. 31:16). That act of disobedience netted Israel a plague that could have wiped out the nation. Although the account of Balaam's activity in Numbers 22–24 seems to portray a prophet reluctant to curse Israel, the notes above provide a different scenario. In truth, he was eager to curse Israel, but God would not allow him to do so.

Balaam actually "loved the wages of unrighteousness" (2 Pet. 2:15 NKJV) and would not come to the light for fear that his deeds would be exposed (John 3:20). He ran after profit with such focus that future followers of greed are tagged with "Balaam's error" (Jude 11). But even going beyond loving unrighteousness and its spoils, Balaam "taught Balak to entice the Israelites to sin by eating food sacrificed to idols and by committing sexual immorality" (Rev. 2:14). Joshua quite bluntly said Balaam "practiced divination" (Josh. 13:22).

So how can we account for Balaam's interaction with God? God allowed Balaam to proceed at certain points, then demonstrated his sovereignty by overruling Balaam's desire to curse Israel. Harrison notes that Balaam, a certain polytheist, would have to know the names and some of the history of local gods if he were to be believed as a seer (329–30). No doubt he heard of God's works in Egypt and the great miracles God had wrought in bringing his chosen people out of that house of bondage. God may have communicated with Balaam, but he did not change his heart and bring the erring prophet into covenant relationship with himself. Balaam, we conclude, was a prophet for hire whose goal was to curse Israel in return for a handsome remuneration. But God "would not listen to Balaam" (Josh. 24:10).

Apparently the curse was in the works (or the conscientious and inten-tional plan of Balaam), but God "turned the curse into a blessing" (Neh. 13:2). He submitted to God because he learned something of the reality of this God, and he could not overcome his power. He had to submit for his own welfare. Balaam's address of God as "the Lord my God" should be taken with the same seriousness as Judas's kiss on the cheek of Jesus.

Harrison correctly concludes: "Balaam was not a genuine Hebrew prophet but was exercising the functions of a Mesopotamian *baru* (seer) when he was used by the God of Israel for the revelation of His will" (331). He bears no resemblance to a true prophet of the Lord, although at times, we admit, he sounded like one.

B. Balaam's Donkey

Critics and skeptics cite Balaam's encounter with his donkey as a clear example of why we cannot take the Bible seriously. Conservatives counter that the God who created the world in six days by speaking it into existence could certainly speak through Balaam's donkey. The miracle demands no more imagination than that required for Jonah's descent into the great fish's belly. Keil notes that "irrational animals have a much keener instinctive pre-sentiment of many natural phenomena, such as earthquakes, storms, etc., than man has with the five senses of his mind" (170). In addition, animals have heightened intuition and can often ascertain things well before their human counterparts. The greatest difficulty rests with an irrational animal speaking with clear rationality. Clearly Balaam heard the beast "who spoke with a man's voice" (2 Pet. 2:16).

C. Blessing and Cursing Israel

Although Balaam wanted to curse Israel rather than bless her, he did bless the nation according to God's providence and purpose. The nation was the covenant people who had been purchased out of the house of bondage to become God's special people. God laid down to Israel the conditions for receiving his blessing in Leviticus 26 and Deuteronomy 28. Israel could either bless or curse herself by how she responded to God's Word. Other nations needed to bless Israel and treat her with respect and kindness. In doing so, they would also receive blessing from God (Gen. 12:3).

But what about our attitude toward modern Israel? Should we still "bless" her as God asked the nations of old to bless her or simply treat her as any other nation? The Bible supplies us with some governing principles to estab-lish our attitudes toward Israel.

First of all, Israel was the covenant nation chosen by God and called to bear his name to the nations. "Theirs is the adoption as sons; theirs the divine glory, the covenants, the receiving of the law, the temple worship and the promises. Theirs are the patriarchs, and from them is traced the human

ancestry of Christ" (Rom. 9:4–5). Hence God entrusted Israel with these privileges and through Israel gave the world the Messiah.

But we must remember that Israel was also supposed to obey God's word
and follow its precepts as covenant nation. This they failed to do, and God
sent them off to captivity. Although the Lord did allow them to return seventy
years later, they continued to have a checkered career as a nation and ultimately were deposed by the Romans. The twentieth century witnessed
sweeping changes in the world brought on by two world wars. Many who
witnessed the horrors of the Holocaust grew more sympathetic with the
plight of modern Israel. Shortly the modern state of Israel came into existence
once again. Some Christians saw this as a fulfillment of biblical prophecy,
while others viewed it differently.

Paul gave us God's own view of Israel when he traced Israel's plight in
Romans 11. Although Israel did reject Christ as Messiah, many in Israel now
make up "a remnant chosen by grace" (v. 5). But the nation did not stumble
so as to fall (v. 11). They indeed have a glorious future, but for now they wait
in the shadows while the Gentiles come to Christ in large numbers (v. 25).
But one day "all Israel will be saved" (v. 26). Scholars view that passage differently, and only time and God's unfolding providence will prove which view is
correct. But we can arrive at some principles that should govern our present
attitude toward the Jewish state:

We should pray for Israel's salvation. This was the cry of God's heart that
drove Paul to tears as he prayed for their salvation (Rom. 9:1–4). The Bible
does indicate God will save many Jews before the time of Christ's return, and
the church should pray to that end.

We should hold Israel accountable to the principles found in the Word of
God. Many prophetic teachers seem to teach that Israel has an unqualified
right to anything it wants, no matter what its present attitude toward God.
Apparently the hope of Christ's return drives them toward this conclusion.
But they misinterpreted Scripture by believing such things. The Lord's blessing upon Israel was always conditioned by her obedience to his commands
(cp. Deut. 28). Israel today has not acknowledged Christ as the Messiah and
at times has shown a reluctance to accommodate Christian missionary activity in Israel. While we should seek friendship with Israel, we should not con-
done actions that are wrong.

Gentile churches should not boast of their present privileges. They must
remember that Israel supports them in the historic order of God's redemptive
blessings (Rom. 11:18). Christians should never dismiss Israel because of her
present attitude toward Messiah, but they should earnestly pray for Israel's
salvation. Some time in the future, God will once again turn his blessing
toward Israel on a grand scale, and the church needs to acknowledge God's
place for Israel. Until that time, both Jew and Gentile need to radiate Christ
in the heart and live out his principles in the world.

VII. TEACHING OUTLINE

A. INTRODUCTION

1. Lead Story: Talk's Cheap
2. Context: As Israel moved toward Canaan, King Balak of Moab became fearful. He knew he didn't have the forces to defend his kingdom against Israel. So he turned to the prophet Balaam and called on him to curse Israel. God used Balaam to offer three prophecies of blessing toward Israel in spite of Balaam's lack of integrity and disobedience. Even though Balaam was unable to put a curse on Israel, he eventually showed Balak how he could bring Israel down.
3. Transition: Today many voices claim to be speaking for God. The God who protected his people from Balaam and Balak still searches the hearts and tests the words of those who claim to speak on his behalf. God's preference is to use clean vessels to communicate his message. But sometimes, as the saying goes, "God uses a crooked stick to draw a straight line."

B. COMMENTARY

1. Balaam the Soothsayer (22:1–41)
2. Balaam's Prophecies (23:1–30)
3. Balaam's Concluding Oracles (24:1–25)
4. Moab Seduces Israel (25:1–18)

C. CONCLUSION: AN INVISIBLE FENCE

VIII. ISSUES FOR DISCUSSION

1. How do you think the circumstances contributed to Balak's being fearful of Israel? And why did he choose Balaam?
2. Balaam's first oracle says a lot about God's expectations for his people and Balak's response to God's desire. Why couldn't Balaam curse Israel?
3. Balak attempted to get Balaam to curse Israel a second time. What lessons can be learned from Balaam's second oracle?
4. Do you see any changes in Balaam's perspective as you read the third oracle? How did Balak respond to this third prophetic utterance? Climb into Balak's sandals and attempt to detect his motivation.
5. What comparisons can you see between today's culture and the idolatry of Numbers 24? Has God's ideal for his people changed over the years? What steps are you taking to maintain purity in your life?

Numbers 26–29

Generation Next for Israel

I. INTRODUCTION
Something More

II. COMMENTARY
A verse-by-verse explanation of these chapters.

III. CONCLUSION
Who Can See?

An overview of the principles and applications from these chapters.

IV. LIFE APPLICATION
Not Alone

Melding these chapters to life.

V. PRAYER
Tying these chapters to life with God.

VI. DEEPER DISCOVERIES
Historical, geographical, and grammatical enrichment of the commentary.

VII. TEACHING OUTLINE
Suggested step-by-step group study of these chapters.

VIII. ISSUES FOR DISCUSSION
Zeroing these chapters in on daily life.

"*S*uccess is never final; failure is never fatal;

it is the courage to continue that counts."

W i n s t o n   C h u r c h i l l

Numbers 26–29

I N   A   N U T S H E L L

*A*ll but a few of the original Israelites who walked from Egypt's slavery toward the promised land are now dead. It is time to enter Canaan, and a new generation must step up to the plate and trust God. First a census must be taken in preparation for the battles ahead (Num. 26); then legal issues for the women of Israel needed resolution (Num. 27); and the spiritual dimension of the people needed some fine-tuning with another discussion of the offerings (Num. 28) and the importance of feast offerings in God's sight (Num. 29).

Generation Next for Israel

I. INTRODUCTION

Something More

At age fifty-four, a Silicon Valley computer software engineer says he has finally found what he was searching for during the sixties. "I was always on a quest. I tried everything. I was a Jew; I studied the Sikh religion in India; and I entered a Hindu monastery. I lived in a tree in Merry Prankster Ken Kesey's front yard. And, of course, I tried taking lots of drugs. None of it worked." He joined Wavy Gravy's traveling Hog Farm Commune. Foster married his wife, Laura, in a memorable ceremony performed by Wavy in New Mexico. The groom wore ice skates, and to seal their vows the happy couple exchanged pork chops. When the Hog Farmers were hired to set up and manage security and facilities at the Woodstock festival, Foster was there. He spent most of his time helping people on bad drug trips into the "freak-out" pen. Although he still keeps in touch with the Hog Farmers, Foster is no longer a part of their family. Now married for twenty-two years, he has three children and is an elder and youth counselor in his church. "The kids of that time were unhappy with what their parents had given them—they wanted something more," he says. "I found that something more in my faith in Christ."

As we near the end of the Book of Numbers, a new generation is looking for something more. This new generation is looking for the promised land, which their parents and grandparents had been talking about for their entire life. But awaiting this new generation are new problems and new battles. So the first item on the agenda before they are given occupancy of the land is another census.

II. COMMENTARY

Generation Next for Israel

MAIN IDEA: *Several matters must be settled before the people enter the land of promise, including a census, legal issues, and spiritual issues.*

A New Census (26:1–65)

SUPPORTING IDEA: *Moses numbers the new generation of fighting men.*

26:1–4. The Israelites prepared themselves for battle, first with the Midianites (see ch. 31), and then ultimately with the inhabitants of Canaan.

Therefore, they needed a fresh numbering that served as a mustering of people to arms. The old generation had died out, with the exception of Caleb and Joshua. But the numbering would also aid Joshua and Eleazar when they began distributing the land. The larger tribes would receive a larger inheritance, and the smaller tribes a smaller share. The census helped determine the needs of each tribe. An accurate count would prevent any suspicion of favoritism when the land was parceled out among the tribes.

Those included in the census were men **twenty years old or more** who were qualified to serve in the army. So Moses and the priest Eleazar **spoke with them** (probably the heads or representatives of the nation), the ones who would carry out the actual numbering of the people.

26:5–11. First counted was the tribe of **Reuben**, some members of which conspired with Korah when he questioned Aaron's authority as a priest. Reuben numbered **43,730**. Reuben forfeited his right to the supreme tribal status due to his illicit relationship with his father's concubine (Gen. 35:22; 49:4). Reuben's children mentioned here were born to him in Egypt. Reuben's new tally actually fell below the previous count of 46,500, probably because of the people who died in the rebellion of Dathan and Abiram, who were members of Reuben's tribe.

26:12–18. The leading clans of **Simeon** were Nemuel, Jamin, Jakin, Zerah, and Shaul. Ohad, mentioned in Genesis 46:10, probably died in childhood or simply had no family. Their total number, which was then the third largest at 59,300, gave way to a reduced **22,200 men**. The seventh son of Jacob (by Zilpah) was **Gad**, who also gave birth to seven sons. They totaled **40,500**, just under their original fighting number.

26:19–22. Judah was the fourth son of Jacob, and he gave birth to Er, who was killed by the Lord for an unspecified reason. Judah then fathered Onan by Shua, followed by Shelah. Onan did not comply with the command to raise up children for his dead brother's name, so the Lord killed him also. Judah's line, therefore, was traced through Shelah. Judah did later father Perez and Zerah by Tamar his daughter-in-law, and these formed a second line of Judah. David and Jesus would come through the line of Perez. See Genesis 38 for details on origin of Judah's line. Just before the conquest of Canaan, they numbered **76,500**, more than their earlier count of 74,600.

26:23–37. Issachar, Jacob's ninth son, had four sons who, in turn, had fruitful families. They were Tola, Puah, Jashub, and Shimron. They stood **64,300** strong. Jacob's tenth son was **Zebulun** (by Leah, Gen. 30:19–20). His own sons were Sered, Elon, and Jahleel. They increased slightly from their original count to **60,500**.

Manasseh, firstborn son of Joseph, lost the birthright to Ephraim on whose head Jacob placed the blessing (Gen. 48:12–20). Manasseh was adopted by Jacob along with his brother Ephraim so the tribes would always number twelve, since Levi received no land inheritance. His line included a strong female representation through Zelophehad, who had no sons. Manasseh numbered **52,700** at this latest census. **Ephraim**, the brother tribe of Manasseh, numbered only **32,500**.

26:38-41. Benjamin, Jacob's youngest son, would become notorious as a tribe for his exploits and publicity brought on by some of its more illustrious sons, such as King Saul and, later, the apostle Paul. But Benjamin would also face near extinction when some of these tribal members committed an unspeakable act and resisted any form of accountability (see Judg. 19-21). Jacob compared his beloved son to a ravenous wolf (Gen. 49:27), a prediction that came true. Although they faced a perilous future, Benjamin's tribe now numbered **45,600**.

26:42-51. Dan, the fifth son of Jacob (by Bilhah, Rachel's handmaid, Gen. 30:4-6), increased to **64,400**, while **Asher** (by Zilpah, Gen. 30:12-13) stood at **53,400**. The tribe of **Naphtali** numbered **45,400**. The total number of warriors eligible to fight came to **601,730**.

26:52-65. The Lord awarded the larger tribes more land than their smaller counterparts, but he also commanded Joshua to parcel out the land **by lot**. Casting lots was one method of determining God's will under certain conditions. The lot, for example, determined which goat would go free on the Day of Atonement (Lev. 16). Thus the Lord alone determined where each tribe would settle.

The Levites were not subject to military service because they tended to the holy things of the Lord. They would receive cities to live in. From these cities they would teach the locals the way of the Lord. The three divisions of the Levites included the families of **Gershon**, **Kohath**, and **Merari** (see Num. 3:21-37 for a summary of their specific duties). From Kohath came **Amram**, the father of Aaron and Moses. Aaron's priesthood fell to his two sons **Eleazar and Ithamar** because his two other sons, **Nadab and Abihu**, burned strange fire and were destroyed by the Lord (Lev. 10:1-2). The Levites numbered **23,000** but again were not counted along with the other Israelites because they received no inheritance among them.

All those who rebelled in the wilderness died according to the word of the Lord—indeed, to the very last man. **Caleb** and **Joshua**, who displayed courage and went against the popular sentiment, did cross over into the land the Lord gave Israel and were rewarded for their faith (Josh. 15:13-19; 19:49-50).

B Zelophehad's Daughters and Moses' Successor (27:1–23)

SUPPORTING IDEA: *The Lord provides for surviving daughters and Moses' successor.*

27:1–4. Land allotments were determined by the size of the various tribes. But the **daughters of Zelophehad** came to Moses and the leaders of Israel with a special request. Their father did not participate in the rebellion of Korah and company in the desert, but **he died for his own sin and left no sons**. He did not leave a male heir, and his surviving daughters feared he would lose his name and they would lose their inheritance. If the daughters were granted an inheritance and married husbands, they could carry on their father's name. Keil notes that such a request matched a common ancient practice in marriages where the wives brought property into the union. The sons would be considered heirs of the grandfather through the mother (213).

27:5–11. Moses brought this difficult question **before the LORD**, and the Lord affirmed the complaint of the daughters. If a man died without leaving a male heir, then the inheritance would go to the surviving daughters. If he did not have a daughter, then they should give his inheritance to his brothers. If he did not have any surviving brothers, then they would give the inheritance to his uncles. Failing that, they were to give it to next of kin. They stipulated this **legal requirement** because the land was not to exchange hands on a permanent basis as long as they were in the land. Later the Lord would supplement these instructions for special problems that arose in regard to inheritance laws (36:1–12).

27:12–14. The Lord informed Moses abruptly that he would soon die. Moses would first ascend a mountain (Mount Nebo) in the **Abarim range** in order to view the land, but he would not enter it because of his sin **at the waters in the Desert of Zin**. The Bible later describes Moses' final days and his death in more detail (Deut. 32:48–52; 34:1–6; for the expression, "gathered to your people," see "Deeper Discoveries").

27:15–23. Moses did not plead for his life, but he asked the Lord to **appoint a man over this community**. He grew concerned for the welfare of these people and asked God to provide a leader for them in his absence.

The Lord chose Moses' chief aide, **Joshua son of Nun**, to succeed him. Joshua had **the spirit** of leadership in him. This spirit meant more than simple wisdom but rather "the higher power inspired by God into the soul, which quickens the moral and religious life and determines its development; in this case, therefore, it was the spiritual endowment requisite for the office he was called to fill" (Keil, 215).

Moses ordained Joshua publicly so the people could view the transference of power. Joshua would minister with Eleazar the priest from this time forth.

The Lord made it clear that Joshua would not inherit all the privileges Moses had—particularly his access to God.

ℂ The Order of the Daily and Special Offerings (28:1–31)

SUPPORTING IDEA: *Moses summarizes the routine and special offerings of Israel.*

28:1–8. Throughout the Book of Numbers, Moses recorded historical events interspersed with priestly concerns (Harrison, 361). Whereas Leviticus focused on the individual's responsibility in sacrifice, Numbers centers its thoughts on the priest's duties in relation to sacrifice. Once the nation entered the promised land, it must know how to maintain fellowship with God. One of the ways was through sacrificial communion as seen in the daily offerings.

The priests would begin each day by preparing **one lamb in the morning and the other at twilight**, and accompany it with a grain (cereal) offering. They also added a **quarter of a hin of oil from pressed olives.** To this burnt offering they added a drink offering (libation) consisting of a **quarter of a hin of fermented drink with each lamb.** They would then repeat this offering again in the evening.

28:9–10. Each regular **Sabbath day**, the priests offered two one-year-old lambs with the accompanying grain and drink offerings. During this weekly remembrance, the nation could consecrate "its total life" as a people of the Lord (Harrison, 363). But the priests would also offer the regular offerings as well.

28:11–15. The months of the Hebrew calendar began with the new moon. **On the first of every month**, the priests offered a larger burnt offering than they did at the regular daily and Sabbath offerings. The offering consisted of **two young bulls, one ram and seven male lambs a year old**, all without defect. Each burnt offering had a prescribed grain offering. Drink offerings must accompany each bull offering. The monthly offering was capped off by a collective sin offering. With the burnt offering came the thought of self-surrender and even national surrender to love and serve the only true God.

28:16–25. Excluding the Day of Atonement, Harrison is quite correct in maintaining that the Passover was "the most important religious celebration in the life of the Hebrews and recapitulates the original celebration in the life of the Hebrews" (365). Strangely, few Passover observances are recorded in the Old Testament, and we have reason to believe that few were ever observed. The next Passover recorded was Joshua's (Josh. 5:10). Hezekiah and Josiah did observe Passover (2 Chr. 30:1–27; 35:1–19). Once again, the Passover offerings would supplement, not replace, the daily offerings. Thus the Lord reminded the nation it must maintain constant communion with him in all of life.

28:26–31. This first day of firstfruits marked the beginning of the Feast of Weeks when the wheat harvest began. It began fifty days following the Feast of Unleavened Bread, hence "Pentecost" (Gr.). Sometimes the writers describe it as the Feast of Harvest. On this day a special Sabbath was observed, and the people did no regular work. The priests would offer the same sacrifices as they did at the Feast of Unleavened Bread. This special observance reminded the Israelites that Yahweh was the Lord of the harvest, the true supplier of all their needs.

Ⅾ Offerings for Israel's Festivals (29:1–40)

SUPPORTING IDEA: *Special offerings and observances highlight Israel's feast celebrations.*

29:1–6. During the seventh month (*Tishri*), three Jewish festivals took place: Feast of Trumpets, Day of Atonement, and Feast of Tabernacles. The festivals anticipated the time when Israel would live in the promised land, primarily as tillers of the soil. The Lord commanded Israel to set aside this special month, a month in which most of the harvest had been gathered, and to **do no regular work**. The entire month was a month of rest from physical labor and a time to approach God for forgiveness and fellowship.

During the first day of the month, they were to **sound the trumpets**, which alerted the nation to the special character of the seventh month. Moses had recorded this instruction in Numbers 10:10. They would offer a single bull, a ram, and seven male lambs as burnt offerings. These offerings would be accompanied by grain and drink offerings. The priests would then offer **one male goat as a sin offering** for atonement (i.e., for the community). And so on the first day of the seventh month, the priests offered the regular morning sacrifice, the regular monthly offerings, the seventh-month offerings, and finally the regular evening offerings. Once again the people were not to suspend the regular offerings during special seasons or observances.

29:7–11. The Day of Atonement began **on the tenth day of this seventh month** (see Lev. 16) and was a solemn fast day where the Israelites did no work. On this day they would **deny themselves** (see Lev. 16:29), which most likely described a fast. The highlight of this day was the offering of a sacrifice that would atone for Israel's sin. Only on this day did the high priest enter into the holy of holies to apply the blood to the mercy seat with the prayer that God would forgive Israel for her sins. See Leviticus 16 for a summary of the sacrifices and observances of this day.

29:12–40. Israel held yet another **sacred assembly** on the fifteenth day of the month—the Feast of Booths, or Tabernacles. Their offering included **thirteen young bulls, two rams and fourteen male lambs a year old**. These were accompanied by the prescribed grain and drink offerings. In contrast to the Day of Atonement, the mood of this festival was festive and celebrated the ingathering of the harvest. But the day also provided them with a special memorial of their wilderness experiences. Their descendants in the land of Canaan would recall how God brought Israel out of Egypt and sustained them in the desert.

On the second day they would sacrifice one less bull, and on the third one less, amounting to eleven, and so on until the seventh day. On the eighth day the Lord called them to a sacred **assembly**, and no regular work was allowed. They offered one bull for a burnt offering, plus one ram and seven young male lambs, each accompanied by the prescribed grain and drink offerings. They capped this observance by offering a male goat for a sin offering.

MAIN IDEA REVIEW: *Several matters must be settled before the people enter the land of promise, including a census, legal issues, and spiritual issues.*

III. CONCLUSION

Who Can See?

In their book *Worship: Rediscovering the Missing Jewel,* Ronald Allen and Gordon Borror tell about a craftsman who traveled to America from Europe to dedicate his life to some of the detail work in a majestic place of worship. One day a sightseer was touring the edifice. He observed the workman laboring near the high ceiling on a symbol which could hardly be seen from the floor. He seemed to be occupied with a detail on the top, out of view of the most observant worshiper. The sightseer said, "Why are you being so exact? No one can even see the detail you are creating from this distance." The busy artist replied, "God can."

What a great picture of a servant doing his job for an audience of one and following through to the smallest detail! One thing we have learned in the Book of Numbers is that God is a God of details. We have seen it in his order of marching for the people of Israel all the way to his detailed offerings and rules. If God sees our lives in this detail, then it makes sense to live life by honoring him with the details of our lives.

PRINCIPLES

- When God makes a promise, he keeps it.
- God does not hold subsequent generations responsible for the sins of their fathers.
- God is concerned with women's rights.

- Sin must be dealt with God's way.
- When we disobey God's Word, we will pay the consequences.
- God always has a gifted leader ready to fill a leadership void.
- God may see potential in a person that no one else sees.

APPLICATIONS

- Each new generation must own their faith and learn to trust God.
- Bring all your needs to God; he cares for his children.
- If God tells you to do something a certain way, at a certain time, do it!
- When you look at the Old Testament offerings, look for the wonder of Jesus.
- Worship is an act of sacrifice, a sweet offering to the Lord.

IV. LIFE APPLICATION

Not Alone

As a POW in Vietnam, Col. Laird Gunnert was beaten and tortured mercilessly. One day, his captors took him to an interrogation room he had not seen before. This time the beating he suffered was especially severe. He crumpled to the floor in excruciating pain, too exhausted and too battered to lift his face from the dirt floor.

Opening his eyes, Gunnert saw something on the wall, about four inches from the floor, right in front of his face. Someone had scrawled in the dirt, "Keep the faith, baby!" In that moment he realized he was not alone. Someone else knew he did not have to succumb to the hopelessness of his situation. He could, with the encouragement of his anonymous benefactor, triumph over his helpless state.

In whatever situation we find ourselves, we can find encouragement in the fact that Jesus Christ has been there before us. Not only has he been there and triumphed there himself, but he has also left us a source of strength. In him we can find strength for the journey toward the promised land.

V. PRAYER

My God and Father, every letter in your Word is important to me. You have given me the details of a census to remind me of your faithfulness to every generation. You have given me the details of a transition in leadership to remind me how you are always on the throne. You have given me details on the numerous offerings you ordained to remind me that you sent your Son to cover my sin with his blood and forgiveness. May my life be lived for him in the details of life. I love you, Lord. Amen!

VI. DEEPER DISCOVERIES

A. Joshua's Qualifications

Joshua came through a lineage of leadership. No doubt he had heard many stories about God's deliverance and guidance throughout the history of Israel. Now he was to succeed the greatest leader Israel had ever known. And some might wonder whether he was qualified.

Born in Egypt, Joshua knew all about slavery. He was the firstborn son in his family (1 Chr. 7:27) and was probably aware of the devastating night when God saved the lives of all the Israelite firstborn through the first Passover. Joshua may have been reminded that he was destined to do something significant for God, and besides, he had a good mentor in Moses. He had seen waters part and God's abundant provision. He had some success militarily when he led the counterattack against Amalek's army at Rephidim (Exod. 17:8–16). He had climbed Mt. Sinai with Moses to receive the Ten Commandments (Exod. 24:12–13). Joshua was indeed Moses' right-hand man. So there was no surprise when the surveillance party was organized to explore the land of Canaan and Joshua was among the twelve (Num. 13–14). God's hand was upon him from the very beginning to fill the shoes of Moses and lead the people of Israel into the promised land.

B. The Importance of Regular Worship

From the very beginning of his relationship with Israel, the Lord planned for regular and continuous fellowship with his people. Even when they left Egypt, God instructed them on proper worship and carefully detailed the construction of the tabernacle, so essential to Israel's spiritual health. Later Solomon would build the temple in Jerusalem. Solomon built an elaborate edifice and offered numerous sacrifices in the name of Yahweh (2 Chr. 7:1–5). Israel squandered their inheritance when the Lord sent them off to captivity (2 Kgs. 17; 25). Jeshua and Zerubbabel led a remnant back from captivity, and immediately they "began to build the altar of the God of Israel" (Ezra 3:1–3). Later they rebuilt the temple of the Lord. They recognized that their top priority was the resumption of regular sacrifice and worship.

By the time we arrive at the New Testament, the early church was eager to meet regularly and to fellowship with one another and the Lord (Acts 2:42). The church grew together because that was the way God designed for it to grow (Eph. 4:13–16). The New Testament closes with a solemn warning from the one who "walks among the seven golden lampstands" (or churches, 1:20;

2:1), indicating he discloses himself to his people in corporate gatherings. As children of God, we should devote our lives to worship God with all our heart, soul, mind, and strength.

VII. TEACHING OUTLINE

A. INTRODUCTION

1. Lead Story: Something More
2. Context: As Israel approached the promised land, God prepared the generation that would possess the land. A new census had to be taken that would show the number of men who were available for the coming battles. Some legal issues regarding the inheritance of women had to be addressed. And finally the subjects of offerings and feast days are treated in detail.
3. Transition: God is concerned about details. Care about details shows that we are concerned not just to live in the sight of other human beings but before God. No act, thought, or motive is unimportant to God.

B. COMMENTARY

1. A New Census (26:1–65)
2. Zelophehad's Daughters and Moses' Successor (27:1–23)
3. The Order of the Daily and Special Offerings (28:1–31)
4. Offerings for Israel's Festivals (29:1–40)

C. CONCLUSION: NOT ALONE

VIII. ISSUES FOR DISCUSSION

1. What do you think was the purpose of the second census? What do you think this new generation had learned from the previous generation?
2. What significance does the story of the daughters of Zelophehad have for women in general? What allowed these women to win their case?
3. Why do you think the monthly offerings were important for the people of Israel? Why do you believe the celebration of the Passover was an appropriate event before entering the promised land?
4. The Feast of Tabernacles is based on what Jewish historical foundation? What would you be thinking about if you were forced to "camp out" in booths before God? What did God want the people of Israel to remember through this observance?

Numbers 30–32

The Next Generation Continues to Learn

"*He* knows, and foreknows, all things, and His foreknowledge is foreordination; He, therefore, will have the last word, both in world history and in the destiny of every man."

J . I . P a c k e r

Numbers 30–32

I N A N U T S H E L L

A new generation is learning the things of God. This section begins with a look at vows from the perspective of women's rights. Then, God's judgment falls upon the Midianites for their disobedience with Balaam in seeking to curse Israel. Moses makes an important decision about the unity and mobilization of Israel as Reuben and Gad ask to remain on the eastern side of the promised land instead of crossing the Jordan River into Canaan.

The Next Generation Continues to Learn

I. INTRODUCTION

Be Sure You Have Your Knife!

*T*he U.S. Government *Peace Corps Manual* for volunteers who work in the Amazon jungle states that if an anaconda attacks you:

1. Do not run. The snake is faster than you are.

2. Lie flat on the ground. Put your arms tight against your sides, your legs tight against one another.

3. Tuck your chin in.

4. The snake will come and begin to nudge and climb over your body.

5. Do not panic.

6. After the snake has examined you, it will begin to swallow you from the feet end—always from the feet end. Permit the snake to swallow your feet and ankles. Do not panic.

7. The snake will now begin to suck your legs into its body. You must lie perfectly still. This will take a long time.

8. When the snake has reached your knees, slowly, and with as little movement as possible, reach down, take your knife and very gently slide it into the side of the snake's mouth between the edge of its mouth and your leg. Then suddenly rip upwards, severing the snake's head.

9. Be sure you have your knife.

10. Be sure your knife is sharp.

Please remember as you approach Numbers 30–32 that this was a new generation and they needed step-by-step, simplified instruction. They must have seen their parents make numerous promises to God, and now they needed instruction on the importance of these vows. They were much younger when Israel faced the "Balaam Controversy," and now they would understand the importance of Midian's influence. They probably didn't understand all the walking in circles their parents had experienced, and Moses needed to review this data with them.

II. COMMENTARY

The Next Generation Continues to Learn

MAIN IDEA: *God continues to prepare his people to take the land he promised.*

A The Law of Vows (30:1–16)

SUPPORTING IDEA: *Moses provides the Israelites with an avenue to express personal commitment.*

30:1–2. A vow was a freely chosen commitment to God. Moses directed these instructions to **the heads of the tribes of Israel** because vows did have familial significance. The governing rule applied to vows was quite simple: If you vowed something, then pay up. The nation's character went only as far as the individual's character, and faithfulness and honesty formed such character. The **pledge** probably involved abstinence of some sort, whether from food or drink. Of course, dietetic restrictions formed part of the Nazirite vow (see ch. 6). These regulations cover four special cases.

30:3–16. The first case involved a young woman who was unmarried and was still living in her father's house. If she were to obligate herself **by a pledge** and her father learned of this pledge but said nothing, then she was fully obligated to fulfill her vow. But if her father heard of it and somehow disagreed with the vow, he had the authority to withdraw the entire vow. The same formula applied to a wife who made a similar vow or pledge before marriage. Once she was married, her husband could withdraw the vow if he felt it unwise. But he had to do it at once (when he first heard of it); otherwise the pledge stood.

A **widow or divorced woman** who uttered a vow must pay it, since she was not under the authority of a father or husband. Finally, if a wife made a vow and her husband heard of it but said nothing, she must pay the vow. The vow remained in force because her husband, by his silence, allowed it. But if the husband heard about it and did not agree with some aspect of it or felt it was uttered rashly, he could withdraw it. But he must do it shortly after hearing of it or the vow stood.

In this way the Lord provided a sensible statue of limitations on vows spoken by women in a married state. The husband would bear responsibility for the wife if she went back on her vow.

B Revenge Against the Midianites (31:1–54)

SUPPORTING IDEA: *Israel executes vengeance against an enemy.*

31:1–12. The Lord had commanded Israel to "treat the Midianites as enemies and kill them" (Num. 25:17). Now by means of the census, the army had been mustered and was prepared to do battle. Overseeing this battle would be one of Moses' last official acts as leader of Israel. The Midianites had led Israel astray into Baal worship through the wicked counsel of Balaam. The Lord described it as **the LORD's vengeance on them**, and such a distinction must be clearly maintained in drawing any theological conclusions. Nations and individuals should always honor the highest standards and motive when going to war, and any retaliation should be authorized by God himself or fall under a scriptural principle. In this case, the Midianites seduction of Israel "had violated the divinity and honor of Jehovah" (Keil, 225).

The Lord did not call for all the warriors of Israel to fight this battle, only **some** of the fighting men. So Moses sent twelve thousand men, a thousand from each tribe, into battle against Midian. Phinehas the priest accompanied the troops and carried with him the signal trumpets. Phinehas upheld the Lord's honor when Israel went astray in Baal worship, and the Lord ended the plague on Israel (Num. 25:6–13).

Israel made short work of Midian and routed them with brute force. They destroyed every man, including **the five kings of Midian**. During the battle, they also killed **Balaam son of Beor**. They burned the cities and towns of Midian and made away with great spoil, which they turned over **to Moses and Eleazar**.

31:13–24. When Moses, Eleazar the priest, and all the leaders of the community went out to meet them **outside the camp**, Moses became angry with the warriors for sparing the Midianite women. He reminded them of how the women seduced them into worshiping Baal so that a plague had struck the Lord's people. He instructed them to kill all boys and **every woman who has slept with a man**. He allowed them to spare those women who were virgins.

Some interpreters have stumbled at this and similar commands to kill women and children. But the Lord instituted Israel as a holy people living in a theocratic society where God's laws influenced all of life. The chief priority was to maintain the distinct purity and holiness of the nation. The married women or prostitutes who survived the battle would have jeopardized the spiritual purity of the nation by introducing their idolatrous rituals. The young virgins, on the other hand, could be positively influenced by the Israelites and were therefore spared. God's command was as much an act of mercy as it was justice. Moses instructed the men who engaged in war to **stay outside the camp seven days** and to observe the usual purification rituals for those who came into contact with a dead body.

To ceremonially purify the spoil, Eleazar the priest told the soldiers to burn any metal articles that usually go through the fire. Then these were to be purified **with the water of cleansing**. Whatever could not pass through the fire intact would also be put through the water of cleansing.

31:25–47. The Lord directed Moses to have Eleazar and the tribal heads count the people and animals that comprised the booty. The prisoners (i.e., the virgins) and animals would be divided between the warriors and congregation. In addition, the Lord would receive from the soldiers' spoils **one out of every five hundred**, whether persons, cattle, donkeys, sheep or goats, as a tribute. From the Israelites' share went **one out of every fifty**, or 2 percent. The plunder taken was massive, including **32,000 women**.

31:48–54. The soldiers met with such remarkable success that they wanted to give a special offering to demonstrate their gratitude. They brought various articles of jewelry taken from the spoils. They offered these **to make atonement**. Harrison notes that the soldiers may have felt guilty for killing so many Midianites while none of their own soldiers died in the battle (390–91). But the men probably didn't feel worthy of such grace that brought about such a resounding victory (Keil, 229). Moses and Eleazar accepted the booty offering, which weighed **16,750 shekels**.

C Settlement of the Transjordan Tribes (32:1–42)

> **SUPPORTING IDEA:** *Moses grants a wish to tribes who desired to settle east of Jordan.*

32:1–5. The tribes of Reuben and Gad owned **large herds and flocks**, so they were attracted to the rich land of Gilead. That land was not part of the original promised land, but the Lord made a special provision in their case. This fertile area served as an excellent pasture for flocks and herds. The tribes approached Moses and Eleazar to inquire whether they could settle in this region east of the Jordan River.

32:6–15. At first Moses balked at the suggestion and questioned their motives: **Shall your countrymen go to war while you sit here?** Such an act, in Moses' view, would surely demoralize their brother tribes in their coming confrontation with the Canaanites. Moses reminded them of the poor example of their fathers who had spied out this territory forty years before, only to bring back an evil report that sapped the moral resolve of the people to take the land. Moses closed his argument with a reminder of God's judgment that fell on the unbelieving people and how Reuben and Gad were following in their footsteps.

32:16–27. The tribes that made the request approached Moses with reassuring words. They would **like to build pens** for their livestock and **cities** for their women and children. But they would cross over with the other tribes to wage battle with the Canaanites until the land was subdued. But they repeated their contention that their inheritance had come to them **on the east side of the Jordan**.

Moses responded positively to their proposal. But he also cautioned them against going back on their commitment to help their brothers fight for Canaan. If they failed to aid them, they could be sure that their sin would find them out. The **Gadites and Reubenites** reiterated their intention of settling their wives, children, and cattle in Gilead, then crossing over the Jordan River with the other tribes to **fight before the LORD.**

32:28–32. Moses instructed Joshua and Eleazar, who would be in charge of distributing the land, to allow Gad and Reuben to cross over and fight but to return east of the Jordan River to settle with their families. But if they failed to assist their fellow Israelites in the battle, then they must receive their inheritance in Canaan just like the other tribes. As it turned out, Reuben and Gad kept their promise to the letter (Josh. 4:12–13; 22:1–4).

32:33–42. Then Moses gave them the land east of the Jordan River that had been taken during the defeat of **Sihon** and **Og.** For the first time the **half-tribe of Manasseh** is mentioned along with Reuben and Gad. They probably stood with Reuben and Gad in their request but let the other two tribes speak on their behalf. At some point the tribe of Manasseh may have split off because of its size and differences in places occupied (Harrison, 399). In addition, the half tribe drove out the people of the land where they wanted to settle (v. 39; see also Calvin, 289).

MAIN IDEA REVIEW: *God continues to prepare his people to take the land he promised.*

III. CONCLUSION

"All Right, Loving"

In an article in *Decision* magazine, Aretta Loving, a Wycliffe missionary, tells about an encounter with a five-year-old neighbor boy. She was washing breakfast dishes when she saw Jimmy headed straight toward the back porch. She had just finished painting the back-porch handrails and was proud of her work. "Come around to the front door, Jimmy," she shouted. "There's wet paint on the porch rails." "I'll be careful," Jimmy replied, now turning from his path. "No, Jimmy! Don't come up the steps," Aretta shouted, knowing of Jimmy's tendency to mess things up. "I'll be careful," he said again, by now dangerously close to the steps. "Jimmy, stop!" Aretta shouted. "I don't want carefulness. I want obedience!" As the words burst from her mouth, she suddenly remembered Samuel's response to King Saul: *To obey is better than sacrifice.*

"How would Jimmy respond?" Aretta wondered. To her relief, he shouted back, "All right, Loving, I'll go around to the front door." He was the only one who called her by her last name like that, and it had endeared him to her from the beginning. As he turned around the house, Aretta thought to herself, "How often am I like Saul or like Jimmy, wanting to go my own way? I rationalize, 'I'll be careful, Lord' as I proceed with my own plans." But He doesn't want carefulness. He wants obedience.

We end this section of the Book of Numbers with the tribes of Reuben and Gad wanting to "climb up the front porch" and live on the eastern side of the Jordan River opposite the land that God had designated as an inheritance for Israel. History records that any time a follower of God chooses to be careful instead of obedient, be sure "your sin will find you out" (Num. 32:23).

PRINCIPLES

- Promises and vows are important in God's eyes, and they must never be made without sincerity and devotion.
- There should be a spiritual separation between the world and the life of a believer.
- Sin can have long-term repercussions.

APPLICATIONS

- The most important commitment you will ever make is your confession of Christ as your Savior.
- A believer must keep his word and follow through on his obligations.
- You will have victory when you treat every battle as a spiritual struggle and you allow God to lead the charge.
- We must choose to remain in the wilderness and wander aimlessly or to move toward the promised land, where we will discover God's blessings.

IV. LIFE APPLICATION

Communicating the Need for Change

Emile Ballard, a missionary with the Telakhon people in Thailand, wrote about the process of communicating the gospel, the good news of the love of God expressed in our Savior Jesus Christ:

> These people talk in allegories and during the discussion with their leaders one of them said to us. "We see ourselves as though we are in a deep hole in the ground. We look up and see the light, but we can't get out. Now we see you come and reach down your hand to help us out, but we can't reach your hand. But don't give up on us—perhaps our children will be able to jump high enough to catch hold of your hand."
>
> This being interpreted means that those of the older generation can't change their ways quickly enough to accept the help we offer but perhaps their children will find a way to adapt.

In another allegory they said, "We're like a little tadpole hiding under a bamboo leaf. The water is getting shallower and the sun is getting hot. What should we do?"

The missionaries replied, "You know the purpose of the tadpole is to become a frog. If it does not become a frog, it dies. But if it becomes a frog, it must adapt. It may have to find another pool, but it still hasn't lost the essence of the tadpole. It's still in the frog."

There are some wonderful truths for us in this illustration. Change is a normal part of the Christian life. The term *sanctification* is a continual process of change experienced over time and growth in the life of a Christian. The next generation of the people of Israel had to learn to change, adapt, and obey. You will too! You won't have to jump higher or try harder; just trust more. God is faithful. He knows the end from the beginning. Yes, be careful, but more importantly, be obedient.

V. PRAYER

Lord, I know that throughout my life I will make promises I cannot keep and make decisions based upon selfish motives. During these times, I give you permission in advance to remind me of the lessons I have learned in the Book of Numbers. I invite your wisdom and guidance into my life and ask that your gentle instruction keep me on my journey to the promised land. Amen.

VI. DEEPER DISCOVERIES

A. The Bible and Vows

The vow involved a person making a voluntary pledge or promise to God. Usually the vow involved obtaining a special favor from God, such as recovery from an illness or deliverance from an enemy. Jephthah, the Gileadite warrior, vowed to offer as a burnt offering "whatever comes out of the door of my house to meet me" (Judg. 11:31), and his daughter came out to meet him (11:34). Jacob vowed to give a tenth to God if only he would be with him and watch over him (Gen. 28:20–22). Hannah vowed to give her son to the Lord's service if only God would open her barren womb (1 Sam. 1:11). The vow must not contradict the Lord's revealed will, as apparently it did in the case of Jephthah. The person making the vow must be competent and mature enough to offer such pledges, and they must pay them.

Paul urged the saints of Achaia to "finish the work" (2 Cor. 8:11) of fulfilling their *promise* of a "generous gift" to the poor Christians at Jerusalem (2 Cor. 9:5). Those who made such vows should consider carefully whether they have the means or the heart to fulfill them. The vow was not to be made reluctantly or by constraint; it was fully voluntary and, as such, should be paid cheerfully.

VII. TEACHING OUTLINE

A. INTRODUCTION
1. Lead Story: Be Sure You Have Your Knife!
2. Context: The Lord commanded Moses to lead one more battle before he died and before Israel entered the promised land. He was to take vengeance on the Midianites for their role in turning Israel against the Lord at Peor. One of the last judgments Moses made as Israel's leader was deciding about the request of the tribe of Reuben, Gad, and the half tribe of Manasseh to settle east of the Jordan River. Moses set the conditions under which this would be permitted.
3. Transition: Obedience to the Lord and vows made to him are closely related. Our circumstances are different from Israel's. But God, who sought obedience from Israel, still requires this of his people.

B. COMMENTARY
1. The Law of Vows (30:1–16)
2. Revenge Against the Midianites (31:1–54)
3. Settlement of the Transjordan Tribes (32:1–42)

C. CONCLUSION: COMMUNICATING THE NEED FOR CHANGE

VIII. ISSUES FOR DISCUSSION

1. After reading Numbers 30, what have you learned about the Jewish culture in relationship to the role of women?
2. Why are vows and promises such a big deal to God? How does your answer affect your view of God's promises to Israel? To you?
3. Why were the Midianites such a great threat to Israel? After the battle, why was a portion of the spoils given to Eleazer and the Levites? What does this say about the victory of Israel's army?
4. Between the lands of Gilead and Jazer were numerous obstacles. What communication headaches would exist for tribes that lived on opposite sides of the Jordan River? What communication problems exist in your church? What must you do to overcome these problems?

Numbers 33–36

Home at Last

Quote

"*D*espots may plan and armies may march, and

the congresses of the nations may seem to think they

are adjusting all the affairs of the world,

but the mighty men of the earth are only the dust

of the chariot wheels of God's providence."

T. D e w i t t T a l m a g e

Numbers 33–36

 I N   A   N U T S H E L L

*U*pon Israel's arrival at the promised land, it is now time for God to distribute the land he has promised (Num. 34), to give some cities to the Levites who were not given any land (Num. 35), and to give one final assurance about the future of the promised land for Israel (Num. 36).

Home at Last

I. INTRODUCTION

A Father's Face

*O*nce a little boy lost his mother, and his father took him to the funeral. But the little boy could not understand what was going on. Where was his mother? Why did she have to go to heaven? "Can we go visit her, Daddy?" he asked.

After the funeral, the father and son went home where the questions kept coming even at bedtime. His father did his best to answer his hurting son's questions, hoping to calm him so he could go to sleep. After a while, the father got up, turned off the light, and went down the hall to his own room.

It was only minutes before the boy began to cry out for his father. His dad went into the boy's room and brought him to his own bed to console him. But the restless child continued to search for answers from his father even after the lights were turned out. Finally, the boy reached out his hand in the darkness and asked, "Daddy, is your face toward me?" His father leaned forward so his son could gain assurance by touching his face and said, "Yes, Son, it is." "If your face is toward me," the boy said, "I think I can sleep now."

People long for their loving Father's face to be toward them. The story of the people of Israel leaving captivity, receiving the law and the offerings, and arriving at the promised land is a picture of God's face toward his people. Now at the end of the Book of Numbers, the people of God reach out to receive the inheritance of the land God had promised them and to gain greater insights into their loving Father's faithfulness.

II. COMMENTARY

Home at Last

> **MAIN IDEA:** *Israel reviews her history, then sets her sights on Canaan by making final preparations.*

A Review of Israel's Past (33:1–56)

> **SUPPORTING IDEA:** *Moses summarizes the travels and key encampments of Israel.*

33:1–2. As Israel stood at the edge of the Jordan River across from Jericho, their history in the wilderness closed with a summary of their wanderings. The list of places where they had traveled brought back memories of

God's sustaining grace and power. The people rarely responded with gratitude fit for the occasion but instead often complained of the conditions of their desert wanderings. "So little disposed, however, were they to that humility, which might have taught them to ask of God by prayer and supplication a remedy for their need, that they rather rebelled against Moses" (Calvin, 298).

33:3–9. Israel departed from Egypt a day following the first Passover **in full view of all the Egyptians.** Even then, Israel was a conquering nation whose destination was elsewhere. God also **brought judgment** on the Egyptian gods (see Exod. 12:12). The Lord shamed the gods who were supposed to protect Egypt.

The major stations leading to the Red Sea included Succoth, Etham, Migdol, Marah, and finally **Elim**, a place where there were **twelve springs and seventy palm trees.** The Lord guided Israel by the pillar of cloud and fire, and each station came by God's clear design.

33:10–49. The encampment at the Red Sea was not mentioned in Exodus, but "it may merely have been a marshaling station" (Harrison, 405). Moses mentioned numerous cities in quick succession, citing only a couple events of importance. At **Rephidim** the people found no water, and **at Mount Hor** Aaron died. Around this time, **Arad**, the Canaanite king, heard that the Israelites were coming and engaged them with initial success. But Israel rallied around a vow to the Lord and routed the Canaanites at Hormah (see 21:1–3). Finally, they arrived at the **plains of Moab** across the Jordan River from Jericho.

33:50–56. The Lord instructed Moses to tell the Israelites to destroy the depraved Canaanites in a campaign that would lead them to conquer the promised land. With all their cult images and seductive sexual ceremonies, the Canaanites were a threat to the pure worship of the Lord. Therefore, they had to drive the Canaanites out of the land. God particularly commanded them to destroy all images or idols and to obliterate any sign of the Canaanite religion.

The land would be parceled out in an orderly manner and according to a plan. Larger tribes would receive a larger share, and smaller tribes a smaller parcel. But they must maintain their tribal distinctions once they were settled in the land.

In a final warning, the Lord predicted what would happen if they failed to drive out the inhabitants of the land. The pagan Canaanites would surely erode Israel's spiritual distinctives and ultimately destroy it. When Israel later succumbed, the Lord subjected them to a fate similar to what was supposed to happen to the Canaanites.

ⓑ The Boundaries of Canaan (34:1–29)

SUPPORTING IDEA: *Moses assigns the general boundaries of Canaan and leaders to distribute the land.*

34:1–2. The land to be allotted to the tribes had precise borders. If anyone should call into question a person or tribe's land rights, they need only appeal to these original borders.

34:3–12. Israel's southern border extended from the wilderness of **Zin**, then followed the border of Edom, moving eastward to the **Salt Sea** ("Dead Sea"). It then moved upwards to **Scorpion Pass** through **Zin** to **Kadesh**. Next it proceeded through **Hazar Addar** and over to **Azmon**, turning northwest to the **Wadi of Egypt**. From there it would extend west all the way to the Mediterranean Sea, a large body of water that served as a natural border.

From the Mediterranean Sea to Mount Hor (not the mountain on which Aaron died, which was quite a distance away, but perhaps Mount Hermon; Harrison, 413) came the northern boundary. That border extended to **Lebo Hamath**, and from there to **Zedad** (modern Sadad), ending at **Hazar Enan**.

Finally, the Lord drew their **eastern boundary** from **Hazar Enan** to **Shepham**, traveling down to **Riblah** along the **Sea of Kinnereth** (named after the Hebrew word that means "harp" because from an elevated view the sea resembled that instrument; see Harrison, 414). Kinnereth later became "Gennesaret," and stood for the place we know today as the Sea of Galilee.

34:13–29. Thus the Lord assigned this land to the **nine and a half tribes** that had not yet received an inheritance. The Lord validated the claims of the **two and a half tribes** that their allotment fell on the eastern side of the Jordan River.

Although lots would decide the specific land assignments, the Lord appointed **Eleazar the priest and Joshua son of Nun** to administer the Lord's will in this matter. Someone had to determine just what the lots indicated and to decide minor disputes. The people also needed the confidence that their inheritance fell to them by God's intention and not by chance. Joshua and Eleazar would be protected from false accusation or prejudice. To aid Joshua and Eleazar in assigning the land and, perhaps, to offset any criticism that too few people administered such a huge undertaking, the Lord appointed **one leader from each tribe to help assign the land**. None of these people except Caleb had been mentioned before as noteworthy characters, but they must have represented the most faithful of the tribal representatives.

Levitical Towns and the Cities of Refuge (35:1–34)

SUPPORTING IDEA: *Moses assigns to the Levites special cities where they will maintain justice and protect the innocent.*

35:1–5. In accordance with the Lord's command that the Levites would receive no permanent inheritance in Canaan, the Lord did not assign them a separate territory. But he did provide them cities to live in. The other tribes needed to set aside a portion of their allotment for such cities. Keil notes that the Levites did not receive these cities as separate inheritances per se, but enough houses to accommodate them (258–59). The tribes also needed to provide sufficient space for cattle grazing. The Lord gave precise measurements for such grazing land to avoid future disputes.

35:6–8. From six of the towns given the Levites would come the **cities of refuge**, where a person accused of murder could flee in order to escape an avenging relative. The Levitical towns would total **forty-eight**. The Lord took these towns from tribes in proportion to their size. He instructed them to take many towns from a tribe with many towns **but few from one that has few.**

35:9–34. Motive determined whether someone should be tried as a first-degree murderer or something less. For example, if a person should strike and kill someone **with an iron object**, he was considered a murderer. Here little doubt remained that the killer intended to murder his victim. On the other hand, if someone killed someone accidentally, then he should not be accounted a murderer. The cities set aside from the Levitical towns would serve as places of refuge where suspected killers could live while judges adjudicated their cases. Six of these towns were located on the western side of the Jordan River and six on the eastern side.

The **avenger of blood** served as the executioner. He was probably a near relative of the victim. But he could not execute someone without first determining whether the accused was guilty. A person's guilt could be determined by ascertaining whether he hated his victim beforehand or demonstrated ill will toward him. When the investigators considered the case and determined that the suspect held a grudge or harbored hatred toward his victim, then the avenger of blood could exact vengeance on the suspect and take his life. But if the alleged crime was an accident, the people needed to restrain the avenger of blood and spare the suspect's life. The authorities were to provide safe conduct to the nearest city of refuge and protect the victim **until the death of the high priest**. Some interpret the death of the high priest as a kind of symbolic sacrifice that atoned for a death even though the authorities could not indict the suspect for the crime (since it was not a capital crime).

Perhaps the accused would grow restless and wander away from the city of refuge or venture home. Confining someone to a small area could prove a special hardship, especially if the town was located far from one's homeland.

Likewise, the accused must remain in protective custody until the high priest died; then he was free to go. But until that time he must stay in that place assigned to him. If he did wander off and the avenger of blood located and killed him, the protecting city would bear no guilt. In addition, the authorities could not prosecute the avenger, since the accused had wandered away from protective custody.

The community could only determine guilt based **on the testimony of witnesses**, but not on a single witness. The accused could not offer bribe money, nor could the authorities award "bail" to a person who put up a sum of money. Bloodshed not properly atoned for by authorized adjudication would surely **pollute the land**. Nothing could remove such a curse from the land.

Marriage Laws for Female Heirs (36:1–13)

> **SUPPORTING IDEA:** *Moses makes a special provision and a requirement to maintain tribal distinctions.*

The daughters of the deceased Zelophehad had appealed to Moses on a previous occasion that he guarantee their inheritance even though they did not have a male heir in the family. The Lord replied by agreeing to uphold their claim and guaranteeing them a permanent inheritance (see 27:1–11). But problems soon arose that the earlier ruling could not account for.

36:1–4. Some **family heads** from **Manasseh** and other leaders approached Moses with a special concern. These men were aware of the earlier ruling granting the female descendants of Zelophehad a permanent land inheritance even though the family had no male to carry on the family name. The name would survive through the male sons of the women. But what would happen if the daughters of Zelophehad married into tribes not belonging to their father? Then their land allotment would fall to their husbands from other tribes and thus upset the previously established land boundaries. They must have imagined what would happen over time with the occurrence of hundreds of such marriages. The entire land allotment would be significantly changed. Furthermore, the land would not revert back to the original tribe in **the Year of Jubilee** in case the new heirs somehow lost it, because then it would go to the women who had married men from other tribes. Hence the Jubilee would result in the transferral of the land to a new tribe.

36:5–13. Moses affirmed the concerns of the men from Manasseh and required that **Zelophehad's daughters** only marry men from their father's tribe, Manasseh (see "Deeper Discoveries"). Once again Moses insisted that **every Israelite shall keep the tribal land inherited from his forefathers**. The daughters did as the Lord commanded them through Moses, and they married their paternal cousins.

From the beginning God was concerned with the plight of the unfortunate and widows and made special provision for them. He protected women from undue oppression from their male counterparts and put these regulations into holy law.

With these final words the Lord closed the Book of Numbers, although he would supplement the law with a final book, Deuteronomy. Israel now stood at the precipice of destiny as they overlooked the land before them. For a generation the Lord had guided them through peril and trial, through trouble to deliverance. Now there was a new generation that did not rebel at the command of the Lord, as their fathers had done. So much of the Book of Numbers dealt with life as it would be once in the land. Now they crept forward, perhaps inching toward a closer view across the **Jordan** and peering toward **Jericho**, armed with a divinely guided history and assured of continued guidance from their covenant God.

Would they hold fast to the commands God had given them at Sinai and throughout their various journeys? Would they not repeat the errors of the past and shrink from the campaign before them? Israel's future would prove tenuous in one sense but final in another: "For not all who are descended from Israel are Israel" (Rom. 9:6).

MAIN IDEA REVIEW: *Israel reviews her history, then sets her sights on Canaan by making final preparations.*

III. CONCLUSION

Ready for Change

When trains were first invented, several "experts" agreed that if a train went at the frightful speed of fifteen miles an hour, the passengers would get nosebleeds and would suffocate when going through tunnels. In 1881, the New York YMCA announced typing lessons for women. Protests were made on the grounds that the female constitution would break down under the strain. When the telephone was first invented, Joshua Coppersmith was arrested in Boston for trying to sell stock in a company to build them. The experts said that all well-informed people knew it was impossible to transmit the human voice over a wire.

How many historians have said that the tiny land of Israel didn't have a chance against their neighboring enemies? Just the thought that Israel would become a nation in 1948 was a radical idea to most people. Just the thought that Jews would begin returning to their homeland brought the comment, "It can't be done." Yet both have happened. How is this possible? God said it; that settles it.

PRINCIPLES

- God takes extreme measures when dealing with idolatry.
- Sometimes God's mercy is demonstrated in his judgment.
- The land of Israel remains important in God's purpose.
- The Levitical tribe was God's possession and God's servant.

APPLICATIONS

- Pray for the peace of Israel.
- Whatever your past, you can find refuge in God's care.
- God walks beside us in our wilderness journey.

IV. LIFE APPLICATION

In the End . . . We Win

The journey is over. It has been a long hard road, and history reveals that the people of Israel had much to learn about obedience and faith in the future. But we take great comfort in knowing that in the end . . . we win.

In Hawaii the major sporting events are usually shown on tape delay so people on the islands can get home and enjoy them. However, the radio broadcasts are always live, so it is possible to listen to the radio and know the outcome of a game before watching the event that evening. This makes watching the game a lot less stressful and the strikeouts and errors less important. Why? Because in the end, they know who wins!

In John 16:33, Jesus said, "I have told you these things, so that in me you may have peace. In this world you will have trouble. But take heart! I have overcome the world." Our Lord is saying to us, "I know the end of the game. I have seen the errors in the wilderness and the hints of obedience. As my child, you will overcome, you will press on toward the prize I have for you, and you will have victory. Don't get discouraged. It is still a nine-inning game, and it's not over for you. And never forget: I know the end from the beginning. You are on tape delay."

V. PRAYER

Lord, with all I read in the newspapers and see on the television about the nation of Israel, it appears that you have placed this land at the vortex of international conflict. And after realizing this land was ordained for your people many years ago, I want to pray for the peace of Israel. Lord, give the Jewish leaders wisdom to make wise decisions. But most importantly, open the Jewish peoples' hearts to the Messiah, Jesus Christ, in whose name I pray. Amen.

VI. DEEPER DISCOVERIES

Courtship in Ancient Israel

The Lord allowed the daughters of Zelophehad to marry anyone they pleased within the tribe of Manasseh, giving us a glimpse into how they went about courtship and what parameters they observed. The Hebrew culture was built on the family and the family on the marriage unit (Knapp, *ISBE,* III, 262). Within that union the man headed the home. The word for *betroth* means "pledge" or "assign." During the time of betrothal, normally around twelve months, a man and a woman entered into a commitment almost as binding as marriage. Sometimes a betrothed couple was referred to as husband and wife (Gen. 29:21; Matt. 1:18–20). If either partner became unfaithful during this time, they committed adultery and could be punished by death (Deut. 22:23–25).

During betrothal, the man would give the woman's family a gift in the form of money or, as in the case of Jacob, service. Samson paid what could have been a marriage gift in clothing (Judg. 14:8–20). Such a bridal price in no way indicated the wife was nothing more than property. The price pointed to the esteemed worth of the bride. The father of the bride would give to the couple a dowry of money, land, or servants.

Before the engagement and before the couple ever met each other, the man's family usually took some initiative in locating a wife for their son. Hagar located a wife for her son Ishmael out of Egypt (Gen. 21:21). Isaac was forty and fully capable of taking a wife on his own, yet Abraham sent his servant to locate a suitable wife for Isaac in Haran (Gen. 24). But Rebekah's father asked her first if she was willing to go (24:57–58). Yet Jacob himself picked Rachel to be his wife and was granted his wish, but not before Rachel's father picked Leah first to be Jacob's wife. Esau also chose his own wives.

So some tension and perhaps flexibility existed between the groom and his family's direct involvement. Here in the case of Zelophehad's daughters, they were given some latitude in choosing their husbands (indicating a mutual agreement between bride and groom and not just the respective families), but the Lord also gave them some clear boundaries. Some today have revived a sort of courtship approach to marriage. But the couple should seek to capture the spirit of the contract instead of the bare letter, remembering that the criterion for any happy marriage is to be united in the Lord (1 Cor. 7:39).

VII. TEACHING OUTLINE

A. INTRODUCTION

1. Lead Story: A Father's Face

2. Context: Israel is about to enter into an inheritance that God promised to give them many years before. As preparation, Moses gives a brief summary of their recent history. He then gives them the boundaries of the land. Moses announces one leader from each tribe who will be responsible for alloting the tribal inheritances.

3. Transition: As we prepare for the future, we need to remember how God has brought us to this point. We need to be open to his guidance in the days to come.

B. COMMENTARY

1. A Review of Israel's Near Past (33:1–56)

2. The Boundaries of Canaan (34:1–29)

3. Levitical Towns and the Cities of Refuge (35:1–34)

4. Marriage Laws for Female Heirs (36:1–13)

C. CONCLUSION: IN THE END . . . WE WIN

VIII. ISSUES FOR DISCUSSION

1. What possible struggles might be initiated by the vows of Numbers 30? Are there any hints in this passage about the Israelite culture and women?

2. In every age, in every culture, God's people have faced opposition from enemies. Why do you think God dealt with Midian as he did?

3. When the time came to enter the promised land, how many of the original Israelites were excited about this event? Why? The major transition to Canaan offered many challenges. Suggest some of the logistical concerns the leaders would face.

4. What additional insights are given in these chapters about the Levites? Why were the cities of refuge necessary?

Bibliography

Archer, Gleason, L. *A Survey of Old Testament Introduction.* Chicago, Ill.: Moody Press, 1974.

Archer, Gleason, L. "The Chronology of the Old Testament." *Expositor's Bible Commentary,* Vol. 1. Edited by Frank E. Gaebelein. Grand Rapids, Mich.: Zondervan Publishing House, 1979.

Berkhof, L. *Systematic Theology.* Grand Rapids, Mich.: Wm. B. Eerdmans Publishing Co., 1941.

Bromiley, Geoffrey W. *The International Standard Bible Encyclopedia.* Vols. 1–4. Grand Rapids, Mich.: William B. Eerdmans Publishing Company, 1979–1985.

Calvin, John. *Commentaries on the Last Four Books of Moses.* Vols. 1–4. Grand Rapids, Mich., Baker Book House, 1981.

Durham, John I. *Exodus.* Word Biblical Commentary. Vol. 3. Waco, Tex.: Word Books, Publisher, 1987.

Gehman, Henry Snyder. *The New Westminster Dictionary of the Bible.* Philadelphia, Pa.: Westminster, 1970.

Hannah, John D. *Exodus.* The Bible Knowledge Commentary, Old Testament. Wheaton, Ill.: SP Publications, Inc. (Victor Books), 1985.

Harrison, R. K. *Exodus.* The Wycliffe Exegetical Commentary. Chicago, Ill.: Moody Press, 1990.

House, Paul R. *Old Testament Theology.* Downers Grove, Ill.: InterVarsity Press, 1998.

Hughes, Philip Edgcumbe. *A Commentary on the Epistle to the Hebrews.* Grand Rapids, Mich.: William B. Eerdmans Publishing Company, 1977.

Jamison, Fausett, and Brown. *Commentary on the Whole Bible.* Grand Rapids, Mich.: Zondervan Publishing House, 1961.

Keil, C. F. *The Pentateuch.* Commentary on the Old Testament in Ten Volumes. Vol. 1. Grand Rapids, Mich.: William B. Eerdmans Publishing Company, 1980.

Leupold, H. C. *Exposition of Genesis.* Vols. 1–2. Grand Rapids, Mich.: Baker Book House, 1942.

Lindsey, F. Duane. *Leviticus.* The Bible Knowledge Commentary, Old Testament. Wheaton, Ill.: SP Publications, Inc. (Victor Books), 1985.

Motyer, J. A. "Old Testament History." *Expositor's Bible Commentary.* Vol. 1. Edited by Frank E. Gaebelein. Grand Rapids, Mich.: Zondervan Publishing House, 1979.

Packer, James I. *The Bible Almanac*. Nashville, Tenn.: Thomas Nelson Publishers, 1980.

Poythress, Vern S. *The Shadow of Christ in the Law of Moses*. Phillipsburg, N.J.: P & R Publishing, 1991.

Rawlinson, George. *Exodus*. The Pulpit Commentary. Vol. I. Peabody, Mass.: Hendrickson Publishers. Reprint.

Reymond, Robert L. *A New Systematic Theology of the Christian Faith*. Nashville, Tenn.: Thomas Nelson Publishers, 1998.

Shedd, William G. T. *Dogmatic Theology*. Vols. I–III. Nashville, Tenn.: Thomas Nelson Publishers, 1980.

Soltau, Henry W. *The Holy Vessels and Furniture of the Tabernacle*. Grand Rapids, Mich.: Kregel Publications, 1971.

Unger, Merrill F. *Nelson's Expository Dictionary of the Old Testament*. Nashville, Tenn.: Thomas Nelson Publishers, 1980.

Vos, Geerhardus, *Biblical Theology*. Carlisle, Penn.: The Banner of Truth Trust, 1975.

Wenham, Gordon J. "The Book of Leviticus." *The New International Commentary on the Old Testament*. Grand Rapids, Mich.: William B. Eerdmans Publishing Company, 1979.

Glossary

atonement—God's way of overcoming sin through Christ's obedience and death to restore believers to a right relationship with God

consecration—Setting apart for God's use

covenant—A contract or agreement expressing God's gracious promises to his people and their consequent relationship to him

election—God's gracious action in choosing people to follow him and obey his commandments

exodus, the—The most important act of national deliverance in the Old Testament when God enabled the Israelites to escape Egypt

expiation—An action directed toward nullifying the effects of sin which breaks the relationship between a person and God; emphasizes the saving event of the atonement of Christ rather than the penalty or punishment endured

fasting—Going without food as a sign of repentance, grief, or devotion to God; often connected with devotion to prayer

firstborn—The oldest son born into a Jewish family or the first offspring of livestock. The firstborn were dedicated to God in a special sense

high priest—The chief religious official for Israel and Judaism appointed as the only person allowed to enter the holy of holies and offer sacrifice on the Day of Atonement

holy—God's distinguishing characteristic that separates him from all creation; the moral ideal for Christians as they seek to reflect the character of God as known in Christ Jesus

holy of holies—The innermost and most sacred area of the tabernacle and temple, where God was present and where sacrifices were made by the high priest on the Day of Atonement

idolatry—The worship of that which is not God

inheritance—Humanly, a legal transmission of property after death; theologically, the rewards God gives his children who are saved through Jesus Christ

law—God's instruction to his people about how to love him and others; when used with the definite article "the," *law* may refer to the Old Testament as a whole but usually to the Pentateuch (Genesis through Deuteronomy)

monotheism—Belief in only one God

Passover—The Jewish feast celebrating the exodus from Egypt (Exod. 12); celebrated by Jesus and his disciples at the Last Supper

Pentateuch—First five books of the Hebrew Bible: Genesis, Exodus, Leviticus, Numbers, Deuteronomy; only Scriptures recognized by Samaritans and by Sadducees

righteousness—The quality or condition of being in right relationship with God; living out the relationship with God in right relationships with other persons

ritual—A symbolic action that points to a spiritual truth

Sabbath—The seventh day of the week corresponding to the seventh day of creation when people in the Old Testament were called on to rest from work and reflect on God

sacrifice—According to Mosaic Law, an offering to God in repentance for sin or as an expression of thanksgiving; Christ as the ultimate Sacrifice for sin

sin—Actions by which humans rebel against God, miss his purpose for their life, and surrender to the power of evil rather than to God

tithe—One-tenth of a person's income and belongings given to God through the church

Yahweh—The Hebrew personal name of God revealed to Moses; this name came to be thought of as too holy to be pronounced by Jews; often translated LORD or Jehovah